BYE FOR NOW

BYE FOR NOW
A Soldiers Story 1943 to 1945

BEVERLY RICHARD BORTHWICK

LitPrime Solutions
21250 Hawthorne Blvd
Suite 500, Torrance, CA 90503
www.litprime.com
Phone: 1 (209) 788-3500

© 2021 Beverly Richard Borthwick. All rights reserved.

No part of this book may be reproduced, stored in a retrieval system, or transmitted by any means without the written permission of the author.

Published by LitPrime Solutions   03/25/2021

ISBN: 978-1-954886-18-6(sc)
ISBN: 978-1-954886-19-3(hc)
ISBN: 978-1-954886-20-9(e)

Library of Congress Control Number: 2021904065

Any people depicted in stock imagery provided by iStock are models, and such images are being used for illustrative purposes only.

Certain stock imagery © iStock.

Because of the dynamic nature of the Internet, any web addresses or links contained in this book may have changed since publication and may no longer be valid. The views expressed in this work are solely those of the author and do not necessarily reflect the views of the publisher, and the publisher hereby disclaims any responsibility for them.

Beverly Richard Borthwick
Camp Roberts, California
July, 1943

For the Great Grandsons
Sasha, Misha and Nicolai

PROLOGUE

When I was a little girl, I remember my father sitting at my grandfather's desk scratching away. Fountain pen in hand, blue lined school paper and the ashes of a cigarette precariously dangling over his work. What he was writing was his odyssey through World War II.

My father, Beverly Richard Borthwick, never talked about these experiences. I was awakened many nights, however, in the bedroom I shared with my parents by screams and my father rushing to the window or door saying, "I know they are out there." What follows, mostly unedited, is the story he could never tell anyone.

"A pen in the hand of my father wrote words that would inspire. The ink that flowed from his pen was a connection to a moment of his experience at that moment in time. The value of his ink was that it absorbed on paper as a gift to be handed down to future generations"

Anonymous

On September 1, 1943 we first sighted land. Far ahead and to our right Africa was slowly coming into view. It seemed good to see something besides water for a change. We had set sail from Norfolk, Virginia on August 15th, so this was the first land we had seen in about eighteen days. Not as long as some of the fellows sailing in the Pacific but long enough for me.

Our voyage across the Atlantic had been grueling and entirely monotonous. It was almost over now and I looked forward to getting my feet on good old terra firma again. What lay in store in these lands across the sea was of a minor nature now, I just wanted to get the hell off this damned boat.

The trip really had been a grueling one. Our "ship" was really only an invasion boat called an L.S.T. (Landing Ship Tank). It was of rather small dimensions and had accommodations for only about one hundred and fifty troops besides the crew. This type of craft was made for carrying tanks and supplies on invasions. They were designed to go right up to the beach and discharge their cargo. Therefore, the thing was flat-bottomed and had no keel. These tubs rocked violently in the slightest of heavy seas. In other words, they were like half a watermelon bobbing on a slop bucket.

The thing was brand new when we boarded her in Norfolk. She was manned by British sailors who had come to the states specifically to pick her up. Besides the hundred and fifty American soldiers aboard the boat carried a cargo of railroad rails and hospital beer. At least they told us that the beer was for malaria patients, and that it was all doped up. Being greenhorns, we accepted this. I now doubt very much that it was the truth. It kept us from going below and breaking into it anyway. On the top deck racks had been constructed on which to place two smaller craft. For some reason they had not been put on this ship although the other ten L.S.T.'s in our convoy were carrying them. There were several reasons besides this ship, to leave plenty to be desired, to make the crossing a pleasant one.

First, the British Navy being in charge didn't help too much. The English themselves weren't so bad and they tolerated us. The crap they served us wasn't fit for a dog. Always half cooked and never any seasoning. As bad as it was we would have eaten a lot more of it if they had served it. There was never half enough to even begin to fill you up. The canteen didn't amount to much, two candy bars per man a day. Even that helped but the supplies ran our three or four days before we reached our destination.

Another thing that made life miserable were some of the characters that were on board. Several of them were Stockade Johnnies. They had spent most of their army careers in the klink. They had been brought down to the boat by M.P.'s. I guess camp commanders had gotten sick of having them around and were sending them over-seas to get rid of them. Maybe they were the kind that had said "to hell" with it, they can't make me fight". And probably some commanding officer had said "No, but we can sure as hell send you where the fighting is". However, most of the guys were regular swell fellows. Just a few undesirables made it more or less unpleasant for everyone. I remember a couple of the troublemakers. One was a guy named Bob Banquet and another was some Greek called Nick. Then there were a few loud mouthed Wops. Not that they did anything too bad but they were always miserable. They were always trying to stir up a stink of some sort. They would never stand guard or do K.P. or even clean their bunks.

The Second Lieutenant in charge of us was a queer duck. He didn't know how to handle men at all. When those characters refused to do anything he just didn't seem to know how to cope with them. He didn't even seem to have the intelligence of a ten year old. I hoped that when I got over into combat he wouldn't be my officer. His name was Blair Armstrong.

On the other side of the ledger there were plenty of nice fellows aboard. Three corporals that I hung around with were swell fellows. Their names were Hopkins, Foss and Thompson. They had washed out of O.C.S. (Officer Candidate School) together. Not that they wouldn't have made competent enough officers but they went to O.C.S. at the wrong time. The Army had decided they had enough officers for the present and was washing them out for anything. Any one of them would have made twice the officer that Armstrong was.

Of course there was John Bixby, the kid I buddied around with on the voyage. We had gone through Basic Training together at Camp Roberts, California. He was a tall, slim kid about twenty-one or twenty-two. He hailed from Hudson, Iowa. Another kid that hung around with us was a fellow by the name of Bob Chapman. He was really the string bean type, about six foot three. Really a nice fellow though. His home town was Marshall, Michigan.

Our voyage had started out rather badly. The very first night out at sea became rough. Almost everyone began to get sick. I was very fortunate and didn't feel too badly. Long before this trip I always figured I would get seasick easily. Even swinging in a lawn swing made me sick, not to mention chair planes and some other carnival rides.

This first night out and the next three days were something. The whole ship was slippery from vomit. There weren't enough not sick to keep the place clean. Even the sailors for the most part were sick. I got a little green around the gills but not bad enough to heave.

The boat really rocked and rolled. First it would roll from side to side. I know what it means to try to get sea legs. It took more than sea legs to stay on this tub in a storm like this. Hanging on the rail one minute you could reach over and touch the water and the next you would be way up in the air and the other railing would be dragging in the water. A couple of rolls like that and then it would buck the other way. First the stern would be way up as we would drop off a giant wave and then we would hit another wave and just about up-end the thing. When the ship hit the waves head on it would shudder and shake so much that everyone thought we would never make it. One L.S.T. was so badly battered it had to turn back to the States. The second day out another had to put in at Bermuda.

On the fourth day the sea began to smooth out much to everyone's relief. The rest of the trip was very smooth sailing. Some days the sea was so smooth it looked like glass.

The days dragged slowly. Nothing much to do but count

the other ships in the convoy or talk among ourselves. Incidentally, there were seventy ships in our convoy. There were ten L.S.T.'s including ours. Most of the other ships were Liberty Ships. One thing we could do on this trip was to get a nice suntan. I took it easy with mine and got one of the best tans I ever had. Many nights we stayed up all night down below playing nickel-dime poker. About all the duties we had were to straighten up around our bunk and to draw occasional watch duty or K.P. I was on K.P. twice on the whole trip.

One bright day a little incident happened to break the monotony. The motors on our boat conked out and we began drifting helplessly around in circles. It was a rather weird feeling to see the rest of the convoy sink out of sight over the horizon. We'd have made a small target for some German Sub that had been following the convoy hoping for an unprotected straggler. After a while they got the motors going again and by going full speed ahead the rest of the day we finally caught up with the rest of the convoy at dusk. It seemed good to be back in the fold again. From that time on we were continually having motor trouble and often dropping behind the rest.

Another little deal happened one night to cause quite a bit of alarm. We were all in our bunks sleeping when there was suddenly a loud and terrifying crash. Some were knocked from their bunks. The same thought flashed through all of our minds. We all figured we had been torpedoed. Everyone was blowing up their life preservers and trying to get upstairs. I lay in my bunk listening for the alarm to ring. When it didn't ring in a minute or two I decided we hadn't been torpedoed but couldn't imagine what had happened. There were several more loud bumping and scraping noises and then all was quiet again.

In the morning we actually found out what had happened. During the night we had been side-swiped by a freighter. A long steel arm that protruded from the freighter was the thing that had done most the damage. It had torn the railing completely off the starboard side, two life rafts going with it. It also had sheared off three funnels. We had a huge dent in the side of our ship where the two hulls had made contact. We were very, very fortunate that it had not been a lot worse. Had that freighter hit us broadside instead of side-swiping us, it would have been curtains. It would have knocked this tin can of ours wide open. We wouldn't have had a chance. We would have gone down in a matter of seconds.

Still on another night we had a little more excitement. There was a lot of firing and depth charges being dropped. Some were close enough to shake the ship some. The convoy also did a few extra changes in course. The next morning we were informed that our convoy had been attacked by a pack of German subs and that we didn't have to worry about torpedoes while we were in a L.S.T. They claimed L.S.T.'s didn't draw enough water. The torpedoes would go right under us. Just the same I wouldn't care to have some sub let one loose at us just to see if it would go under or not.

Now we knew that our voyage was about over. Africa was becoming more and more visible. A little later Spain hove into sight on our left.

About noon we entered the Straits of Gibraltar and a little later the Big Rock could be seen. One of our L.S. T.'s put in at Gibraltar. I was hoping our boat would follow it. However, after a short pause we started moving on. When we got on the east side of the rock we could look back and see it more clearly. It certainly looked mighty formidable.

We were now looking forward to getting to our destination which was Oran, Algeria, North Africa. The captain of the ship had told us a few days before that Oran was to be our destination. Up until that time we had spent much of our time trying to guess where we might go. We knew we wouldn't get to Oran until the following day but we became impatient to get there.

We were now sailing on the Mediterranean Sea. It was as smooth as glass and was a beautiful blue. I have never seen water so blue.

Near the Straits of the Atlantic side we had seen many porpoises. They were about the only fish we had seen on the voyage with the exception of many little flying fish.

We sailed all that night and in the morning land was again in sight. About noon we turned and started heading for the shoreline. A couple of hours later we were at the outer Oran harbor. The inner harbor was jammed with ships of all types, predominately cargo vessels. There wasn't enough room to get our ship in so we dropped anchor just outside the inner harbor. From where we were we could look in on the city of Oran. From here it looked quite large and modern. For some reason I had always kind of pictured North Africa as all desert, Arabs and huts. From here it looked as if I had been all wrong.

After the ship anchored we were allowed to go swimming off the side of the ship. The water was as warm as the weather and it was really swell. I was really enjoying myself until a human turd hit me in the face. In fact I damned near swallowed it. That was the end of my swimming that day.

That night we were allowed to sit up on the open deck after nightfall. It was the first time since we had left the States. We sat up on the deck, smoked and talked way into the night. We could look in on the bright light of the harbor and the sprinkling of lights throughout the city.

Early the next morning our boat weighed anchor and we moved slowly into the inner harbor. Inside there was a beehive of activity. Ships unloading, small vessels scurrying to and fro. We pulled in and finally got up alongside a large American transport. On the way into the harbor we saw some war torn ships. There was one destroyer that was just a twisted mass of steel.

The fellows on the transport started throwing us candy, cookies, etc. We all were so hungry we scrambled and fought over the food like a bunch of beggars.

We waited all day expecting to get off this tub any second. The rumor had it that we were to go to some camp near here. I wanted to go anywhere. Anything to get off this scow. Night came and Lt. Armstrong said he hadn't been able to find a thing about what was to become of us. No one seemed to know we were even here. We knew we would be on the ship until the next day anyway.

That night Bixby, Chapman and I were so hungry we sneaked into the galley and stole some potatoes. We sat around on the deck in the dark and munched the raw spuds. The things really tasted good.

The next day was the same story. Nothing happened in regard to our leaving the ship. However, one thing what helped the situation was that the British Navy quit feeding us. They told us we would have to start eating the American "C" rations that were aboard. They acted like they had been doing us a big favor feeding that crap they fixed. I knew the "C" rations couldn't be much worse than the food we had been getting. We opened cases of "C" rations and distributed them. This was my introduction to the famous Army Type "C". The one I got that day was hash. We were so hungry that this stuff seemed like the best food we had ever eaten. It was quite filling anyway.

All that day we hung around on the ship wondering when we would get off. We watched the activity of the harbor and stared in at what we could see of the city. On a high cliff that rose up from the harbor stood an ancient fort or castle of some kind. It must have really been a stronghold in its day. I wondered about its history.

I hadn't heard too much about Oran until the war. The British and French fleets had quite a battle here in the early part of the war. One of the Limey sailors aboard had been on a British warship during that action.

That night, as we sat around on the deck talking, the air-raid sirens began to blow. All the lights in the harbor, on the boats and in the town went off immediately. To our relief, no planes showed up. They said that any time German planes came over the whole North Africa coast blacked out. Tunis and Algiers were much closer to German airfields than Oran so probably one of those places was getting raided The alert lasted about forty-five minutes and then a long blast on the sirens notified everyone that the raid was over.

The next day, September 4th, 1943 was the day we had been waiting for. Finally we got our orders to leave the ship. We gathered our "A" and "B" bags and prepared to move off. To get to the dock we had to climb up on the transport we were tied to. We were so loaded down with our two barracks bags we staggered up onto the transport and out onto the dock. We finally made it and here we were again on solid ground. What a long way from home though. I figured I was about seven thousand miles from California. Oh well, what the Hell. This is what I wanted. To get around a little and see what the rest of the world looked like.

The dock hands and street cleaners were odd looking characters. They were a crumby bunch of Arabs. They wore long baggy pants and either turbans or fez's on their heads. They were a filthy lot, too. They didn't look very clean and some had sores on their legs. They really worked hard, too. They would take a step about every two or three minutes.

After the usual amount of screwing around we loaded on Army trucks and took off. As we whisked through the city we were able to get glimpses of it. It looked interesting. I was hoping I would get a good chance to look this place over soon.

We left Oran and tore down the open highway. It was a black-top road but had been pretty well beat up by the heavy traffic and it was rough. We traveled down this road for three or four miles. Suddenly, we rounded a bend in the road and our camp came into view. The camp consisted of hundreds of large tents situated around a small resort village called Canastel. Canastel is located near a high cliff overlooking the sea.

We dismounted from the trucks and were shown which piece of desert was to be our area. We divided into groups of six or eight and went to work putting up the tent which was to be ours. Bixby, Chapman and I stuck together. A noncom was to be in charge of each tent. The non-com assigned to our tent happened to be Corporal Thompson. There were only six including Thompson in our group. There were supposed to eight but there had been a mix up of some kind. We were pleased with the set up. All the fellows were a swell bunch and willing to do his share. At least we were going to get along with ourselves in our own tent anyway.

We had no more gotten our tent up and half way situated when the order came down to get ready for a physical. We had to strip and put on our raincoats. We were also told to take a towel because we would have a shower after the physical.

We were soon all ready and were marched down to a building in the village. As we passed through the village you could tell that it had been quite a resort in its day. Before the war that is. The houses and cottages were all in pastel colors. All the places were pretty nice. There were plenty of trees and shrubs growing around them. There was a large casino built right on the edge of the cliff. The side facing the sea was almost completely solid glass. This had probably been quite a gambling and drinking establishment before the war.

Our physical consisted of the usual short-arm examination. No doubt we had picked up something on the trip over here. After the physical we were taken to the showers. The showers were quite a deal. It consisted of water running at a bare drizzle for two minutes to soap up in and then two minutes were to wash off in.

After the shower was completed we went to our tents, changed clothes and went up to chow. Italian prisoners were doing the K.P. The food we got was still "C" rations but at least they were heated. After our mess-kits were filled we went over to some stand tables a short distance away to eat. The tables were built high enough so that when you stood at them you didn't have too far from your mess-kit to your mouth.

It was Sunday so we didn't have to do anything by the way of training. We spent most of the afternoon looking over our new camp. Our particular area was right across the road from the village. Our dirty company street slanted down towards the drill field. Before the drill field were the wooden latrines, concrete washing stands and a couple of blister bags for drinking water.

Looking straight out to the west we could see the edge of the bluff and the sea. This wouldn't be a good place for a sleep walker. That cliff was several hundred feet high. Looking to the east you could see row after row of tents until they disappeared over a small hill quite some distance away.

After chow that evening Bixby, Chapman and I went to a movie. The place where they showed the movie wasn't far from our area. The theater was an open air affair. Your seat was on the ground with about a foot of dust for a cushion. The picture was several years old but I hadn't seen it so enjoyed it very much.

After the movie we came back to our tents, crawled under our mosquito netting and settled down in our bunks for the night. Our bunks were rather crude affairs. The uprights were made out of anything from about a two by two to a twelve by twelve. Every one of the posts on my bunk was of different dimensions. Instead of springs or canvas to lay on rope had been used. A mattress cover with about a handful of straw completed the set up with the exception of your two blankets.

In the morning at Camp Canastel we were awakened by one of the cadre noncoms coming down the company street blowing a whistle. Reveille here was at 6:00 A.M.

Our second day was not strenuous either. We had a clothing check and most of our O.D. clothing was taken away from us. We also turned in all of our gas impregnated clothing. The processing took until about noon and we had the rest of the day off.

The second evening we were here we had to stand retreat. Retreat here at Canastel was something to dread. We had to dress all up in our suntans and march up to the parade ground through ankle deep dust. Then, after juggling and moving around and having more dress right commands than you could count, we were ready to pass in review. After retreat we waded back through the fogging dust to our areas.

The third day here things really began to get down to business. Right after morning chow we had tent inspections. The inspection wasn't too tough, but everything did have to be more or less in place.

A really funny thing happened during the very first inspection. Our steel helmets were all supposed to be hung over the backs of our bunks. When our company commander, a First Looey came in to inspect our tent for some reason he took off his helmet and laid it on a bunk. I didn't see him do it so I was amazed to see a helmet lying there. I thought that some damned fool in the bunch had forgotten to hang up his helmet. When the lieutenant stepped outside for a minute to check around the tent I grabbed the helmet and quickly hung it on my bunk. I didn't want the tent to be gigged. The officer came back in and made his final inspection. Then he started looking for his helmet. He looked on the bunks, under the bunks on the floor and all over the place. He didn't look for it hanging on the end of the bunk. He knew he hadn't hung it there. I realized what I had done but what the hell could I do? I just stood there at attention and sweated it out. Finally, the company commander left sort of mumbling to himself. After he left I told the rest what I had done. They all got a big bang out of it. I asked Thompson what the heck to do with the thing. He said that was my problem. I wasn't going to take it to the C.O. and try to explain where it had been and why. I waited until he was inspecting a few tents down the line and then pitched his helmet out into the company street.

I watched while the C.O. walked back up the company street. He spotted his helmet and stood there and stared at it for about a minute in disbelief. He knew it was his because it had the First Lieutenants bar painted on it. He looked around to see if anyone was looking, picked it up and went on towards the orderly room shaking his head. He probably reported to the psycho ward as soon as he could get there. He probably figured this African heat was getting him.

After inspection in the mornings we would go down to the drill field. The first hour we would have close order drill. The second hour we had sitting up exercises. The third hour we played rough games. The games were really rough, too. I remember one little gem in particular. We were divided into groups of twelve. One man was "it" to start the thing off. The object of the thing was for the man to try to cross the line that had been drawn in the dirt. Another line had been drawn about twenty-five yards away. You had to run to that line while the other eleven fellows were trying to bring you down. If you succeeded in making it across the goal you were given a pass to Oran the next day. However, if anyone did make it the ones who had let them do it had to do extra detail in the hot afternoon. So it was a vicious thing. I don't think they worried about giving out any passes.

Each man was given three chances to make it. You could get a running start and cross the starting line at full speed if you wanted to. When it was my turn to try to make it everyone was hot, dirty and in a nasty mood. They were beginning to take it out on the runner. The first crack I made about ten yards. After I went down I could feel the bastards piling on. My face smashed down in the dust and I almost suffocated before they unpiled. The second try was about the same thing only they jumped harder when they were piling on. It made me sore, in fact pretty damn mad. For the last try I backed off an extra few yards and came charging like a mad bull. The first fellow that got in my way happened to be a little fellow. He probably didn't weigh more than a hundred and forty pounds at most. I weighed 195 pounds and was going at top speed while he was standing still to meet me. We hit head on and I mean head on. I was running with my head down and somehow the top of my head hit him flush in the face. I bowled him over and kept going. I saw daylight and for a second I thought I was going to make it. Some guy somehow grabbed my arm. I pulled free but it had slowed me down just enough. The next thing someone grabbed my head and just about tore it off my shoulders. Then another grabbed me then another and it was the same old piling on again. When the dust cleared the poor guy I had hit was out like a light. His nose was smashed all over his face. He was finally revived and led away to the medics. Later I learned that he was O.K., just a broken nose. I had hoped to see the kid and tell him how sorry I was it had happened. I never seemed to see him around while I was at this camp. Of course, I'm sure he knew it was unintentional. Anyway I know how a fullback feels when he has no interference at all. Had it been football though I would have made at least forty-five yards on those three tries. There's a fifteen yard penalty in football for unnecessary roughness and piling on. Needless to say no one got a pass for Oran.

The last hour before noon we marched and doubled time up and down the road. This was if any of us were capable after the games. It was quite a rugged morning to say the least.

The dust here was terrific. Every step we took the stuff fogged up. The dust was so fine that it sifted through our clothing and leggings. By noon we were always caked with a layer of reddish brown dirt. Bathing facilities here at the camp were very poor, too. We had only one very poor shower a week. Our daily allowance of water for bathing, washing clothes, shaving etc. was one helmet full. It was impossible to even keep half clean. About all you could do was to keep your faces from getting too caked up. The rest of our body had to go to heck.

Our clothes became absolutely filthy. It showed up especially on our underwear. At the time they were white. The Army later changed the color to O.D. Maybe to keep them from showing the dirt so much was one of the reasons.

Drinking water was a problem, too. We had about all of it that we wanted. Drinking the stuff was the problem. It hung out in the sun all day in Blister Bags. Therefore it was always near the boiling point. It was so doped up that it was hardly recognizable as water. It was the vilest tasting stuff imaginable.

Everyone, including myself, got sick the first few days at Canastel. There was an epidemic of the G.I.'s. You had to line up to get into the latrines and sometimes it was hard to wait. Everything from dirty mess kits to the fruit that some of the men were buying from the Arabs was blamed. I personally think it was caused from that lousy doped up water we had to drink. Some of the fellows got so sick they had to be hospitalized.

About the third or fourth day in camp our company caught guard. They got the guard roster by alphabetical order so naturally I got the call. Bixby and Chapman were also stuck.

We were excused from drill but had to go down and practice for guard. We had to practice guard mounts, say our general orders etc. One thing I could say about the training at Camp Roberts it must have been good. As much as I hated the place and the way they drove us

I had to admit they had crammed a lot into us in those thirteen weeks of basic. I had noticed in Camp Shenango, Pennsylvania that the Robert's boys could drill better and knew more about the army generally than the other rookies from other training camps. It was the same here. Many of the fellows were sloppy drilling. They couldn't do the manual of arms worth a damn. Some had no idea about guard, general orders or anything else.

The officers in charge were raising hell. We had to practice over and over. Some even had to study their general orders out of the manual.

All of us had to learn a few words in French to use with the Arabs. They were "arret" for halt, "allez" for scram and "habe vous permission" for have you a pass. I didn't know what would happen if any one of us had challenged an Arab with any of those and he had answered. I figured allez was the best on to use. That eliminated any further discussion.

We were warned to watch out for the Arabs and not let one of them sneak up on you. Some guards had been found with a knife in their backs and their clothes gone.

We practiced all morning. We were issued bayonets and then we returned to our area. We all had to get haircuts, shave and clean our rifles, clothes and web equipment. This was quite a chore considering the dust and the limited facilities around here.

About five thirty we marched down to the drill field where guard mount was to be held. The guard inspection wasn't as tough as we were led to believe it might be.

Bixby, Chapman and I all drew the third relief. After the first relief had been posted Bixby and I went back to our tent to get a couple of blankets. Suddenly a huge cheer swept the camp. We stuck our heads out of the tent to see what was up. The big news was that Italy had surrendered. It made us feel pretty good because we felt it might help shorten the war some. So on the seventh day of September 1943, Italy had thrown in the towel.

We went back to the guard tent. Everyone there, including the O.D., were sitting around talking excitedly about the news.

Time for relief came and we were led to our posts. I got a dark, forbidding looking spot. The post was about two hundred yards long. It was a narrow path that led down through waist high brush. I had visions of an Arab waiting behind some brush ready to leap out on me. The first couple of turns around the post I kept throwing glances over my shoulder. I wouldn't have been able to see anything anyway because it was pitch black. I soon forgot about the Arabs and felt at ease. It was sure black though and jackals barking in the distance added a weird touch.

I soon discovered that Bixby's post started where mine left off. At the end of each turn we timed it to meet and would spend several minutes talking. Strictly against the orders of the day but it helped to pass the time away.

Finally, at midnight our bunch was relieved and we went back to the guard tent to try to catch a few winks of sleep. We took our other turn from 4:00 to 6:00 A.M. This was the last relief of guard. Guard here was only during the hours of darkness. At six all guards went up and had breakfast. No drill for us today so we went to our tents to try to get a little sleep before it got hot.

That same night our company got its first passes issued. The passes were also given by alphabetical order. This was one time I was glad my name started with "B". If it had started very far down the alphabet, I'd have never gotten to Oran. They were only in the "G's" when we were shipped out. Bix and I got passes but Chapman didn't quite make this one.

BYE FOR NOW

As soon as retreat was over Bix and I got ready and beat it down to the highway and started hitching a ride. We soon hooked a ride on a G.I. track and were taken right into the middle of Oran.

Oran was a strange city alright. Dirty barefooted Arabs were to be seen everywhere. Arabs with donkeys were moving along the streets. There was also a cleaner better looking class of Arabs. Their clothes were clean and their bodies looked clean. The women wore white flowing garments. This class of women wore gold earrings, arm and leg bracelets. Almost all of the Arab women were veiled. A lot of the young girls, even down to the very small ones, had scarves on their foreheads. I understood this was more or less of a brand. All these girls belonged to some rich Arab and when they were of age they would be in his harem or at least slaves.

Most of the permanent populations of Oran were French. They dressed and looked like the people in any American city. The city was alive with all kinds of troops. Americans made up the biggest part of them but there were also British, French and French Colonials. Many vehicles, practically all American army trucks and jeeps, dashed madly through the streets.

There were many nice ultra-modern buildings here as well as a lot of broken down ones. Some of the bars and cafes were pretty good looking comparable to those in the States. There were a couple of nice looking stream line hotels here. One I remember in particular was the Continental Hotel. The American Red Cross was set up there.

As Bixby and I were going up a street we ran into Bob Banquet and his pal, a guy named Balentine. We didn't care for either of them but we figured that Bab was just screwy enough to have a good time with in a place like this.

First, we all agreed that we very definitely needed something to drink. We found a pretty good looking bar and went in to have a few to start the evening off.

First we ordered a round of beers. The beer was cold, tasty and nice but seemed to be plenty weak. After a couple of glasses of beer we decided we needed something stronger and so began to order wine. The wine had more kick to it and soon we began to get in good spirits. I saw a thing here that was never in the States. A French kid about ten years old came in and ordered a glass of beer. The bar tender gave it to him as if he was a guy who was forty years old. In other words it wasn't uncommon for a ten year old kid to come into a bar and order beer. I have no idea what the laws of liquor and minors are here but they couldn't have been too tough. Maybe stronger stuff is harder to get. This beer seemed hardly more than a soft drink. Of course over here in the old country I found people use liquor differently than we do in the States. It was really more common here than at home but the people seemed to know how to drink better than the Americans. They grew up with the stuff and it was part of their life just like a hamburger was to an American. No doubt there was a lot less alcoholism in Europe than in the States. The English and Germans seemed to come nearer to our way of drinking than any of the others.

After about four bottles of wine we decided we were hungry. A Frenchman directed us to a respectable restaurant called The Normandy. The place was really nice. Nice atmosphere with music and all. We found that the meals they served were rather limited. The only thing they had on the menu was an egg omelet or spaghetti and meat balls. We decided on the spaghetti and meat balls. The meal was pretty good. We had soup, salad and wine and all the trimmings.

A couple of French Marines sat at the next table and we tried to converse with them a little. It was pretty rough not being able to speak French.

Things were going along pretty fine until the meal was almost over. Then that wise punk Balentine got a wise idea in his head. His idea was to just get up and walk out without paying for the meal. I guess he figured these Frenchmen were too dumb to know what the score was. I didn't think much of the idea but the rest seemed to want to try it so I didn't want to be a wet blanket.

We got up and walked nonchalantly out of the place. About half a block down the street I was beginning to think we were going to get away with it. We hadn't though. A waiter came running down the sidewalk after us with the check. He was a little excited but he tried to be nice about it all. Of course Banquet and Balentine started arguing with the fellow. I told them hell, we had been caught so forget it and I would pay for the meal. I went back with the waiter trying to apologize for trying to pull a sneak. I was really sorry and felt ashamed of myself.

I paid for dinner and thought that ended the unpleasant incident. When I got back to where I left the rest of the fellows Banquet and Balentine were talking to a M.P. Bixby said they were telling the M.P. that we had to pay for the meal twice. That was enough for Bixby and me and we took off. As we rounded the corner we looked back and saw the M.P. and those characters going back to The Normandy. We were glad to get away from those men.

Bixby and I went to another bar and had a few more drinks. We were glad to get rid of those characters and enjoyed ourselves the rest of the evening.

Quite late we decided to go back to camp. We walked to the edge of the city and waited to catch a ride. As we stood there waiting for a ride Banquet and Ballantine caught up with us. They were feeling pretty proud of themselves. They had convinced the M.P. that they had been forced to pay for the meal twice. Of course the M.P. had taken their part and demanded that the Frenchman cough up. Of course they refused and the M.P. told them that the place would be closed up. The place was closed the next day, too. Chapman got his pass the next evening and we had him go by the place and take a look. He said the place was closed tighter than a drum. I was surprised that such drastic action was taken. I hoped it wouldn't be closed long. It probably wasn't. I always felt real bad about that little incident.

The effects of the heavy drinking didn't start working on Bix or me until we got back to camp. We began to feel really high and acted accordingly. We had our clothes strung all over the place. We finally made it to bed and settled down for the night.

Life at Camp Canastel was pretty routine. Every day the old grind was about the same. In the mornings we always had the drilling, calisthenics, marching and double timing. Due to the intense heat of the afternoon our activities were limited to a lecture on one thing or another. Sometimes it was water discipline or chemical warfare. Of course there was always the military courtesy lectures.

The entertainment at Canastel was surprisingly good. The camp had about three open air theaters. I went to a different movie about every night. There were also G.I. and Red Cross shows put on the outdoor stages. One night a bunch of girls from Oran put on a nice show for us. They sang, danced and played musical instruments. Most of them were very talented. Their teacher had been a big star in the Folies Bergere for years. One girl could speak English and led in singing songs community style.

We sang songs like "You Are My Sunshine", "Deep in the Heart of Texas", "California Here I Come" and other popular numbers. All of the girls were good looking and scantily attired. Some were really stacked, too. It was a very enjoyable evening. They ended the program by singing "La Marseillaise" and "Over There".

One of the G.I. shows I saw while I was here was pretty good, too. There were several highly talented musicians and singers on the program. No doubt most of them had been professionals in civilian life. One of the highlights of the show was a sword swallower. He stuck everything imaginable down his throat including a huge pair of scissors and a bayonet. He also swallowed a lighted neon tube and we could see it shine in him. This sort of stuff gave me the willies.

A Negro sergeant on the same program made a few predictions. He was supposed to be very good at this sort of thing. He had hit the invasions of Sicily and Italy and the surrender of Italy right on the day. This time however, he really went overboard. He predicted Northern France would be invaded by October (1943) and Germany would fall by Christmas (1943). Of course we found out later how wrong he had been. And I do mean far wrong.

The weather around Canastel was pretty nice. It was getting towards the middle of September and although the days were still plenty hot I guess they were nice compared to July and August. The evenings were nice and cool and made it nice for sleeping. The weather here now reminded me a lot of the San Joaquin Valley back in California. The nights were always clear and we had some beautiful starry, moonlit nights.

Some of the jokers that had made the voyage over on the boat with us were beginning to get worried. They figured that some of us might be sent to the front pretty soon and they didn't want to be named "it". They began to go on sick call every day. They complained about everything from a toe ache to an aching back. They had been a brave bunch until they thought there was a possibility of being sent somewhere where they might really get hurt. The sad part of it was that most of them got away with it. Nearly all of them were re-classified and put into some non-combat outfit. I guess the rest of us were the suckers.

Time at Camp Canastel was running out. On the evening of September 14th our battalion was alerted. Our company commander told us that practically every one of us would be shipped out the next day. Most of us were anxious to get going. We were pretty excited and curious to know where we were going. We packed our barracks and musette bags and sat around half the night talking. That night it began to rain.

The next morning it was still raining. We had breakfast in the rain and then stood around the downpour and listened to the shipping orders. Sure enough I was on them. I was really glad. I didn't know where we were going but I wanted to get going anyway. Those on orders carried their barracks bags up to the motor pool early. At noon we all sloshed up to the motor pool ourselves.

By now the rain was coming down in cloudburst proportions. We stood there in the torrent for three hours waiting to get on trucks. Not once in that time did the rain slacken. The water kept getting deeper and deeper and soon it was half way up to our knees. Boy! What a rainstorm. When it did rain here in North Africa it really rained. I had foolishly put my field jacket in my barracks bag thinking this would only be a short shower and that the sun would be out bright and hot in a short time. The raincoat I was wearing didn't shed the rain it just strained it. Even a field jacket under it wouldn't have kept me from getting soaked in this rain but it would have helped keep me warm. I was soaked through and through and chilled to the bone.

While we were standing there in the downpour we had a physical examination. It was really a lulu. A medical officer came sloshing down the line asking each man if he felt alright. It was comical to see everyone all hunched over looking miserable say, "Yes Sir" when he was asked if he felt in good shape. What a damned bunch of liars. If anyone of us had put in a much more miserable afternoon I'd like to know when it was.

Just before our three hours of waiting were up the camp commander showed up to give us a little farewell speech. His name was Colonel Crisenberry, a full colonel. He was driven right up to the stand in his staff car. He got out draped in a couple of raincoats and carrying his little riding stick. He said, "Men, I like to see you standing there in the rain and mud. It shows me how tough the American soldier really is". He went onto say that we were leaving here and going on a little nearer to the Front. "Never mind that", he said, "Even if you do get to the Front there isn't any danger. When the war is won come back to Oran. I will still be here. Just say, Colonel Crisenberry let's have one more parade and go home". With that little ditty he climbed into his car and drove off. What a speech! How inspiring! From that and the speech we had gotten from him when we arrived I was convinced the man was mad.

Finally, when it looked as if we were going to be left in the motor pool to drown, our trucks showed up.

We piled on the trucks and soon were tearing down the highway. We were, I understood, going to a place called St. Cloud to board the train. The official deal had it that we were going by train to Bizerete.

The ride was a miserable one. The rain continued to pour down. The speed of the truck created a wind that cut through us. We all stood there in the truck shivering and too miserable to even talk.

The country we were passing through wouldn't have been bad if we could have enjoyed it. The countryside looked quite prosperous. There were many vineyards and orange groves. We passed through a couple of small towns in route. Parts of them, the French section, were pretty nice but the Arab side was crumby. In the country we saw several nice country houses. Probably belonged to some well to do farmer.

It was beginning to get dark when we pulled into the railroad yards at St. Cloud. We had come about twenty miserable miles. I was surprised at the appearance of the trains here. The engine and cars were so much smaller than those in the States. They almost looked like toys. Even the whistle on the engine sounded like that of miniature ones.

We were informed that we were to travel by coach instead of boxcar. The boxcars were not available at the last minute. This was a bad break. Boxcars are better because there would be more room and a chance to lie down.

We struggled around in the rain and knee deep mud trying to get organized. We retrieved our barracks bags which were now water logged. We waded over to boxcars into which they were tossed. Finally, as dusk was settling we clambered aboard the train.

European coaches are much smaller than American ones and are divided up into compartments. There were nine of us crammed into each compartment. Ordinarily these compartments were made to accommodate four. It was quite a trick for nine men and the musette bags to squeeze into one of these compartments. Bixby, Thompson, Fowler and a fellow named Anderson, another one we called Kansas and three other jokers jammed into a compartment. Immediately three of the fellows left looking for more room. The rest of us sat there pretty miserable. We were all soaking wet and had no change of clothes. All of our other clothes were in our barracks bags in one of the boxcars on the train. It didn't matter anyway because they were soaked, too. We just had to sit there and let our stuff dry out.

At dark the train began to move. So on the 15th of September 1943 we left Canastel and headed for Bizerete, Tunisia.

The first night of travel we stayed awake and talked most of the time. We were so crowded we had to sit in a very upright position. We couldn't relax a little without crowding the other guy. Our clothes were soaked and so cold and miserable sleep was almost impossible anyway. Toward morning we began falling asleep from sheer exhaustion.

You would just be dozing off when the train would stop so suddenly you would be thrown from your seat. When everyone got untangled and settled back in your seat the train would start up with a jerk that your head would bounce on the back of the seat. Incidentally, the seats in this compartment were just plain hard benches of wood and wooden backs. No doubt this car we were in was one of the oldest in captivity.

The next morning, we were traveling in much the same kind of country as that around Oran. Vineyards, orchards and of course those dirty Arabs everywhere.

The weather had cleared up now and the sun was shining down brightly. It wasn't too hot though, just right.

It was easy to tell that there had been plenty of G.I.s

through here before. In every town, village and hamlet we passed through all the Arab kids turned out by the tracks and set up a cry for candy. They would call to us, "Hey, Joe gimme bonbon." I heard that so much on the way to Bizerete I could have scalped me a few kids.

Our rations for the trip were good old "C" rations. Each morning we each received a can of hash, one can of meat and beans and a can of vegetable stew. With this we got three component cans that held the crackers three pieces of candy and some kind of drink. The drink was either lemon powder, bouillon cubes or some soluble coffee. The bouillon cubes and coffee needed hot water and the lemon powder was as solid as a rock and impossible to dissolve. The stuff didn't solve any problems for something to drink. The first few times you didn't mind "C" rations but soon you began to hate the things. I liked the hash the best of any of them. The meat and beans seemed to be the choice of almost everyone though. I liked the beans alright but the meat they put in it was awful. To get an idea, to me it tasted like a wet stinking dog smells.

The "C" rations were highly seasoned, and they got pretty hard to take after eating them cold for a couple of days. It seems when the rations are eaten cold they cause a lot of gas on the stomach. There was usually a lovely smell floating through the car caused by escaping gas. After a day or two you could detect whether the gas was of the hash, meat and beans or vegetable stew variety. Sometimes it got so bad you had to stick your head out of the window for fresh air.

In the afternoon of our first day of travel we entered the city of Algiers. We lay over here in the railroad yards for two or three hours. There was lots of activity going on in the city. Plenty of troops and army vehicles of every description. Everything here seemed to be about 90%

British. Algiers had seen the war. For blocks on both sides of the tracks it was devastated. Probably both Allied and German planes had hit this place.

While we were sitting there sweating it out, another troop train pulled into the yards. It was a train load of French Colonial Troops. All had a fairly dark complexion, probably from Morocco or some other North African territory. They wore colorful red and blue uniforms. From the looks of the boxcars full of horses they must have been a cavalry outfit. We saw several trainloads of these troops all the way to Bizerete.

Toward evening we pulled out of Algiers and started rolling eastward again. It was the same story again that night. We jolted, bounced, rocked, swayed and jerked along all night. Sleep was just about impossible so Bixby, Fowler, Anderson and I sat there talking most of the night.

Sometime during the night we began groaning through some mountains. They were really rugged. In the moonlight they looked big and barren. They were big alright. Our train labored and struggled so hard getting up the grades I was afraid it would start rolling backwards. When the train finally made it to the top of the grade it would really take off down the other side. We got going so fast and swaying we were sure that any second we would leave the tracks and plunge off into space.

The next morning, we were almost out of the mountains. The climate now seemed hotter and drier. The countryside definitely took on the appearance of desert. There would be a mile or two of quite productive land and then long stretches of pretty desolate looking country.

Our train stopped at every little town and siding. It would no more than grind to a halt when all of the G.I.'s would be off racing around looking for something to eat or drink. The officers wouldn't let us buy anything to eat or drink from the Arabs. If you were caught with anything we had to throw it away. The officers were actually doing us a big favor although some of them were just trying their rank. Most of the officers were right out of O.C.S. and were green themselves.

They were right about the food though. Those crumby Arabs never took a bath. I think it was against their religions or something. Most of them had sores on their arms and legs and sore mattery eyes. You would see little kids standing around with matter oozing out of their eyes. Hundreds of flies would be crawling in their faces and feasting on the matter. What a low bunch of people. Imagine eating eggs, melons and other stuff they had to sell. Water was scarce so there was not any way of even washing the stuff. They even fertilized their melons and crops with human manure. I don't know what diseases they had but I would hate to think.

Fowler and I were crazy enough to want some wine anyway. In a small town we found an Arab selling the stuff. He filled our canteens for four bits. The officers didn't check our canteens when we got back on the train. I guess they figured we had gotten off to get water.

That night after dark we got out our canteens and drank the stuff. It was vile tasting crap, hardly recognizable as wine. However on just a canteen foe each of us we began to feel real queer. I had stories of the Arabs mixing marijuana in with their wine. I wondered if this was some of it. I had heard stories from official sources that many G. I.'s had gone blind, crazy and everything from the stuff. Maybe propaganda to keep you away from it but I don't doubt it. It was a thought anyway. Anyway we felt a lot weirder than we should have on such a small amount of ordinary wine. However, most of the bumps and jerks seemed to have gone out of the train that night.

The next day we crossed over into Tunisia. Tunisia looked the same as the country we had traveled the day before. Of course there was no reason why it should look different. One thing Algeria and Tunisia for sure in common were those damned Arabs.

I understand that when the first trains ran across North Africa with American soldiers they carried their guns with them. They had taken so many pot-shots at the Arabs from the windows of the trains that now our guns were issued again not at the end of the trip. I can understand how the G.I.'s must have been tempted. Besides being dirty and miserable, you had to watch them or they would steal everything you had. Murder wasn't beyond them either.

Here in Tunisia we began to see many signs of fighting. Along the railroad bed there were thousands of fox holes and slit trenches. The ground for long stretches at a time would be pitted with countless thousands of shell holes. Across the landscape knocked out tanks and other war equipment lay strewn. Some had German markings, others American. Although salvaging of this stuff had been going on for several months there was still plenty scattered around. In some of the towns we saw huge graveyards of wrecked tanks, trucks, planes and other equipment.

Late in the afternoon we arrived in the town of Mateur. This was as far as we were to go by train. Mateur wasn't a very large or prosperous town. It looked worse than ever now. It was just shambles. There had been some bitter fighting here. I remembered reading about ever coming over to it. We moved slowly through the town and pulled up to what was left of the railroad station.

We dismounted and assembled in an open lot near the station. Our train trip was finally over. It had taken us three days and nights to come approximately 900 miles.

We sat around the lot waiting for something to happen. Finally, a couple of hours later some trucks showed up and we climbed aboard.

We rushed down dusty roads hanging on for dear life. Approximately seven miles from Mateur we turned into a camp that had a lighted sign by the road. The sign read "29th Repl. Bn.

At least this place looked like someone was expecting us. Some lieutenant that was trying to get tough by smoking a big cigar came out and called roll call. Everyone seemed to be here but a couple of guys who had been left back in the desert. They had gotten off to get water and the train had left them. I had nearly been left myself. The train would never give any warning when it was going to leave. It would just start up and take off. One time I had been getting water in my canteen quite some distance from the train. Suddenly the damned thing just took off. I raced for the thing and was just barely able to grab on to the last ear. If it hadn't taken so long to get moving I would have been left behind. Well, most of us had made it anyway.

After roll call we were showed to a spot to bed down on. We threw our blankets down on the ground and leaped on them. I was travel weary and it seemed good to stretch out again. The ground even seemed good and I had a swell night's sleep.

We were up early the next morning anxious to know what was up. We had breakfast of "C" rations. They were warmed up this time anyway. We were given instructions to hang around mighty close because there was going to be a shipment today. They weren't wasting any time on us.

Sure enough right after noon chow the shipping list was called off. Bixby, Anderson and I all got the nod. Fowler didn't make this one. I was hoping we could stick together for we always had good times together. The only other I knew on this shipment besides Bix and Anderson were those characters Banquet and Balentine.

We were supposed to leave about 3:00 p.m. Our bags were supposed to show up before we left. They never did of course. We were issued rifles, the old .03's and ammunition. It was beginning to look like we might be going somewhere we might need them. They also issued us gas masks.

Just as we were loading onto the trucks to shove off a couple of Red Cross Officers of some sort showed up. They had cigarettes for us. They just didn't hand them out though. They said they wouldn't sell the cigarettes but contributions would be appreciated. We hadn't hardly had any cigarettes since we got off the boat so we didn't ask any questions and paid for them. None of us had small change so most of the cigarettes cost us anywhere from two bits to four bits a pack. On the seal of the packages were seals saying, "For American Overseas troops. Not to be sold". Those bastards really had a racket. The Army gave them the cigarettes to distribute and they were getting money out them. No doubt they were just pocketing the money. Probably get rich before the war was over. They just showed up when a bunch was pulling out and no one thought too much about what was going on. They also knew we were going a long ways from here and would never be back. They figured that away from here other things would make us soon forget about the deal and the chances of being reported were remote. Even if someone did remember and later put up a squawk they would say, "Why those men gladly contributed a little for the cigarettes". They were pretty safe with their racket alright. It was still a lousy trick. Oh, well what the Hell.

We pulled out and headed down the road toward Bizerete. The 29th Repl. Bn. Had been located half way between Mateur and Bizerete. As we rode along some one pointed out a hill and said it was hill 609, famous in the North African fighting. All the way to Bizerete we saw large stacks of shells, gasoline and other supplies in the fields off the road a ways. A few well-placed bombs could have raised heck with the things around here.

On the edge of Bizerete we were driven into an olive orchard and dumped off. From our position here we could look at the activity in part of the docks. There were several L.S.T.'s pulled up and being loaded with all kinds of war equipment. There were lots of tanks and other vehicles driving into the L.S.T.'s. After two hours of waiting here in the orchard we marched on down to the docks.

After the usual checking and rechecking of names we boarded a L.S.T. that was tied to the dock. Three hundred of us boarded this particular L.S.T. It had accommodations for one hundred and fifty troops so there were lots of us left without accommodations. Bixby and I put our stuff under a half-track up on the top deck.

After the troops were on the ship they began to load it below with 105mm artillery shells. It sure would have been swell if something had started them going. We wouldn't have known what had happened. There were several L.S.T.'s tied up along the docks and they were all being loaded with tanks, shells, etc.

The Navy fed us that night. After chow that night we had a movie up on the open deck. After the show Bix and I crawled under our half-track, spread our blankets and were soon sawing logs.

All next day we lay in the harbor. We watched the

activity of the loading and other activities of the port. We all talked, guessed and argued as to where we might be going. It did seem now that we had a good chance of going to Italy and right into the fighting. The battle of Salerno was just winding up and the causalities had been high.

All along I had thought that most of us would join outfits that we were training over here somewhere. First I thought it would be around Oran and then when we moved east I figured it would be around Bizerete. Now I was beginning to doubt that. Unless we stopped in Sicily it looked like the front for me.

I felt that I was hardly prepared for radio work in actual combat. I had only thirteen weeks of training and there were so many things to learn. If we were really going to the front as replacements it did seem as though they could have gotten a more seasoned bunch than us with all the men they had in the army. We were barely more than raw recruits. None of us had been on maneuvers and some of the boys had never even spent any time in the field at all.

I felt I was better off than many as far as practical training went. Basic at Camp Roberts had been hell but they had pounded a smattering of everything into us. I realized that more and more after talking to recruits from other training camps. At least I knew how to fire the .03 I had been issued as well as the carbine. Many had trained on different weapons and had never fired this type of rifle. I had at least spent a few days in the field. Many hadn't even done this. I also felt that if the pressure was really on I could get along some on the radio. I was able to take about thirteen words or so a minute. Thirteen words a minute had been required to get out of basic as a radio operator. I had been away from it several weeks now and might be a little rusty. Anyway we were going to find out what the score was pretty soon because at dusk our L.S.T. began to move. Anyway quit griping Borthwick, this was what you wanted.

Bizerete harbor was full of sunken ships. Just the masts of many of them was all that remained above the water. The sterns of others stuck out above the water. One ship that must have been carrying ammunition was really devastated. It nearly had been blown clear out of the water on to the land. In fact, large pieces of it were rusting on dry land.

As we passed slowly out of the harbor we got a pretty good look at the city. Bizerete was supposed to be the worse bombed place of the war up to date. I didn't doubt it a bit. The place was absolutely flat.

We finally cleared the harbor out into the open sea. The old L.S.T. began to shudder as the motors were opened up to full speed. We could look back and see search lights stabbing into the skies above Bizerete. It was pretty definite now that we were going to Italy. The sailors said we were going to Salerno, Italy.

The next morning, we could see land now and then. The sailors said we were passing off the coast of Sicily. The day passes without event.

That night there were about thirty guards taken from the three hundred troops aboard for watch duty. Of course I had to be one of the unfortunate ones caught on this detail. One thing that was good about this detail was that we only had to stand one two hour watch.

Bixby and I happened to be assigned to the same post. Our post was in the 20mm gun turret in the bow of the boat. What our duties were we were never quite sure. There was a sailor in the turret with us. He had a headphone and was in touch with the brains of the ship. He reported every flash of light or anything else that seemed to be worth reporting. Nothing much happened but far ahead we could see flashes.

Bix and I were sitting there in the dark when Anderson appeared carrying a case of "K" rations. He had gone down in the hole and swiped them. This was the first time any of us had ever had "K" rations. We opened up the rations and took out the chocolate bars, cigarettes and whatever else we wanted. The canned meat, crackers and drink we pitched overboard. We started to save the dextrose tablets until we tasted them, then overboard they went. Those dextrose tablets must have been the brainstorm of some idiot.

The next morning, we could see land in the distance in front and on both sides of us. We realized that this must be the Gulf of Salerno.

Around noon our L.S.T. attempted to pull up to the beach. A couple of hundred yards out were hung up on a sandbar and were unable to get any closer. The ship would back up and make another run for the shore but would hang up again. After several unsuccessful attempts to make it to the beach our L.S.T. moved up the beach a few hundred yards to try again. We passed several L.S.T.s that had been sunk. Either the bow or the stern was all that stuck out of the water. Our boat took a tremendous run at the beach. We were close enough anyway and a small floating wharf was brought out from the shore. Almost immediately the trucks loaded with the 105mm shells started driving off.

The troops were soon organized and we walked across the wharf and onto the beach. Here we were in another country, Italy. It was the fourth country and third continent I had been in in about a month. Also, I had seen Spain in the distance.

The road we took off on was dirt. It wasn't really a

road but just sort of a dusty trail. The dirt had been pounded into a fine powder from the heavy equipment using it so much. Three hundred men stomping through it made the dust fog up fifty feet. Some of the poor guys in the middle of the column were almost passing out from the suffocation. Some of the men that were in charge of the wharfs and nearby supply dumps razzed us about marching in columns of four. They said if some Jerry planes swooped down on us they would slaughter us like cattle. A very sobering thought.

We headed into a large field and were told to take it easy. It seemed strange to be here in Italy. I'd studied about it in school and had always hoped to see this place as well as North Africa. I never really had expected to ever get over here but here I was. I had always been interested In Roman history. So here I was in the land of it and not too far from where it had started, Rome. It could have been a little more enjoyable under better circumstances but you can't have everything. Well, anyway here I was in Italy. This was September 23rd, 1943.

We were supposedly in the rich Salerno Valley. The land where we were was quite level. It sloped gradually towards the towering mountains to the east. To the north and south the land was table like. Of course to the west was the sea. There were a couple of houses nearby and they looked anything but prosperous.

About half a mile to the north was an airfield. Planes were continually taking off and landing there. Every time one took off it raised a huge cloud of dust. Most of the planes headed toward the north, the front.

Amphibious trucks "dukw (ducks) were going back and forth from the beach out to the ships they were unloading. To me those "dukws" looked like giant crocodiles. You would see them emerge from the brush and go right out into the water without hardly changing pace. They were long and low like a crocodile.

We hailed on one of these "dukws" that was loaded with "C" rations. They threw off several cases to us. We had cold "C" rations for supper that night.

At night Bixby and I bedded down together. To the north we could see the flames and hear the grumble of artillery. Boy! We were getting nearer and nearer.

For breakfast the next morning we had more cold "C" rations. One of the "dukws" dropped off some 10 to 1 rations. It was comical to see those replacements officers trying to divide up the stuff. They acted like a bunch of old school teachers. In fact that is what they; had been, at least a lot of them. It was disgusting to see those jokers stumble and fumble around with the stuff. They wanted everyone to buddy up with someone else so Bixby and I got together. When they got through farting around with the stuff and we got our share. We received two packages of toilet paper and a pound of butter. Bix and I had to be satisfied with cold "C" rations again.

Later we needed water so went to a nearby farmhouse. There were a bunch of women from about eight to eighty washing clothes in the back yard. We got our water from an open well. Probably it wasn't too clean but it was wet and tasted good.

In the afternoon trucks came to pick us up. We didn't go many miles but lots of that was straight up. Up on a high mountain they had made replacement depot. It was a replacement depot as of last night. Of course there were not buildings, tents or anything. Just a wooded area on a mountainside that was called a replacement depot. Last night a bunch of infantrymen had been here and had left this morning. We were the second bunch to inhabit the place. We were told to park any place in the immediate vicinity. Bixby and I found a fairly level spot that we claimed as our own by putting our equipment there. Not only did you have trouble finding a level spot but also a clean one. The Germans had used this area for a few days before. They used any place to go to the toilet and so there were loads all over the place. The bunch that had been here last night had added to the collection so it was pretty thick around here. If we had come into the area after dark I hate to think of what the results might have been.

It's no wonder the Germans had used this area for their use. From here they could see every inch of the beach and were still hidden by the heavy foliage.

A makeshift kitchen had been set up on a level spot in an orchard. Here they heated the cans of "C" rations in large tubs. We lined up to get the chow in a line that wound around the trees for a good many yards.

The first night here passed without event. Some guys that had been here in Italy for a few days were nervous. He kept yelling at us to quit smoking. He said that the beach had been raided for the last three nights. He said they had always hit the beach but if they could see cigarettes here we would liable get it. We were lucky I guess. No planes showed up at all. The rocks and twigs dug into our backs and we kept rolling down the hill. Otherwise we had a good night's sleep.

The next day Bixby and I were lolling around taking it easy and some guy took our names for guard detail. Good old guard. I just couldn't miss it.

My post was at the bottom of a hill. My first stint was from 8 to 10. The second relief. When I was relieved at 10 o'clock the corporal or the guard told me in the general direction of where the guards were supposed to stay. It took me two hours of stumbling around, sweating and swearing to find the place.

At two o'clock I was led back to my post. While standing there at my post a shot rang our up on the hill somewhere. The shot was followed by the yelping of a dog. I found out later a guard had shot and killed a dog. We heard something crashing around in the brush and challenged it. When there was no response he had fired. Even firing blind he had hit the dog.

Finally, at five thirty an hour and a half later I was relieved. It griped you to be relieved late, but you expected something like that in a situation like this.

The following day, September 26th, the big day. This was the day we were assigned to the 45th Infantry Division. The officer told us that the 45th was a crack outfit and one to be proud of. I was assigned to the 158th Field Artillery. Bixby and Banquet were to go to the 160th F.A,

We were told that we would do the jobs that we had been trained for. This was a relief. I hated to think of trying to do a job I knew even less about. Soon some rucks from the different outfits arrived to pick us up. There were about twenty five of us assigned to the 158th Field Artillery Battalion. We climbed on trucks marked that way.

Men as well as animals had died along this road. There were burned out tanks, riddled helmets and other war equipment scattered around.

Boy! This was it. We guessed it wouldn't be long now. I began to have a funny feeling in my stomach.

The trucks really took off. Down the mountainside and soon hit a main highway. The highway was a pretty nice concrete one. There were plenty of signs of fighting all along the road. Buildings in shambles and broken from shell fire. Off in the fields all kinds of stock lay dead from artillery shells. They were all bloated and the smell was terrific.

The first town we came to was named Battipaglia. The town was just one big pile of rubble. They had cleared a path through the middle of it so equipment could go on. It had really taken a terrific pounding from artillery and bombing. There wasn't a building that didn't look like a pile of gravel or wasn't destroyed beyond repair. Bizerete couldn't have been any worse than this. Of course, Bizerete hadn't been a large town. I can't imagine a town in this shape even being rebuilt or even cleaned up. It would be much easier to move to another sight and erect a new town.

As we passed through Battipaglia on down the road we saw huge craters on either side of the road. Misses that had no doubt been directed at the town.

Soon we turned off the main highway onto a secondary road. The road had a surface of crushed rock packed down solidly. We soon began to wind into the mountains.

We passed a couple of old, small decrepit villages. The houses were jammed up against the hillside so tight they almost appeared like caves. I was amazed to see how miserably the people around here lived. They weren't much better off than the Arabs. I had always thought of Italy as one of the leading European countries. It certainly didn't look like it around these parts anyway.

On many of the hills, particularly the extra steep ones and that sat more or less apart from the regular range, perched forts and small villages. They were old. Probably dating from medieval or more ancient times. They had been placed on these steep hills for protection. These old fortresses and fortified towns were to become a familiar sight here in Italy. We weren't the first G.I.'s down through the centuries to move through these parts.

There were hundreds of interesting ancient things here in Italy. I would like sometime to have time to look the country over as a tourist.

We wound around through the mountains for miles. In many places there were signs of fighting. The retreating Germans had blown out every bridge. We had to detour even for many of the shallow streams.

We knew that we were getting near the front now. We began to see tanks, trucks, half-tracks and all kinds of vehicles grinding up and down the grades.

We saw a plane flying slowly towards our lines with smoke streaming from it. It was a fighter type of some kind. It suddenly hesitated and then plunged down into a mountainside. Nor parachute opened so I guess the pilot went down with it. Maybe he was badly wounded and couldn't bail out.

It began to grow dark and the weather began to threaten. An occasional drop of rain spattered down on us. Everyone became pretty quiet. I guess our spirits were reaching a new low.

It was well after dark when we turned off the road and drove up a very steep hill. About half way up we stopped and the driver got out. We learned that we were at the Headquarters Battery of the 158th Field Artillery Battalion. The driver went in to CP but returned immediately.

We drove back the way we came. About two miles back we turned off the road and into an olive orchard. This was the battalion service battery. We dismounted and were told to flop anywhere for the night.

We stumbled around in the dark trying to find a smooth place to bed down. I was a lone wolf. Most of the fellows were lucky enough to stick with someone they knew all the way from the States. All of my friends had been left behind or sent to different outfits. I didn't know a soul in this bunch and felt pretty lonesome when all of the others were buddying up with their friends.

We must have been near the front alright because it began to rain. The old story of the front and rain of World War I seemed to be holding true. It was a cold miserable rain, too.

By the time I found a place reasonably level and free of rocks and roots it was pouring. I threw my two blankets down and threw my shelter half over me. The rain began to come down in cloud burst proportions. I kept pretty dry for a while, but only for a short time. The down pour turned the slope we were flopped on into a small river. Rivulets of water came running down under my half shelter and drenched me thoroughly. From the cursing and moaning around me I knew others were having the same trouble. The down pour continued until my blankets were as soaked as myself. I stood around an hour or so until the rain slowed down. Now I was sold, wet. Miserable and lonely. I laid down on my wet blankets and finally went to sleep.

The next morning was a damp, miserable and dismal day. The clouds hung low and were very threatening. The fellows of the outfit said that this was the first rain they had seen since coming overseas in June. We ate from the service Battery chow line.

Right after breakfast it began to pour again and continued to rain all day. I was so soaked now but instinctively tried to devise means to protect myself from the elements. I had very little luck however. I had one brainstorm that I thought would work. I spread my shelter half over a fox hole after me. Everything was fine until the shelter half collected about thirty gallons of water and caved in on me.

Towards evening the rain let up and I got a pretty

good night's sleep in spite of being wet, miserable and sleeping on waterlogged blankets.

The next day the weather had definitely taken a turn for the better. The rain stopped, the clouds lifted considerably, and the sun was trying mighty hard to peep out.

All of us replacements began to cluster around some of the veterans and fire questions. We were all anxious to find out something about the outfit and what combat was like. We were told that we were sitting her for a couple of days while the 34 Division and a few other smaller units passed through us. They told us not to worry because the Germans were out of range. The day before we had arrived however some of the firing batters had been shelled and had casualties. We learned that the 45th Division had originally been an Oklahoma National Guard outfit. It had left the States in June. It had landed in Sicily and fought through the campaign there. It had also landed at Salerno and fought its way up to where we were now. They also told us that we would be assigned to different batteries either today or tomorrow. We asked about battle and casualties. We got comforting answers and some not so comforting ones, depending on whether the guys we were talking to were trying to make us feel at ease or trying to scare the hell out of us.

We spend most of the day out by the road watching the equipment roll by. Lots of tanks and guns were moving up. Near the road were three German graves. Above each was a neatly carved cross with the soldiers name etc. On each cross hung the man's helmet.

In the afternoon a major form the headquarters came down. We learned his name was Major Hubert. He took our names and asked us a few questions. He seemed surprised when he found out that most of us were fresh out of basic.

Late in the afternoon of the following day the same major came down with a list of our assignments. I was assigned to Headquarters Battery along with five others. The rest either stayed at Service Battery or were assigned to the firing batteries.

Toward evening a truck drove the five of us assigned to Headquarters Battery up to their position. When we were dumped off someone told us to bed down near the wire truck. We sat up quite late talking to some of the older members of the outfit.

About the time we started to turn in it started to rain again. A couple of us crawled under the six by wire truck. An old timer called to us cheerfully from the cab that this was a jinxed truck. It had backed over one sleeping soldier and had crushed this head in. Another time it had run into another G.I. and had crippled him for life. A cheerful thought. We found out later that was exactly what had happened. We were in luck tonight though. The truck didn't roll over us and it didn't rain very long.

The next day was sunny but definitely cooler. We hung around in the vicinity of the wire section wondering what was up. As the afternoon wore on and nothing happened, we began to think that we had been forgotten.

We hadn't though, because a little later the first sergeant, Alf Talent, came and got us. He took us up and introduced us to the Battery Commander, Captain Beverly A. Finkle. Captain Finkle was a red headed fellow and looked to be in his early thirties. He talked a little about the situation and assigned us to our sections. The fellow, Adams, Smith, Ward and Kitchens were assigned to the anti-tank platoon. Mairop went to the wire section. I was assigned to the radio section. The First Sergeant then took us down to the supply truck and issued a few things. We received 30 caliber ammunition for rifles. We also got a few things we didn't have. Our barracks bags hadn't shown up yet so we were lacking a lot of things. I got part of the things I needed. The thing I needed the most they didn't have. That was a field jacket.

After chow that night we were introduced to our section chiefs. Mine was Staff Sergeant Bridenbach. He in turn introduced me to the rest of the radio section. In the section were Sgt. Joyce, Sgt. Kuza, T/S Ruhs, Sgt. Massie, Sgt. Kegler, Pvt. Bell, Pvt. Brumbach, Pvt. Mutheart, Pvt. Matinovich, T/5 Kitchens, Pvt. Regan, Pvt. Schwartz, P.F.C. Marshall, T/5 Gill and now myself, Pvt. Borthwick.

Well, for the first time in my army career I had something definite. I was now a private in the radio section of the Headquarters Battery, 158th Field Artillery Battalion of the 45th Infantry Division. Bridenbach said I would be in Gill's fire direction section. In the same breath he told me I was to be a guard that night. That damned guard again.

There were two guards to a post. I got on with an old guy named Sample. He was sort of a handyman around the battery. Sort of a queer duck. Gill was the corporal of the relief. He sat with me quite a while and talked. He seemed like a swell fellow. He hailed from Logansport, Indiana.

The "probably" about moving early in the morning proved to be a fact. Just after I had turned in after my second relief they came around getting everyone up to move. I stumbled around in the black getting my stuff together. I had some trouble finding Regan's weapon carrier, the vehicle I was supposed to ride on. Ruhs, Bell and Dorozio also rode on the same truck. Our convoy pulled onto the road. Headquarters Battery went first, followed by the firing batteries.

It was plenty cold on this morning and here I was still without a field jacket. I was really miserably cold. Bell brought out a blanket and offered me part of it. It was the only thing that kept me from turning into an icicle.

We traveled a considerable distance that morning. There were plenty signs of battle along the way. There were blown out bridges and all sorts of destruction everywhere. Many houses and other buildings were in shambles.

We pulled alongside a small burned out car. In the back seat were two charred bodies with their arms drawn up over their heads. The bodies were burned beyond recognition but the type of auto had to be German. They were actually the first dead from battle that I had seen in the war.

We went on down the road and passed through a town called Avellino. We continue on the improved road for a short distance more and then turned off onto sort of a cow trail road.

All along the road, different outfits were camped in the fields. Some of the fields were full of tanks and other trucks. In places the roads were jammed with quartermaster trucks taking supplies towards the front. All of the quartermaster trucks were driven by Negroes.

Finally, after we had gone perhaps twenty miles, we pulled off into a lane. The C.P. section stopped immediately but the radio section and kitchens followed up the land quite some distance before they found a suitable place to stop.

Our area was in a small ravine with lots of grapes growing on arbors. There were signs that the Germans had been here before us. There were empty German cigarette boxes and sardine cans for one thing. There was also a big pile of trash the Krauts had left. Among letters and other stuff there were a couple of painted pictures of Hitler.

Schwartz and I pitched a tent together. We didn't know how long we were going to be here, but the weather began to look threatening again.

I was beginning to get acquainted with a few of the fellows a little. Gill, Ruhs and Bell were among the first fellows in the outfit that I got very acquainted with. Harry Bell was a tall good looking fellow of about twenty-five. He hailed from somewhere in Pennsylvania. He had been with the 1st Division in both North Africa and Sicily. When the 1st Division had been broken up after the Sicilian Campaign he and some others had been sent to the 45th. He said he had a bad case of battle nerves and didn't know how much longer he would be able to take it. He thought that a little more combat and he would fall to pieces. He said he had met a girl in Scotland while with the 1st Division the he hoped to marry her someday.

Henry "Hank" Ruhs was a swell fellow, too. He hailed form New York City. As a civilian he had been a janitor in a subway station. He was always joking about his civilian occupation. He was twenty-four, blond and of medium build. He wasn't much on looks but his sense of humor and personality more than made up for that. I liked him immensely.

Ray Gill was another of my first buddies in the outfit. He was chief of the fire direction radio section although he was only a T/5. He came from Logansport, Indiana. He was pretty proud of his home state and was always talking about it. He was friendly though and tried to tell you, to the best of his knowledge, any information you might want to know.

That night passed without event. We didn't move up. Schwartz had to work on the radio, so I had the tent to myself. It began to rain a little that night but not enough to do any damage.

The next day we stayed in the same area waiting for orders to move up. The day passed without event. That night I worked on the C.P. (Command Post) radio set for the first time. It was a 608 radio and it had tower receivers. It was the push button type and had several different channels. It was a cabinet set mounted in a jeep. I had only seen this set a few times while at Camp Roberts and had operated one for about five minutes. I didn't have much idea what it was all about.

Gill and Grady Marshall were at the set when I got there. They showed me a couple of things about the set. They gave me a list of different officers' names and some call signs. They told me who to wake up when my two hours were up.

The list of names and call signs were Greek to me. I was nervous about whether I could handle everything that might come over the set. Fortunately, the traffic was light. Even so, every time something would come over the set I would get so excited I would about leap out of the jeep. I would drop my pencil or message book. By the time I found them I wouldn't be able to find my blue lensed flashlight.

The pay-off came when Major Hubert came out and wanted to send a message. He asked me if I was connected to the service battery. Being flustered anyway I didn't realize what he meant. I thought there must be an auxiliary battery or something to keep the radio going when the jeep battery began to weaken. I told him I didn't know whether I was connected to the service battery or not. Major Hubert stood there a minute and then took the mike out of my hand and called the Service Battery himself. My face really burned when I realized what he had asked me. He didn't say a word to me. I don't know if he was too disgusted to give me hell or he had had experiences with raw recruits before. I was really glad when my two hours were up and I went to wake up Jim Mutheart.

The next day we moved out of this position. We moved only a few miles and pulled up in a large vineyard. It was raining for some now. I was on the pre-dawn shift and it was plenty cold. I still didn't have a field jacket.

About noon we hit the road again. We moved up a few more miles. We knew that we were getting near the front. We began passing infantrymen walking up the road in single file and at about ten-yard intervals.

A couple of minutes later I realized that we had reached the front. Just as we started to pull off the road a smoke shell burst in the road a couple of hundred yards up ahead. I had been munching on some hard candy but now I crammed my mouth full and really started chomping away.

We took up a position about two hundred yards off the road. We had no more than dismounted when a shell smashed in about a hundred yards up ahead. A piece of shrapnel came ripping through the trees clipping off leaves and small branches. It dropped at my feet. I touched it. It was hot. Another shell screamed over our heads and smashed in back of us. It landed much closer. I was scared stiff. Everyone was digging like mad. One over, one short. They had us bracketed. The next one dropped right in on us. Shrapnel screamed in all directions. You had to try to dig lying flat on your stomach. Rocks and roots were too thick so it made it rough.

The last shell had gotten some of the boys. A couple

pretty bad. It had landed a few yards in back of us. I threw a glance in the directions. One of the guys was just lying there staring wide eyed. I recognized Mairop, one of the guys that had just joined the outfit with me. He looked hurt and was trying to crawl under a weapons carrier for protection. Someone was calling for the medics. Another shell landed close. It smashed in near a weapons carrier. The fragments from it blew out a couple of tires and riddled the body.

Fire missions were pouring into our radio from both Forward Observers up ahead with the infantry and the Piper Cub Observation plane. Most of the missions were enemy gun positions. I was glad they had been spotted.

Grady Marshall was on the set. He was lying under the jeep. The cord on the mike was just long enough to let him do it. He was an experienced operator. It took one to handle the amount of traffic that was coming over the set and in those circumstances.

More shells crashed in throwing dirt and rocks on us. I about gave up trying to dig a slit trench with only a little entrenching tool. The hard ground, rocks and roots made it impossible anyway. I had been able to dig down only a few inches.

When I had gotten in the Army I was afraid the war would be over before I got over here and saw any action. It wasn't that I saw flags flying in front of my eyes or even especially hated the Nazis, I was curious to know what it was all about. Now that I had seen some of it I was ready for cease firing orders already. I was afraid the war was going to last longer than I was.

When a couple of more shells smashed in close, I thought to myself, "Why don't those bastards give up? They know they can't win." They were a long way from through yet.

Finally, our howitzers began to open up. They really started blasting away. Some of the German shells now began to whine over our heads and smash down in back of us trying for our guns.

Our 105's must have been hitting home with their shells for some of the incoming mail began to slacken. About dusk things became quite quiet.

All four of the wounded men were evacuated to the rear hospital after dark. I understood one of them died there. He never came back anyway. Mairop was the only one of them I ever knew. I never became acquainted with the rest because they never came back to the outfit. Mairop had a piece of shrapnel through his leg above his ankle a ways. He wasn't supposed to be hurt too badly. I almost envied him. I wished I could go back home to some nice hospital and get the hell out of here. However, Mairop returned to the outfit in a few weeks.

After dark the Germans began to plaster the road that was about two hundred yards to our right. That was too close for comfort. Quite a lot of shrapnel came dropping around. Most of it was pretty well spent by the time it reached our area but some of it could still make a nice gash in you if you got in its way.

The older fellows with the outfit said this was typical of the warfare since The Battle of Salerno. The Krauts would battle during the day and raise all kinds of hell and under the cover of darkness they would withdraw. They would leave rear guards and shell the road and by-passes to hinder our moving up.

The Germans hit the road to our right spasmodically during the night. Our own guns spoke occasionally during the night. They were probably interdicting some town or some crossroad deep in the German Lines to hinder their withdrawal. October 4th, 1943, my baptism of fire.

We stayed in this same position all the next day. We didn't receive any artillery right on us but they kept interdicting the road near us occasionally. More of their shells were landing up ahead about a quarter of a mile or so. The poor infantry was catching it. Our guns were blasting away pretty heavily all day. I got on the radio a couple of times but always got into trouble and had to have help.

We stayed in this position all that night. It was about the same as the night before. The Krauts interdicting the road and our own guns firing some.

The next day passed quietly. Our own guns fired very little. The retreating Germans were getting out of range. Late that afternoon we moved forward again. Three miles down the road we came to the town of Benevento. This town was where a lot of the German artillery that had been shelling us for the last couple of days had been located. This place had also been one of the main targets for our own artillery.

It was hard to judge how large this town had been in peace time. Of course, now the place was completely deserted. It had been a Fascist city and a German stronghold. Now it was nothing but rubble. Most of the buildings had been laid flat by the bombing and shelling. We could smell the sickening odor of the dead.

We wound around, over and through, piles of rubble and debris. Huge craters were everywhere. There was lots of German field telephone wire strung around. It was easy to tell the Kraut wire. It was made of some sort of plastic or composition and was a bright red.

We moved through Benevento and took up a position about a mile north of the town. Our new position was on a hillside partly covered with trees.

Shells kept whining over and smacking on the road

between us and Benevento. It was dark when we got situated in our new position.

Matinovich had found some liquor when he passed through Benevento. He gave me a slug of the stuff. It was a green, sweet, thick looking substance. Whatever it was it seemed to be really potent. He said he thought it was called Strega.

Gill had found a spot in a nearby barn for the fire direction radio operators to bed down in. The fire direction operators were: Gill, Marshall, Martinovich, Mutheart and myself. At the end of my two hours on the set I came to wake Mutheart. As he was leaving he said there was a drink of booze in the corner if I wanted it. I went to bed instead.

I was the last one up in the morning. In the corner I spied the "drink" Mutheart had referred to. It was a two gallon jug almost full of that "green stuff". I decided to have a couple of slugs. I didn't have to go back on the set for a longtime so we sat the sipping on the stuff. An hour later I had consumed a considerable amount. I began to feel mighty peculiar and everything began to get a little blurry and unsteady. I managed to get down the ladder from the loft but knew I was in no condition to be seen around the C.P. or the brass. I wandered a ways and came upon a haystack. There were several of Headquarters Battery boys sprawled there sleeping off the effects of the green stuff. I leaned against the haystack and relaxed. It started to rain and it felt so good spattering down in my face. I finally passed out. I woke up in an hour or so. The rest of the drunks were still sprawled where they had been. They must have drunk more of the stuff than I had. I felt a little groggy but ready to take my turn on the radio. Pretty soon Gill came around to check up on me. He said that Major Ford was sore because so many guys had gotten tight while we were on the line. Years later, I happened to read an article about the green stuff. It was called Strega and in fact had been first discovered and made right here in Benevento for several hundred years. The name of it meant "Witches Brew". That I can believe.

It didn't seem that we were too near the front. The only incoming shells were crashing a considerable distance ahead of us. The Germans were apparently on the retreat again.

Our guns weren't quite out of range yet. They did quite a bit of firing. In the afternoon I got on the radio and got into trouble as usual. There were about three fire missions as well as other messages coming over all at once. A lot for an experienced operator to handle to say nothing about an unexperienced replacement like myself. If I had had only a few hours of training on this set back in the States it wouldn't have been so bad.

My worst problem seemed to be hearing. I had perfect hearing but something was wrong. One of the troubles was that I did not know the sequences of the fire commands and the routine procedure of firing. If something did not come over quite plain I had to ask for a repeat. I know those F. O.'s (forward observers) must have loved my lousy operating. I know later, when I was a F. O., when sometimes every second counted it made you sore to have to repeat several times. The harder I tried the more nervous I became and consequently the more I screwed up. I made several glaring mistakes. Captain Sheafers, the S3, screamed at me a few times. He was a miserable bastard anyway.

In spite of my grief I was improving a little and knew that before long I would be able to handle the thing as well as any of them. I could do better than poor old

Mutheart already. He had been trying to operate for quite a while but still fouled up miserably. In fact, he was finally transferred to the anti-tank platoon.

We stayed in this position until dark. We fired a few more missions, but the Krauts were just about out of range again.

That night we moved up again. We traveled a few miles up the road and pulled off onto an old gnarled olive orchard situated on a muddy hill. We groped around in the dark trying to get things set up.

I ran across Bell. He was supposed to be an L.C. (liaison officer). I asked him what he was doing here. He said it had been pretty hot where they were so he had taken off. He said his nerves were shot. I didn't imagine that Capt. Finkle was going to like this very well. Bell, I'm sure, wasn't a cowardly type but he was definitely a battle fatigue victim.

Rain was threatening so Gill and I pitched a tent together on one of the rocky slopes.

I did my shift on the radio. To my satisfaction I seemed to be improving and could handle the set better.

I turned in at midnight. I was so hungry I could hardly sleep. I had been hungry ever since I had hit this outfit. I just couldn't seem to get enough to eat. The rations weren't plentiful either. Eating was pretty slim. That was, of course, because everything still had to be brought from North Africa.

As I lay there I could hear machine gun fire and rifle fire up ahead. The infantry was mixing it up with the Krauts. You could easily tell when a German was firing or when one of our boys were firing. The German machine guns really spit out the lead. It made the rat-tat-tat of our thirty and fifty caliber machine guns sound slow in comparison.

Just as I was dozing off shells suddenly began screaming over the hill. They were hitting on the road about a hundred yards to our left and down the hill. They must have been skimming right over the hill we were on from the sound.

I was wide awake now and could hear others rousing up. The shells came in a steady stream. They were all landing on a curve in the road. That showed you how well the Germans knew this country and had it zeroed in. They knew that there was a sharp curve there and vehicles would have to go slowly there. Also, the Germans had blown out a small bridge right at the curve to slow things down even more. It happened that there were not convoys on that particular piece of road at that moment. That was luck, too.

The shelling stopped as suddenly as it had started. That seemed to be all they were going to shell around here tonight. I soon fell asleep again.

The next day I worked on the radio quite a bit. I was getting along better all the time. I still had some trouble though now and then. Everything was fairly quiet. The Germans were retreating out of range again.

Everything was pretty tranquil until chow that night. Just as we lined up for chow things began to pop. There were some terrific explosions and some popping, cracking noises. I didn't know what was up but knew something was haywire from the way everyone was hitting the ground and taking cover. A split second later I knew what it was all about. Eight Jerry planes came roaring over the hill, low and wide. I hardly had time to hit the ground before they passed over. It would have been curtains for most of us if they had had their guns blazing when they broke over the crest of the hill.

I was looking toward the ground as I hit the dirt.

One of the planes was over the road with all its guns blazing. There were men and vehicles on the road. There was another crash as the plane dropped its bombs. They were all gone in a flash. They hardly gave you time to get scared.

Our immediate area had escaped unscathed. However, a lot of damage had been done. Down on the road by us a couple of fellows had been killed and others wounded. It was a wire outfit and they had been laying some phone lines. One of the fellows killed was up on a pole. He still hung there in his belt. One of the bombs had demolished their truck. Back down the road an ammo truck had been blown to smithereens. A couple of ambulances had been destroyed too. Three fellows from our "C' Battery came walking over to the aid station. "C" Battery had been strafed but they were the only casualties and their wounds did not amount to much. Getting close though.

The planes the Germans had been raiding with were M.E. 109's. They were fast and heavily armed. On those raids they carried a couple of small bombs. They hedgehopped to keep down out of our anti-aircraft fire.

The Germans had moved out of range again, so we were just waiting here for orders to move up. About all the news that was coming over the radio were unimportant messages or communications.

The next day was a cold, bleak, miserable thing. I was beginning to wonder about that "Sunny Italy" stuff. It was getting towards the middle of October so I guess you could expect lousy weather.

I had made friends with several fellows in the outfit by now. I got pretty well acquainted with a couple of the fellows that worked in the S-2 Section.

Bob Perkins was one of their names. He was thirty-one years of age. He hailed from Morganstown, North

Carolina. He was a graduate of the University of North Carolina. He had gotten a degree in journalism. He had worked on some papers and written some articles for magazines before the war. He had come over from the States as an infantry replacement but had somehow wound up in the artillery.

The other fellow was just a kid named George Bouncher. He was only nineteen but he acted like fifteen. His home was in Butte, Montana. He was a likeable fellow even though he did act silly part of the time. He had also been an infantry replacement but had come to the artillery with Perkins. They had joined the outfit two days before our bunch had.

In spite of the cold weather we decided to go down to the Volturno River and take a bath. I was ready for it because I hadn't been able to take a bath since leaving Camp Canastel. Even the ones there had been next to nothing.

We headed for the river which was only about three hundred yards from our position. We hoped when we go out in the open we wouldn't get strafed. On the way down we crossed the road. The wreckage of the wire truck was still there but it had been shoved off the road. A little way from the road was a single railroad track. The retreating Krauts had made sure that it wouldn't be used for some time to come. They had done a very detailed bit of sabotage. Besides breaking practically every time they had knocked a piece out of every rail. They must have had special equipment to do such a thorough job. Of course, they had quite a bit of time to do it.

At the river we stripped and tried to get in the water. It was icy cold. We got in up to our knees and that was all we could possibly stand. Our legs soon became numb. We splashed a little water on us and had to get out.

Twice later in the day German planes came over bombing and strafing. They didn't hit any targets in our immediate vicinity. In fact they didn't try for anything near. We could hear bombs exploding some distance away. They came over our position though. They were very low. The big black crosses were very plain. You could even see the pilot very plainly.

Night came and things were fairly quiet. Ahead we could hear the rumble of guns. The front had moved up a ways in the last couple of days. The Germans had been retiring slowly northward. They weren't in flight by any means. They were holding up our advances all they could without taking a chance of losing too heavily right now. They were giving troops behind them time to prepare a strong line where they could make a real stand.

The last couple of nights had been as clear as a bell. The moon had come up over the mountains and had shone brightly. Also, during the last two moonlit nights, German planes could be heard buzzing around low overhead. You could tell the German planes by the sound of their motors. At least it was easy to distinguish their two motored planes from ours. Their motors were not synchronized like our own and had more of an unsteady sound. They were probably recon planes taking pictures or looking for lights of convoys or something to bomb.

The next day passed uneventfully. At dark we prepared to move. We moved up towards the Front in the brilliance of the moon. We passed infantry men sitting by the roadside resting on their march to the Front.

We traveled on up the road several miles. As we neared the Front, we could see the flashes and hear the reports of many artillery pieces. The American artillery was giving something a terrific pasting.

We turned off the road and wound our way up a long

driveway to a large hotel sitting out here by itself. It was surrounded by lots of trees. In the moonlight it looked like it might have been quite swank in its day. However, we didn't check into it or sleep in any beds that night. Actually, the place was abandoned.

The C.P. section set itself up in the hotel lobby but the rest of us took up positions around the grounds of the place. Our radio jeep was parked about fifty yards from the hotel so we strung telephone wire to it. Now the operators had telephones as well as radios to contend with.

A terrific artillery duel was taking place and all hell was breaking loose. On all sides American artillery was laying down a terrific barrage. The ground shook from concussion. Our twelve 105's joined in the barrage and added to the din.

All the artillery wasn't outgoing either. The Germans were throwing plenty back. We could hear the nasty crack from the exploding shells on all sides. Fortunately for us none of the shells were landing right in our immediate area but we could hear them whining over. Several landed close enough the shrapnel came whipping through the trees.

On this particular night I became acquainted with another famous German weapon. I was already familiar with their famous artillery piece. Now this other weapon was the Nebelwerfer or six barrel mortar. The Americans called it the "Screaming Meemie". This weapon could fire six projectiles without reloading, either one at a time or all at once. The projectiles it fired were not pointed like artillery shells but pretty blunt. They made a weird sound cutting through the air. A horrible high pitched moaning sound. When two or three of the Nebelwerfers were fired at once the sound they made defies description. Being in the impact area of a mess like that would be something, too. They were supposed to be inaccurate and the Krauts weren't able to tell within a quarter of a mile where they were going to land. They covered a wide area though and a misplaced shell can kill you just as dead if it hit you.

The din continued all night and sleep was impossible. At dawn things began to quiet down considerably. We looked over our new position. The hotel, for an Italian one, must have been pretty nice in its day but was now pretty well frayed around the edges. The Jerry's had also used this position before us. There were always two familiar sights that marked their departed presence in the place. They were cigarette boxes and sardine cans. I was beginning to wonder if that was all those guys lived on. They really must have loved sardines. All these sardines had been put up in Portugal.

A fellow in the outfit informed me that there was wine to be had in the cellar of the hotel. I figured a few good drinks would bolster my morale so went to investigate.

I had to grope my way in the inky blackness. After quite some time and a box of matches I found some wine. I was afraid of setting off a booby trap any second so was about to give up my adventure. I was particularly suspicious of booby traps. I had already learned that the Germans were artists at that kind of work. They had a habit of planting booby traps before leaving a place. They had used this hotel and this dark cellar would be an ideal place to set a trap.

Just as I had decided to find my way out of the place, I chanced upon a group of about ten Italians. They were huddled together in the dark jabbering. They had evidently come here for protection from the bombing and shelling.

A girl came towards me with a dim flashlight. She must have known I was after wine for without a word she beckoned me to follow her. She led me to a small room. The place reeked from the smell of wine. A small window near the top of the room on the ground level let in enough light for me to see that this had been a wine cellar. The girl jabbered at me in a steady stream. From what I gathered the Germans had taken off with all the good stuff. What they hadn't they had broken open and let run out. The girl had found a couple of bottles that weren't damaged and a couple the crumby glasses. I used half a bottle of cognac washing cobwebs and rat turds out of the glass. We sat on a couple of empty wine barrels and finished off the other bottle and a half. Although the girl apologized for the bad liquor I enjoyed it very much. I didn't know much about cognac but this stuff tasted alright to me.

The little window let in enough light for me to get a good look at the girl. She wasn't bad looking, small and probably about twenty-six or twenty-eight. I made out that her home was in Naples but she had taken off to stay here with relatives when things got hot around Naples.

We finished off the cognac and I gave the girl a pack of cigarettes for her troubles and then took off. With quite a lot of cognac under my belt things looked brighter and cheerier on the outside.

Twice during the afternoon German planes came over and bombed and strafed. The Kraut air force was becoming more and more active. They bombed a bridge and a convoy quite near our position and did considerable damage.

When a group of German planes would come roaring over our position everyone would scatter. Some would go into the hotel, others would go into the thicket or dive under vehicles. We were lucky and no bombs were dropped right in our area. Either we were hidden in the foliage around the hotel or the planes were after heavy equipment or guns. I imagine they saw so many good targets they hardly knew which ones to go for.

Some of the fellows took pot shots at the planes with their M1's. Rifle fire is pretty ineffective on planes unless they are low flying and the fire is concentrated. Most of the planes they were banging away at were out of range anyway. I took a few shots at them myself with my .03.

The next day was about the same. The artillery fire had died down because the Germans were dropping back again. The Luftwaffe was active again though. Apparently during the night a lot of anti-aircraft guns had moved into and around our position. The 37 and 44 mm guns were throwing up a lot of flak. I liked to watch and listen to the 40mm guns as they fired. Because of the trees and shrubs around our position it was impossible to see if any of the planes were brought down.

The Italian girl in the cellar the day before came out and hung around. She wasn't bad looking at all in the bright light. She did a lot of panhandling for cigarettes. I had only a few left and had given her a pack the day before so I had to go sparingly. She was doing alright for herself though. Gray Marshall was particularly generous. He was trying to make a big hit with her and was handing out the butts like toothpicks. He could be generous because he didn't smoke.

The next afternoon we moved out of this position. The German Air Force was very active now and it would be murder to be caught out on the open road during strafing. However, we moved only a couple of thousand yards and mostly across fields. We were still lucky that no planes came at that particular time. We took up a position around a farmhouse.

Even though we had moved forward only a little over a

mile things seemed to be much livelier again. From here we could see the Germans shelling hell out of a small village. Smoke would geyser up when a shell hit. Our infantry was in that town. We could hear two or three "Screaming Meemies" in action. At dusk 88 shells began to whine over our position and crash in back trying for our guns.

Perkins found an empty room in the farmhouse and a few bottles of wine. We went up to the room, blacked out the window and lighted a candle. We sat down and played Five Hundred Rummy and drank wine. Perkins had been drinking the wine for quite some time and was pretty oiled up. We remarked it was rather novel playing a game of cards in the middle of an artillery duel. I wasn't able to stay in the house all night because I had to go on the radio at 2:00 am and the guy I was supposed to relieve wouldn't be able to find me.

The next day was fairly quiet. A few shells whined over our position heading in the direction of our guns. That night orders came down for our battalion to join in a corps concentration. The target was a small town up ahead. The Krauts were supposed to be making a strong stand in this town. They had blown the bridge in front of it. The town almost had to be taken before any advances could be made. The corps was to throw in 1500 rounds of all sizes into the town in a half hour.

The barrage was set for midnight and at that exact time the guns opened up. They sky lighted up from the artillery and the bombing was terrific. That town was taking a shellacking alright. I sure would have hated to be in it. Our guns continued heavy interdictory fire all night. We kept shelling the town and all roads that led to it. The infantry was to attack the place at dawn.

The next afternoon we moved up again. We passed

through the village that had received the 1500 rounds and more. It had really taken a beating alright. I felt bad about the bridge the Germans had blown up. It was over two thousand years old and had been built by the Romans. We forded the river about three hundred yards from the blown out bridge at a shallow point. This was the Volturno River we were crossing. We crossed the river, then crossed it again about a mile further on, then turned off into an olive orchard situated a few yards off the road.

We had moved up far enough to get back in range of the Germans. We hurriedly set up and started receiving fire missions. Incoming Jerry shells whined in and smashed on the nearby road. Shell fragments whined in all directions. Everyone, including myself, were digging.

One shell hit near a truck shuttling infantry up the road. Some were killed and several were wounded. The wounded were coming into our aid station. Shells kept crashing up and down the road. Shrapnel kept whipping around us and we all stayed mighty low. Grady and I were lying on the ground by the jeep trying to handle fire missions and other traffic over the radio. Shrapnel from one of the shells ripped through the body of the jeep just above our heads. At dark things quieted down. Probably the Germans were getting ready to pull out under the cover of darkness.

Bell came sneaking in with a hunted look in his eyes. He said that as we were both sleeping alone we might as well bed down together. I agreed but almost immediately wished I hadn't. Bell was too nervous to be any company. He began to worry about a safe place to sleep. He tried to figure out the line of fire and pick a place accordingly. I finally talked him into sleeping in a nearby barn. I was afraid it was going to rain and wanted some kind of shelter. He finally agreed and we got some straw from a nearby stack and spread it on the dirt floor. Soon after dark the Jerrys threw in a few more rounds in on the road. We figured they were departing shots as they hit the retreat trail again. A couple of pieces of fragments ricocheted off from the tile roof of our barn.

During the night sometime it began to rain. I was tickled that we had picked this barn to bed down in. Also, during the night Bob Perkins came wandering in looking for a place to bed down. He was all excited about his new job. When it was time for me to go on the radio he followed me out to the jeep to tell me all about it. It seemed an order had come down for each battalion to have a correspondent. Perkins was the logical one for our battalion because of his journalism background. Already tonight he had been out with Major Huburt to get a story. This job sounded like a good deal. He was practically his own boss. I wished I could get something like that.

The next morning the rumor was around that as soon as Piedmonte fell the 45th would have a few days' rest. The infantry was nearing Piedmonte now and it might fall in a day or two.

All that day our guns blasted away without much return fire. Fire mission after fire mission were coming in from our F.O.'s (Forward Observers). I was on the radio for several hours and handled things pretty well. I had gained a lot of confidence in myself and felt I was able to handle the thing almost as well as any of them.

In the afternoon a British officer who was in charge of propaganda came to our C.P. (Command Post). The Britton was neatly dressed and came up with a snappy salute. Our Major Ford was lounging in the C.P. with his shoes and shirt off. He was so surprised to see the British officer he returned the salute halfheartedly and from a sitting position. The British officer wanted to see Colonel Funk. Someone sent for him. Colonel Funk had been up about all night and was trying to get a few winks. When he was roused up he came rushing out of his tent still about half asleep. He was barefoot, helmetless and his shirttail was flapping in the breeze. This "Limey Officer:" must have thought that this was a sloppy outfit. I guess maybe he was right too.

The area we were now in had been plastered with plenty of artillery before we had arrived. The whole orchard was pitted with shell holes and many limbs and tree trunks had been shattered and lay strew around. The shelling had been effective on the enemy too. By a stone wall were four German graves. The Germans evidently buried many of their men where they were killed. All along since I had joined this outfit and even before in Tunisia I had noticed the German graves. Sometimes there was only one grave. Other times three of four or even ten or more. After big battles the Germans would dig large common graves with bulldozers if they were retreating fast and didn't have time to make individual graves.

The next day was October 19th, 1943 my twenty-fourth birthday. I wondered if I would be around for my twenty-fifth and if, where. It was definite now that we were going to get a rest. In fact, we were practically in it now. Piedmonte had fallen and the Germans were slowly retreating to the north. Tomorrow we would officially start our rest period. My birthday passed pretty quietly. A bunch of us sat around an argued on the progress of the war. Marshall and a fellow names John Priest maintained that the Germans would keep retreating like this all the way to northern Italy. Italy was several hundred miles long and the way we were going it would take a long, long time to get to the Po Valley. They argued that when the Po Valley was reached we still wouldn't be any place. We wouldn't be able to go over the Alps into Germany. It sounded logical at that. At the rate we were going even though it was fairly steady advance it would take months to get to the Po Valley. Italy isn't very wide but it is several hundred miles long. Now we were just barely up the leg of the country. About up to the ankle.

The Germans were masters at this retreat business. As good as they were at offense, I guess they should be. It seemed the art of war is a national pastime in Germany. Something like baseball is to the Americans.

They used every delaying action and used it wisely. They used mining, blowing bridges, blasting high banks down onto the roads, etc. They even used demolition on buildings to blow them down onto the streets. They did this in villages where only one narrow street wound through it. They planted thousands of road and personnel mines. They booby trapped everything from a grapevine to a dead body. They would leave a few men with a machinegun and an inexhaustible supply of ammunition in a key position. These men were usually placed overlooking a road or a small ravine. They would be well camouflaged and protected. Sometimes they could hold up the advance of a company or two for quite some time. They put their artillery in positions that they could shell by passes, crossroads or bends in the road. They were pretty clever in the use of their mines. They would blow a bridge and then mine heavily the most logical place to make the crossing. At the blown out bridges they knew our traffic would be slow and congested so they would have it zeroed in and shell it heavily. Another nice little trick was to stretch piano wire across the road. It was set just high enough to hit a man around the head or neck while riding in a jeep. It could snip a man's head off easily or cut him up badly. This stunt was easily overcome by each jeep having an iron bar welded to a bumper. The bar was about five feet high and hooked on top. It would catch any wire and break it before anyone got hurt.

Gaining ground against a well-organized and clever enemy is tough anyway. They have all the advantages in the knowledge of the terrain. They have time to prepare key positions. It doesn't take anywhere near the men and equipment for a defending army to hold the one trying to advance. It's as if there were two desperate criminals holed up in a solid rock house on a barren hill and heavily armed. You sure as hell wouldn't send two men with the same amount of equipment out to get them. It couldn't be done. Then there was always the problems of supply and communication. The advancing army always had tougher problems with extending supply lines.

Anyway, Grady, Curtis and Priest argued that the Krauts would continue this sort of rear guard action all the way up Italy and make their stand in Northern Italy. They predicted that we would be in Rome by at least Christmas. Gill, Bell and I argued almost the opposite. We figured the Germans would make a strong stand and soon somewhere before Rome. They were either dropping back to terrain more favorable to make a stand or to prepare positions. To us it seemed that they had rather make Italy the battleground than let us get almost to Germany. The farther they held us down in Italy the further it was to the Fatherland. It made our bombers go several hundred miles to Germany proper from this theater. We generals spent most of the day on the strategy of the war. We got into some pretty heated arguments trying to prove our points.

The next day, October 20th, we moved up a mile or so and into an area that was to be our rest area. The place was sort of a grassy and tree covered glen. There were the familiar signs of the Krauts being here before us. We always seemed to use a spot that the Germans had used. Nothing strange about that I guess. After all they were in this war, too.

A thicket nearby showed signs of our artillery. Shelling had ripped thousands of saplings to shreds. A farmhouse just beyond the thicket had been shattered. The shell had made a direct hit in the doorway really enlarging it.

We were beginning to wonder what kind of a rest this was going to be. Our "B" Battery a few yards from us was shelled and a couple of fellows killed. A hell of a note to be killed by artillery fire while you were in a "rest" area. Artillery of the 34th Division fired from behind us for a couple of days. From where we were we could see and hear German shells smashing into a wooded area a little ways ahead. However, we put up our pup-tents and prepared to stay a while. In a day or two the battle moved up a short distance and things began to quiet down.

We hadn't been in the area long before the Italian civilians began to show up. At first they just stood around and watched but soon they began to beg for food and cigarettes. The kids all hung around and pestered us for candy. "Caramella" they called it. The kids as well as the adults would steal anything that wasn't nailed down if they got a chance.

George Bouncher and I pitched our tent together. However, the first couple of nights we slept outside of it. The nights were beginning to get pretty damp and cold though and we decided we had better use our tent while we had a chance.

The nearest town to our area was a small village named Calvisi. It was about a mile from our area. One of the first days here in our rest, Bell and I paid a visit to the place. The town was very small, probably didn't even have a population of more than a very few hundred. It was a dirty, miserable hole, too. It had one narrow main street winding through it. The main street was filthy and had pigs and chickens running up and down it. I even saw a woman throw the contents from a piss-pot from a second story onto the street. At least in the town were a couple of places that sold wine. On our first visit to one of these dark, dingy places we sat at a table and consumed several bottles of vile tasting wine and played Bell's favorite card game, Casino. There were no windows in the place and the only light besides what came in through the door was one tiny candle. Once I stepped to the door to watch a couple of German planes fly over. Our antiaircraft fire had attracted my attention. In the light of the sun I happened to look down at the glass of wine I still had in my hand. The stuff was full of gnats and other unidentifiable objects floating around in it. No wonder the stuff tasted so lousy.

As we were wandering around the village an Italian family invited us in for bread and wine. Their home was typical to the place, was crude almost beyond belief. They had no regular stove, no plumbing of any kind and practically no furniture and very little lighting. These people were really poor.

As we headed back through the town towards home a woman came out with a jug of wine and a couple of glasses. She could speak a few words of English. She said that she had lived in the United States for a while in Erie, Pennsylvania. By now Bell and I were up to our ears in wine but she insisted. We sat down on the curb and she stood over us with that damned wine jug. Every time we took a mouthful she would fill our glasses up again. The woman wasn't giving us the wine entirely out of the goodness of her heart or to cement international relations. She made us a proposition that if we brought her husband a pair of shoes we could have all the wine, bread or anything else we wanted to eat. The old guy certainly needed some alright. About all that was left to his shoes were the laces. We told the woman we would see what we could do. I had in mind an extra pair of shoes I had in my barracks bag. The next thing was to sneak them up here. The Army took a dim view of the G.I.'s giving their stuff away.

At dark we started back to our area. At the edge of town we passed the village church. Bell suggested that we go in. Neither of us were Catholic and didn't know what to do but went in any way to see what was going on. We piled our guns and helmets in the hallway and went on in. A couple of fellows seemed pleased to see us and got chairs and placed them where we could see. The church was a beautiful thing. It had a beautiful altar. The roof was supported by beautiful marble columns. I wondered how much a miserably poor town in which the people didn't live in much more than a pig sty could afford such a beautiful church. For one thing I guess this was their only entertainment. There were not theaters, ballparks or anything around here. Still, this church must have more value than the rest of the town put together.

After the service we left the church and headed back towards our area. Off towards the southwest we could see flares and red tracers crisscrossing the sky. The Germans were raiding the Naples area. Naples was probably forty air miles from where we were. We watched the show for an hour. They were giving it a pretty good going over.

The next day Bell and I returned to Calvisi. I had dug up the extra pair of G.I. shoes and brought them along. The whole family screamed when I presented the man with the shoes. They invited us in their home to have wine and something to eat. Their home was old, decrepit and poorly furnished. Instead of a stove they just had a hearth sort of a deal for heating and cooling. No stove pipe, just a hole in the roof to let the smoke go out. The wall clear to the ceiling was black from the smoke. This family consisted of the parents and three children ranging in age from about four to ten years old. The man poured us glass after glass of wine while his wife fixed us cornbread. We hated to take the bread for we felt they needed it much worse than we did. The wine was different here in Italy. I'm sure there was much more wine than water. They also gave us dried figs and walnuts. They even cracked the nuts and took out the meat for us. We tried to make them stop and save the food for themselves but they insisted so much we were almost forced to take the stuff. At least these people were some of the very few who seemed to appreciate anything done for them. Most of the Wops just seemed to take it for granted and expected you to help them. We did compensate for some of the food by giving the wife and kids a few rolls of Life Savers and the man a few cigarettes, both very much a luxury to them. We sat there, ate, drank and talked for about three hours. Going back to our area that night I felt pretty good. I felt those blooming shoes had made one family a little happier in such a miserable circumstance.

Another time when Bell, Bouncher and I were in Calvisi we had a little excitement. We were sitting, leaning up against a wall killing a little time. Suddenly a couple of shells smashed into the roof above our heads. Italians went screaming in all directions. My first thought was some German tank must have sneaked up close enough to shell the town. I couldn't imagine why though for there was nothing here. Even we seemed to be the only

G.I's that ever came here. We knew the front wasn't far up ahead but we should be out of artillery range. We lay low for a minute and when no more shells dropped in we got up to investigate. We soon discovered that the shells were a couple of 40mm shells from our own anti-aircraft. They had been picking away at a couple of German recon planes away up there all night. Apparently these shells hadn't exploded until they had come down and hit the building. I don't know why 50mm guns had been firing at the recon planes anyway. They must have been way too high for 40mm's to even some close.

The shells knocked a couple of sizeable holes in the roof of the place. Little damage had been done inside of the building except showering everything with tile and debris from the roof. Fortunately no one was in the room when the shells hit. The three of us also thanked our lucky stars that the shells hadn't dropped right in our laps.

During the rest Bell and I also went into the town of Piedmonte. Piedmonte was a fair sized town up the main road three of four miles from where we were camped. One day we hitched a ride on a tank destroyer into town. Although the railroad yards and a couple of small buildings along the tracks had been destroyed the town was not damaged too badly. The main street was a wide affair with a park running down the middle of it. The town was the best looking place by far I had seen in Italy yet. The stores in the place all seemed to be open for business. The only store that seemed to have anything to sell were the dry goods stores and the variety stores. The grocery stores were practically bare. The only thing they had in any quantity was some kind of canned fish, pickled olives, dried figs and a few other things.

The town had several nice bars and liquor, particularly

wine, vermouth and brandy were plentiful. We stopped in a couple of the bars and had a few drinks. One of the places was particularly nice. It was modern with a clever design. Even the doorway was different. Instead of a door it had an arch shaped opening with a beaded sort of affair something like a beaded curtain. I imagine in peacetime this place had been the place around here. Even now it seemed to be the favorite place of the civilians.

We wandered around the residential part of Piedmonte, most of which was situated on a hill. Several homes and large buildings had been bombed out. Men and women from six to sixty were slowly pecking away at the piles of rubble. They had practically no equipment, only a few picks and shovels. It seemed trying to clean up a mess with this kind of equipment. It would be a fruitless job. The town hadn't been hit badly either.

We eventually wandered down to the business district of the town. We wanted a haircut and a shave and asked a civilian where a good barber shop was. We were having a little trouble trying to make the fellow understand what we wanted. A woman passing by overheard our conversation, stopped and asked us in perfect English what we wanted. When we asked her where she had learned to speak English she told us that she had been born in New Haven, Connecticut. She was an American, or at least had been one until she married an Italian and then had come over here to Italy. She immediately started on us asking us why the Americans hadn't brought in trucks loaded with food for them yet. She wanted to know why the Americans hadn't started rebuilding their homes and bridges. She also wanted to know when we were going to take up all the mines that the Germans had planted. She said America was rich and had plenty of food and money. This kind of crap burned us up. We reminded her that the United States and Italy had been at war for a couple of years and that hostilities had only ended a couple of months ago. She just shrugged and said that Italy was on our side now. The Wops will always be on the winning side. They switch their position to the one who is getting the best of it. When it looked like Germany was going to conquer the world they were only too happy to be on their side.

After our shaves and haircuts we decided it was time to ear. There wasn't much in Piedmonte by the way of food. All that was left in the grocery stores was stuff that even the Italians wouldn't eat. We did however buy a dimes worth of pickled olives each.

We were sitting on a curb eating our olives when an Italian soldier, still in his army uniform, came up and started talking to us. He couldn't speak a word of English but between Bell's and my twenty word Italian vocabulary we carried on some sort of conversation. The fellow invited us to his home to eat and of course we accepted.

His home was above one of the stores right on the main street not far from where we were sitting. His place had a balcony overlooking the street and it had a nice view from there. His wife and three small children were introduced to us. His wife was quite nice looking. The wife and the kids looked clean. In fact, they were the cleanest looking Italians I had seen yet. The soldier brought out wine and we sat there drinking and trying to carry on a conversation. He told us he had been in the Italian army for ten years. He claimed he hated Mussolini and the Fascists. Later he brought out his picture album and showed us his army pictures. Some were taken during the Ethiopian and Albanian campaigns. On almost every page he had written "Viva Mussolini". Evidently when things were going right he had thought a lot more of

Duce. When I pointed to his writing he just shrugged. These Italians certainly could pass things off with just a shrug. We took several more glasses of wine. When the wife started to prepare the meal we made her understand not to fix anything for us. We figured that they didn't have the food to entertain us with. We gave the soldier a few cigarettes and the kids some candy and took off.

We caught a ride back to our area on a supply truck. We arrived back just in time to hear a concert presented by the 45th Division Band. The band sounded good and everyone enjoyed the music. No doubt these fellows had been professionals in civilian life or at least had been exposed to a lot of music. All of the musicians were pretty loaded. They all had a bug jug of booze at their feet and drank hardily after each number. It didn't seem to affect their playing. No doubt they were used to this sort of thing.

The days of the rest were flying by. No one knew exactly how long the rest would be but knew it wouldn't last more than a week or ten days.

We had very little routine things to do while in camp. Just the bare necessities. Guard and K.P. were the main items. I drew guard a couple of times and even that didn't amount to much. Also, during the rest we had a V.D. and tooth examination.

There was a little other entertainment for us. One day a G.I. swing band showed up and played for us for a couple of hours. On another afternoon a few girls, the "45th Donut Dollies" showed up and handed us each a donut. One night we tried to have a movie but the machine broke down before they even got it going. It was just as well because German planes passed over every night on their way to bomb Naples. If they had seen a bright light below them they probably would have dropped a few bombs just for luck. One show that we could see every night was the bombing raids on Naples and vicinity.

On clear nights we could see the dull red glow from Mt. Vesuvius in the distance. We must have been seventy miles from the volcano, but it showed up quite brightly.

Our battery took on a couple of replacements while in the rest. One of the fellow's name was Seth Leacock from Houston, Texas. The other fellow was named Haddow. I never knew his first name. He was a big burly fellow and was soon dubbed "moose". Leacock was assigned to the S-3 section and Haddow to the anti-tank platoon.

The 25th of October was a day I had been waiting for. I received my first mail since coming overseas. I hadn't received any mail since August 9th, the day I left Shenango. Most of the letters had been forwarded from Shenango and a few from North Africa. I received about twenty letters and enjoyed every line of them. Most of them, of course, were from Bernice.

Our rest was just about over. Already part of the division had gone back in to the line. Our outfit would move up in a day or two. On the afternoon of November 1st we pulled out of our rest area and started moving toward the Front. We had been in rest about eleven days.

We had only a few miles to go to get to the Front. The line hadn't advanced very far in those eleven days. Things seemed to be getting tougher and tougher and slower all the time. We didn't pull out of our area until late afternoon and it was getting dark before we reached our destination. As usual I was riding on Regan's weapon carrier. Just as we were about to pull into our position a huge Sherman tank loomed up in the black. The tank came to a grinding halt but not quite quick enough and it nudged us a trifle. Even just ticking us ever so slightly it smashed a fender badly. We were lucky though. A split second later and we would have been smashed flat. We reached our new position by driving over a cow trail road. It was plenty muddy and some of the vehicles slid off the road into a small ravine. I didn't like the looks of the new position at all. We set up in an open field with no hills very near and very little foliage for concealment. We were informed that Jerry planes had bombed and strafed around here this afternoon. That made a very pleasant thought.

Up ahead we could hear incoming shells and they sounded like big stuff, too. About midnight a single German plane flew over low. It was evidently taking recon pictures. There were bright flashes from it that looked like pictures at night. Sometime during the night we saw a couple of explosions and heard some screaming from a field a few yards to the north of us. We wondered what the heck was up. We soon learned that some outfit had been unloading some shells and a couple had somehow gone off. A couple of guys were killed and some others wounded.

The next day passed rather quietly. We were actually in support of the 160th F.A. (Field Artillery). Our own guns were barely in range of the Germans. That afternoon we loaded up again. At the last minute I was told I was to be a road marker. They wanted a marker from Regan's truck and being a private and the newest one in the outfit on this particular truck I was named "it". The P.F.C.'s must have been damned glad they had one stripe. A Private like myself is a low bastard and doesn't have a hell of a lot to look forward to but the crumby details. Bell was one of the lucky boys too.

A few minutes before the convoy pulled out onto the road the road guides loaded on a jeep and headed down the road. We were dumped off at various places along the road. There were cross-roads or side roads where some vehicle from the convoy might pull off on to by mistake in the dark. It was our job to keep them on the right track. I was dropped off where a "T" road came in and joined the main road. There was another guide there from the 171 1st F. A. (Field Artillery). Soon my outfit came by and I directed it on down the right road. The service truck of the Headquarters Battery was supposed to pick up the road guides. Our outfit passed by then another and still no service truck. I finally decided they had missed me and I would have to stay here all night and try to find the outfit in the morning. It was bitterly cold and the thought of staying out here with the little clothing I had and no blankets wasn't too pleasant. I had only my O.D.'s (Olive Drabs) and a field jacket. I wished they would hurry up and issue winter clothes, things like an overcoat, long johns and gloves. It was getting pretty cold at night lately. After all is was November 2nd. I could sure have used a few warmer things right now.

The poor guy from the 171st had been here since afternoon and hadn't been picked up yet. His outfit had passed hours before. He was griping like hell and I didn't blame him a bit.

Several huge engineer trucks kept going back and forth on the side road where they were apparently building a bridge across the Vultrane River a short distance away. One of these big trucks was nearly our undoing. The 171st was so disgusted that he sat down and leaned up against a road sign and started dozing. I was standing practically in the middle of the road. It was so dark I was afraid my truck would pass me by without seeing me. Suddenly, one of huge engineer trucks loomed up in the black. The driver seemed to hesitate for a second trying to decide which road to take and then rushed right at us.

I dove out of the way just in time. As I leaped I heard the other guy holler, "Hey" and heard the post against which he had been leaning snap. I was almost afraid to look. I expected to see the kid squashed under one of the wheels. He had somehow just rolled out of the way in time and was unhurt. He didn't know how he had done it himself. The truck backed up and went rumbling off down the side road. It was a big job with a crane on the back of it.

Accidents on the roads could hardly be helped. All vehicles, of course, drove blackout. With many vehicles of all sizes and kinds and usually poor narrow roads, it's a wonder there weren't more accidents than there were.

The night dragged on and it wasn't getting any warmer. Up ahead on the hillside several fires burned brightly. Most of the fires had been set by artillery fire. One fire was burning more brightly than the rest. The 171st man said he had seen it just before it hit and didn't know whether it was one of ours or German. We both kept wishing that we were near one of those fires to get a little warmth from it.

Finally, when I had resigned myself to staying here all night, much to my surprise the service truck showed up. The 171st man was still there when we pulled away.

We bumped along through the blackness. The road guides were crammed into the truck with a lot of other equipment. We tried to catch a few winks as we bounced along but it was pretty tough going. Some of us were just dozing when we arrived in our new position.

The new place was on a heavily wooded hillside. Bell and I thrashed around in the underbrush trying to find our bedrolls. I found Regan's truck pretty easily and got mine but Bell couldn't locate the truck with his roll. It was getting towards morning anyway so we decided to let my blankets be enough.

Just as we were dozing off shells began to crash in not too far away. They were big ones, too. They weren't close enough to harm us but it was a clear night and the sound really carried. The shells made a nasty crack and probably sounded closer than they actually were, but they were big ones. No mistake about that. This was a hell of a night to get some sleep anyway. Bell became pretty nervous and wanted to move. We gathered our stuff and went around to the other side of the hill. It was 4:30 when I finally got to sleep.

The next morning we were awakened by the sound of planes going through the works. There was a dog fight going on up above. The trees were too thick to see much of what was going on. Later in the day Bell and I hiked up a high hill to an O.P. (Observation Post). It was a static O.P. back quite a ways from the actual Front. It was more for general observation than anything else. There was a F.O. (Forward Observer) party there from the 15th Brigade. They were an independent outfit and had been supporting our outfit considerably. They each had a big red 15 on a yellow background painted on their helmets. One of their party was a fellow I had come over on the boat with from the States. I only knew him as Jimmy.

This spot was an ideal place for an O.P. From here we could look miles in every direction. You could look back towards our lines and see much plainer that you could see the Germans. Surely the Krauts had used this for an O.P. before us.

We could see incoming shells landing in different places. All of them were landing so far away from us that their reports weren't too loud. However, we could plainly see the smoke and dirt they kicked up when they hit.

They were shelling a large wood down to our left quite heavily. Out almost straight ahead of us they were interdicting a cross-roads. To the right they were interdicting an open stretch of road with a four gun battery. About every minute four shells would land on the road. They were never over or short but right in the middle of the road. It was beautiful to watch. The cross road was being shelled with about one shell a minute with the same degree of accuracy. The shelling of the woods was different. It was the searching type of fire. First they would shell the outer fringe and slowly work the shells farther into the woods. Then they would move the fire to the right and left. They know American men and equipment were in there and were giving them a working over. Quite a few of our tanks were going up the road the Krauts were shelling. They would stop near where the shells were hitting and after a salvo they would tear down the road past the spot. They couldn't really go too fast because the road was pretty well battered by the shelling but you can bet they were moving as fast as possible. Later that afternoon Bell and I went down the hill and returned to the battery.

The next morning I was again awakened by the sound of airplanes and motors under terrific strain. I was in a better spot to see this time but they were so high up there I could barely see them. A couple went down but I couldn't tell if they were theirs or ours.

Late that afternoon we moved up again. At one cross roads we hesitated for a minute. I became rather nervous for the delay because I recognized this cross road as the one I had seen being shelled from the O.P. There were plenty of signs that the cross road had taken a beating, too. The road was full of holes and the trees around it had been ripped to shreds.

We turned left at this cross road and then soon again off this road and ground down a dirt road. We approached a tree covered hill that stood by itself. It was several miles from any other hills. We took up a position in a small rock strewn ravine.

Just at dusk a Battery Officer reported into Headquarters for something or other. We soon left in his jeep back down the dirt trail up which he had come. He had only gone a few yards when there was a terrific explosion. The officer's jeep had run over a mine killing both him and the driver. It completely demolished the jeep. The odd part was that all of the Headquarters vehicles had come up that trail and not one had run over the mine. Probably the jeep had gotten a little off the trail. The Germans usually placed their mines on the edges of the road instead of the middle. They knew that the middle of the road would be watched close and he mines would be easily found.

As night fell several German tanks down in the valley began to open. They sent shell after shell screaming over our hill. Apparently they were trying for our gun positions. The shells seemed to be just skimming over our heads and the sound from them was blood curdling. Our guns never opened up, probably no one was able to spot the tanks. Even if they had been spotted it was pretty tough to fire at tanks effectively after dark. The tanks would fire a few rounds and then move a few hundred yards under the cover of darkness and fire again. By the time you had zeroed in on where you had seen the flashes the tanks had moved to another position and was firing again.

The night passed rather quietly with only an occasional shell from the tanks whining over. The shells weren't landing too close but were annoying. They also seemed to be pretty close to our hill. The nights were plenty sharp and damp now and I wished they would hurry up and issue winter clothing.

The next day rumor began floating around that things had definitely become tougher. The infantry was having plenty of trouble crossing the Vultrane in any force. Reports from the civilians were that the Germans were well dug in on the mountains on the other side of the river. Also, the reports had it that the Germans had been packing artillery and supplies up into the mountains for months. Evidently Captain Cleverdon our S-2 hadn't received any official information about the rumors. In fact, he was optimistic about the situation and figured at the present rate we would be in Rome by Christmas. Time was going to tell.

We were to go forward that night but things were too hot up ahead to move so the move was postponed for another day. It was beginning to look like the advance was really slowing down to a walk. That night it began to rain again. A slow, cold, miserable drizzle. Bouncher and I didn't have a sign of shelter so consequently we got pretty damp.

The next day was a drab thing. It rained spasmodically throughout the day. Just at dark as we were going to move I was informed I was to be a road guide again. Bell had gotten the call too.

The road guides were dumped out along different sections of the route the convoy was going to take. Lt. Block in charge of the guides must have saved Bell and I for the town of Venefro. He dumped Bell off and myself on a dark miserable corner several blocks on. In fact I was the further most guide. It was cold, dark and miserable. It wasn't raining hard but just enough to drench you. I had a raincoat on with a field jacket on underneath but was still cold and miserable. I was sort of uneasy too. Things seemed pretty tense.

I had just gotten out of the truck when a M.P. came by

with some cheering news. He said to be careful because there was a German machine gun emplacement on the hill just above here. He said that it sprayed the street here every once in a while. He had no more gotten the words out of his mouth when the machine gun opened up. The bullets from it were ricocheting off the street. The M.P. and I leaped behind a huge wooden beam that lay by the side of the road. The machine gun spurted a few more bursts and then stopped. The M.P. remembered he had important business elsewhere and was off at a gallop.

I decided that this was going to be a lovely place to wait for a convoy. I tried to stay near the beam as I could and still be near enough to the street, not to miss my outfit when it came through. Trucks, guns and heavy equipment were lumbering by in the darkness. My outfit had to make a hair pin turn at the corner where I stood. The gun trucks would have to back up a couple of times to make it. I was hoping that machine guns wouldn't open up when one of the gun trucks was trying to make the corner. Our drivers were experts. Most of them had been doing this kind of work for some time now. They had to be good. Driving on strange roads, blacked out with a truck full of men and dragging a 105 Howitzer hooked on behind.

An M.P. marched a couple of German prisoners past us. They had just been captured on the outskirts of town. They were still in their full gear. I almost envied them for they had overcoats on. The Germans had beat us to issuing winter clothing.

Big German shells began to crash into the town not far away. The ground shook form their impact. I kept hoping Bell would hold fast and not take off or something. If he did that it might foul up the company to say nothing of himself. The big gun continued to shell the town. It was probably a 170 (mortar). They started scorching the town with it. They moved to the right and to the left but seemed to keep the range about the same. I hoped they wouldn't extend the range a little. The shells were too close for comfort now. I was hoping the service truck would hurry up and get here. I wanted to get the hell out of here before they dropped a shell on me or that the machine gun opened up again.

Finally, my outfit showed up. I didn't tell anyone about the machine gun while they were backing up the two or three times to make the hairpin turn. I figured it would only scare someone and the drivers might get in a hurry and really foul things up. I kept my fingers crossed though. We were lucky though and it didn't open up until all were passed the turn.

We pulled out of town and onto a narrow road. A short distance up this road we came upon a battalion medic truck off in the ditch. It had slipped off from the slippery going. It had slipped off about a ten foot embankment and was resting on its side. It was impossible to do anything with the medic truck now. We loaded supplies from it onto our truck and went on.

Our new position was about a mile and a half north of Venefro. Headquarters Battery was being set up right tight against a steep hill. About ten yards back from the hill was a cemetery. A lovely place for a position. The cemetery had a thick wall running around it. The C. P. (Command Post) was put up against the base of the hill. The radio jeep was parked by the cemetery wall about ten or fifteen yards from the C.P. tent.

I had no more gotten to or new position and gobbled down a few mouthfuls of cold chow when I was informed that it was my turn on the radio. Just as I got into the jeep and took over on the set a snappy mortar barrage began crashing in. The shells were landing between us and a tiny village called Pizzoli that was situated about three hundred yards to the north of us. The shells were landing close enough to make a nasty crack and shrapnel sung through the air. Fellows that weren't on duty doing something important came down to the cemetery to get protection from the walls. Our guns were just using charged ones. All back through the valley we could see the flashes and hear the rumble of many guns. Some of them looked to be back there several miles, too. When you are in the range of mortar fire you just about as close as you can get. To near for artillery really.

The night had cleared off and it was crisp and the moon shined down brightly. I wasn't enjoying the nice evening much though. There were some 4.2 chemical mortars set up at the bottom of our hill almost in position. They were shelling a ridge just above Pizzoli. They were using white phosphorus shells. From where we were we could plainly see them hitting. They would flare up in brilliant red and white flashes when they hit. It was kind of pretty in sort of a gruesome way. It would be rough to be under barrage of phosphorous shells. They just burned and burned and burned. War is a swell pastime.

Our own guns were using such a short range that it was hard to tell whether the shells cracking were our own or incoming. The mortars near us apparently began to draw fire. It seemed that you could hear the shells that were trying for them whine all the way from the gun. You could hear the German gun fire and then the scream of the shell for several seconds. That is the only time during the whole war I had ever heard it exactly like this. I guess it was the angle that they were firing them from.

The Krauts were really pouring in the artillery and

mortars. They were giving the top of our hill a terrific shellacking. They were probably trying to get the shells right down on us. They were getting too close for comfort as it was now. Shrapnel whined over our heads and rocks and dirt and pieces of trees showered down on us. Other German shells went whining overhead and crashing around the gun batteries farther back in the valley. They were also sending them into the town of Venefro as well as plastering Pizzoli.

Perkins and I decided to put our blankets down alongside a rock wall that ran along right at the base of the hill. We figured that the Germans were going to have a pretty hard time putting their shells on the reverse side of this hill. We also figured the wall would give us some protection from the flying shrapnel and other debris. Bell wanted to sleep with us. He was pretty nervous and shaky.

Shells continued to crash on or near the top of our hill showering stuff down on us. Others kept going on farther into the valley in a steady stream. They were crashing among the gun batteries and on the road. With all the incoming stuff the thundering of our own guns sleep was practically impossible.

About the biggest guy in the outfit, a fellow named Hunnicutt, was so scared he was just about in tears. He wouldn't even go down to his vehicle and get his blankets. We tried to comfort him and Bell but it was tough with the shells getting closer all the time. One shell hit real close and shrapnel really tore through the air. That was all for Hunnicutt and Bell. They got up and started running. I don't know where they thought they were going to go but getting up like that is one way to get hurt for sure. Neither one showed up until morning. It looked like the Germans were going to make their winter line here alright. They certainly seemed to have plenty of artillery up in the mountains and the mountains looked pretty rugged, too. It looked as if things were going to get really tough from now on.

Things weren't any better in the morning. Shells were still crashing in. Just after daylight German planes bombed Venefro. After they dropped their bombs they came scooting down the valley. They were low to the ground to keep out of the anti-aircraft fire and they came wide open. They were so low they just barely skimmed over the cypress trees in our cemetery. Just beyond Pizzoli was a small opening between where our own hill left off and another one started. They used this route on their way towards our lines. The planes flew over us so low that the big black crosses painted on the wings could be seen clearly. Even the pilots could be easily seen. Some of us fired our rifles at them. I don't know how effective rifle fire is on planes but at least they were in range. It looked like the tracers from my gun were going right through the fuselage. In the days to come we took lots of pot shots at them as they came roaring over.

A couple of fellows came down from the vicinity of our medic station. They said the medics were working hard with the causalities. They said the Germans had pulled quite a stunt. Up the road away they said a group of about fifty Germans came down the road, apparently to give up. A bunch of infantrymen had approached them to take over. Everyone thought that everything was normal because the Germans carried white flags and the rest had their hands up in the air. The boys had approached the Krauts not expecting anything. Some of them still had their guns slung over their shoulders. Suddenly, at a command the Krauts in front threw themselves on the ground. About eight of them in the back of the group had machine pistols and opened up. It naturally took the G.I.'s off guard and a bunch of them were mowed down. It took some time to get organized and blast the bastards. The characters that had thrown themselves on the ground kept insisting that they wanted to give up. They said that they were Poles not Germans. They said the Germans had used them to set the trap. They were told to do what they did or they would get it in the back. Anyway it was a lousy trick. Our aid station was the nearest and the dead and wounded had been brought here. Captain Kalin was the only doctor in the battalion so he and his P.F.C. medics were swamped. These guys told of some pretty gruesome sights. They said the dead were just dumped and forgotten about. One American had been shot through both eyes. Another was bleeding from the mouth and gurgling his last. Several others were hurt badly. Several more had minor flesh wounds and the like. One German had a leg hanging by just a little skin. They said one of the P.F.C.'s took a pair of scissors and just snipped the skin and tossed the leg to the side.

Another thing that didn't make things any nicer here the first few days were the snipers. They were up on Mt. Cavallo and harassed us day and night. They were shooting from great distances and didn't seem to hit anyone in our immediate vicinity. It was plenty annoying though to have bullets whizzing around all the time. In fact, every time you moved you had to move quickly and get behind something for protection. At night the snipers really opened up. Of course they were firing blind but a lucky shot can kill you just as dead. The first couple of nights I was on the radio bullets splattered around pretty close.

Another thing to make things around here extra pleasant were the thousands of mines planted in our immediate area. The large olive orchards a short distance behind the cemetery was thick with mines. A creek bed just a little beyond was just as bad. The whole area between our position and the village was almost one solid mine field. The engineers had taken out the ones they absolutely had to. They swept areas outfits wanted for positions and nothing more. Three men had already been badly wounded from the mines.

This was no doubt to be the German winter line. Reports were that we had been stopped cold and the going ahead looked tough. The British Eighth Army driving up the Adriatic coast of Italy had been stopped cold too.

The elements were turning against us, too. It began to rain and I do mean rain. We were to be here on the line for sixty-three days and it was to rain fifty-nine of them. Of course, that does not mean that it poured every minute of every day. Some days it rained very little. Other days it poured down all day long but it did rain at least some during fifty-nine of the sixty three days. The ground here soon became a sea of mud. The unimproved roads, and they were practically all unimproved, were soon almost impassable. The rain was tough on the men too. Being wet isn't very morale building. It was getting colder every day too.

The second and third day we were in a constant downpour. In the afternoon of the second day Perkins and I found that we had lost the battle of trying to keep dry. We, and our blankets and other equipment were soaked. We decided to move into the cemetery and into one of the tombs.

The tomb we moved into was about ten by twelve. It had plastered walls and a marble floor. It was bare except for an altar in the north end of it. In the middle of the floor was an iron trap door affair. Below was the vault where they kept the bodies. There were crevices where the caskets were kept. Most of the crevices were already sealed up. There were several still unoccupied though. It looked rather forbidding down there. It was dark and lots of cobwebs were hanging around. Real cozy looking. It was about eight feet to the floor of the vault below but there were no stairs. The same afternoon we moved into the tomb some Italians showed up and brought a baby along with them. They did however have the body in a wooden box, a casket. They lowered him into the vault and put his box on one of the unoccupied crevices. They never took the time to seal over the place. They were in a sweat to get out of there before they got hit with a shell or something. They probably didn't have the equipment to do the job anyway. Our new "buddy" wasn't going to keep us out of our tomb. We disliked the elements and were a lot more afraid of the German shelling than we were of the dead men and ghosts. The dead couldn't hurt you. It was the live ones.

We put our blankets on the floor and made things as comfortable as possible. We hung a shelter-half over the iron grating deal at the opening. The shelter-half would help keep out the cold rain and also block out the place. Our beds on the marble floor weren't going to be particularly comfortable but at least they would be dry. We would be a little safer too. This place would keep flying shrapnel, rocks, debris and things like that from getting us. Stuff could come through the grating but at least three sides of the walls would stop it. Our tomb wouldn't do much good in case of a direct hit from a shell or a bomb.

The fellows were really cramming into the tomb right beside us toward the hill. The guys were flocking into it because it was much more suited to live in than ours. To start with it was much lower than ours. Ours towered on high. I was afraid it would get one of those low skimming shells. Also, their tomb was cleaner and nicer below. Most of the crevices were empty and they made swell bunks. They also had an iron ladder leading down to their vault. Well, at least our tomb had plenty of room, at first anyway.

That night the shells really began to roar again. They came roaring over the hill, just skimming over the cemetery and crashing into the orchard just behind it. These shells really whined and chilled our blood. The whole area was showered with shrapnel and flying debris. Lots of stuff was bouncing off the roof and walls of our tomb. Perkins and I kept hoping that one of those low shells wouldn't hit the roof of our tomb. The thing wasn't too high, probably only eighteen feet at the most, but now it seemed like it towered up a mile high. Pieces of shrapnel really were hanging off the wall of the tomb and other pieces went singing past. It seemed that the air was full of stuff.

When I returned to the tomb after my shift on the radio, I found that several more fellows had moved in with us. One of the fellows was a guy named Jones from the anti-tank section. He had climbed on the back of his truck to try to keep dry. He made his bed on three hundred rounds of 37mm ammunition. He had really started sweating when shrapnel went ripping through his weapons carrier. He decided to find a place elsewhere to sleep.

The next day several more fellows moved into our tomb. It was now as crowded as the one next door. All of the fire direction radio operators moved in with the exception of Curtis. He was holed up next door. The fellows that now occupied the place were Gill, Marshall, Burbach, Jones,

Perkins and myself. With a few more fellows in the place at least it made it a little more cheerful. Christ.

The German air force had become much more active since we had moved into this position. Almost every day they would come over and bomb Venefro. Sometimes only three or four planes would make the raid. Other times there would be quite a force. Some days they would hit the town and try for gun positions. They usually used Messerschmitt 109s. They needed something light and fast. They would swoop in over the mountains, hit Venefro and scoot back up the valley strafing as they came.

Things were always pretty lively around here. Besides the Kraut planes there was continuous shelling day and night. Shells pounded all around our area and endless streams went whining overhead going farther out into the valley and into Venefro. This Venefro Valley was soon dubbed "Purple Heart Flat". The area between us and the village seemed to be hit harder than some of the others. The 189th F.A. (Field Artillery) in position there took quite a beating. They were losing men and equipment quite heavily and regularly. Several of the 156 Batteries were bombed and strafed. One German plane was shot down and crashed into one of our Howitzers.

When we operated the fire direction radio we had to stay pretty low. We had our jeep parked right beside the cemetery wall and when things got too hot we would lie on the ground between the jeep and the wall. After a time or two having shrapnel rip through the jeep we decided we needed something a little safer. We dug a hole about head high between the jeep and the wall. We piled sandbags around the top of the hole and put a camouflage net over both the jeep and the hole. We felt a little more secure when the shells started slamming in. We would rather sit in the jeep then stand in the hole but when things started to get hot we would quickly jump into the hole.

The day before we dug the hole I had quite a little thrill. I was sitting in the jeep operating the set when a shell smashed near the top of the hill. I didn't think too much about that first one but when the next one smacked in a little closer I began to wonder. I decided I was about as safe sitting right in the jeep as anywhere. The next shell hit right above the C.P. (Command Post) and sent shrapnel singing past my ears and that made up my mind to move. I tumbled out of the jeep and crawled over to a rock terrace right at the foot of the hill. The shells started coming in with machine gun speed. The scream they made almost defies description. It sounded something like locomotives rushing over you at a thousand miles an hour. The shells were landing awfully close. Like a damned fool I kept raising my head to see where they were landing. I didn't have far to look. The shells were landing right beside the anti-aircraft half-track about fifteen yards away. I was lucky. I didn't get a piece of shrapnel through my head the way I kept looking up. Plenty of shrapnel was screaming past my ears and bouncing around. Pebbles and dirt were bouncing off my helmet. The shelling suddenly stopped. They had thrown in about twenty shells in a small area in just a matter of seconds. I had been handling a fire mission when the fireworks started and now I heard the F. O. (Forward Observer) asking what had happened to his mission. I sneaked over to the radio and asked him to wait a minute. Again the shells began to crash in and I dove back beside the terrace. The shells landed in almost the same places and there were about the same number. The shelling stopped about as suddenly as it had started.

In about a minute or two the heads of G.I.s began to

pop out here and there. Fortunately no one was hit but we all had a few years growth scared out of us. Most of the Battery were living in one of the four tombs in the cemetery. The ones that weren't were dug in pretty deep with some sort of cover over them. We were lucky that the shells hadn't landed in the cemetery. The cemetery was unquestionably what the Krauts were trying for and they hadn't missed it by more than ten yards. Ten or fifteen yards to the north and the story would have been much different as far as casualties were concerned. However, several vehicles were damaged. What we hadn't figured was how the Krauts had gotten 88 shells on the reverse side of this hill. The 88 gun was supposed to be a flat trajectory weapon. They sure could put them on the reverse side and at the base of a hill sometimes apparently.

It was quite apparent now that our forward progress had been halted. We had been right here at the cemetery now for several days and not even any talk of moving forward. Reports and rumors had it that the Eighth Army had been halted too. Just one glance at the terrain and you didn't have to be a military expert to see what had happened. From where we were we could see mountains raising beyond mountains. The Germans had picked this spot to make their line. They were dug in and well-armed up in the mountains. They had taken months to prepare this line. At this point Italy is only about seventy-five miles across. This also made it easier for them to defend. The elements had turned in their favor too. Continuous rain had turned the roads, fields and mountains into a big mud hole.

The mountains around here made radio communications bad a lot of the time. One day when communication was particularly bad it was decided to move a radio out into an open field away from the hill. It was hoped that we could get better communications from the F.O.'s (Forward Observers). Good and clear messages from the F.O.'s were absolutely imperative for effective artillery support of the infantry.

The way the guns are fired as far as the artillery communications go is a little complicated but effective. The forward observers spot their target and radio back the map coordinates, nature of the target, etc. The radio operator at fire direction gives it to the computer. There is one computer for each battery in the battalion which number three. The computers take the information from the F.O. and changes it into miles, get the range, site and elevation. They send this information down to the guns by phone and the gunners set their guns accordingly. The computers get most of their information by using a slide rule. At first a round of smoke is fired so it is easier for the F.O. to pick it up and send back his bearings from it. If the round of smoke is right in the area usually fire for effect follows immediately. The amount of shells used in firing on the target depends on how important the s-3, a Major, thinks it is. If the target is only a few men, usually a battery of three rounds or twelve shells would be used. If the target was a large group of men, vehicles or tanks, many shells might be expended. If the target warranted it, the whole battalion could be brought to bear on it. This would mean twelve Howitzers firing. For instance, a battalion five rounds would mean sixty rounds. That would usually be enough to neutralize or disperse any ordinary target. In the case of a counter attack or some extra juicy target, the amount of shells could be almost unlimited. Even division artillery and supporting units were called upon. This seldom happened however.

Although the system sounded complicated and

cumbersome it actually was not. Artillery could be brought on a target in a few seconds. I understood that the European armies, including the Germans, used only one battery that had direct communication. It is harder for them to get a concentrated barrage on one particular target so quickly. They may have used only the battery system because their batteries were usually larger than the Americans. I know the British had either six or eight to their batteries while our batteries had four guns.

Anyway, I took a jeep and headed out away from the hill to try to get better reception on this particular day. I only went three or four hundred yards away. I started sweating it out when I drove into an olive orchard. There weren't any guns or anything in position there so I figured it hadn't been checked for mines yet. I got in safely however and got the radio into action. Another thing that didn't look too good was that there were many shell holes from the German artillery. This was one area they seemed to plaster pretty often although there wasn't anything too close around. A few shells right here right now might do them some good, but I hoped they would refrain for a while.

I had no more gotten organized and dug a hole than I noticed I had company. I was surprised to see Bixby drive into the orchard. He was out to do the same thing that I was. He was to relay to his outfit, the 160 F.O. (Forward Observers)

A little later four German planes came scooting down the valley. The way they were roaring and maneuvering up and down reminded me of a bunch of angry bees. They stayed in a pretty tight little formation. As they neared us they began to strafe, probably not particularly at us but most likely the road nearby. It was too close for comfort and I headed for my hole, but was too late. Bixby had beaten me to it. We both stayed in the area most of the day relaying for our outfits. Bixby was handling a mission from the 160th F.O. when suddenly the talking came to an abrupt halt. After several minutes a shaky, unsteady voice came over the set. It was the Sgt. of the party. He said that they had been shelled and the Lieutenant and two of the other men had been killed. He was the only one left in the party. One of the Privates that had been killed was John Anderson, a kid Bixby and I had gotten pretty well acquainted with. We had ridden in the same compartment on the train from Oran to Bizerette. The Sgt. up there really had guts though. He continued on with the fire mission. At first he was pretty shaky and confused but finally got going. A fellow like that deserves a lot of credit for carrying on like that. He probably never even got a thanks much less any recognition. At dusk communications were much improved at our respective fire directions so we both returned to our outfits.

We were fortunate in having picked the cemetery and its immediate surrounding area for our position. Captain Finkle probably saved a lot of lives for picking this particular spot. Colonel Funk, the Battalion Commander, who was very shrewd and very well liked, had not made such a good decision here as it turned out. He had first wanted to make our position across the road from the cemetery. Had we set up there we would have lost many men. That area across the road was often heavily shelled. Captain Finkle, the Battery Commander, insisted that we take up position as we did tight up against the hill by the cemetery. In my opinion that decision was the thing that saved many of our lives. The Germans couldn't see so it was hard to get many shells right at the base of the hill where we were. They put them to the right and left and behind us. The 189th Headquarters position started where ours left off and towards the village. They were shelled very heavily many times and lost many men and lots of equipment. One of their firing batteries, still a little nearer the village, was shelled so badly and lost so many men they were forced to move to another location. Even shells hitting a hundred or even two hundred yards away can kill you just as well as one hitting two yards away. Naturally, fragments traveling a couple of hundred yards have more of a chance to disperse and so cut down the odds in getting you. Incidentally, most people in this war still called the fragments from shells shrapnel. In a sense this is incorrect. In World War I they did use shrapnel percussion shells. These were shells filled with nuts, bolts, jagged pieces of metal, etc. The high explosive shells of this war were different in that the shell itself broke into thousands of pieces. The fragments from the shells were jagged and razor sharp. They traveled farther, faster and were much more dangerous.

One night, Gill, Grady, Burbach, Perkins and I were in the tomb playing cards by candlelight when suddenly there was a horrible roar and wham! The shells coming in this time weren't 88s but bigger, much bigger. 170s or something. The ground really shook when they hit. We all huddled against the wall expecting to get it any second. The old tomb was really quivering and shaking. Fragments and large rocks splattered against its walls. When the shelling stopped we went outside to look around. The shells had done damage this time for sure. About twenty yards away from the tomb four anti-aircraft fellows had been killed and two more were badly wounded. The only one of the bunch that had escaped without even a scratch was their officer, Captain Farrell. Their half-track had been riddled by shell fragments. Pieces had gone through the half inch armor on it like it had been tissue paper.

Curtis had been our fire direction radioman just a few feet away and he was mighty lucky not to have been killed. Luckily he had rolled out of the jeep onto the ground. Shrapnel had gone through the spare tire, the back of the jeep and through the radio. Both of the rear tires had been blown too.

The next morning we examined the damage more closely. Those shell fragments were powerful. They had clipped off many tombstones and had gone through olive trees several inches thick. One thing I wouldn't have believed if I hadn't seen it myself was the way a couple of fragments had gone through the cemetery wall. The wall was about eighteen inches thick. It was made of dirt with about a half inch of cement coating covering the outside. It had to have power to go through something like that. One could imagine what happens to a man hit with flying stuff like that. One shell had hit a large boulder near the C.P. (Command Post) and where I had put up my pup tent. It had made powder out of part of the boulder and my shelter half was just a bunch of string. That would have been my last day on earth if I had remained in my tent instead of moving into the tomb.

Our area was getting well pockmarked with shell holes now. The trees, cemetery walls and tombs were getting pretty battle scarred. Every one of our vehicles had holes in them made from shrapnel. Many tires had been blown too.

There were the smaller shell holes of the 88 quick fuses and larger holes from the 88 delayed fuses. Then there were the still larger holes of the 170s. There was no doubt the Germans had been trying for the cemetery. Our particular location had made them only partially successful but they had gotten lots of them mighty close and some right where they wanted to. Naturally, having no 105s in our battery we weren't going to receive counter battery fire. Though if they had any idea that an area was being used as a headquarters they would of course given it special attention. A headquarters was the brains of a lot of men and artillery pieces and to destroy it would actually be of more value than knocking out some guns. The guns could be more easily replaced than a lot of higher ranking officers with lots of field experience. We believed that through their intelligence or airplanes or some way they knew that the cemetery area held headquarters. We figured it must be this for there were no guns, tanks or hardly any heavy equipment in our exact spot. The Krauts had too many good targets to keep wasting ammunition on light vehicles and a few troops. Anyway, they sure seemed to be trying especially hard for the cemetery. Knowing that we were probably well dug in there they used lots of delayed fuse shells. A tomb would not have been of any use against a 170 delayed fuse or even an 88 for that matter.

In "our" tomb the fire direction radio gang had made ourselves as comfortable as possible. We hung a couple of shelter halves in front of the grating like a door to make it warmer and to also black out the place. We also rigged up some charcoal burners out of tin cans. The burners made it warmer but we got headaches from the fumes and it was a wonder we hadn't all suffocated. Candles were scarce so we rounded up some olive oil and rigged up some oil lamps.

After one heavy shelling when plenty of stuff bounced off the tomb we decided to move right down into the bottom of the vault and use the empty crevices for bunks. We spent most of the day burning spider webs with gun powder. There were several empty ledges awaiting more permanent occupants. Just the right length for a bunk.

All the crevices that contained a body were sealed except the one where the man had been placed the day we had moved in here. A reddish black substance oozed from the guys box. We dared one another to open the box to have a look but no one did it. I've slept in better and more cheerful places than this hole.

That night I felt much safer as far as the shelling was concerned. I had a tough time getting to sleep though because of the sickening odor of the dead man. It was almost unbearable. Boy! Talk about Dracula stories. This wasn't watching one in a movie. This was living it.

The next morning, we all moved back onto the ground floor. We decided that we had rather put up with the shelling than try to endure the smell of the rotting flesh.

In the tomb next door to ours was a great place to do a little gambling when you had a chance or were so inclined. This particular tomb was convenient because the vault below could be used. The smell was O.K. and no leaking coffins. One wooden box that was used to put the casket in made the table. For chairs the players used boxes of bones.

These Italian cemeteries were rather weird affairs. Land here must have really been at a premium. Of course, in several hundred years of burying everyone in separate graves it would have taken away acres of land even in a small community like here. They apparently had solved the problem of how to keep the cemeteries from spreading out. It seemed that a few of the more well-to-do families in the vicinity had the quite elaborate tombs. Then there were the ordinary graves throughout the cemetery. However, the family plots apparently never grew in size regardless how many died down through the years. Evidently, when someone died they dug up one of the older graves and pitched the bones into a huge pit in the middle of the cemetery. Then the new corpse was placed in the hole just reactivated. In a pit in the middle of the cemetery there seemed to be hundreds of skeletons. The pit was covered by a heavy door. It was a pretty gruesome sight to lift up the door and see the dozens of skulls looking up at you. Probably in the States if there was a setup like this guys would be tossed down in there as part of some college frat initiation. It would probably be impossible to get out without a ladder and would be a hell of a place to spend a night by yourself.

Some of the richer people must have taken pity on some of their poor relations. Apparently, when it was their turn to be thrown in the pit, they took their bones, boxed them in a little wooden box and placed them in the bottom of their respective family tombs. These boxes of the "poor relatives" made the seats for the gamblers.

One night the Jerrys were shelling particularly heavy and everyone was sweating it out as usual. Stuff was screaming through the air and bouncing around. It was pretty rough. Suddenly Bell appeared in the tomb and announced that he couldn't stand it out on the radio any more. He was really shaky and had a hunted look in his eyes. Bell said he wouldn't go back out on the set under any circumstances. Gill argued with him but it was no soap. It was an hour until it was my turn on the set but I told Gill that I would take over now. I felt sorry for Bell and I liked him. He was in bad shape and couldn't help it. I know he wasn't putting on. As I went around the cemetery wall on the way to the set a shell whined in low and crashed into the olive orchard a few yards away. I figured it would just be my luck to get it when I was trying to do a guy a favor.

Bell was still awake when my time was up on the radio. He was in bad shape and his nerves were completely gone. He told me that he couldn't take it any longer and as soon as it was daylight he was taking off. He had been in the North African and Sicilian Campaigns and had seen quite a bit of action. He said that this was the worst continuous German shelling he had ever seen. I told him that taking off was the worst thing he could possibly do. I told him to go to Colonel Funk instead of Captain Finkle to see if something could be done for him. He had been to Captain Finkle before and hadn't gotten any satisfaction. Although I liked Captain Finkle, I thought he was unfair with Bell. He didn't like Bell and thought he was yellow. Bell had come to the 45h from the 1st Division and Captain Finkle had overheard him make a comparison between the two outfits that he didn't think was complimentary to the 45th. This didn't make him feel any kindlier towards Bell either.

Early the next morning Bell went to see the colonel. He said the colonel was very understanding and had the medical officer make arrangements for him to go back to Naples for observation. I was glad he was going to get a break. Some of the fellows said he was just yellow, etc. It was just one of those cases of ones nerves going bad.

As Bell packed to leave for Naples he made me a present of his carbine and bed roll. The bedroll wasn't much but would make the tomb floor a little softer. The carbine was the real prize. There were very few of them around yet. Only a few officers had them. In fact, Bell had gotten his off a dead officer in Sicily. It was a lot better to have than the old .06. I kept the .06 however for there was a good chance that some 2nd Looey would pull his rank on me and take the carbine for himself.

I never saw Bell again as I knew I wouldn't. I knew after an examination he would be declared unfit. That's how sure I knew his battle fatigue was real. I did receive about three letters from him. The last one was from North Africa. He had been reclassified and put into limited service. I often wondered if he ever got back to Scotland and married his girl.

The days dragged on and on. Each one the repetition of the day before. The usual shellings and air raids. The thundering of our own artillery and the almost continuous rain. Our tomb was beginning to crack up. Not from incoming shells but mostly from the concussions from our own guns. The constant booming and vibrating, especially from the 155s not too far away. The plaster had begun to crack on the ceiling and walls. Even small pieces were beginning to drop off.

Thanksgiving Day arrived and we did have turkey and cranberry sauce. It was raining cats and dogs when we went up to the mess truck for chow. Some turkey and cranberry sauce was tossed into a mess kit with some other food. We all stood around in ankle deep mud and water trying to eat. It was raining so hard that our food was sloppy and tasteless because it had taken on so much rain water. A couple of shells whacked in close and everyone hit the mud. Most of the stuff that was left in our mess kit slopped out on to the ground. Yes, it was quite a Thanksgiving and quite a meal. I guess someone had wanted to bring a little home to us with the turkey etc. No one seemed to gripe too much at that. I guess we figured things could be worse and I guess we felt lucky to still be alive.

We couldn't complain too much about food under the circumstances generally. Although we did get "C" rations often we did have a variety of food and usually enough. Our static position was the reason we probably ate as much food as we did. Most of the gun positions hadn't moved a foot during the two months we were here on the line. When a move was made it was usually a few yards to get away from a place that was being shelled. We also had a good cook. He could even make the "C" rations taste better. He really tried to please the fellows, sometimes staying up all night to make doughnuts or fritters or something a little extra. His facilities for cooking were pretty limited as well as there was a lack of different seasonings. Our cook even made pancakes for us using G.I. toothpowder instead of baking powder, which seemed to be one of the scarce items. I guess about all that G.I. toothpaste was salt and soda anyway.

We didn't have a decent place to eat. We just stood around or squatted down in the mud. We gobbled up our food as quickly as we could. Another thing that didn't do much to help our mealtimes was a sudden shelling or a plane or two strafing around.

One day we actually had steak. It was the first time I had had any meat or anything like this since coming overseas. Although it was tough I knew it was going to be good. I was just getting ready to carve mine when a German plane zoomed over low and everybody scattered. One guy came charging by me, hit my mess kit and knocked it about thirty feet. I raced after my steak but before I could pick it up someone else stepped on it and almost drove it out of sight in the mud. I dug it out of the mud and washed it off a little. I wasn't going to let good food like that get away.

At most of our meals there was what we called the "bucket brigade". It was a line of Italians, usually kids, lined up with small buckets to get our scraps. They came under pretty dangerous conditions. There were many killed and maimed along the front from shells and mines. When you are hungry though, a person will take chances they never thought of in normal times.

BYE FOR NOW

Most of the kids were pretty ragged and hungry looking. They begged for our left overs and would take any scraps, no matter how small. There were about six to twelve kids that came to our area at mealtimes. That's the only time you ever saw them. They just seemed to come out of nowhere. What few scraps that were left over didn't go very far so there was a lot of jockeying around to get into position where they thought they would get the most food. I could never figure out whether the older people were too proud or too scared to come out and beg. Maybe they figured they wouldn't have much in competition with the kids anyway.

One little girl sort of became a favorite with us. She was around nine or ten and a very pretty little girl. When she first came down to our area she would stand shyly away from the rest of the kids. She never screamed and hollered and begged at you. The first few days she went away empty handed and wasn't even noticed. She always came back though, hoping I guess, that she would get a little to eat. The guys began to notice her and how she acted. Anything a G.I. hates is to be hounded by beggars or someone trying to sell him something, whether it was here or in Naples. We began to give this quiet little girl practically all of our scraps. She always blushed and seemed embarrassed, which is unusual for Italians. She may have been putting on an act or had been coached by someone in the weaknesses of G.I.s or just humble and appreciative. I sincerely believed the latter. She soon began to get more than she could carry in one bucket so someone rigged her up with another one. I also surmised that the cooks were sneaking out a loaf of bread or some canned meat to her once in a while. Maybe it wasn't right the way we were dividing up the food. At least that little girl, her parents and probably a few relatives were eating a little better.

There were the usual rumors floating around the outfit. There were a couple that were honeys. One had it that the 45th Division was going back to the States and make a movie called "The Fighting Forty-Fifth". Some actually believed this. Another rumor was supposed to have come from a big shot chaplain. The poor chaplains seemed to keep up the morale more from the rumors that were supposed to come from them than their actual duties. Anyway, this one had it that around Christmas we would be relieved and sent back to Sicily or North Africa for a long rest. This rumor seemed a little more logical, for the division had been on the line quite a while and could stand a rest and complete revamping. The Division had fought through Sicily, Salerno and up Italy to this point without much rest. The companies were there the whole time. It seemed as though if enough man power had been brought to bear on the Germans here we could have overpowered them with sheer weight. Of course, it would have been bloodier for a while but probably no worse than sitting here and being blasted at for months and getting nowhere at all. I suppose the generals and whoever was supposed to be running this war knew what they were doing but it made you wonder sometimes.

Of course, the odds were terrific here in Italy. The Germans had taken a lot of time preparing this line. They were up in the mountains and with all the advantages. They were well dug in with plenty of artillery and other equipment. The few narrow roads through the passes were heavily guarded and were all zeroed in with artillery. It would be impossible to try to go over them. All around were thousands of mines planted everywhere. Civilians and stock would be blown up by these mines around Venefro and up in the mountains for years to come. I imagined that the whole front across Italy was about the same.

One day some shells landed in our other radio station. One fellow, realizing he had been hit, hot footed it for the medics. He didn't think his wounds were too bad at first. As he jumped over a rock terrace blood spurted from a couple of holes in his chest which really scared him. He made it to the medics O.K. but it did turn out that he was wounded pretty badly. He was sent to the hospital where he spent two or three months. He eventually rejoined the outfit.

One day in the middle of December I was informed that I was to go up on a L.O. (Look Out) Party. It was to be Lt. Lindsey's party. Two other fellows, also from Headquarters Battery, made up the rest of the party. The other fellows were Hank Pulsey and Eddie Grates. Pulsey was an original member of the 45th. He was a Sgt. from the anti-tank platoon section. Grates was a corporal in the survey section. He hailed from somewhere in Michigan. At the last minute Burbach was added to the party making a total of four enlisted men and one officer.

We started up the mountain early the next morning. All we had to take with us were our guns and a blanket. We would use the radio of the L.O. party we were to relieve. It was a break not to have to take a radio for it was to be quite a climb at best. The trail that we were to take started at the bottom of a mountain where our "C" Battery was in position. The trail was a muddy affair and had been churned up by the feet of hundreds of men and mules. Here, along the trail, we passed and met many mules and their skinners. Everything had to be brought into the mountains in our sector by mules or the backs of men. No kind of vehicle could get up the mountain even part of the way. There were no roads of any kind and the mountains went straight up. The mules had to carry everything to keep a bunch of infantrymen going and fighting so they were packing everything imaginable. The mules going up the trail were loaded with ammunition, rations, water and all sorts of equipment. Most of the mules coming down the trail were traveling pretty light. Some of them were loaded with empty water cans and odds and ends. We met a couple with the corpses of our own G.I.s.

Having to take everything up in the mountains on mules was another thing that made moving on this front just about impossible. When even drinking water had to be packed for miles up steep and slippery trails you knew things were rough. I couldn't imagine bringing a badly wounded man down on a jolting, staggering mule.

The mules that were being used were local ones. They weren't as strong and tough as the American breed. I guess they were about as stubborn though. You would see some G.I. tugging and swearing at an old mule. The mule would pull his head back and set his legs stiff. Maybe the skinner didn't know how to cuss them out in Italian. Most of the poor skinners were inexperienced in this type of work. Hell, this was a modern war and everything moved on wheels. Where the trail wasn't slippery from mud it was slippery because of the solid rock. In some of the narrow places men and mules had gone over the side. We saw a couple of mules off down the side of the mountain dead. They had probably gone over the side and had broken a leg or something and had to be shot. I felt sorry for the poor damned mules as well as the men. This was a tough, miserable and dangerous job.

We struggled up the trail and the farther we went the steeper it got. We had a nice day for our trek. It was bright and sunny which was unusual. From up here we could look back into the Volturno Valley. In the distance we could see the Volturno River shining in the sunlight. The whole view below us was beautiful. The Germans certainly had good observation from up here. We could see trucks and other vehicles moving on the road far below. We stopped at a tiny village smashed against the side of the mountain. The infantry's rear C.P. (Command Post) was set up there. Lt. Lindsey went into the C.P. for one thing or another and the rest of us flopped down on the ground to rest. Soon Lt. Lindsey came out and we continued up the mountain.

We finally reached our destination, a place that was called the "Goat Shed". No doubt that's what it had been, too. It was a fairly long but narrow, crudely constructed stone building. It had a flimsy make-shift tile roof on it. It was built up against a sheer solid rock bank with the bank acting as one wall. The top of the roof was flush with the top of the bank. The whole thing was flimsy and very poorly built. Anyway, this was the end of the line for us. We were to stay here at the battalion forward C. P. and work with the battalion commander who was Colonel Brown of the Third Battalion. We went into the shed and relieved Captain Hayes and his party. There was very little ceremony. Smith, the radio operator, just handed me the mike and they took off. They seemed to be in a hurry to get going and I didn't blame them. The duties of a L.O. (Liaison Officer) is to work with the battalion commander. It helps give better support to the infantry and the artillery.

Things here seemed very quiet. You would hardly know that you were very near the Front at all. Right now it was a lot quieter than back in the valley. Back there if there weren't incoming shells our own guns at least would be banging away. I guessed that this was one of those unnatural lulls. I stayed on the radio for the rest of the day. I had to handle just routine stuff, relaying fire missions, coded messages to the F. O.'s etc. It was quite late in the evening when I was relieved by Grates.

Burbach and I went out to try to find the place where we were supposed to sleep. The place was supposed to be a shelter-half stretched over two piles of rocks. Here may have been the only place in the war where a fox hole or slit trench was built instead of being dug. On top of this mountain most of our immediate area was solid rock or in some places just a couple of inches of dirt. Right where we were there wasn't any place that had dirt deep enough to dig down in. The only way to get a little protection was to gather up rocks and build little walls with them. This was the type of thing Burbach and I were looking for. We finally found the place after wandering around through "shit alley" for about two hours. There were plenty of loads around on the ground here. The infantry had been here quite a while and the rock was pretty hard to dig in. Probably another reason for the mess was when the boys first moved into this position they didn't know they would be stuck here so long and they had been careless about their disposals. When we did find the place, after wandering all over the landscape, it was only about thirty yards from the C.P. We crawled under the shelter-half and took off our shoes and put them outside. In a few minutes we had to put them on again to keep our feet from freezing. Even if our shoes were slimy and stinky it was a little more comfortable with them on.

All night long shells went sailing over going both directions. We could see the flashes of both the Germans and American guns. The German guns seemed to be much closer than ours. We could plainly see the German shells flare up as they hit way down in the valley. We figured they were landing in Fozilli and in our positions around and near the cemetery. Our own shells seemed to labor as they came over us. All of the shells seemed to be low, just skilling over the top of the mountain. They seemed so low that we could have reached up and touched them. No doubt, in this sort of terrain, where you had to shoot over steep mountains, the shells did just skim over the tops of them.

It was bitterly cold out in the shelter. We huddled together in our blankets trying in vain to keep warm. The ground was wet and that made matters worse. We were cold and miserable all night and only got a few winks of sleep.

The next day was about the same as the one before but it began to rain some again. It was slow, cold, miserable rain. I couldn't see how it could rain when it was so cold. It should be snowing. That night it was colder than ever, so we decided to sleep right in the shed. Most of the Headquarter bunch slept there and it was pretty crowded.

In spite of winter underwear, regular O.D.s (Olive Drabs), a field jacket and over coat I was still cold. I found that draping a blanket over my head seemed to make it a little warmer. I guess by not letting your warm breath escape makes it a little warmer. I just sat up all night. Might as well, the place was so crowded you had to sit up to sleep anyway. Actually, I was the only regular radio operator in the L.O. party and the rest were a little reluctant to get on the set if they could get out of it. I didn't mind. It was something to do and keep from getting too bored.

From here at the goat shed, we could hear mortar shells whacking in a short distance away. The boys said that the goat shed area itself hadn't been shelled in several days. The shed itself had never been hit but there were some near misses. The location of the shed made it almost impossible to get a direct hit. It was flush against a rock bank with another one rising just beyond the first one. Mortar shells can be dropped in almost any place, but still it would be pretty hard to get one right in on top of us. A few yards from the goat shed was the forward terminal of the mule trains. Mortar shells had landed there often and both men and animals had been killed.

The mule train terminal was always busy. There were almost always mules being loaded or unloaded there. A large area at the terminal had been churned up into knee deep mud by the mules.

A wounded German soldier was brought into the C.P. He had been wounded about three days before and had lain out in "no man's land" all that time. He must have suffered a great deal from the cold as well as his wounds. He didn't appear to be in too bad of shape, but was awfully pale and very weak. I imagined he would pull through O.K. He was loaded onto a mule and taken down the mountain to a hospital and then eventually a P.O.W. (Prisoner of War) camp.

The morale of the Germans was supposed to be pretty low along this winter line. It may have been, but they were doing a good job of holding us. In fact, the Allies were at a standstill here for a total of about seven months altogether.

I wouldn't say that the American morale was too high, or even the least bit high. The miserable weather, tough terrain and stubborn enemy didn't make anyone too happy. No replacements, no one to relieve us, no "Second Front" didn't help morale any. We were fed with hundreds of rumors and propaganda to try to keep our spirits up. The stories about the German morale being low was part of the propaganda to keep our morale up. No doubt there was a lot of despair among the German troops. A few did give up but mostly they were Poles that were forced into the German Army and didn't want to fight anyway. The German morale certainly must have been shaken by knowing that they had been driven out of North Africa, Sicily and had been driven well up the boot of Italy. They were being pushed back on the Russian Front and their homes were being heavily bombed. That should be enough to ruin anyone's morale. The American morale was pretty low because of being stopped. I can't imagine what it might have been if we had been pushed backward. Some of the prisoners would say that the war was lost for Germany and they were glad to give up and get it over with. Other prisoners said they thought Germany still had a good chance. Some of them said they didn't mind so much losing ground for a year or two. After all they reasoned that they had nothing but victories for several years and should expect some serious reverses. They expressed the opinion that they would come out with some new weapon and get going again and win the war. Some thought that the German strategy right now was to conserve their forces and then lash out at an opportune moment and win the war quickly. Maybe they had been fed some high powered propaganda at that.

German censorship of mail wasn't as strict as ours. Letters taken from prisoners and their dead proved that. They seemed to write back home anything they wanted to. They told of battles, hardships, casualties or even their exact locations. In our letters we couldn't even write what kind of weather we were having. We couldn't say where we were or what outfit we were with. It seemed that a lot of the German letters struck a gloomy note. They usually wrote of the hardships, etc. Our letters would have been very similar if we had been allowed to do so. I guess the War Department didn't want the people back in the States to worry. It's too damned bad they didn't know a little more about what was going on. I guess it would have been too bad, after goofing off all day at a shipyard or aircraft plant, to take a chance of spoiling their time at the beer joint. All they heard about were the glorious victories of the American armies. They made it seem in the news accounts that we were much smarter, tougher and braver than the Krauts. They tried to make it seem that the going was easy and that the Krauts were the ones that were taking all the punishment. Even Roosevelt once said something about the "soft underside of the Fustang Europa".

The headquarters of the 157th Infantry regiment, 3rd Battalion, the one we were working with, at last prepared to move. They were not moving forward but moving anyway, probably to more comfortable quarters. I never got to the new quarters. One afternoon the whole outfit moved out. Even Lt. Lindsey, Gates and Pulsey. Brumbach and I, with the radio, were all alone in the goat shed. We were to relay the messages on back. A radio had been brought up the mountain for the rest of them to use. By the middle of the afternoon the goat shed was deserted except for Burbank, myself and two infantry boys that were left to guard the rations and ammunition at the pack train terminal. Everything seemed deserted and quiet now. Even the pack train route was changed so we were pretty well isolated.

We had plenty of room now. Only four where there must have been fifty before. We moved right into the part of the shed where the Colonel had slept. There was a makeshift fireplace. We stoked up a big fire, which was O.K. because the one small window in the place was easily blacked out. We had plenty of "C" rations and cigarettes and with lots of room we were more comfortable than we had been in days. Our biggest problem was drinking water. We didn't have a bit and with the pack train being rerouted the chance of getting any was next to nothing.

That first night the four of us sat around the fire and talked for hours. We talked mostly of home and better times. It would have been hard to believe a few short months ago that I would be stuck up here on the top of some mountain in Italy. About midnight Brumbach and the two infantry boys turned in. I told Brumbach that I would stay on the radio until 3:30 and then wake him up. About 2:00 a.m. a strange voice came in over the radio. It was definitely a German voice and I could feel the hair on my head beginning to rise. Several thoughts flashed through my mind. First of all, I didn't have the slightest idea about the situation. I knew the Germans were only a short distance away, but didn't know if there were friendly troops between us and them. I naturally supposed that there were. I thought how stupid could we be not having a lookout. We had just laid around in here taking it easy. A whole division could have moved in and we wouldn't have known it. I also wondered if the Germans had some way gotten on our frequency. Some of the boys told me it had happened in Salerno. Another sobering thought was that a German patrol had gotten through our lines and were very close. Sometimes a radio pretty close would come over your set. We had heard tank conversations a few times. The guttural voices sounded again. It sounded like it said "ach der lieber" or something. I grabbed my rifle and strained my ears to try to hear footsteps or anything outside. My imagination didn't run away with me. I couldn't hear a thing. I was wondering whether to wake up the other fellows. If it was nothing I would feel pretty foolish, but I sure did feel lonesome. I listened intently for a few minutes and nothing more came over the radio or I heard nothing outside, so I began to relax a little. I later asked at the Fire Direction and some of the F.O.s about this particular night. No one had heard anything. I know I had though and hadn't been dreaming or imagining it. Just one of those things I guess.

The next day was a dull affair. The weather was threatening and it was dark and gloomy. I relayed fire missions and other messaging all day. The only thing that bothered us was the lack of water and we were all beginning to get mighty thirsty. Toward evening Pulsey came down from the other position. Lt. Lindsey sent him down to see if we were O.K. and if we needed anything. Pulsey hung around for a while and just at dusk he started back. About two hours later Lt. Lindsey called us and asked if Pulsey had left yet. When I told him he had left a couple of hours before he was really worried. He kept calling us every few minutes throughout the night. Pulsey never showed up there or returned back to our place all night. I didn't worry too much about Pulsey. I figured he had lost his way in the dark and had laid down by the trail some place to wait out the night. Of course there was always the chance he had wandered off the trail in the dark and had gotten into a mine field. There were thousands of mines around here both German and ours. It was also possible that he had wandered into German lines or had been picked up by a patrol. Any of our fears were relieved early the next morning when Lt. Lindsey called and said Pulsey had shown up. It was just like I figured. He had gotten lost in the dark and instead of taking any chances he sat down and waited for daylight.

The next day went about the same as the one before. There was one thing that was different and that was that our thirst was much worse. By now it was almost unbearable. We decided that we were going to get water if we had to go clear to the Vultrane River after it. That night we decided on a plan to help our thirst. We went out and dipped water out of the holes made by the mule's hooves down at the terminal. It was black grimy stuff. We took it to the shed and boiled the stuff. As we drank it we drank a lot of mule manure and other unidentifiable objects. We figured by boiling the stuff it wouldn't poison us and it did quench our thirst.

On this night more than the average amount of shells passed over our shed going both ways. Both sides were interdicting known targets, such as roads, gun positions and towns. We wondered if the boys back at the cemetery were doing alright. Actually, we seemed further away from the war up here than we did back in the valley, even though we were only a few hundred yards from the German Infantry. It was much quieter here most of the time. Mortar barrages dropped fairly close at times and spasmodic machine gun and rifle fire could often be heard a way to the north and west of us. No big incoming stuff like down in the valley and also not the booming of our own guns. No air activity either. We had seen some German planes attacking something along our lines quite a distance away. We could see them plainly and hear the machine guns firing and hear the personnel bombs exploding. It was considerably far away though. This terrain wasn't very good for very effective use of fighter planes.

Late that night a rather humorous thing happened. Very late we heard someone walking on the roof of the shed. We could tell that it was only one man but on the loosely fitting tile it sounded like an army. We challenged him and he called out that he was Lt. So and So and was lost from his outfit. He sounded bewildered and couldn't figure out where he was or where our voices were coming from. He had apparently followed along the bank and walked out on our roof without knowing it. Suddenly he let out a yell and we hear him crash into a pile of empty "C" ration cans at one end of the shed. We opened the door and he staggered in looking confused. Blood was streaming from his hand. It's a wonder he hadn't cut himself up worse than he had falling into that pile of cans, for those open edges are razor sharp. We got his hand fixed up and gave him the directions to the rear C.P. He stumbled out into the darkness still in a state of confusion. It was obvious he couldn't figure out what the score was. He couldn't seem to figure out how he had fallen ten feet into a pile of tin cans and found himself right at the door of our place. I think he thought we were in a cave or something. Anyway, we never bothered to try to set him straight.

The next morning Graves came over from the other position and said that we had been relieved and the new L.O. (Look Out) party was already there. We gathered up our stuff, put the radio on our backs and started down the mountain. Just as we left the shed it started to rain and it poured all the way down. The going was easier going down. About the closest call we had on this deal was a German plane which had apparently been raiding Venefro or something. It was scooting down the valley towards the low place they generally headed for on their lines. Our anti-aircraft was firing at them. Shells either 37 or 40 mm started hitting the mountainside near us. Damned poor shooting we thought and cursed them. Someone said it must be that Negro "ack ack outfit" down there that fired at anything that flew from a sparrow to our planes. I didn't know who was doing it but it gave us a few anxious seconds. We made good time getting back to the battery but we were thoroughly soaked when we got there. We had been up on the mountain a week so we had quite a lot of mail to read. We also had a chance to wash up, shave and put on clean underwear.

Christmas was drawing close and all of the fellows began to receive things from home. Every night someone in the tomb would get something from home. It was usually fruit cake, cookies, candy, cigars or cigarettes. Whenever anyone got candy or cake it was passed around to everyone. Most of the times the cookies would be mostly crumbs and the cake would be stale and dry. Some of the fruit cakes would be moldy. We enjoyed then though and made a big deal out of every package. Everyone seemed to be getting a little Christmas spirit in spite of the circumstances.

Everyone was receiving presents too. Most of them were either funny or sad depending on the way you looked at it. One fellow received a blue polka dot tie. Another a pair of gaudy pajamas. Some got swim suits, ping pong sets, tennis rackets, etc. We kidded fellows about sleeping in the pajamas, having a few fast games of ping pong or going for a dip in some mud hole. Mine didn't seem to be as funny although one thing I got was kind of amusing although usable. It was a few bars of Camay soap. On the label it said "Camay the soap of beautiful women". Being dirty, grimy and changing clothes only about once in three months, somehow the beautiful women bit just didn't seem to fit in. Things like pajamas were really out. We wore our G.I.s twenty four hours a day. We just took off our shoes when we could when we lay down to sleep. Swim trunks were just as bad. However, some of the rear echelon troops might have been able to use some of this stuff. The blue polka dot tie was out for anyone as long as the war was on and you were in the army.

Some of the things that were sent made you damned mad at the merchants who sold them and the bastards that manufactured them. They were getting rich off of well-meaning parents, wives and sweethearts that wanted to do something for the "boys". It made you fighting mad and almost want to cry at some of the stuff they had conned some into buying. I remember one little gem in particular. It was called a "fox hole pillow". It was a horse collar affair that you were supposed to put around your neck and then you could lean back against the side of your fox hole and be comfortable. I understand that they cost several dollars but couldn't have cost more than a few cents to make. Those crooks were getting rich off of innocent people. I suppose that to be a parent, wife or sweetheart who was trying desperately to find something nice to send to their man overseas the pillow did make sense but what a crime. Talk about war criminals.

Christmas Eve finally arrived. We took up a collection and coaxed an Italian to come to our area with his accordion and sing and play. At first he sang some Christmas songs and carols, but that made everyone too homesick. We had him sing things like "You Are My Sunshine" and "Roll out the Barrel". The guy couldn't sing or even play very well but we enjoyed it.

Christmas morning we each had one fresh egg for breakfast. Just being December 25th didn't make it much different. The day was about the same as any other. I had heard stories about in World War I all of the fighting stopped. Even gifts were supposed to have been exchanged between the Germans and the Americans. It was different this time, at least in our particular sector. There were the usual artillery exchanges and I doubt if the infantry and the Krauts were exchanging hankies for Christmas either. It rained all day Christmas which was also normal. The weather was at its worst now, raining every day and always low hanging clouds. It was a lot colder than it had been when we moved here almost two months ago.

1943 was rapidly coming to an end. Only a few more days left. Rumors were really strong now that we would be relieved shortly after the New Year. Most of us believed that this rumor was the real thing. After all, after two months on the line one might expect relief.

A few officers and non-coms from the 8th Division came up to the Front to see how things were supposed to be done. There were both artillerymen and infantrymen to observe what was going on. The rest of the Division was still back in North Africa, and these guys were to go back with what they saw and learned and pass it on to the rest. They were all full of questions and seemed to want to find out as much as they could. It was amazing to watch them when a shell whined over or crashed in pretty close. They looked and acted like I must have in my first shelling back near Benevento. They would dive down in the mud or a latrine trench or anything else that was handy. It went to show you how you could get used to the shelling. Of course, they never stopped scaring the daylights out of you and when they were right in on you all you could do was lay there and hope for the best. When you were in an area as long as we had been in this one you knew the spots that were the most frequently shelled. You could never tell though and it didn't pay to be too careless. From the instant we heard the whine we couldn't tell if they were going to be close or go way past us. The ones right in on you didn't give much warning, just a very short scream. Like they say, you never hear the one that gets you. Until the 88th boys got here we had forgotten how little attention we paid to the shells going over us farther out into the valley. Now with these green troops we realized how used we had gotten to it. They jumped, ducked, cowered or scattered every time a shell whined, no matter how close they were going to hit. In a day or two a lot of them were getting the idea and not acting so ridiculous. No one made fun of them though because it's not a very funny thing to see a man badly frightened and most of us remembered how it had been with us in the beginning.

Anyway, a rumor now sprang up that the 88th Division would probably relieve us. We didn't care who in the Hell it was, just so someone did, and we could get away from this damned cemetery.

We had a couple of sunny days toward the end of the year. Groups of our heavy bombers came over heading for the German lines. We hadn't seen many of our bombers lately as the flying weather hadn't been very good. They never seemed to fly unless the sky was cloudless. A few dive-bombers strafed and bombed the front lines occasionally. We marked the towns of Concasale and Acquafondata in the German lines with colored smoke for the dive bombers.

One day we saw a formation of bombers coming our direction from the German lines. They were big and looked like ours so we just figured they were returning from a mission. They were our bombers alright but they didn't seem to know where they were. They began dropping bombs behind our lines. Fortunately for us they were some distance from our position, but we could hear the bombs plainly exploding. Our own anti-aircraft began to fire at them and they slowly wheeled around and headed back towards the German lines again. Their bombs had caused causalities among our own troops. I suppose it was fairly easy to get turned around here. With all the mountains and valleys and little villages the landscape from several thousand feet up must have looked pretty much the same. I was told after we left here, but never found out for sure, that Venefro had been hit hard by our bombers killing many of our troops. I imagine if it had happened the War Department would have kept it as quiet as possible. It was possible however because it was well-known that our troops had been bombed and strafed by our own planes by mistake.

One day in late December, Perkins told me that a woman up in the village had some nice jewelry to sell. I had wanted to get some gift to send to Bernice but had never been able to get any place where I could buy something half decent. I decided to go up to the village and look the woman up.

I found the lady. An elderly person who spoke perfect English with a Scottish brogue. She was Italian herself but had married a Scottish doctor and had lived in Scotland for many years. She had only necklaces for sale so the selection wasn't much. She claimed to be real hard up for cash and was forced to sell her jewelry. There was only one necklace I cared anything about but it wasn't really what I wanted to send home. I didn't know when I would get any place to get anything better so I decided to take it. The price was 1500 Lira, in other words about $15. That was quite a bit of money here in Italy but the woman assured me the stuff was good and that the price was really a good one. It was supposed to be gold but didn't know the name of the lavender stones in it. Cheap glass I guessed.

The rumors that we were going to be relieved seemed to be really true. We were supposed to be relieved by the

French and not the 88th. We were beginning to believe the rumors for we heard the names of the towns we were to go to on our rest.

Around New Years the French did begin to move in. The first of the troops we saw were an Arab looking type of Colonial Troop. I didn't know whether they were supposed to be infantry or cavalry. They were a tough looking bunch riding horses and carrying a long, old type of rifle.

The few Italians we came in contact with here dreaded to see the French move in. I suppose through the centuries they had had their differences. That stab in the back by the Italians back in 1940 probably hadn't made the relationship between the two countries any better.

New Year's came and so did a German greeting. At one minute to twelve the Germans sent in a snappy barrage. Our own artillery was supposed to give the Krauts a pretty nice greeting right at midnight. No doubt they had anticipated this and had beaten us to the punch by starting theirs a minute earlier. Some of their shells had landed right in the battery that was preparing to fire our barrage and rained all kinds of Hell. In fact, it was so bad they had to call off their barrage.

Right after New Year's the French began to move in in force. They had American equipment throughout. They even had American uniforms. The only difference was their own insignia was sewn on them. The only items that weren't American were their shoes and helmets. The shoes were British and the helmets were their own.

We soon made friends with several of them and they seemed like nice guys. I got pretty well acquainted with on fellow named George. He had lived in Marseilles before the war and had been a newspaper reporter. When the Germans took over France he had gotten to North Africa some way and joined the French forces there. Incidentally, to make us able to understand each other he spoke a little English.

The French had a little tough luck the first day they moved into our position. A group of them were standing in the olive orchard talking when a shell whined in and crashed right next to them. One was killed and another very badly wounded. They were lucky that more of them had not been killed. They buried the one that was killed at the far side of the cemetery. They gave him a military burial with a squad firing a salute over his grave.

It was definite now that we would be relieved. The 158th would pull back on January 9th. It sounded almost too good to be true. We all began to get more cautious now and didn't take any unnecessary chances. We didn't want to expose ourselves any more than we had to. We didn't want to get knocked off just before we got relieved.

The French that were moving in moved right into our position. They put the C.P. (Command Post) by our C.P. When one of our guns was taken out of position one of their guns was put where it had been. The idea was to move out slowly, each gun being replaced by one of theirs one at a time so there wouldn't be any differences in the amount of fire power available. Doing it in this manner it was easier for the French to get adjusted.

I happened to be in the village when a company or two of French moved into the town. I could see that the Italian's fear of them was somewhat justified.

An officer and a few men would go into a house or building to inspect it. If the place was suitable to quarter men, out would come the Dagoes through doors and windows. I didn't blame the French. Our own troops should have been able to take over any building that would have been useful or made it more comfortable for them. Instead, our troops had to stay out in the elements. I guess it was because the Italians were supposed to be our allies now. I guess maybe we were better off outside anyway. Most of the houses looked pretty crummy and I imagine one could easily pick up lice in them.

One night we had a little party in the bottom of one of the tombs. Some of the fellows had gotten hold of two five gallon cans of wine. I invited George and a couple of his buddies down to celebrate with us. I guess we were celebrating the fact that we were going to be relieved shortly. There was plenty of wine and it flowed freely. Most of us got pretty tight. We all sang songs, laughed and had a good time. George and his French buddies sang some French songs. We ignored the shells when they began whacking in around midnight. I got pretty high and also pretty sick. That damned Dago wine.

The time here on the Gustave Line was rapidly running out. Seventy days here. There had been some narrow escapes, heartbreaks, miserable weather and a few laughs. We were all anxious to get the Hell out of here.

Some odd things happened while we were here. One thing, it was discovered that Perkins was sort of fruity. I don't think queer in the real sense but something not quite normal. When I first met him I thought he acted a little on the queer side but he seemed like a pretty good guy and never made any funny moves. However, after we reached this position he seemed to change. I hadn't noticed it and had bedded down with him. One night he started fooling around and I gave him Hell. He said he was sorry and wouldn't do it anymore. I guess he was just testing. I may have been getting hard up but that sort of thing just didn't seem at all appealing. He never made any other advances and as far as I was concerned the matter was closed. I never said anything to anyone about the incident. I liked Perkins in spite of this and didn't want him to get in trouble. The lid blew off though when I was up on the mountain on L.O. (Look Out). Perkins sacked up with Matinovich. He started the same stuff with Marty. It made Marty sore as Hell and he really chewed Perkins out. He was so mad that he told several other guys and then the truth about Perkins was all over the battery. From then on Perkins was usually referred to as "Ma Perkins".

The kid George Boucher fouled up. He began to get nervous in the service and neglected his work. He finally got so bad he was of no use to anyone. He was sent back to the rear echelon in Naples. I never ran across the kid again.

Our outfit had been very, very lucky here in this position. Our casualties had been pretty light considering everything. Being in the exact spot that we were was the only thing that had saved us. The 189th just a few yards away from us had received many, many casualties. So had other outfits on all sides. Even lots of the outfits way back in the valley had been hit a lot worse than we had. Being jammed against the mountain had done the trick as well as this exact spot. Yep, we had been very, very lucky. Fortunes of war I guess.

The minefields around us were still claiming victims. An Italian man and his son were killed just a few days before we left the area. They had been out gathering firewood and had wandered into the mines. Every so often some G.I. would get it from them.

Most of the German's mines used for foot troops were wicked things called "Bouncing Bettys". When they were stepped on they would bounce up about waist high before they exploded. More often than not the victim would live. That's where a lot of legless veterans came from. The victim would usually lose one or both legs and have the lower parts of his body mangled. Usually it was worse than if they had been outright killed. Apparently, that was what the Germans had in mind in designing this type of mine. Maim but not necessarily kill. When a man is dead that's all. But a badly wounded one takes a lot to take care of him. It is harder on morale of the other troops to say nothing of how it effects the folks back home to have one of the boys come home legless or horribly disfigured.

Finally, the 9th of January 1944, the day we had been waiting for so long had arrived. Early in the morning we loaded in our battle scarred vehicles and prepared to move. Just before we left a Wop kid that had been hanging around the battery lately began to cry and begged to go with us. He was a kid of about seventeen or eighteen and claimed to be an orphan. The guys on the kitchen truck felt sorry for him and told him to hop on.

We headed down the road through Venefro and on back. The farther away from the Front we got the easier we began to breathe. Down below Venefro we figured we were out of artillery range and the only thing to worry about now was the aircraft.

We passed on down through places that we had fought through. We went through Piedmonte and passed the area where we had had our rest back in October. It seemed a long time ago since we had been here.

We finally reached our destination, probably forty miles from the Front. Some of the infantry outfits were having their rest areas around a town called Amorosi. Amorosi was a small town, probably a place of two or three thousand in normal times. It was a pretty poor looking place with narrow cobblestone streets. Our area was in a big vacant lot in town right in back of the main drag. The rest of the outfits of the 159th were clustered around the northern outskirts of the town.

An advance detail had left the Front a few days early to get the camp in some sort of shape. About all they had done was to put up a few large army tents. They had been drunk the rest of the time.

Each section was assigned a tent. The radio and wire sections had several tents right together. Curtis, Joyce, Regan, Gill, Martinovich, Brumbach and I had a tent together. We all pitched our stuff into the tent and took off to look the town over and do some heavy drinking,

The town wasn't much but we found a couple of places that sold liquor and they sold a lot of it. We began to drink wine, vermouth and anisette. It didn't take us too long to begin to feel the effects.

As Joyce, Regan and I were walking down the street, Regan and I got a bright idea. We saw a horse and buggy parked at the curb and decided to take it for a little joy ride. We climbed in and I took the reins. The horse took off at a fast trot. The harder I tried to slow him down the faster he went. Finally, the horse was going down the street wide open. Seeing we couldn't stop him Regan and I hit the pavement. The last we saw was the horse and buggy going around a corner on two wheels with an Italian, probably the owner, racing madly after it. Another incident to cement relations between two friendly countries.

A little later some "Second Louie" stopped us and gave us a bad time. We were wearing our wool caps instead of our steel helmets which we were supposed to have on. The Lt. gave us hell for a while. He was a very nasty character. We tried to reason with him, because we didn't think it was necessary to wear our steel helmets forty miles from the Front. He really blew up and threatened to have us thrown in the brig and have Joyce, the only non-com among us, busted. We finally got away from him and continued on our way. A fellow from the Battery informed me that I was on guard that night. A fine thing, the first night back from the Front and I drew guard. It was that old alphabetical order again.

I was supposed to go on guard at twelve so I returned to the tent about ten-thirty; my night was ruined anyway. I felt kind of drunk and pretty sick. I wanted to get a little sleep before I went on post. I flopped down on the cold ground floor of the tent and pulled a blanket over me. I awoke hours later from the cold. I sensed that it was much later than twelve but the corporal of the guard hadn't come around to get me up so I wasn't going to worry about it. I was so cold I could hardly go back to sleep again.

The next morning the corporal of the guard looked me up. He said he didn't know where I was sleeping so he couldn't find me to go on guard. He didn't seem too happy, but it wasn't my fault. I had been ready and able. He said I could do my two shifts at one time. At noon I went down to the area where the communications vehicles and equipment were parked. I relieved Smith who was sitting in a jeep, and just like him, listening to music instead of walking up and down watching things like you are supposed to do.

A little later the rest of the Battery took off for Piedmonte for showers and clean clothes. I wished I was going with them for I hadn't had a bath for months. The clothes I was wearing were really grimy.

A couple of little kids were playing near the Jeep, playing of all things, war. I gave one of them a "K" ration I found in the Jeep. The kid disappeared into the house a few feet away and soon emerged with a man I figured was his father. He had evidently seen the "K" ration and to show his appreciation brought me a bottle of wine. The wine was pretty good stuff, not the usual crappy stuff.

I tried to carry on a conversation with the man but had a pretty rough time doing it. By repetition, sign language and a mixture of Italian and English we understood each other a little. I learned he owned his home here and a small farm. He seemed like a real nice fellow and was polite and friendly. I judged he was a fellow in his early forties. He certainly hadn't gotten around much. Although Naples was only about forty miles away he said he had only been there once. He had never been to Rome or even as far north as Venefro. This was almost hard to believe. Rome was only around a hundred miles from here and it seemed as if he would have gone there out of curiosity if nothing else. He must have been a little better off than the average too. His house was nice compared to most of the others in these parts. He said he owned the small farm here which I think was unusual. I understood that about 85% of Italy was owned by the other 15%. I guess most of the farmers were sort of share croppers or just tenants. This was supposed to be one of the reasons the poor people of Italy were so poor. Anyway, this fellow hadn't gotten around much. Maybe he had been working so hard to pay for his farm or maybe people just didn't travel much. Another thing that made traveling hard was the lack of transportation. I learned that in this area there had only been one car for every 160 people. That was in peace time of course. Now, no civilians had a car here. I guess they had been taken over by the Italian or German armies. I had seen no railroad in the area and I doubt even in peace time there had been any bus service to this out of the way town. The man did seem interested in the progress of the war though. He wondered if the

Americans had taken Casino yet. He seemed to know that it was a tough nut to crack.

Late in the afternoon I was relieved just as the rest of the battery was coming back from taking showers. After chow we sat around and talked for several hours. We also tried to fix up our beds a little more comfortably. We pooled our blankets, putting half of them down on a little straw and the rest were put over us. It was like seven men sleeping in one bed. Boy! I'd be glad when I was able to take off my clothes again and sleep in a real bed.

The next morning after chow we began to work on our equipment. The radio section started cleaning up our radios, mikes, etc. In the afternoon Brockett, Burbach and I went down to the river to wash up Brockett's truck. We found a good wide, shallow place in the river to clean it up.

It was a beautiful, sunny day and quite warm. The weather reminded me of the weather in the San Joaquin Valley in California. Sunny and warm in January and off in the distance we could see snowcapped mountains. Very similar to home.

The next day we began hauling gravel to make driveways and walks around the area. The bunch I was working with were putting a driveway in near the kitchen. There were several bottles of wine in the bunch and we kept knocking off for ten about every fifteen minutes to have a few snorts. The kitchen bunch gave us a lot of tangerines. I knew when I tasted one that it was frost bitten or something but I ate a lot of them anyway.

After chow that night Ruhs and I took a long hike. I began to feel sick and the further we went the sicker I got. The frozen tangerines and the wine were catching up with me. By the time I got back to the tent I was really feeling lousy. I turned in early and being so early I was the only one in our tent. Burbach happened to pop in to get something and it was lucky for our bed he did. I hollered for him to get a helmet, anyone's helmet. He got one to me just in time. I heaved it half full. I immediately began to feel better and soon dropped off to sleep.

The next morning the ones who had missed showers the first time got to go. Several of us piled on Regan's weapon carrier and took off for Piedmonte. In Piedmonte the showers were set up in several small tents. It felt good to have a real honest-to-goodness shower. The clean clothes felt good too. The ones I drew must have been surplus from the Civil War. They were a funny brindle color and fit like Hell but at least they were clean.

When we got back Charlie Joyce had a big proposition to make to me. This time he claimed he knew where he could get some honest-to-goodness champagne. Not the usual rot gut. Cheap too. He said it was only $3.50 a bottle. Joyce and I both bought two quarts of the stuff. A bunch of us sat around the rest of the day drinking the "champagne" and some of the ordinary rot gut stuff. You couldn't tell the difference between our "champagne" and the two-bit stuff.

That evening Reagan, Joyce and I went to a movie. The "theater" was set up in a field out in the country a ways. The side of a barn was used for the screen and the cold, muddy ground were our seats. When they were adjusting the sound it let out a scream like an incoming shell. A thousand men hit the mud. The movie was "Sahara" with Humphrey Bogart. The thing stunk pretty badly. In real action you didn't go running around with shells landing at your feet and live. Also, a single tank, cornered and out of gas holding off a whole German battalion was a joke. I guess to the people back home it looked logical and inspiring.

One day we hiked to Telese to see Bogart in person. The hike there and back was part of our "training" program. We hung around Telese all afternoon but the bum never showed up. Another time we hiked to Telese to see Joe E. Brown. He did show up and put on a good show too.

One morning after chow we were sitting around in our tents talking when someone stuck their head in the tent and asked if Dick Borthwick was in there. To my great surprise the head belonged to Bob McMullen an old friend from Dinuba. We shook hands for about ten minutes. Both of us seemed at a loss for words. He was with the 36th General Hospital which was in Naples. He had learned that our outfit was back from the Front and where we were located. I was really glad to see him. He was the only person I had seen from home since joining the army.

Bob and I walked around most of the day and talked over old times. We sat in a small bar for a long time, drinking vermouth and marveling how two friends from a tiny town in California should happen to get together in another tiny town in Italy, six thousand miles or so from home.

That night we sat talking far into the night. He told me of the nice cot he had in a warm room in Naples or rather Caserta. The good food, movies, operas and shows he was able to attend. In fact, they were staying at the king's palace in Caserta. I didn't blame him to seem rather reluctant to lie down on our humble bed on the cold ground.

The next morning Bob decided he had better get back to Caserta. He told me he had several days off if he wanted them. I tried to talk him into staying at least one more night. He would have no part of it. I had an idea that sleeping on the ground had made his decision. I had sensed during the night that he wasn't resting well and it was cold. I don't imagine the chow we were having went over big either after having steaks, fresh eggs and the like. I thought we had things fairly good here but realized it must have been pretty rough on anyone used to living like he was. Just before he left a rather comical thing happened. We were walking around the area talking when Colonel Funk happened by. Of course Bob, being used to rear echelon regulations etc., came to a snappy salute. I was dumb-founded. Saluting officers in our outfit was unheard of. I got my hand about as high as my nose and started scratching it. The colonel himself was so startled that he gave a very sloppy, half-hearted return salute. After chow Bob prepared to take off. I told him I'd get a pass the following weekend and come and see him.

One night Joyce, Marshall, Reagan and I went to some Italian people's house that Joyce had gotten acquainted with. There were four in the family, the father, mother, a girl about twenty and a boy about twenty-five or so. The old man could speak about five words of English and I spent a very boring evening listening to "Americano bono", "Tedeschi no bono". We had only one lousy glass of wine at that. I guess the big attraction was the girl. Joyce did get a date with her for church the following Sunday so I guess the trip to their house wasn't entirely wasted.

During our stay here in Amorosi we spent most of our idle time in bars and drinking, and we had plenty of idle time. One thing I sure liked about the 45th was when you were back at rest you were back at rest. We didn't have full field inspections and a lot of corny training like a lot of the outfits had. Probably outfits that were regular army like the 1st or the 3rd Divisions took a dim view of the 45th's lack of enthusiasm for spit and polish while at rest. They probably figured we were a rout order outfit which was a National Guard Division. National Guard or not I sincerely believed it was one of the top division if not the best in the war. Naturally, I could be a little prejudice, but I really believed it. There was no reason to think otherwise. First of all, the original outfit was made up of men from Oklahoma, Texas, New Mexico and some other southwestern states. For some reason fellows from this area seemed to have a little more spirit and love of country than some other parts of the country. The men weren't the wise acres that you found from say some of the eastern cities. They seemed to have a greater sense of loyalty to their country and were willing to defend it without asking too many questions. You very seldom found the barracks type of orator that knew all of the answers. They griped some of course, but not the vicious bellyaching and crying of being done wrong as some from some sections. I don't mean to imply that the guys from the East and other sections of the country were cowards or disloyal at all, but lots of the time the attitude was just different. It is hard to explain. I also found the fellows from the Deep South, Alabama, Georgia, Mississippi and the like to possess an even fiercer devotion. I sometimes got disgusted with the southerners for still fighting the Civil War and a few other things, but individually they were tops as soldiers. Anyway, back to the 45th. A lot of the men had years in the guard. Sure, maybe only one night a week and a couple of weeks in the summer, but they were in touch. When I went in the army I didn't know a single thing about anything. Most of the officers, or at least a lot of them, were graduates from Oklahoma A and M. They had a good military background although most of them were not professional soldiers. I understood that even Colonel Funk had been some sort of an executive for a chain shoe outfit. Maybe not just being all military gave them a better view of the situation. The 45th, as a division, had had all kinds of training as a complete unit. They were the first National Guard outfit activated back in 1940. They had training in the swamps of Louisiana, the mountains of North Carolina and the beaches of the New England States. They even had spent one winter in Watertown, New York with the snow up to the eaves. They had had training in all kinds of terrains and climates. Just because some outfit has a nucleus of professional soldiers does not necessarily mean that it is superior. Sometimes I think the set-up with the strict, by the manual can be bad. I know when I joined the 45th, as a replacement, I was surprised with the treatment. Before, in the presence of a high ranking non-com, to say nothing of an officer, I was ill at ease and not relaxed. It was all salute, heel clicking, etc., the way I was taught and had to practice before I got in this outfit. Here, most of the non-coms and the officers were friendly and treated you like a human instead of some dog. I'm not an advocate of no discipline because without it you have no army. Actually, the 45th had discipline even if there wasn't the bowing and scraping and the lousy disciplinary action for every little mistake. Everyone respected rank and obeyed orders without question. I think probably the 45th was unique among the outfits with this mutual understanding. Maybe it wouldn't have worked in any other outfit.

As for inspections and a lot of training in rest periods it is a lot of bunk. If something new has to be learned that is different, but just to keep the troops occupied to stay out of trouble is for the birds. Probably the guys of the 45th, at least H.Q. Battery of the 158th, had more free time than any other outfit while at rest. There was very little trouble from our boys among themselves or with civilians. I think their record would have been hard to beat. A lot of drinking, of course, but a pretty orderly bunch with only an occasional fight.

I believed in the Forty-fifth's attitude for a rest period. Just do the things necessary and to Hell with too much crap. You didn't learn anything from having a full field inspection and it didn't make you any tougher or braver. Anyway, I was proud of the 45th and at least thought I belonged to the best division ever to represent the United States. I guess practically every guy in the army, especially the combat outfits, thought theirs was the best. A good healthy sign.

We ran into a few English speaking Italians around here. All of them that could speak English lived in the United States at one time or another. They either lived in New Haven, New York, Philadelphia, Erie or some other eastern city. They all moaned about the Fascists and Mussolini and all claimed they hated both. I'll bet when Italy was taking over Albania and Ethiopia and Italy seemed to be a world power, their tune had been different. They all complained about being taxed too much. Building armies took lots of money just like in any other country. One guy, a storekeeper, was pointed out by the villagers as a Fascist. He did have plenty of things in his store to sell to the G.I.'s for nice high prices. Most of the other stores in town had empty shelves.

Others complained, especially the farmers, how hard it was to get anyone to work on their farms now. The pay for a day's work on a farm was fifty cents a day and a bottle of wine. That was supposed to be an average and pretty good wage. The local farmers said no one would work while the Americans were in the area. They could make more money trading wine for cigarettes and then taking the cigarettes to some town where there were no troops and sell them for a fortune.

I was beginning to learn the value and power of an American cigarette. It seemed that cigarettes actually had more value than money. American cigarettes seemed to be very valuable. Everyone seemed to prefer them much more than their own. I could hardly figure out why an American cigarette, with mass production methods, could be as good as European ones. Italy grew tobacco as did Turkey and other Near East places. I had to admit though that the American cigarettes seemed to be quit superior to the others but I didn't know what their secret was.

In spite of just mostly loafing, the days of our rest passed rapidly. Of course, there were the usual rumors floating around. The rumors ranged from making a beachhead in Norway to going home. Most of us actually believed it would be to the same old places. News from the Casino Front hinted that it was still a stalemate.

We lost a man while we were in rest. John Priest, Colonel Funk's driver, was killed in an accident. The report stated that he was run off the road by a truck.

One day I was informed that I was to go to driver's school. I guess they had to do something along training. The class was to have its primary training right here in the area with road problems coming later. Captain Hayes was to be the instructor. That morning, Smith and I and a few other privates gathered at the designated place to begin classes. As we gathered we noticed a difference in things. It was a fine, sunny day without a cloud in the sky. We noticed many, many formations of our heavy bombers going over, heading north. From the unusually large number of formations we wondered if something big was up or if they were just taking advantage of the perfect flying weather. We were so busy watching flight after flight of bombers overhead we hardly listened to what Captain Hayes had to say. He finally blew up and gave us Hell. He said to never mind what was going on up above and pay attention to him. He almost sounded like some of those characters back at Camp Roberts. I don't think he was original 45th anyway so maybe that explains it.

The next day was a nice one as well. Hundreds more of our heavy bombers flew over. We got the report that they were bombing up around Rome. That evening the news was pretty hot. About a thousand bombs were being dropped in the vicinity of Rome. We wondered what was up.

The next day news broke. Landings had been made at Anzio, about forty miles south of Rome. The first news was that the assault waves had met practically no opposition. Our hopes began to rise that Rome might fall before we had expected it to.

That evening a bunch of us went to a show in an open air theater. The movie was "Arsenic and Old Lace" with Raymond Massey and Peter Lorre and it was pretty good. When we returned to our area later that night we were informed that our outfit had been alerted. No more passes and we were to stick around in the immediate area and to be ready at a moment's notice. There went my passes to Caserta. I had gotten permission to have a pass into Caserta for the week end coming up. I was going to go on Friday afternoon and stay until Monday. I had even made arrangements for a ride there and back. I had dreamed about staying at the King's Palace, having a cot to sleep on, good food and a chance to have a little fun. That was all out the window now. The story of my Army career. A party, that was to be thrown by the battery, was also knocked in the head. We had rented a hall in

Telese to throw the affair. There were even supposed to be a few Italian girls there for one thing or another. That night they dished out the liquor that was to be used at the party. There even wasn't much of that left now. The officers had stolen most of it.

That night Gill, Martinovich, Joyce, Marshall and I went over to an Italian place for dinner. We had been giving them a few things from time to time and they wanted to show their appreciation I guess. We took a pair of shoes with us.

We did have a good meal there. The woman did a fine job preparing the meal with what she had to work with. We had sort of a grass like salad, meat, potatoes and wine. She even baked some little cakes, apparently without sugar, but they were not bad. It was the idea that she had tried so hard. We ate by candlelight, not for the atmosphere, but because the electricity of the town was still off. They wanted us to stay with them all night. We were given a bedroom with a big shell hole still in the roof. That hole must have been there from the fighting around here four months ago. They were not able to repair it. That was something I didn't understand about the Italians. You could come back to an area a month later and the war damage never seemed to be touched. I could never figure out whether they were too poor or just didn't give a damn if anything was ever fixed up again or not. These Italians seemed to be a little better off than most too. They owned this home and a small farm adjoining. I guess this family was small by Italian standards. They had only two small boys. We spent a most enjoyable evening with this family. After dinner we sat around for several hours drinking wine and trying to carry on some sort of a conversation. Quite late, when we retired to our bedroom, we drew straws to see who would sleep in the bed. With my luck I had to sleep on the floor. Even sleeping on the floor in a house was better than sleeping in a tent and on the cold ground. I sure wished that I could have slept in that real bed though.

The next morning we gathered our stuff and put it in the trucks that were lined up in convoy formation. Everything was ready. All we needed now was the word to move out. We figured that when we did move out we would go to Naples, load on ships and go to Anzio. Of course, being in the army, you could never figure anything for sure. With the big wheels turning somewhere anything could happen. Even a surprise landing farther north or anywhere was possible.

One thing I did like about the army. You never knew what was next or where you were going. I say that sincerely and not sarcastically. I liked to move even though it might be something not too pleasant. Every time, even back in the States, it always gave me a big thrill. I liked to be going someplace regardless and to see something new. I never could understand guys that liked to stay in the same place because they had a good deal or something going for them. To me, it was like people who actually bragged about never being out of the county in which they were born. I never had pictured myself as particularly the adventurous or pioneer type, but one thing I knew, I liked to move and see things.

A little later we were informed that we probably wouldn't move that day, but to stay close and keep the vehicles in formation, just in case. A. P. Curtis and I wandered over to one of the local bars. It was only a short distance from where our convoy was lined up. If there was going to be any movement among them we would know it. The bar was run by a woman named Mary. In fact, she had set up the bar in her home. Quite the entrepreneur. She did serve pretty good wine so Curtis and I sat there drinking and talking for a couple of hours. Curtis was an interesting person. He actually was from Baltimore, Maryland, but for some reason had come west to Oklahoma where he had gotten involved with the 45th. He looked something like a gangster but was a really nice guy. He loved to gamble and spent a lot of his time doing it. A good drinking man too. I was sort of fascinated by the fact that his girlfriend was a strip tease artist in an Oklahoma City burlesque house. He had plans, when the war was over, to return to Oklahoma City and open a bar. He said he would call it the "Thunderbird" and have a big neon sign of a thunderbird above the door.

The next morning we were still in the same position. Everything lined up and waiting. Everyone just hung around waiting for the word to move. We were curious to get going now. Especially me. All day fellows came by with bottles. Lacrosse had gotten some cherry brandy. Another fellow some anisette. Still another champagne. Joyce and I had gotten some pretty good wine. Lacrosse took some pictures of some of the gang.

The news we were getting back from the beachhead were encouraging. So far, the resistance had been light. We figured maybe the Germans were going to abandon the Casino front and Rome and withdraw further north.

Around noon we received word that we would definitely move out at dusk. There was a ripple of excitement and everyone speculated as to what was coming up and what we might be in for. For once a rumor had been right. Just after dusk we moved out onto the road and headed in the direction of Naples.

The convoy crawled along in the blackness. We were crowded into the vehicles and the road was bumpy with lots of by passes. What seemed like hours later we pulled off the road and into what appeared to be some kind of orchard. Everyone began looking for some kind of a place to sleep. Regan spread a tarp over the back of his truck to protect some equipment on it. I decided to stay under the tarp. This seemed to be the best place considering how dark it was. I unrolled my blankets and laid down on the wooden seat that ran the length of the side of the truck. I felt pretty snug for a few minutes when I heard rain begin to patter down on the tarp.

The next morning they had us up bright and early checking and working on our equipment. We knew we weren't in a staging area yet for we were still a considerable distance from the harbor. What I had thought to be an orchard last night turned out to be a vineyard. The vines were growing on high arbors and one would need a ladder to harvest most of the grapes.

In the afternoon the Battery had to go on a five mile hike. The brass suddenly began to get excited about a little physical training. Fortunately, I had to do some work on some radios. It was the only thing that saved me. I had just gotten a new pair of combat boots and they were killing my feet. I couldn't have hiked five miles in them if my life depended on it. The boots were plenty big but they kinked into my ankle when I walked.

We were informed that we wouldn't move out that night so Ruhs, Reagan and I went to a movie in a nearby field. After the movie we returned to the trucks and I crawled under my tarp again to sleep.

The next day was a rather dull, slow passing one. There were lots of rumors floating around. The news from the beachhead were about the same but it did seem as though resistance was stiffening. About the only other thing that happened that day was that we were issued pro. (Prophylactic) kits. Victory kits they were called. It made it seem like we might be going where there might be some wicked women. Maybe they expected us to be in Rome in a few days at that. Just as we turned in that night we were told that we would move out at four in the morning.

At 3:30 we got up and at 4:00 a.m. we were out on the road moving. After traveling down the road a few miles, for no apparent reason, we pulled off the road and stopped. We stayed here in the middle of an open field for several hours. There were a few Italians around selling apples. Most of us either bought or traded something for a few of them. One of the women among the vendors had a small baby in her arms. Some wise G.I. gave the kid one of the tubes out of the Pro. Kit and the baby started eating the stuff. I guess the mother thought it was candy or something. Oh well, I guess it wouldn't hurt the kid anyway.

Around three o'clock we pulled out onto the road again and went on into Naples and right down to the docks. Our outfit stopped at a staging area called the Texas area. Around dark we found out that we wouldn't load onto the boats until the next day.

Joyce, Ruhs, Burbach, Marty, Regan and I all decided to try to sleep in Regan's truck. It was bitterly cold and we figured that even if it was awfully crowded in the weapon carrier it would be better than trying to sleep on the cold ground. We had gotten partly settled down when Rudy Bohn wandered by and wanted to know if it was OK for him to sleep with us. Rudy was actually from "B" Battery that was lined up close by. I didn't know him myself but most of the other fellows did. We squeezed him in some way. We all sat there for a long time talking, mostly speculating how Anzio would be. Finally, we tried to get as comfortable as possible to try and catch a few winks. During the night our anti-aircraft guns let loose. I couldn't hear any planes or bombs dropping but there were plenty of pieces of flak dropping around.

The next morning we got out Regan's little Coleman stove and heated some "C" rations for breakfast. Most of the rest of the day we just looked around the immediate area and talked and wondered what was up. The area here contained many acres and it was crammed with hundreds of vehicles and thousands of troops. If the enemy could place a lot of well-directed bombs right here they could probably do more damage in a few minutes than being a month at the Front.

Ruhs and I took a walk over to an Italian steel mill a few yards away. It had been completely destroyed by the Germans before they pulled out. The place was a bunch of twisted girders and piles of debris. Later I went over to where some of the Sixteenth's vehicles were located. I looked up Bixby and we had a little talk.

In the afternoon Gill, Marty, Marshall and I had our picture taken by a wandering Italian photographer. He had just gotten the picture developed as our convoy started to move. We had to run to catch up with our trucks. The trucks hadn't gone very far. We just moved down to the docks and drove right onto a L.S.T. without much ado. Burbach and I raced upstairs and were lucky enough to get a bunk each. This was going to be the best bed I had slept in for months.

At dusk the L.S.T. slowly pulled out of Naples harbor. By dark we were out of the harbor and going full speed. We were heading north. This was it. We would soon be at Anzio. The sea got rough during the night and the bouncing around woke me up a couple of times.

We were up on deck the next morning to see what was going on. It was a nice, sunny, beautiful day, January 29th, 1944. We could see Anzio off in the distance. We could also see the distant puffs of black smoke from anti-aircraft so we knew the harbor was being raided by the Germans.

Eventually we reached the harbor and pulled in. Everything seemed serene and peaceful. We were hoping to get out of here before another raid. The town itself showed plenty of signs of naval bombardment and bombing.

We pulled up to a makeshift wharf and unloaded without a hitch. As soon as our trucks were unloaded we climbed aboard them and headed out. The whole operation of unloading had taken only a few minutes. We got a pretty good look at Anzio as we passed through it. It looked like it had been a pretty nice resort town before the war. There were many modernistic homes overlooking the sea. It had taken a pretty good beating already though. Parts of buildings and trees were down in the streets.

We passed on through the town and out into the country a short distance and pulled into a field and stopped. We quickly camouflaged our vehicles with nets because there was no natural camouflage in this field. We set up communications and waited to find out what to do next. Near where we had stopped there was a German plane that had been shot down. The pilot was still in it with his brains splattered all over the instrument panel. The plane didn't seem too badly damaged. It looked as if it had come down at a slow speed and hit the ground comparatively easy. Maybe the plane had been crippled and the pilot had been trying to land it.

We could hear the rumble of guns on all sides of us.

We figured that the front would be farther inland by now. No question about it. Things must not be going as well as had been reported. Late in the afternoon German planes came over in quite a large formation and bombed the harbor. It was a good thing for us that we weren't unloading at that time.

Just at dusk German planes came over again. We saw something strange and new. The German Focke-Wulf. It had a small plane attached under it. Long before they got to the harbor they released the small planes which were controlled by radio from the larger planes. The smaller remote controlled planes were actually a flying bomb. They guided them right over the harbor and down at a target. A tiny red flame streamed out from behind the bomb. It was quite a sight. Our anti-aircraft guns fired away at them but didn't seem to be able to bring them down.

Flak from our anti-aircraft was dropping all around us. Suddenly Haddow let out a yell, fell to the ground hollering that he had been hit. We rushed over to him expecting him to be gasping his last. We couldn't find a mark on him although he had been hit by a piece of flak alright. The fragment had gone through his coat and hit his address book in his shirt pocket as well as breaking a pipe in the same pocket. It had cut part way through the address book and if it had not been for the address book he could have been badly wounded. All he was now was just scared. So badly, in fact, that he could hardly talk.

Sometime after dark we got orders to prepare to move out. We finally got all the vehicles lined up on the little dirt road and awaited orders to move out onto the black topped highway. We were all lined up bumper to bumper. Just as we were going to move German planes came over and dropped flares over the harbor. The flares really lit up the sky. Our anti-aircraft guns were sending hundreds of tracers across the sky. We figured they were going to bomb the harbor again and we were watching the show with interest. The word was passed down that we had better dismount just in case. We had no more than jumped from the trucks when we heard a plane dive and a bomb screaming. What a horrible sound. I'll never forget it. I hit the ground about the same time the bomb did. It was close. Only a few yards away. There was an ear splitting report and I saw fire and dirt go gysering up. I felt dirt and rock showering down on me. We started crawling into the vineyard beside the road. More bombs came crashing down close and I heard the screams of the wounded. Boy, was I scared. I was looking for a hole, any kind of hole, but there were none.

More flares were kicked out right overhead now and it was brighter than day. More bombs came screaming down and crashed, making a terrible din. Dirt and rocks fell like rain. I stopped crawling. The bombs were falling on all sides and I knew I was just as safe here as a few yards on. This was the end anyway. By the light of the flares I could see men crouching and crawling. They looked weird in their overcoats and helmets and for a fleeting second it looked like scenes I had seen in movies about World War I. I wished to hell that I was watching a movie instead of being in the real thing. Joyce came crawling up beside me and said, "Borth old boy, this looks like it." I agreed. We lay there sweating it out and trying to comfort each other that it would soon be over one way or another. More bombs dropped but now it was the harbor area and then the drone of the planes slowly died away. I felt thankful that I was alive but knew we had been hurt and hurt badly. Several fires near us and in the vicinity of Anzio, were burning brightly. Headquarters had been lucky again. We had been incredibly lucky. "B" Battery, which had been lined up right beside us and was close enough that we had been able to talk to one another in normal voices, had been hit terribly. Several men had been killed and many wounded, some very badly. Two or three were burned beyond recognition. One of these was Rudy Bohn, the guy who had crowded in our truck with us in Naples a couple of nights ago. Every one of their prime movers had been knocked out as well as their kitchen truck. In fact, they had only a few vehicles capable of moving.

We were pretty shaky as we loaded onto our trucks and headed for the black topped highway. We passed through Anzio and headed inland still on the black topped road. The sky was bright from the flashes of artillery and the roar from the guns was terrific.

We finally pulled into a large wooded area with lots of big trees. It was around 4:30 a.m. now but no one had slept yet. We set up communications and started looking for a place to take a few winks. I had no luck however because it was decided, by someone, that it was my turn to be on the set.

The traffic on the radio was heavy, especially from "B" Battery. They were calling for help. They badly needed men and vehicles. A few minutes after I had taken over on the set a huge red flash lit up the sky. Big red streamers went flying out in all directions. I thought the Germans must have been trying out another secret weapon on us. I thought the big flash and sky rocket streamers had come from the direction of the Front. The next morning I found I had been completely turned around. The flash had come from the harbor. Some ship had been hit and it had been the ammunition aboard that had gone up. I was only on the set a short time when Gill took over. I took blankets and flopped on the ground to try to get a few winks.

I had just started to doze when a big German gun began to speak off in the distance. It was a big gun. In fact it was huge. Probably a railroad gun or something just as large. I had never heard anything that sounded so big. The shells from the gun, or guns, were landing a considerable distance away but they made a nasty crack. I hoped that our woods weren't one of the targets for that monster tonight.

Raymond Gill, Peter Burbach, Dick Borthwick, William Regan
Anzio Beachhead
October 1943

Daylight came and we looked over our new position. The place was heavily wooded with tall, old looking trees. There were practically no small trees, saplings or underbrush. We didn't care too much for our new position. It seemed as though our woods would stand out like a sore thumb. The rest of the beachhead, as far as we could see, seemed to be flat and void of foliage. The Germans must surely know that someone was hiding out here in these woods.

There were a couple of companies of tanks from the 1st Armored dug in near our position. They didn't seem to know what the score was any more than we did.

We were pretty busy on the radio. War guns were set up in positions in the outer fringes of the woods and were doing quite a bit of firing. At the moment our guns were supporting an English attack. The English were in the process of taking some fortified buildings and things seemed to be going pretty well with them. I don't know why we weren't supporting our own 157th. I thought they had landed on the beachhead a day or two before us.

We already had the feeling that things weren't going well on the beachhead. It was already over a week and very little progress had been made. The Germans could still take the harbor easily even with their smaller caliber artillery. That alone proved that the beachhead could only be a very few miles deep. Their aircraft were very active too. Although we were only about twenty five miles from Rome, we now had a feeling we weren't going to be there in a day or two. In fact, everyone seemed to have a feeling that something disastrous was pending.

Most of the day was a gloomy thing with low hanging clouds. In spite of the weather several of our F-40's patrolled over the beachhead all of the time. They flew low, only about a few hundred feet above the ground.

They gave us a feeling of some security. The trouble was that there were no landing fields on the beachhead and after a few minutes of patrolling they would have to go back to the vicinity of Naples to refuel.

In the middle of the afternoon the drizzle subsided and the clouds lifted a little. Shortly after the clouds lifted eighteen German planes came over and raided the harbor. I saw one plane go down in smoke. I also saw black smoke drifting up from the ground. Either some ship had been hit or some ammo dump or supply dump on the shore. Towards evening another group of eighteen German planes came over and again raided the harbor. Apparently no planes were brought down in spite of the intense anti-aircraft fire.

Night approached and again that big German gun began to speak. The shells seemed to be landing in about the same place they had the night before. I would have hated to be in the impact area of those big shells. The sky was continually lighted up all night by the flashes of artillery. There was also the steady din of many artillery pieces firing.

The next day was another cloudy day with the threat of rain. Air activity on both sides was quite limited. Our guns kept banging away all day and the traffic on the radio was quite heavy. So far we hadn't had any shells come too near us and we hoped it would stay that way. We hoped they still believed that no one was so stupid to take up a position in such an obvious place. Around noon orders came down that we would move at nightfall. Of course, I was one of those unfortunate ones that was picked to be a road guide again.

I was dropped off at a crossroads. Our outfit was to turn off the main highway and onto a small dirt road. It was my job to keep them from going down the highway.

There was a British guard nearby who was guarding a railroad crossing. He was really on the ball and business like, challenging every vehicle. I hoped this wasn't the crossroads that the big gun might have been shelling for the last two nights. I figured it wasn't though because everything was pretty much intact. If that big gun had been pumping them in here there would have been lots of damage and some sizable shell holes.

The outfit soon came along and I got them on the right road. I was then picked up by the last vehicle in the convoy. We soon got far behind the rest because we had to stop ever so often to pick up a road guide. When all the guides were picked up we discovered we were lost. All we knew was that we were on a cow trail road out in the middle of open plains. The road was muddy and rough and our truck nearly bogged down a couple of times. The sky was lit up on all sides from artillery flashing and made it seem that we were right in the middle of everything.

We eventually arrived at another hard topped road which we hoped was the one that was called the Coast Road. A bunch of Limeys were at the intersection so we stopped to ask them a few directions. They didn't know the score any more than we did. One of them was really funny though. He swore like a pirate and talked with a definite Cockney twang. He did tell us he had heard a lot of vehicles moving north and figured they were probably our outfit.

We turned north and headed up the black topped road. We kept driving down the road wondering where to turn off. After quite a ride we were halted by a guard. He told us to turn around and get the hell out of there. Come to find out we were at an American road block. We had damned near driven right through the German lines. The guys at the outpost wanted us to get out of there before we began to draw fire. They said no vehicle as large as ours had made it this far up the road. We turned around and sped back down the road. After inquiring several times we finally located our outfit.

Gill and Marty had the radio set up and going. They had a pretty good-sized hole dug near the radio jeep. I flopped down on the ground and got a little shut eye before my radio shift.

Early the next morning we were awakened bright and early by the crashing of anti-aircraft guns. I looked up and saw a bunch of Folk-Wolfes heading for the harbor. There were at least two dozen of them and they were going full speed. We watched them dive down and saw the bombs falling. We could plainly hear the bombs exploding and see smoke rising from the harbor area.

Soon after the German raid a couple of large formations of our own bombers came over. They were certainly a welcome sight. About noon it clouded up again and that put an end to air activity.

It was still drizzling that night and there were low hanging clouds. We naturally supposed that there would be no German air activity in this kind of weather. We were in for a surprise and something new as far as I was concerned. Shortly after dark we heard the uneven drone of a German bomber. It was flying very low and came down our ravine just a few feet over our heads. Just as it passed over us a battery of guns down the ravine opened up. We then heard the sharp crackling of many explosions. We couldn't figure out what was causing the noise. We were sure it wasn't strafing for it was too loud and uneven. This was my introduction to the German anti-personnel bombs. I had heard of them before but we had never been in an area where they were being dropped. We called these bombs butterfly bombs or popcorn balls. The way I understood how they worked was that a lot of small bombs were put in a large bomb casing. The smaller bombs ranged from the size of hand grenades up to several pounds. When the bomb was dropped the large casing exploded in mid-air and then smaller bombs rained down in a wide area. On this particular night the German planes had been flying low looking for a target. When those artillery pieces in our ravine fired the personnel bombs had been dropped where the flashes had been seen. These bombs were just another thing we were going to have to put up with for the next few months.

The next day was a damp dismal thing. There was no air activity in our area but there was lots of firing and lots of work on the radio.

We began to hear a really big German gun or guns speak now. They were German railroad guns. When one fired the report sounded louder than our own 195's just a few yards away. It sounded like it was just over the hill from us although it was twenty-six miles away. When the shells from it passed over it sounded like box cars banging together. We soon dubbed it "The Anzio Express". This was another thing that we were going to have to live with for the next few months.

Toward evening it began to clear and that night turned out to be clear as a bell. Also that night, we had a terrible air-raid. The raid lasted most of the night. The German planes seemed to come over in waves. Flares were dropped all over the place. They were dropped right over us, to the north and over the harbor. Everything was lighted up as bright as day. The flares seemed to burn forever as we crouched there sweating it out. The Germans were bombing the whole beachhead as well as the harbor. Big bombs crashed down and the ground shook with their impact. Personnel bombs cracked all around. Our ack-ack (anti-aircraft) boys were sending up plenty of flak. Thousands of red tracers crisscrossed the sky. From the light of the flares and tracers and the pounding of the ack-ack guns it made this night a horrible nightmare. Before one wave of German planes finished bombing another wave would fly over. We just sat there in our holes hoping for the best. One thing for sure was that we saw a fantastic fireworks display. Besides, the German bombs we were also endangered from our own ack-ack fragments. They were raining down by the thousands. They whizzed and thudded down all around. Even whole shells whined down. They were duds from our anti-aircraft guns. If a large piece of fragment hit a man it could easily kill or badly wound him. In our open holes we had very little protection from the falling stuff.

The next day everyone began to put rooves over their foxholes. The night that had just passed made everyone realize that they were going to have to try to get more protection. Thus started the movement of a whole army moving underground. I wasn't going to sleep on top of the ground for some time to come.

Putting rooves on the holes would do some good. They would at least stop falling fragments. If they were constructed strong enough they could even stop some of the smaller personnel bombs. Of course, they were useless against larger bombs or direct hits by artillery shells.

Curtis and I cut down a couple of very small trees and with a few planks we rounded up, we made a roof over our hole. After we laid the trees and planks over the hole we filled sandbags and placed them over the trees and planks. We then shoveled a foot or two of dirt over the sandbags. Then we stretched a couple of shelter-halves over the top to help water-proof our dugout. We finished the job by putting branches and sod on top to camouflage it. Our dugout wasn't as fancy or well-constructed as some but we were proud of it.

That night we felt pretty snug in our little dugout. Having a roof over our heads made it possible to smoke at night. The roof on our hole gave us a more secure feeling. It was a lot of false security because we were far from being absolutely safe, but after being out in the open it seemed a lot safer. In fact, I felt so much more secure I didn't even wake up later in the night when there was an air raid. Some bombs had landed pretty close too.

The next day passed rather quietly. The big German railroad gun fired into Anzio off and on all day long. A couple of flights of German planes came over and dropped bombs on the harbor. We saw four planes going at it in dog fights. They were up so high that we could barely see them. One plane came down in flames but we couldn't tell if it was one of ours or German.

The weather here in Italy was what you would call mild. It had been very rainy since about November and had frosted a few times. In the mountains around Venafro it had snowed some and gotten pretty cold. There had been some cases of Trench Foot. Generally though, for wintertime, the weather had been pretty mild. None of that below zero stuff with deep snow. The incessant rain had been the biggest problem. The natives said it had been one of the wettest years on record. Being out in the weather all the time made one more conscious of the elements. When you are out where you get wet every time it rains it makes it seem like it is raining more than normal. Living out in the field and combating the elements can be a trying thing. It always seems too cold or to hot or something. It had rained a lot this winter. I have no doubt that it was an extra wet one. Looking back through history it seems like every war was fought in the mud. Stories of mud in World War I were told and retold. Some claimed that the artillery and bombing causes it to rain more. I don't know if this was actually a scientific fact or not but most of the men believed it.

There were quite a few British here on the beachhead. It was sort of hard to tell how many they had here. It seemed as though many of their outfits were smaller units, maybe a battalion size or something like that. If the Americans had so many divisions in an area you could tell something near the amount of men there were. These British outfits, being smaller and of different strength, made it more difficult if you weren't acquainted with the different outfits and their sizes. There were outfits like the Gordons or the Queen's Own. They were old organizations with a lot of history and tradition behind them. They did have one regular division that I knew of there on the beachhead. It was the British 1st. I suppose their divisions are somewhat the same size as ours.

The British artillery was quite different from ours. While the 105th was the backbone of the American field artillery, theirs was what they called a twenty-five pounder. The twenty-five pounders were smaller than our 105s. They were roughly equivalent to a 75. They were pretty much of a flat trajectory gun and I believed they out-ranged our 105's some. The shells from them weighed about twenty-five pounds against our 105's thirty-three. I guess our 105's packed a little more power but not the range. They used their guns a little differently too. Instead of putting them behind a hill like we did they put them right on the crest of the hill. I guess it was more practical with the flat trajectory type of weapon. The twenty-five pounders had a peculiar sound when they were fired. To me they sounded like huge air rifles. Incidentally, they had about six or eight guns to a battery instead of the four like we did.

One soon learned the different sounds of the different artillery on the beachhead. There was the air rifle sound of the twenty-five pounder. Our 105's made quite a sharp report and the 155 Howitzers made still a larger report. The 155 rifles or "Long Toms" as we called them, made a very loud and sharp report. If they were directly behind you, even though a good many yards away, they sounded as though they were only a short distance away. The 155 rifle was about the largest artillery piece on the beachhead early in the campaign.

Of course, the Germans had their 88. It was probably the most famous and most talked about artillery piece in the war. It was an all-purpose gun. It could be used as artillery, anti-tank, anti-aircraft and they had 88's on their tanks. It was a very high velocity, flat trajectory weapon. Its range was somewhat greater than our 105's. The speed of the 88 shells was terrific. The scream from them chilled your blood. Poems, songs and jokes were made up about the 88 but few saw any humor in them. The German larger guns were the 105's, 150's and the 170's. I don't know what their biggest gun at Anzio was but I did know they were using those railroad guns and they were huge.

Early in February it was obvious things on the beachhead weren't so hot. Reports had it that the Germans were concentrating a large force around the beachhead and would probably launch an all-out attack soon. They had a good chance to push us right out into the sea too. We didn't have many men here. Some of the outfits that were here had taken a terrific beating and were way under strength. They didn't seem in any hurry to put more on the beachhead either. This landing had really been fouled up. The idea of the landing had been a good piece of strategy. The idea here had been to make highways six and seven the main arteries to the Casino Front. The landings had taken the Germans completely by surprise. It had been a golden opportunity to pour men in there while the Germans were off balance and completely rout them. There had been a good chance of trapping the troops around Casino and the rest of the winter line. This wasn't achieved however. It seemed to me they hadn't used near enough men for an undertaking like this. They might have known the Germans would act violently when they found that the rear of their main line was being threatened. Maybe our brass thought the Germans would get excited by the landings and withdraw the whole line instead of taking a chance of getting trapped. Whatever the thinking had been it had been wrong and we were in a bind now. The Germans needed a victory for the morale at home and they could see it right here by driving us into the sea. Things were beginning to shape up as pretty grim for us.

The Germans kept up their air activity day and night. During the day they would usually raid the harbor several times. Flights of their fighter bombers ranging in numbers from eight to two dozen would come rushing in going like mad. At night they would come over and drop flares and bomb the harbor. In the last couple of days they had bombed just the harbor. They seemed to be trying to knock out the harbor facilities and also sink the supply ships that were coming into the harbor. They were doing some good too. In the day time we could see big columns of black smoke rising up from the direction of the harbor. At night we could see fires burning brightly in the direction of Anzio and hear the crackling and popping of ammo dumps that had been hit.

A British artillery outfit began moving into our position. They were to take over our position and we were to move to another sector. They set their twenty-five pounders right on the crest of our hill. It seemed odd to see them do that rather than to put them at the bottom of the hill like we did. At night, when they fired their guns, they made a large red flash. It was much larger than the flash from our 150's.

We got acquainted with some of the English. They seemed like a pretty good bunch. On average they seemed quite a bit older than us. Probably as long as England had been in this war they were getting a little low on manpower. They were probably taking older men into the army than we were.

We had gotten orders that we would move at any minute and to get ready to move out in a minutes notice. We wondered what was up. In the afternoon large formations of our bombers came over and bombed the front lines. It must be true that the Germans were about to launch an all-out attack because we had never seen our bombers bombing so near our lines. They were probably trying to break up infantry and armor concentrations. Several waves of them came over during the afternoon and it was morale building to see them. Several of our bombers were brought down. It was something to see one of those big planes hit. When one was hit it would pull slowly out of the formation. It would then start going so fast the whole plane would break to pieces. From some of the planes several parachutes would blossom out. From others only one or two. Probably all of the fellows that did get out alive were captured as they must have had to land behind German lines. One time I saw a lone German fighter plane dive at a formation of our Flying Forts. The plane just stayed in its dive and never pulled out. I didn't see a parachute open from it either. We saw another sight that was rather different. A bunch of Folk-Wolfs came over heading for the harbor at the same time a flight of our heavy bombers were passing over the beachhead. The German planes turned and engaged the Forts. Of course, the Folk-Wolfes were faster than our big bombers. They flew around them like a bunch of sparrows after an eagle. Our Forts never broke formation but just kept heading towards the target. We saw two of our Forts and two Folk-Wolfes go down. The German planes finally broke off the engagement and headed back toward their lines. They never dropped their load of bombs on this trip anyway.

Things were tense here on the beachhead and everyone sensed it. The reports had it that the Germans had ten infantry divisions and lots of armor and artillery ringing the beachhead and more were pouring in every hour. We figured we must be badly outnumbered. There were only two American divisions here, the 3rd and the 45th. Part of the 1st Armored Division was here along with a couple of miscellaneous regiments, battalions of Rangers, paratroopers and the 36th Engineers. There were some British here but not in any strength. The Germans had us in a bind and were going to take advantage of it. An all-out attack was expected momentarily.

That night everyone was routed out and put on alert. No one was to sleep. When I went into the C.P. (Command Post) to take over on the radio everyone was tense and grim-faced. The situation was bad. The Germans were attacking all along the beachhead, especially in the central sector from the direction of the "factory". Already their attack had made some progress and some of our infantry outfits were forced to fall back. Some of the outfits that had their ground were being encircled.

All of our guns were blazing away. The sky was lit up from the flashes and the booming was terrific and steady. German planes were over in force bombing everywhere. Reports coming in weren't encouraging at all. The Germans were advancing and their attack in the central sector seemed to be going well. Here they were making their maximum effort. Their strategy was apparently to drive us to the sea and divide the beachhead and that would be it.

The next morning we were told that we would move that night. We wondered if we were going to get the hell out of here. There had been strong rumors that the beachhead was going to be abandoned. It seemed that the big decision of the big brass was whether to try to hold or withdraw from the beachhead. If we started withdrawing now many could escape. If we tried to hold and failed and the beachhead was cut in two the results would be complete disaster. Once in a while I guess the big brass did have to make a tough decision. Probably either way there were politics and careers at stake.

When it was definite we were going to move some of the English fellows that only had temporary make shift shelters started taking over our dugouts. Curtis and I invited a couple of them to have ours. I remarked to one of them that our particular place had escaped shelling and felt it was a pretty good position. He said, "Yes. Isn't it lovely?" I almost had to laugh. I never thought of a position in a war zone, especially on this beachhead, as "lovely". I got a kick out of the English and liked them a lot.

In the afternoon there were several air-raids. Our

planes seemed to be strangely absent when the German planes flew over. I suppose they stayed away from the beachhead to stay out of the flak that was thrown up. They probably waited on the outer fringes of the beachhead to try to intercept the Germans or lay for them on their return towards their lines.

We had, for the most part, the 99th Air Force supporting us. It was a colored outfit and they flew P-40's. I didn't know much about aircraft but it seemed to me that the P-40 seemed rather obsolete in this stage of the war. I had seen M.E, 109's scoot past them like they were standing still. The P-40 was still supposed to be the best for dive bombing and strafing though. Those fellows were supposed to be experts at that sort of thing. There were also quite a few of our P-51 Mustangs around and the British and their Spitfires were quite numerous.

That afternoon several flights of our Forts came over and pounded the German lines. They received considerable flak and we saw several of them go down. We had lost several bombers here in the last couple of days so I guess everything wasn't always milk and honey for the "Fly Boys".

As soon as it was dark we rounded up our stuff and got ready to move. Soon after dark German planes began coming over in large numbers again. We had to hold up moving because it wasn't wise to get on the highway while so much bombing was going on. It was the same old story again. Sky bright as day, tracers crisscrossing and the ground trembling from the bombs crashing down. We could see fires burning brightly toward Anzio.

The raid lasted for hours. Finally, at about 2:30 A.M., things quieted down a bit and our convoy started moving. We hit the black topped road and headed north. Heading north toward the Germans dispelled any rumors that we were going to the docks and leave the beachhead. In fact, we took a dim view of artillery moving up while the infantry was being pushed back. It didn't look good at all to us. We went a mile or so on the blacktop and turned off again and made our way through some open, muddy fields. It was really flat out here and barren with no sign of trees at all. We all felt that this was going to be a hot spot. We spotted a tank or two sitting around in the fields.

After grinding slowly through the mud for a short distance we reached our position in a very narrow, shallow ravine. We quickly set up our radio and got communications established with our guns. Although our guns weren't in position yet, it wouldn't be long, for they needed all the artillery they could get up ahead. We must have been the furthest ahead of the artillery because we could look back and see the flashes of hundreds of artillery pieces. We could hear hundreds of shells whining overhead going both ways. At the moment the bulk of them seemed to be going toward the German lines.

Gill took over on the radio so the rest of the operators started looking for a place to sleep. You could hear the sounds of picks and shovels tearing at the earth. Everyone was digging now and not waiting until morning. With thousands of shells sailing over and some already landing close you could never tell when some would come right in on us. We also figured that when it was daylight we might be under observation from the Germans even though we were down in a slight depression.

All Curtis and I had to dig with was one small entrenching tool. The digging here wasn't easy like it had been back in the other position. The ground was full of roots and there were a lot of rocks. About three inches down we hit hard clay. After working about ten minutes we saw it would take hours to get down any distance with this tool. We decided to wait until morning and borrow some larger tools from one of the vehicles and dig our hole much quicker. Besides it was now 5:00 A.M and it would be daylight in a couple of hours. We also figured the air activity would be quiet until daylight.

We were wrong again. We had no more than lain down when here came the German planes again. There were lots of them too. The anti-aircraft reported later that there were 270 planes in this raid. That's a lot of planes for a target as small as this beachhead.

The German planes came over just a few feet above the ground. They sounded like a bunch of angry bees. Our anti-aircraft was sending up thousands of shells. They weren't very effective however because they were bursting high up in the air nowhere near the planes that were hovering just above the ground. The Germans flew low not only to get out of the anti-aircraft fire but it was quite moonlit and they could probably see targets on the ground. They didn't drop flares. They could see without them. The flashes of the artillery could be seen and artillery was a choice target too.

We lay there sweating it out. In the moonlight we could see the planes passing over low. They were dropping bombs and personnel bombs everywhere and some were coming mighty close. These planes, which the Germans used to bomb at night, were larger and slower. They may have been Hienkles or Dorniers. Anyway, they carried tail gunners and they were busy.

We heard something crashing through the underbrush and the splash of water. It was Haddow. He had gotten so scared he ran down to the small creek that ran along the bottom of the ravine and jumped in. He was a lot braver than I was to jump into icy water on a cold night like this.

There was no doubt that the Germans were making an all-out effort to drive us from the beachhead and so far they were making progress. Their air force was really supporting their ground troops. They were doing everything possible to bomb artillery, troop and tank concentrations and to disrupt communications and supplies. This raid lasted about an hour and a half and then the planes droned away with the first gray of the dawn in the east.

At the crack of dawn everyone was digging like mad. Everyone was so anxious to get a fox hole dug that we hated to take time out to do our regular jobs. Curtis and I were unable to get larger tools because there were only a few in the battery and there was a long waiting line to use them. We dug the best we could with our little shovel. The clay or hard pan that was about three inches below the surface had to be chipped away about a teaspoon at a time. We kept taking turns working at it. Curtis wasn't thinking about a poker game now. He just wanted to dig a hole. We knew we were close to the front lines. We could hear mortar shells landing out a short distance ahead. German artillery was whining overhead. They laid a barrage of high bursts in on our "B" Battery. It caused considerable causalities. Poor "B" battery was a hard luck outfit.

It took Curtis and me almost all day to get our hole dug. Even then we were down only about two feet. We couldn't go any lower without hitting water. We cut a few small trees and placed them over the hole. On top of this we put some sandbags and dirt. Still on top of this we placed bundles of sapling, which were all around. The

Italians had evidently cut and bundled them for some reason.

Our little dugout was very hard to get in and out of. The entrance was very small. Just large enough to squeeze into. When we got in there was barely room for the two of us. We had to lay straight and it was almost impossible to turn over because the roof was so low. I almost got claustrophobia at first when we were both in the dugout. However, it was much better than sweating out the shelling and bombings on the open ground. We felt much safer that night when the German planes came over. The raid was almost as bad as the one the night before too.

The next day things were pretty hot and the Germans had renewed their attack. All day armor piercing shells came whizzing into our area and plunking onto the ground. Fortunately, no one was hurt but it was annoying. We figured they were misses and overs from the tank battle a little way ahead. About noon we saw vapor streaks of planes that were very high and heading in for the sea. At first, we thought that they were some of our bombers. As they got closer we realized that they were German planes trying to sneak in from the sea. They came in dropping lower at incredible speed. The coming formation looked like a huge scythe. Right over our heads the planes split up. Half of them headed for the harbor and the other half started diving down. We watched the planes discharge their bombs behind us and watched the usual columns of black smoke go rolling up. They had been on target with something. The flak was really peppering the sky and we saw two of the raiders go down.

By night things had reached a critical point. The Germans were throwing everything into the attack and it seemed as though our lines might not be able to hold. The German planes were over again in larger numbers and were plastering the whole beachhead. While I was on the fire control radio in the C. P. some shells crashed right into our area. The C.P. was dug down about two feet but, of course, had no cover on it. It only had the heavy canvas sidewalls and top. Everyone in the C.P. lay in the mud on the floor utilizing that two feet. Shrapnel ripped through the canvas walls of the tent. It riddled some slide rules and other computer equipment that were hanging on the wall.

Our F.O.'s were pleading for more artillery. Things up ahead had gone from bad to worse. Lt. Robinson's party was completely surrounded. They had holed up in a house with no chance of escape unless some of our other units got to them. Lt. Robinson had been killed and another man in the party was badly wounded. A fellow by the name of Wilsey, a corporal, was directing fire. All that day half of his fire missions had been aimed behind him. They had barricaded themselves into one room of the house and were trying to old out. They had mortars dropped on the house, hand grenades thrown at them and had been sniped at. They still held out.

Wilsey kept calling that the situation was hopeless and asked if there were any instructions before they destroyed the radio. Colonel Funk had me tell them to try to hold out a little longer. Col. Funk was trying to get two or three tanks to make a rush in and try to rescue them. The plan never materialized.

Wilsey and his bunch really had guts, there was no question about that. Holding out like that and still directing artillery fire after his officer had been killed was something! Fellows like that deserve medals and recognition but the hell of it is that they never get it.

BYE FOR NOW

You had a better chance if you kissed some Major's ass around headquarters here. Guys like Wilsey and other F.O.'s never got much credit, medals or anything else.

Finally, Wilsey called and said a mob of Germans and a couple of tanks were approaching the house. He said the jig was up and he was destroying the radio. His last words were, "This is it." Someone finally heard from his family months later. He and John Silver had been taken prisoner and were in Germany.

The German attack was mounting in fury. We were instructed that if the word came to pull out we were not to take unimportant items. Just yourself and your rifle and pile on the nearest truck. I found out later that one tank outfit had gone as far as to pile all extra equipment into a big pile and stood by with gallons of gasoline ready for the word to soak the stuff and set it on fire. They were all out of ammunition and knew they couldn't help any in stopping an attack.

The F.O. (Forward Observer) kept calling in and pleading for more artillery. Our guns had started out firing one round a minute and were now up to five. We also called on some British twenty-five pounders. They were firing two rounds per minute per gun. We also got Voodoo, a 155 outfit, to help support.

The different batteries kept calling in and saying their guns were red hot and would burn up. They were throwing water on them to try to keep them cool. The guns were so hot that when they put the shell in and closed the breach it fired without even having to pull the lanyard. One of the F.O.'s called in and said, "For God's sake, keep the artillery coming". Fat assed Major Sheaffers grabbed the mike from my hand and screamed, "Never mind the asinine instruction, you sense them and we'll fire them." That lousy bastard anyway. He had gone up on L.O. (Look Out) once for about a day and one of the guys that went with him said he was scared stiff and stayed in a hole most of the time. L.O.ing was nothing like F.O.ing either, particularly in a predicament like this. That's the way it is though. If you kissed this guy's ass or brought his chow to his hole you had a good chance of getting a promotion or a Bronze Star or something. I could see that I wasn't going to get any medals. However, we were doing all we could. Five rounds a minute from our guns was really far beyond their capability for very long. Just the same, under the circumstances, crap like that was uncalled for.

We were mixing the shells up using H.E. (High Explosive) but also quite a few phosphorus shells. The phosphorus shells had a twofold purpose. Besides burning the Krauts and causing confusion among them, they lit up long enough for the infantry boys to see the oncoming enemy and shoot them.

German planes were over in droves again and plastering bombs all over. Our guns didn't usually fire when enemy planes were detected directly overhead. The Krauts would pick up the gun flashes and know where our guns were positioned.

Col. Funk ordered us to keep firing. We couldn't let up for a second now. If the German attack was successful everything would be lost anyway. "A" Battery kept banging away. It was a tense situation. We were expecting to get blown off the face of the earth any second by German bombs. However, no bombs were dropped right in our immediate area.

Our guns became so hot they had to be rested one at a time. After about three hours of heavy shelling the attack seemed to have slowed down some and things became a little quieter. Our battalion alone had fired

8,500 rounds this night. Ammo was getting mighty low and if the Germans continued to attack much longer everyone would be out of ammunition.

The artillery played a big part in stopping the Germans here at Anzio. Of course, the infantry bears the real brunt of the thing, but if it hadn't been for the tons and tons of shells hurled into the oncoming German troops and tanks they never would have been able to hold. The infantry admitted that they wouldn't have stood a chance without the artillery and of course it was vice-versa. There was plenty of good feelings between the artillery and the infantry. Back in the States there had always been arguments and fights between them. It was a lot different here though. They were the closest of friends and had nothing but praise for one another.

Another thing that had helped immensely to save the beachhead was the radio communication. There had always been arguments as to which was the best means of communication. Wire or radio. During the big German push I think it was settled once and for all that radio was much superior. When the chips were down it is imperative that there be communication. There is no comparison between the two. Had we had nothing but wire the artillery would have been almost at a loss to add effective help. The German bombing and shelling had practically destroyed all wire communication. The lines to the F.O.'s were especially hit hard. The repair crew couldn't begin to keep them going. If it hadn't been for radios fellows like Wilsey would have been completely cut off from the outside. They would never have been able to do the effective firing he had radioed back. Radios very seldom went out of order. Batteries going dead was the biggest problem. Usually a F.O. party carried a couple of extra batteries with them. If a vehicle was handy the radio could run off of its battery.

Most of the officers hated the radio, mainly for one thing. A radio message had to be short and to the point. Officers liked to shoot the bull with their fellow officers and they couldn't do it on the radio. They had to be brief and business like. On the phone they could carry on a lot of nonsense. One disadvantage the radio did have however was that everything had to be coded. At least anything important at all. It was possible for the enemy to pick up our frequency and to listen to what was going on. If a radio got captured the enemy could easily listen in.

The German attack had been slowed but not entirely stopped. They were regrouping and bringing in fresh reserves and more equipment. They continued to shell the whole beachhead as well as the harbor. They were trying to keep our artillery down and to keep more troops and supplies from coming in.

In the afternoon I was sitting near my dugout trying to scratch out a few words to home. LaCoss, Gill and Curtis were all sitting around nearby reading or writing. Suddenly, a shell screamed and hit near the top of the knoll and shrapnel went singing in all directions. In about one second all four of us had disappeared into our dugouts. Curtis and I had always cursed the entrance to our dugout and the amount of time it took us to wiggle in and out of it. This time however, we got into it in nothing flat. Curtis did a jack-knife and a half gainer diving into it and I followed the same way right on his heels. Curtis remarked, "Hell, that entrance hole isn't that small after all". The Germans really laid in a barrage mixing H. E. (high explosives), delayed fuses and armor piercing shells. We could hear the German guns firing. It sounded like there were about eight. The shells were coming in with machine gun speed. Some were landing so close they made our ears ring. The whole ravine was being shelled. The way the shells were screaming in and crashing did make a person a little panicky. I could see why some guys got up and ran during a shelling although that was, of course, the worst thing you could do. I think Curtis and I both felt like trying to get the hell out of there but controlled ourselves. The Germans laid about two hundred shells into the ravine in just a few minutes. Again, we were very lucky. No one in Headquarters Battery was hit. Several vehicles received considerable damage though. "A" Battery, down the ravine, had also been shelled, causing casualties. One shell made a direct hit on a dugout killing two men.

We knew that we were going to be shelled but didn't know when. The evening before the Germans had put two high bursts over our area. They had been the really high bursts, the adjusting kind. The Germans adjusted their artillery differently than we did. They used high bursts over the target and somehow adjusted that way. They were pretty tricky about it too. They would seldom shell an area just after they had adjusted on it. They knew everyone would be on the alert and probably holed up. They would wait for several hours for firing effect. Sometimes they would wait as long as twenty-four to thirty-six hours. Then they would throw them in and fast, catching everyone flat-footed. This is what they had done over our ravine just about twenty-four hours before. We knew they knew we were in here and we were one of their concentration numbers. We could expect artillery in here at any time from now on.

The Germans were after our observation planes too.

They knew that from our position on this flat terrain of the beachhead we didn't have very good observation. They knew that the Cubs were our best way of getting ground information. In fact, the only way to get decent observation. I had never before seen them bother with the Cubs. They seldom fired at them for fear of giving gun positions away. They seldom sent fighter planes after them either. Here on the beachhead they were doing both. You often saw anti-aircraft fire popping up at the flitting Cubs. They also sent their fighter planes to try to knock them off.

One day a Cub came scooting over our position, just skimming the ground. Then there was a big roar as a M.E. 109 raced over the knoll after it. The Cub swerved just as a German M.E. (Messerschmitt) let go with a burst of machine gun fire. The M.E. missed and went roaring pass. The M.E. was going so fast it took several miles for it to turn around and start back. By the time it started back the Cub was on the ground and our anti-aircraft had taken the German fighter under fire. The M.E. roared back toward its own lines.

Lt. Lindsey was now observing from a Cub. One time he had a very narrow escape. While they were out doing a little observing they ran into a lot of trouble. Six M.E.109's attacked them. Imagine six fighter planes going at speeds of three hundred miles an hour and with several machine guns each, taking on a Cub. The Cub had the speed of about seventy-five miles per hour and no weapons at all. Three German planes got below the Cub and three above. Lindsey and his pilot thought it was curtains for them. Somehow a miracle happened and they got to the ground some way. Their plane was riddled with bullets and Lindsey had bashed his head on something bruising him up pretty badly. He said he had had enough of that old crap and I didn't blame him. The Germans had been fairly successful against our Cubs. In February our division alone had lost four of them.

Orders came down for us to move. We were to move toward the middle of the beachhead. We were supposed to be getting in a position that was more favorable to support our outfit. There wasn't any artillery moving into this position, British or American, to take over for us. I wondered if we weren't retreating a little as we were the furthest forward.

The next morning, February 22, Washington's Birthday, we prepared to move. At first we were going to wait until dark to move. It was such a cloudy, rainy day and the visibility was so poor we figured we might get away with moving during the daylight hours. Most of us were glad to be getting out of this position. The tension seemed to be mounting. The Germans were throwing in plenty of high bursts as though they were getting ready to give the whole ravine along here a hell of a bombardment. They had already begun to shell heavily up and down the line. They were shelling heavily in the back of us as well as in the front.

In the downpour we hurriedly got our stuff together. We had to empty our sandbags if we wanted them as they were scarce on the beachhead. When Curtis and I took the bags off of our dugout we found that several of them had been knocked open. Pieces of shell fragments had cut through the sacks and embedded in the sand. Those sandbags had undoubtedly saved us from being killed or at least badly wounded.

We finally got our stuff together and Curtis and I jumped on the service truck. The other C.P. (Command Post) vehicles had already left. We made our way slowly along the muddy slope of the ravine. One truck and a jeep ahead of us had slipped down to the bottom of the ravine. Artillery shells were popping around pretty close and we hated the slow speed that the truck had to travel. We wanted to get the hell out of there in a hurry. After traveling through open fields we finally reached the black topped road and turned south. When we hit the black top the driver of the truck didn't spare the horses. He must have pushed his foot clear through the carburetor for we really went tearing down the road. Soon we turned east on another hard topped road and sailed down this road too. We passed a place where some gun positions were being shelled. They were in a position about a hundred and fifty yards from the road. The damp rainy weather must have deadened the sound of the shell bursts. Although the shells were landing less than two hundred yards away the report from them didn't seem to be so loud. However, we didn't stick around and listen. Soon we turned off the hard topped road into muddy fields. We moved along slowly through the mud. Twice the truck bogged down and we all had to get off and push. We reached sort of a thicket with a small muddy road running through it. The truck got to moving better and disappeared around the bend. Curtis and I had been off pushing and the truck went off and left us. We walked on toward our new position.

The rain was really coming down now by the bucketful. Curtis and I sloshed along in the mud and downpour cursing like pirates. We were soon drenched to the skin. We walked about three quarters of a mile and came upon our new position.

Our new position was in a small ravine that was pretty well hidden by a thicket. For the most part the thicket consisted of lots of saplings growing close together. There were a few trees mixed in that ranged up to a few inches in diameter.

At the new position everyone was busy digging. The C.P. dugout and many individual dugouts were in the process of being dug. The C.P. dugout was to be quite an affair. It was to be about seven feet deep, eight feet wide and twenty feet long. They were busy cutting larger trees to put across the top. Then came the sandbags and dirt.

Curtis and I selected a spot on the reverse side of a gentle slope on which to dig our hole. There was a large bomb crater about ten yards from where we were working. The top soil was pretty sandy and easy to dig in. All we had to dig with was our little entrenching tool making the work hard. The rain beat down on us all the time as we worked. When we were down almost deep enough Curtis said he was going off to find something better to dig with. He didn't show up again until late that afternoon. He had found some of the boys playing poker in a dugout and that was it. He just couldn't resist a poker game no matter what.

I had to finish digging the hole and chop the small logs for the top of it. I also filled the sandbags and some shell casings and put them over the top. Then I put a shelter half over the whole works. I was soaked to the skin and miserable when I finished the job. It was still pouring when I moved our stuff into the dugout. I had no more than settled down when the roof began to leak. I got out another shelter half and threw it over the top and shoveled a couple more feet of dirt on top. The roof didn't leak for the present at least.

It continued to rain the rest of the day and into the night. About midnight I woke up and found I was sleeping in a small lake. The water didn't leak in through the roof but came in on the sides. The water ran in where the top soil and the clay met. Curtis was still snoozing away. It seemed as though I was sleeping on the low side.

After cursing a while I finally got up and went into the C.P. Martinovich was on the radio. Although he had just come on the set I told him to go back to bed and I would take over. I was too wet and miserable to sleep anyway so I just stayed on the set all night. I didn't wake anyone up to relieve me. About dawn my clothes began to dry out pretty well.

The next day was another wet and miserable thing. Things had definitely quieted down though. The German attack had apparently been stopped for the time being at least. It was lucky they stopped their all-out effort when they did. Most of the ammunition as well as the men on the beachhead had been expended. One more day of German attacks and our lines would probably have collapsed and we would have been run right into the sea.

Our division had taken quite a beating in the month of February. Losses for our division alone for the twenty-nine days (from the History of the 45th) were 88 trucks, 16 trailers, 36 anti-aircraft guns, 159 machine guns, 61 mortars, 101 automatic rifles, 364 rifles, 108 Carbines, 219 pistols, 12 Tommy Guns, 674 bayonets, 398 trench knives, 288 sets of binoculars and 122 wrist watches. The division artillery lost four Piper Cubs. The 191st Tank Battalion lost 21 tanks and the 645th T.D. (Tank Division) Battalion lost 17 tank destroyers. Of course, there was a lot of equipment and personal stuff that could never be counted.

Losses of men were greater than the division had had in any other period. There were 5, 709 causalities during the 29 days of February as compared with a total of 13,129 for the previous 120 days including and following Salerno.

Our division had fired a good many rounds of ammunition during the month too. Here are some of the figures on that:

> Sicilian Campaign: 25 day of combat, 14,697 rounds.
> Naples-Foggia: Four months of fighting, 167,153 rounds
> Anzio Beachhead: 158th F.A. Battalion, Feb. 17, 18 and 19: 20,961
> Division Artillery: February 17, 18, 19: 41,525
> Total for Division for 29 days of February: 129, 732

These figures just went to show how much more terrific the fighting had been here. For instance, the 158th Battalion alone fired more rounds in three days than the whole division had in twenty-three days in Sicily. In 29 days here on the beachhead the Division hadn't fired any fewer than the four months of fighting from Salerno to the Gustave Line.

On the three days of the 17, 18 and 19[th of] February, during the time the Germans had been driving their hardest, the division had fired 41,525 rounds. The 158th Battalion alone had fired 20, 961 rounds or a little over half of the divisions allotment. That proved that the good old 158th had been right up there pitching in. Even the 171st and the 160th Battalions griped about us firing so much they wanted to know if we were trying to make a name for ourselves or something. Well, we knew what our job was supposed to be and that was to support the infantry to the utmost. That is exactly what we had done.

The Germans must have lost heavily too. Probably more than we had. Naturally, there was no way of really knowing but attacking forces usually lose more. Carter, one of the boys from Headquarters, gave us a little dope on it. He had been up with the 2nd Battalion during "the Battle of the Caves" and had been captured. He had been taken to a stockade up around Rome. While he was being taken there he had a chance to see what went on behind the German lines. He saw some of the havoc we had heaped on the Germans. He saw a German bulldozer digging a trench for the German dead. He said he saw piles of bodies, and 150 or more in a pile waiting to be buried. He had also seen several hundred dead along the route to Rome who were killed by our artillery.

Carter escaped from the enclosure in Rome and after several days had made his way back to our lines. He brought back a lot of valuable information with him as to the location of German troops, gun and tank concentrations. He was able to pick out some important targets on maps and air photos for the artillery and air-force. For his efforts he received a much deserved Silver Star and a promise to be sent home in the near future.

The first of March came and the days dragged on. The German planes came over day and night, weather permitting. The day time raids differed from the ones at night. In the day time they used their fast fighter-bombers, the Focke-Wolfe. They usually used smaller numbers of planes in any single raid but might come over several times a day. They generally headed for the harbor but they had plenty of good targets everywhere. Our anti-aircraft would make it so hot for them they didn't take much time to pick out a good target. They knew if they dropped their bombs anywhere on this small beachhead they would probably kill someone or destroy some material.

The night raids were quite different. The Germans always came over with more and larger bombers. They took a lot more time too. Sometimes the raid would last an hour or two and sometimes there were more than one raid a night. Sometimes they dropped flares and sometimes they didn't. They always dropped plenty of bombs from their anti-personnel type bombs to the huge block busters. They made our nights miserable and uneasy. Even though they often came over you, you never got used to them. As soon as we would hear the drone of the planes and the crashing of anti-aircraft we would begin to feel uneasy. Time after time the ground would quake and tremble from the concussions of the bombs. Dirt would rattle in on us from the rooves of our dugouts. Several times personnel bombs were dropped in and around our area. Fortunately, no one in our outfit was ever killed but they caused many anxious moments. Two of our trucks were badly damaged by bombing.

Things around here were shelled often too. The 189th had a battery of their 155's up the ravine a short distance. They were shelled several times and lost men. Over to one side, about three hundred yards away and across another ravine our "C" Battery was in position. They had been shelled several times and men had been killed. One thing happened over in "C" Battery that was more or less a mystery. Two fellows were sleeping in a dugout one night when an armor piercing shell ripped through the top of their dugout and buried into the ground between them. One of the fellows woke and was naturally afraid. He asked his buddy if he was O.K. When there was no answer he reached over and discovered the fellow was dead. He was examined by the medical officer and there wasn't a mark of any kind on him. The puzzle was, how did the fellow die? Some thought he might have been awake when the shell came in and could have died of fright. It was remotely possible that he had died of heart failure or some other natural cause even before the shell hit. It was a rather odd case anyway. His buddy had felt no concussion because armor piercing shells do not explode. The fellow could not have died of concussion.

Shells landed in and all around our position. Many shells pounded on to the opposite slope of our ravine. Many just fell short of our position.

One night they were laying a few pretty close. The three H.E. (High Explosive) shells, delayed fuses, armored piercing and phosphorus shells. They really scared the daylights out of everyone. Again we were lucky. We had only one man slightly wounded. One phosphorus shell hit near his hole and started the boards and straw around his dugout burning. He climbed out to get away from the fire and was hit in the head with a piece of shrapnel. He was just grazed with a pretty nasty head wound, but nothing serious.

There were several kinds of shells that both sides used. They were the H.E. or high explosive shells. This type was used mostly against troops. Usually they used the H.E. shells with a quick fuse. The instant they hit the ground they exploded and sent thousands of fragments flying in all directions. They exploded so fast when they hit the ground that they hardly made much of a hole at all. Usually they just cleared a place on the ground of all sod, twigs, rocks etc. for a few feet in diameter.

Delayed fuse shells are H.E. shells with the fuse set longer. When they hit the ground they would bury in several feet before they exploded. This type of shell was used in areas where men and equipment were dug in.

It's used on buildings to pierce through the roof or walls and explode inside.

Then there are the phosphorus shells. These shells would hit, burst and scatter phosphorus all around. They can inflict serious burn wounds on the enemy. They are also used to set buildings, haystacks, woods or anything else that will burn that the enemy might be hiding in.

I didn't know much about piercing shells, but I believe they were just a chunk of metal that was able to pierce thick metal. Of course these shells were used against tanks. They were also effective against pill boxes or other fortifications with thick walls.

The high burst was an H.E. shell with a short fuse. They were timed to burst just above the ground. These were used effectively against men in open foxholes of slit trenches.

The Germans didn't seem to have white phosphorus shells. I guess they lacked the materials to make them. They had shells that were filled with gasoline or some kind of chemical that splashed and burned when they hit. Not very pleasant to be around their impact area.

The defense against artillery shells is the good old ground. For instance, an 88 H.E. shell could be effective on upright troops for a radius of a hundred yards. Larger shells could be effective a much greater distance. Advancing into an artillery barrage was murderous. If you were in a slit trench a H.E. shell had to make almost a direct hit to get you. If you had a couple of feet of earth over you, you were safe from most high bursts too.

A lot of artillery is fired by maps as well as observation. Observation is the best, of course, on an attack or where a person could be in a position to observe enemy movements. Maps were used many times to direct fire. Sometimes a main highway or an important crossroad behind the German lines would be interdicted. This was done by firing from maps. The maps had to be pretty accurate to be able to drop a shell on a crossroad five or six miles away.

The Germans usually had the advantage in blind firing. As they retreated they carefully surveyed all important cross roads and bypasses. They could almost always put their shells right where they wanted them. It seemed like they always had the advantage in observation too. They always seemed to be up in the hills while we were down on the flat. They planned it that way. They only defended terrain that was advantageous to them. That is an advantage that a retreating defensive army does have. Even here on Anzio they controlled all of the hills ringing the beachhead and we were down on the flat, open country.

The weather here in the first part of March was lousy, rainy and raw. The weather did seem to be getting a little warmer however and as the month dragged along it seemed to improve some.

Toward the end of March we prepared to move. We weren't going to move forward but just to another part of the beachhead. Colonel Funk and Captain Finkle went on reconnaissance several times before they found a good position. It wasn't exactly a "good" position either. It was right out in the open. There was no foliage for cover and practically no uneven ground for protection. The fact that the new position was so much in the open it was decided that about half the battery would go there at a time. The rest of Headquarters would go to the Service Battery area which was better hidden. We would take turns every few days going to the new position to relieve one another. I was supposed to go to the new position with the first bunch. I loaded a lot of my stuff, including my .03 rifle. At the last moment there was a switch and I was sent to the Service Battery area. The vehicle with my rifle and some other stuff went to the new position.

Marshall, Matinovich and I all of the fire direction radio section, went to the Service Battery. This position was located in very flat country. There was quite a bit of brush and some very small trees to afford some kind of camouflage, but all in all, it was pretty well in the open.

As soon as we arrived there we began digging our dugout. We decided we would dig enough for the three of us. The ground was sandy and the digging was easy. In a short time we had a large hole. It was about eight feet long, five feet deep and six feet across. We cut down some small trees and with some boards that we were able to round up, we put a framework over the top. Over this we put sandbags and shell cases filled with sand. We lined the inside walls with shelter halves. We even stuck two small shell cases in the back corners on a slant to give us a little more ventilation. We were proud of our dugout. We topped it all off by digging a trench about six feet long leading into it. It was the best dugout by far any of us had had yet.

Just a few yards from our new position was a British mortar outfit. They used this area more or less the way we were going to use it. They were rotating their men back and forth between two positions the way we were going to do. Marty and I soon became acquainted with some of the English. They were all friendly and a nice bunch of fellows. A couple offered us tea. A couple others gave us a couple of quarts of beer. That's what I liked about the English Army, their beer ration. They got a weekly allowance of beer. We were tickled to get the beer as it was the first we had seen since we had left the States. In return we gave them "D" bars and a few cans of "C" rations which they were equally glad to get. The English always seemed to go for our "C" rations. I didn't know whether it was because not getting anything like it they didn't get tired of it or the stuff was seasoned more like the food they ate at home. They always seemed to enjoy them though.

One fellow that hung around with us all the time was a red headed kid named Ted Billings. He hailed from London and was a real cockney. At first it was hard to understand him. Billings hung around with us more than he did his own outfit. There were several of the British boys that we got to know well. In spite of the propaganda that I'd always heard against them I found, for the most part, that they were a swell bunch of fellows. They always seemed polite, nice to talk to and not the blow hard types or anything like that.

The weather here on the Anzio Beachhead really began to improve around the first of April. From then on we began to have nice warm weather and had only a few little showers. The appearance of an early spring reminded me a great deal of the weather for this time of year back home in California.

Another thing we began to notice on the beachhead was the increasing amount of German artillery. For the first month or so about the only big stuff that we had heard passing over was the Anzio Express. Every day now more and more big shells went screaming overhead. There was a large ammunition dump about four hundred yards from us. The Germans interdicted it day and night. They set fires in it several times. I guess since the Germans found that they couldn't drive us off the beachhead they were going to slaughter us with plenty of artillery.

Our area was shelled so much more than the other position. The boys there didn't want to be relieved. They had rather take double shifts than to come here to our position. Marty eventually did go and take Curtis' place but Grady and I never did get to go.

The first week or so we were in this position and before the shelling got so bad we would go over to where an English service outfit was in position and do a little community singing. The Limeys had gotten a piano and some other musical instruments. I guess they had liberated them in Anzio or Nettuno. Among the Americans and the British there were fellows that could play piano, sax, clarinet and the accordion. Besides playing we did a lot of singing. What seemed strange to me was that the British knew the words to our own American popular songs better than we did. They had very few tunes of their own. They liked the American songs the best. One explained to me why they knew the words to the songs so well. He said that in English bars, or pubs as they called them, they seldom had a jukebox. Instead they all sang the songs community style. It seemed to me that was a better way and more fun and congenial than our system of the juke box.

One night we were over there singing when German planes began to come over and drop bombs. Everyone headed for dugouts. I found a dugout and started to dive in. I didn't know whose dugout it was but I wasn't waiting to find out. Just as I started to get into it a rather funny thing happened. A Limey, who had been pounding right at my heels, grabbed me, pulled me back and jumped into the dugout first. It reminded me of some comedies I had seen in the movies. It's funny what can happen in the heat of excitement. It was a good thing everyone had taken cover quickly. Bombs dropped right in our area. The Germans also began to lay plenty of shells in too. Some of them were big ones too.

The next day we found out the piano had received a direct hit. Most of the other instruments were destroyed too. That ended our little musical get-togethers .

The get-togethers would have ended anyway. From then on our whole area was shelled heavily, especially at night. Around dark it would commence and the shelling would last all night. They usually covered the whole beachhead. They fired everything from the Express on down to about 57mms at us. With the German Air Force over us every night it made things mighty tough.

The 36th Engineers were in a position about a hundred and fifty yards from us. They seemed to lose men and equipment almost every night. The British, who were only about fifty yards away, also lost men and equipment. Our luck continued to hold out. Lady Luck wasn't just smiling at us, she was laughing out loud. We were losing some equipment however.

The Germans often timed their air raids with their artillery barrages. There were a couple of reasons for doing this. Besides adding to the hell of an air raid, the artillery helped down our anti-aircraft fire. During the combined artillery and bombing jobs they always shelled all known anti-aircraft gun positions.

It was really hell on earth to sweat out an air-raid and barrage of artillery at the same time. Planes droning overhead, bombs screaming down and crashing, shells screaming in, anti-aircraft banging away. All this made things very unpleasant. After a shelling and bombing raid or either of the other, we could stick our heads out of our holes and see the whole beachhead lighted up from burning fires. Gasoline and ammo dumps going up in smoke. You could hear the crackling and popping of shells as they burned.

We had many close calls here. If some of them had

been any closer I wouldn't be around to talk about it. One night a fuse quick 88 shell hit two feet at the back of our dugout. Another night a string of personnel bombs were dropped about ten yards from us. One night Grady and I were sitting out a bombing raid. We heard the first one hit and then the next one that was even closer. They were strung our way. The next one was going to be right in on us. We held our breath. It crashed down close and the walls of our dugout started caving in. We let our breath out as the next one crashed a few yards further on.

The next morning we found that the bomb had landed only about twenty-five yards from our hole. It made a pretty good sized hole. Had it hit our dugout we would never have known what had happened. The one that had landed about fifty yards away had made a direct hit on a British supply truck. Of all things it had hit the truck that carried the beer and liquor rations.

About the closest call we had in this particular area also happened at night. Huge shells were really finding our area. We believed that it was the Anzio Express falling short of the town for some reason. We could hear the big guns booming plainly although they were located around Albano, twenty-six miles away. On this occasion Grady, Billings, the Limey and I were in our dugout. Those big shells were landing close. They made no scream when they came in. We could hear the big gun fire and then the ground would shake violently when they hit. There was no whine or roar of the shell, just the angry sound of huge pieces of shrapnel ripping the air. The ground trembled and churned and dirt rattled down from the top and sides of the dugout. Needless to say the three of us lay there sweating it out and scared stiff. Suddenly they were bouncing right off the ground and the walls of the dugout caved in. That one had come mighty close and had really jarred us up. Finally, the big shells stopped much to our relief.

The next morning we found out how close that one had really come. Billings was the first one to stick his head out of the dugout in the morning. He just about fell back in from shock. He groaned and said, "My God Borthwick, look how close those bloody Jerrys came." Grady and I crawled out and were also taken aback by what we saw. There was a huge shell crater near our hole. It had uprooted some stumps and had filled the small road a few yards from our dugout with dirt and debris. This one had almost gotten us. From the edge of our dugout to the edge of the crater was only about five yards. No wonder we were shaken up so much.

There was another odd thing about it that was fortunate for us. The rest of these big shells, nine to be exact, that had landed in our area were all delayed fuses except this one. Had this shell been a delayed fuse it would have gone far enough underground to explode right in our dugout as it was heading in the right direction. Even a quick fuse like this one would have gotten us if it had been five yards further. A roof wouldn't have made any difference with this size shell. Lady Luck was still grinning. One British dugout had received a direct hit. What a mess. One of the Service Battery trucks was ruined from one of the shells. There was a big dud nearby. They were big shells alright. Nice and shiny. You could see the hole where it had gone into the ground and had ripped out without exploding. It was just lying there on the ground. Some engineers came and took the thing away. I sure would have hated to have the job of fooling around with some damned dud like that.

The German aircraft were plenty active here. As time on the beachhead wore on their day raids became less but they stepped up their night raids. I guess they were losing too many planes to our anti-aircraft during the day.

One of the last daylight raids was a pretty big one though. In fact, the most enemy planes I had seen them use. There were somewhere between fifty to fifty-five planes. I understand about a hundred of them had taken off from airports around Rome but part of them had been intercepted and engaged by our own planes.

These fifty some odd planes that did get through came zooming out of the sky late one afternoon. About half of them were going to the harbor. The sky was black from our anti-aircraft fire. It didn't seem possible that any of the planes could get through it. The planes seemed to start dropping their bombs any place. They wanted to get the hell out of the flak. I guess it didn't make much difference where the bombs were dropped. A bomb dropped on this crowded beachhead had an excellent chance of hitting something. When some of the planes came scooting our way dropping bombs we hit our dugouts. Some bombs were dropped on a nearby ammunition dump.

It seemed impossible that any of the planes could get through that intense flak. We only saw three planes actually go down. I would bet my bottom dollar that a good many of the planes never got back to their bases. Even if a plane was badly hit or even if the pilot was dead it would be possible for the plane to travel a good many miles farther at the speed they were traveling. They could easily get clear out of sight before they went down. In fact, infantry outfits would report planes going down that we probably had not been able to see. Also, when I say we saw only three planes go down I'm not sure that is even correct. We noticed a large puff of smoke among the German planes. These puffs of smoke were much larger bursts than any of the anti-aircraft bursts. It was possible that these large bursts were German planes receiving hits and exploding. If this was so, they must have had their bombs explode on them and they were completely disintegrated in mid-air. We never seemed to see any of the pieces of the plane coming down. We had seen those big puffs previously during air raids but were never able to determine what they were. Anyway, we knew they lost more than three planes out of the fifty or more or they would have never discontinued the daylight bombing.

The ammunition dump a few hundred yards away that had been hit was burning fiercely. We could hear the shells crackling and popping as they burned. Suddenly there was a huge blinding red flash and a terrifying explosion. The wind from the concussion nearly blew the helmets from our heads. We all dove back into our dugouts. It was good that we had too. The whole area was showered with pieces of flying shell fragments. We could hear big pieces dropping around outside. We found hundreds of pieces of shell lying around, twisted from the heat. From the size of some of the pieces, some of the shells must have been 240's. The big blast had also killed a bunch of engineers working on a road nearby the ammo dump.

Shortly after the air raid the Germans threw in a snappy artillery barrage. I was almost caught flat footed. Everyone tumbled into the nearest dugout. I happened to land into Brocket's. Several 88's landed right into our area. One rooted up a stump right outside Brocket's hole. Another had missed my dugout by a foot. Marshall was alone in it and when I got over there his ears were still ringing.

As the days passed the German artillery seemed to be getting heavier and heavier. They were apparently going to throw in so much stuff that they would keep things on the beachhead in constant turmoil. They could also keep killing men, destroying supplies and keep things too disorganized for us to launch an attack to get out of here.

This beachhead was like being on an artillery range. Our foot hold here was only a few square miles. The depth of the beachhead was so shallow that the Germans could shell the whole beachhead, clear to the harbor with all of their artillery. We often wondered if they brought artillery recruits down here to give them some practice firing at live targets.

Things got so bad that everyone made it a point to be underground at dark. That's when the fireworks really started although it wasn't exactly dead during the day. It was just the opposite with the infantry. They had to lay low during the day and might be able to move a little at night.

The whole beachhead was shelled at night with the rear areas being shelled very heavily. Those blasted planes would come over every night too. We had many, many sleepless hours. During the raid you would lay there wide awake sweating it out. As soon as an air-raid was over or the shelling stopped, a wonderful feeling came over you and you would drop right off to sleep. It wasn't the hours of sleep you missed that made you drop off to sleep it was the mental relief you got.

The fellows here on the beachhead began to make little radio sets in their spare time. They were weird affairs and you would never have believed they would work if you hadn't seen it. They were made out of some copper wire, a piece of round stick or beer bottle or anything round, some old razor blades, an aerial and a pair of earphones.

Grady Howell and I made one. We were lucky to get a pair of earphones and some wire from the radio truck. We got a piece of board about a foot square to build the set on. We took the copper wire and wrapped it around a beer bottle to make the coil. We nailed a few old rusty razor blades in a cluster on the board to act as crystals. We then hooked up the aerial and a ground. We began moving the feeler wire around the razor blades and much to our amazement we were able to pick up a station or two.

Another thing about the sets that also amazed us was that we could sometimes communicate between dugouts. It wasn't from the connections or anything we had, but rather the sound coming through the ground someway. I never did figure out how by shouting into your earphones you could sometimes talk to someone in another dugout a couple of hundred yards away. This would happen on rare occasions though. Sometimes we could pick up the switchboard and hear phone conversations. This seldom happened. The set that Grady and I built was a dandy. We could always get one station really well and sometimes another pretty well. This one station came in so well that sometimes we could hang the earphones on the roof of the dugout and listen at the same time. Most of the time though we had to take turns with the earphones.

About the only thing that was consistently good over the set were the German propaganda programs. It was interesting though and we enjoyed it. The Germans called it Jerry Front Calling. Axis Sally became very familiar to all of us.

About six o'clock in the afternoon Axis Sally had a program for the British. They always started the program off by playing the famous English marching song Lily Marlene.

Some of the German propaganda was pretty clever. It never made any impression on anyone that I knew of, but it was pretty clever just the same. When we first got to the beachhead one bunch of propaganda showed old King Neptune sitting on his throne. Fish were swimming around wearing American helmets. Under the drawing were words that went something like this, "You've been in Italy so long now, of course your Nettuno was named after King Neptune. He has already claimed many of your boats and equipment and is now anxiously awaiting your nice uniforms which he will get when we drive you back into the sea."

Other propaganda pamphlets we got had a series of cartoon type short stories on them. One was a story about Betty and Bob. It showed Bob leaving for overseas and Betty telling him how true she would be. Next we see Bob in a fox hole being shot at. Then it shows Betty back home with a big, fat, hooked nosed Jew. He is making love to her and telling her of all the things he will buy for her. Of course he has gotten rich on money from graft and war contracts. Betty finally gives in and the last picture shows her in bed and the fat Jew taking off his pants getting ready to get in to her.

Another little ditty they showered on the British was one showing a scene in England. It showed some American Staff Sgt. spending his big pay on some English gal and making a big impression on her. It finally shows the gal in bed and the Sgt. with his pants off ready to join her. Under the drawing it said. "This is what your American ally is doing with your women while you are away fighting."

All in all I thought the German propaganda was pretty good. It was better than ours. We shot over menus for instance, telling them what they would get to eat if they surrendered. That might have been good propaganda in World War I but not so hot in this one. The German front line troops were eating just as well as us if not better. Some of our propaganda seemed to be pretty good. One I figured might be a little convincing was the one about them fighting for a madman-Hitler. Quit following him while there is still a chance and before Germany was completely destroyed. Another one that surely must have hit home was the one telling them they were losing on all sides and their cause was hopeless. We even shot tickets over to them. The ticket would admit the bearer safely through our lines. I thought that one was corny but I knew that at least one incidence it had worked. Some Germans approached our boys with the tickets. Not only that but they said there were a bunch more holed up somewhere who didn't have tickets and they wondered if it was alright for them to come anyway. They must have been sick of the whole thing.

A good part of Sally's stuff was naturally directed at the beachhead forces. She mentioned the different outfits that were on the beachhead. She told of locations like one of the outfits that was in the pines. She was usually right too. Of the 45th she said, "There is one of the 45th Division that is dead, another wounded and another prisoner." That wasn't too far wrong either.

The morale of the soldiers didn't seem to be affected by the propaganda. We enjoyed listening to Sally's programs for the music and the Crosby records. Of course, the propaganda was part of warfare and we accepted it strictly as such. Very few, if any, G.I.s paid any attention to the political end of this war. For instance, the reports of the casualties were pretty close. Over all the propaganda failed to have any adverse effect. I doubt if our propaganda had too much effect on the Germans either.

Things on the beachhead went on about the same day after day. The same old shelling and air raids. It was nerve wracking and several of the fellows began to get "nervous in the service". It was very hard on a person mentally to be in a place where they knew shells could come in any second of the day or night. Bombs and shells landing close to you doesn't do any good either. When you see what can happen to other people it starts you thinking that you may be next.

It seems almost everyone in battle zones figures by the law of averages. They figure if you keep going on you are going to get it sooner or later with no way out. After a fellow has gone on quite a while he begins to feel more and more that his number is surely up.

There were many theories about figuring when a man's time is up. If a fellow was killed by a stray piece of shell fragment or under some rather usual circumstances guys would shrug and say, "Well, his time was just up". If a guy went through hell and maybe was the only one of his group to come back then they would say, "Well, it wasn't his time to go". Some were convinced that if your number was up you would get it even if you were on the moon. Some believed, like the old belief of World War I, that there was a shell or a bullet with your name on it. I never did quite figure that one out. Most though, including myself, believed that if you were in the right place at the right time you would get it. I felt it was just a matter of luck. No amount of skill or brains could help you where bombs or shells were concerned. When artillery shells are lobbed in from several miles away and all over the landscape or bombs dropped at random you are either where they hit or you're not. There were a few who believed your chances depended on how good of a Christian you were as to whether you lived or died.

Most fellows had some little thing they did more or less for good luck. Subconsciously I really had a couple.

One way, probably brought on by movies I had seen or stories I had read, was about to never be the third man on a match. A great many had that little superstition though. Another one was strictly my own. I always ended my letters with, "Bye for now". Silly of course, but I ended the hundreds of letters I wrote that way.

It did seem that some fellows had better luck than others. For instance, back on the other front in the cemetery position, I had moved from my tent into the tomb just two days before my tent, which was still up, was completely shredded by shrapnel. In that same area a 189th fellow had just come back from Naples after a short rest and had just crawled into his hole when a piece of shell ripped into his heart killing him. Just one of those things. If you were in the right place at the wrong time it could be rough.

Here on the beachhead towards the end of April, I guess our high command decided to do something about the German observations. Smoke machines were set up around at different points on the beachhead. They really poured out a lot of whitish smoke. From then on a lot of the beachhead was always under a haze. It seemed as though it was almost too late for anything like this. By now the Germans knew where everything was and they didn't need to see where they were firing. It would help though because troops and vehicles could be moved more easily without being as easily detected. The Germans must have had good observation here. They even seemed to fire at a single vehicle.

One time Kitchens and I were driving up to our other position in a weapons carrier. As we were moving slowly through some swampy ground, a couple of high bursts popped in over our heads. Kitchens really crammed down on the gas. We were lucky in our haste that we didn't go off the narrow trail and bury us in the mud. We were lucky to be able to get on up the road quickly because a snappy barrage was laid on the road where we had been only seconds before. We wondered if they had been trying for us or had just happened to shell that particular section of road when we had happened to be there.

It was becoming more dangerous traveling on the roads at night. Although they couldn't see us they shelled the roads heavily at night. They knew that the vehicle movement was under the cover of night. You never knew what stretch of road they might shell or when.

I used to do quite a bit of traveling around with some of the boys taking things up to the other position and different places. I got tired of sticking so close around our little area so much. I had offered to go to the C.P. and work on the radio. The guys that were there didn't want to change because they weren't shelled in that position as much as ours. They had rather do double time than to change places.

One day I went with Regan on some strictly unofficial business. Regan liked his beer and didn't care how he got it. The British had the beer and they liked our "C" or "E" rations so there was only one way for him to get the beer. He had guts enough to drive into a ration dump, load on a bunch of cases of "C" rations and drive off. If he had been caught swiping them he would have spent the rest of his life in the stockade. Now that he had the stuff he wanted to peddle it to the British for beer. The price of beer had gone up considerably from what it had been when we first got on the beachhead. At first you could get a quart of beer for one or two cans of "C" rations or a "D" bar. Now too many supply drivers in route to the different outfits had done a little trading on the side. Having plenty of "C" rations and afraid of being caught, they didn't take time to do any bargaining. They would just pitch out a few cases of "C" rations for a few bottles of beer. So now it was hard to get any beer without plenty of "C" rations. Regan and I went around doing a little trading. He only managed to come up with three or four quarts of beer. On the way back to our area we had to hold up for a while. The road ahead of us was being shelled heavily.

> *A container of C Rations consisted of a chocolate bar, toilet paper, powdered fruit juice, four packs of cigarettes, chewing gum, biscuits, graham crackers, sugar tablets, can of ham, can of chicken, sausages, fruit bar, caramel, bouillon cubes, lemon powder, wooden spoon, matches. A container of K rations consisted of breakfast: a can of ham and eggs, biscuits, sugar tablets, dried fruit bar, pre-made oatmeal, water purification tablets, chewing gum, instant coffee, and sugar. For lunch: canned pork meat, American cheese, bacon, biscuits, malted milk tablets, five caramels, sugar, salt, four packs of cigarettes, gum, powdered fruit juice, canned meat with carrots or apples, biscuits.*

Night travel was becoming more ticklish all the time. One night Brockett and I took some stuff up where they were digging some new positions along the Mussolini Canal. It was quite a long trip, at least for this small beachhead. There was always the danger of colliding with another vehicle driving blackout. This particular night was pitch black too. We went through a little village called Campomorte or Camp of Death. We found the place that we were to turn off the road and make our way over to the canal. The ground in front of the canal was heavily mined. There were two small strips of white ribbon marking the path cleared of mines. I got out of the truck and went ahead to make sure Brockett didn't get off in the mines.

We finally got our sandbags and other stuff unloaded and headed back. From back on the road we could see a fire fight going on between one of our machines guns and German machine guns. Red tracers and the German white ones seemed to be flying at each other by the thousands. German artillery was becoming very active. One shell crashed in near us as we sped down the road. It flared up an angry red. Brockett really tore down the road and I was almost as afraid of cracking up as I was of the shelling. As we neared our area we had to stop and pull off the road. The Germans were shelling the ammunition dump near our position. A couple of fires had been set in it and they were burning brightly. When the shelling stopped we scooted on in and made it to our respective dugouts pretty fast.

The outfit had lost men and equipment on the roads. Two men were killed, and their jeep destroyed by shelling. They had been running wire during daylight hours. There had been some other bad breaks and some collisions too.

Liquor was pretty hard to get here on the beachhead. There wasn't any to be had except for the few bottles of beer we could get from the British. I believe the British ration was two bottles a week. Even if they had traded it all to the G.I.'s it wouldn't have amounted to much. The Americans outnumbered the British here considerably. Lately it had been impossible to get any anyway, it was going to the guys who had excess TP (toilet paper) in the most rations.

A couple of the boys had gotten a five gallon gasoline can full of some kind of alcohol. They called it medic alcohol but I suspected that somewhere on the beachhead some enterprising G.I. had a still going. The stuff was clear like water and was 190 proof. They took this stuff and put it in British beer bottles and sold it for ten bucks a copy. They sold everything they had too. I invested in a couple of bottles of the stuff myself.

The "medic alcohol" was really potent stuff. It didn't take much to get you loaded. We would take the stuff, put a small amount in a canteen cup and cut it with grapefruit juice and water. Even then it was pretty hard to get down. For a couple or three nights while the stuff lasted we would sit around, drink the stuff and talk. The last night that there was any left I drank too much and got sick. That night when the shells came in I was so sick I was hoping our dugout got a direct hit. That was the only time there seemed to be any of that stuff available which was just as well.

Eventually we were sent a little beer up from Naples. It was brewed there by G.I. brew masters. It was real crap, green and hard to drink. It cost fifteen cents a canteen cup full and we were limited to one cup full. That was plenty of that stuff. The "medic alcohol" was better.

On May 5th I was notified that I had been transferred to "C" Battery. I knew that meant I was to be a permanent radio operator on a F.O. (Forward Observer) party. I didn't mind much. In fact, I was glad. This sweating it out on the beachhead without much to do was getting old. I hadn't even operated a radio in about a month. As long as a person was here and in danger anyway, he felt like he ought to be doing all he could. Those bastards at the C.P. wouldn't let us rotate with them. Even though they worked many extra hours on the radio they wanted to stay just where they were. Things weren't quite so hot in their particular position either.

I was sort of glad to get out of Headquarters Battery anyway. There were a bunch of suck asses that were always hanging around the officers and waiting on them hand and foot. I was glad to get away from all that brass too. Although most of them were O.K., it was just the idea of them being around.

There were fellows that I was going to miss too. All of the fire direction gang and radio bunch were swell guys. Grady Marshall, Ray Gill, Marty Martinovich, Art Lacrosse and A.P Curtis. Other guys I would miss were Burbach, Charlie Joyce and a Jewish kid named Saul Goldberg. This Goldberg kid had come to our outfit as a replacement after we had come to the beachhead. When I first met him he had made some wise remark to me that had made me sore. I hated the kid at first and rode him badly. I called him all kinds of uncomplimentary things, among them, lousy Jew. He could sure take it though. He seemed to like me and he finally won me over and I actually liked the guy. He seemed like a big dumb Jew from the Bronx. He was just a kid though, only nineteen. He used to read me letters from his girl. It was all I could do to keep from laughing. She would tell him she was going to send his tennis racket, bathing suit and dark glasses now that he was in a resort area. She wasn't kidding either. When Goldberg found out I was going to be transferred he wanted to go with me. He even went to the Captain and asked to be transferred with me. What a character. Another fellow I was going to miss was John Smith. We had come into the outfit together. We hadn't seen too much of each other. He was the radio operator on Captain Hayes' L.O. (Look Out) party and was gone quite a while. We did get together often though and had long talks.

Although I had transferred to another battery I didn't have to move. "C" Battery was also leaving part of their men in this area for the same reason and Headquarters was still here.

I soon became acquainted with several of the "C" Battery boys. There were Corporal Dull, the Battery clerk. Sgt. Shoemaker, who was his own forward observer party. Sgt. Wilhelm, also had his own F.O. party. Then there was Porter Roth, the supply corporal. Others I got acquainted with the first day or two were Green, Hines and Queen.

Very shortly after I transferred I felt a difference in the atmosphere and the attitude of the men. The "C" Battery men were more of buddies to one another. There weren't the little cliques like in the H.Q. Battery with a few being the fair haired boys. From the very first day I was glad that I had been transferred. Everyone was friendly and I felt at home right from the start.

In a firing battery there wasn't too much brass either. There was a Captain, the Battery Commander, one First Lieutenant as Battery Executive and then two or three Second Lieutenants. There weren't all the Captains, Major and Colonels that were hanging around H.Q. Battery. There, even a low ranked general was liable to blow in. They didn't bother me so much but you had to be a little bit more on guard.

Incidentally, one of those Generals that blew into Headquarters C.P. occasionally was nearly my undoing. When we had moved from the thicket, things had gotten fouled up. At first, I was supposed to go to the new H.Q. position, but at the last second I was sent to our present position with part of the battery. Thinking I was going to the other position I had loaded some of my surplus stuff, including my .03 rifle, on a truck going that way.

The driver had naturally pitched my stuff on the ground at the new position expecting it to be claimed right away. It was raining the day we moved and I never got a chance to go up to the new position for some time. Consequently, my stuff laid out in the rain and mud for some time.

The General of the 45th Division happened to visit the 158th, F. A. (Field Artillery) H.Q., C.P. one day. Of course, he spied my rifle right away. He picked it up and couldn't even get the bolt open. He was in a rage and took the gun to Col. Funk and told him to find the man who owned it and have him court martialed.

Many of the boys and probably some of the officers knew whose gun it was but they were all real buddies and no one squealed. The Supply Sgt. had all the serial numbers of the guns that had been issued by the battery. Fortunately, I had gotten my rifle in North Africa so they had no record of it. They even had each outfit have an inspection. The brass thought it was odd that I was almost the only one in the battalion that had a carbine but they let it go. I breathed easier after a couple of days and the whole thing was forgotten. I don't know what they would have done with me if they found out that it was my rifle. Probably shot at sunrise or something. It really wasn't my fault about the gun but I suppose I should have turned it in months before. The only reason I hadn't was because I figured some officer would pull his rank on me and take the carbine. Lots of them preferred them to a side arm and there were very few carbines available at this point in the war.

Soon after being transferred to "C" Battery I found out that I had been assigned to Lt. Liggett's F.O. Party. The next night Lt. Liggett sent word around that he wanted to see all the members of his party in his dugout at seven o'clock. I just naturally figured that we were going to go forward.

At seven o'clock we all gathered at the dugout that Lt. Liggett and Lt. Olson shared. They had a little sign by the entrance with "Flak Shack" printed on it. Lt. Olsen was up forward right now. Both Lt. Liggett and Lt. Olsen were new to the outfit, joining it here in Anzio. Lt. Liggett had only been up forward once or twice, both times with different and make shift parties. We were going to make up a permanent party for him. This little get together turned out to be a sort of get acquainted meeting.

I hadn't seen any of the fellows before that were to make up the party, including Lt. Liggett. As soon as we all arrived introductions were made all around. First there was Lt. Liggett. He was a graduate from the University of Nebraska. His home was Denman, Nebraska, a very small town, a few miles from Lincoln. He was fairly tall and slender and a rather good looking fellow. He was about my age, twenty-four.

Then there was Sgt. Smith. He was quite a big fellow. He was considerably older that the rest of us. He was thirty-eight but actually looked quite a bit younger. His home was Philadelphia, Pennsylvania. He had been connected with the jewelry business for many years and just before he was drafted he had opened his own store with a partner. He had come over from the States with the 45th.

Next there was Rupert Rodriquez. He originally had been from Puerto Rico, but was now living in New York City. He claimed to be Spanish but he must have surely had mostly Negro blood in him. He was black, blacker than many Negroes. He had the Negro features, kinky hair etc. He had gotten into a white man's outfit someway though. He wasn't a bad looking fellow. He was just my age and had five or six kids already. In New York he worked as an interpreter for a law firm that had a large Spanish speaking clientele. Naturally, being born, raised and educated in Puerto Rico, he could speak Spanish fluently.

Harris was to be the driver for the party. As long as we were together I don't believe I ever heard his first name. He was always just Harris. He was the youngest of our group, twenty. His home was in Washington, North Carolina. Harris hadn't done much before coming into the army besides going to school. In my estimation he turned out to be the best driver in the outfit, or maybe the whole battalion. Then there was me, to make up the rest of the party.

We were quite a mixture. We were of all national origins and from all parts of the States. Smith and Rodriquez were Catholic and the rest of us were supposed to be Protestant.

After all the introductions were made Liggett said he hadn't heard anything about us going forward but had only wanted us to get together and get acquainted. Liggett got out a bottle of gin and we passed it around. The officers were just now beginning to get a liquor ration. The gin was Italian stuff and pretty rough. All we had for a chaser was water and it was about all we could do to get the stuff down. When our little get together was over we had to hole up in Liggett's dugout for a while before returning to our respective dugouts. The Germans were throwing them in again.

The first few days of May dragged by. We knew that soon we were going to start a big push. Ammunition and supply dumps were getting larger and larger. Many new dumps were being made. There were millions of rounds of small arms ammunitions. There were thousands upon thousands of artillery shells of all sizes. There was just a tension in the air that made us feel that something big was up.

The Germans seemed to know it too. Their artillery barrages increased, and their air force stepped up their nightly bombings. They shelled our supply dumps day and night. They destroyed thousands of shells and lots of our supplies. We were bringing in stuff faster than they could destroy it though.

The beachhead was really showing signs of wear and tear. The whole beachhead was pitted with bomb craters and shell holes. The holes were so close together that there were only a few feet between them. No part of the beachhead had escaped. In and around our new position it was dotted with hundreds of holes of all sizes. The "Pines", where a lot of our army stayed a good deal of the time, had received constant shelling. The twin towns of Anzio and Nettuno had been battered down to rubble. Even our cemetery had been shelled and several female nurses had been killed. The small landing field for the observation cubs had been hit. Nothing, nowhere had escaped. We had heard about the English "Block Buster" bomb. The Germans must have had a few too. I could hardly believe the first crater that was made. It was so wide and so deep I figured it surely must have been dug that way with a steam shovel. It had been dug alright, with a huge bomb. I saw where another had hit beside a road lined with trees. It had made a huge crater and had completely uprooted two huge trees right out of the ground.

Toward the middle of May we received news which we had been waiting and hoping for. Our force on the Casino Front had launched an all-out drive. We were hoping it would be a lot more successful than the one during the winter that had been stopped in its tracks. We knew that whether their attack was successful or not it would only be a matter of days before we made a big push to break out of the beachhead.

For days now we had noted considerable truck and equipment movement. Supplies and ammunition were being moved as close to the front as possible for the jump off. Our own outfit was having new positions dug along the big Mussolini Canal. A large, well-constructed dugout was being prepared for the Headquarters C.P. as well as smaller ones for the firing batteries C.P.s. All of the digging was done under the cover of darkness.

We noticed many, many tanks and tank destroyers clogging the road at night as we moved up and back from the canal. We watched the news of the progress of the fighting to the south anxiously. Things seemed to be going well. Casino had fallen and the drive northward seemed to be going along nicely.

Finally, we learned that the big day was to be May 23rd. Liggett's F.O. party drew the assignment to be with the assault infantry. We had pretty much expected it as we had been passed over when it had actually been our time to go forward before. They were saving us for the rough deal.

At dusk on the evening of May 22nd our party gathered up our stuff and prepared to go forward. We climbed on the jeep and went up to Headquarters for last-minute instructions. The 3rd Battalion of the 157th Infantry was to be the assault outfit. While Liggett talked to the Colonel I went down to the radio section and picked up the radio call signs and the code.

At about nine o'clock we climbed back onto the jeep and headed up forward. We stopped for a while at the 157th Battalion Headquarters for more instructions. We moved up towards "K" Company's Position. This was the company we were going to attack with. We talked to some of the infantry boys. They were talking it up among themselves, sort of like before a big football game. They said they were going to do their best. We kept telling everyone we would give them all the artillery support that was humanly possible. Some of them were pretty gloomy and said, "Yeah, we're all going to be in mattress cover cases."

We finally reached "K" Company. Harris dumped us off, turned around and headed back. We got final instructions from the "K" Company C.O. What the hell could he say though? This was it. At 6:30 in the morning we would go "over the top".

We began to look for a place to bed down. Mortars were crashing in nearby and an occasional shell screamed in and exploded close. A fire was burning brightly out in front. Machine guns were exchanging fire and clattered madly. The party was all split up but we all found holes to climb into. I climbed into a dugout with a couple of infantry boys. They were machine gunners and had been here only a week.

I had just started to doze off when orders came down the line to get ready to move out. We loaded our stuff on our backs and the F.O.'s (Forward Observers) got together.

We moved off to the right about three hundred yards and stopped again. We just sat there for about three hours. I didn't have any idea what time it was. I did know it was plenty cold and the dew was settling on the grass making it miserable to lie on. We were traveling light for the attack so we didn't have blankets to keep us warm. Things were quiet, strangely quiet. Only an occasional flare was shot up by the Germans.

We finally started to move again. This time we moved

to our left angling towards the German Lines. We were moving across flat, grassy, open fields. Everyone was moving as quietly as possible. It was amazing how quietly more than two hundred men could move when they had to. No one even as much as whispered. One of the connections on the radio was clinking on the set as I walked. I didn't like it but couldn't reach back without taking the damned thing clear off of my back. An infantry boy came up and tucked it in without a word.

When the Germans would shoot up a flare we would all freeze and turn our faces away and towards the ground. We went through this process several times. Things still seemed oddly quiet. Just the flares and an occasional zing of a rifle bullet or an occasional shell sailing over heading way back. The lull before the storm I thought to myself.

Soon we began walking along the slope of a big canal. The steepness of the slope and the wet slippery grass made the going tough. The radio I was carrying was heavy and dead weight.

I kept slipping down and sliding almost to the bottom of the canal. I would scramble up and try to get going again only to slip down again. I had my clothes torn and my hands and knees were bleeding from being torn on berry briars and barbed wire. Rod was having the same trouble. He was carrying the battery pack that was also pretty heavy. I could hear him falling and cursing and groaning softly. Smith and Liggett were traveling light and were soon up the line way ahead of us. I got thoroughly pooped and things began to become dark. When I thought I couldn't walk another step we arrived at our destination.

It was now 3 A.M. We had three and a half hours before "H" hour. Everyone sat there quietly waiting, not even whispering to one another. I guess everyone was too deep in their own thoughts.

We knew that this was to be one of the biggest days in our lives. We had been cooped up on this tiny beachhead for four months and knew it would be an all-out effort to break out. It was going to be tough. Probably tougher than any of us realized.

We knew that the Germans, as well as ourselves, had every inch of the beachhead zeroed in. They had every canal, road, by pass, field, ravine, ditch, tree and every possible attack route well zeroed in. We knew the moment we jumped off we would be right out in the open. As soon as the Germans knew that a major attack was under way they would start throwing in all their defensive fires. Yes, it was going to be rough. The German infantry was well dug in. They had every advantage with us having to come out on the flat, open fields towards them. They had a series of trenches dug along the tops of many knolls. They had many well-hidden machine gun emplacements. They also had the beachhead ringed with plenty of armor and artillery.

Everyone just sat through the lone black hours of early morning. Everyone was thinking of home and loved ones. Some were probably saying prayers. For we all knew many of us were living their last hours.

Dawn began to break slowly in the east. We were momentarily expecting our artillery barrage. All night things had been pretty quiet on both sides. A few shells sailed over now and then went both ways. The Germans had shot up a lot of flares during the night like they were nervous.

Our artillery preparation was to be quite a show. Hundreds of guns from 37mm up to the big navel guns of ships lying off shore were to be fired. It was all prearranged fire. It was to last for thirty minutes and then there was to be a rolling barrage to be kept in front of the advancing infantry.

At 6:00 A.M., May 23rd, 1944, a gigantic roar broke loose. The barrage was on. It was too horrible and awful to even try to describe. One would have had to be there even to comprehend the meaning of it. Hundreds of guns were firing at full blast and thousands of shells screamed overhead and crashed out in front of us. So many were crashing down that it sounded, to me, like slat backs thousands of feet high crashing down in a gigantic avalanche. The whole battlefield ahead of us was churned up into a mass of smoke, dust and flying debris. A pale or whitish smoke hung over everything.

It was absolutely terrifying. The terrible din made your blood run cold. There had probably never been an artillery barrage like it. Thousands of artillery pieces consolidated in such a small area. The big barrages of World War I were supposed to be something. Lots of times they were strung out for miles.

Everyone was wide awake and alert now. We tried to laugh and joke to ease the tension. You would try to light up a cigarette and your hand would shake so much you could hardly hold your hand steady. Some were trying to eat their "K" rations without much luck. I took a mouthful of "K" ration meat but couldn't realize any taste. After one bite I threw the rest away. I just wasn't hungry.

Somehow I kept thinking of movies of the last war where the men were waiting to go over the top. I wished that this was a movie instead of the real thing. I wished some of the people from back home could be here for just fifteen seconds. I would have liked for them to hear the artillery and see the looks on the men's faces. I thought to myself, "If I ever happen to get back to the States and someone told me how patriotic they had been by buying bonds as a nice safe investment, I was going to hit them". If they could have been with us just a few seconds and know they had to go on this attack they would have gladly given ninety percent of their earnings for the rest of their life to get out of it.

The Zero Hour was almost here and everyone was watching their watches closely. Everyone was scared stiff too. Some trembled all over, others' teeth chattered, others stood around with their eyes closed. One guy was trying to take a leak and the stream was a violent zig-zag. I was scared. I just felt numb.

The first wave was getting ready to go. The company commander told Liggett and Smith to go with them. They were to take a phone and combat wire and would send back to me the lifts for the rolling barrage and I would radio it back to fire direction. The idea was to keep the artillery just a hundred yards ahead of the advancing infantry. When the end of one hundred yards was reached they would notify me to have the artillery fire moved up another hundred yards. Rod and I were to follow up with the third wave. At first Rod and I thought that might be a break for us but we were soon to find out that the third wave was to have it the roughest.

The fellows of the first wave grabbed their rifles, tommy guns, B.A.R.'s (Browning Automatic Rifles) or whatever weapon they were carrying and climbed to the top of the canal. They were a worried, scared bunch with faces drawn and they looked old. They looked determined though. Some of them were as white as a sheet. Their first objective was the cemetery about five hundred yards away.

This was it. The C.O., a Captain, was checking his watch. The Catholic boys were crossing themselves. The

Captain jumped up to the top of the canal. He simply said, "Let's go" and led his men out of the canal. Not one of the fellows hesitated or hung back. I knew that they were all scared to death. It took plenty of intestinal fortitude to go out into that unknown hell. It made me really proud of the boys. Maybe the Americans weren't too bad as soldiers.

Just as our bunch leaped out of the canal I could hear a bugle further down the line playing "Charge". It was probably some British or Scottish outfit. They went in for that sort of thing more than we did. I'll bet all of the British boys had a good stiff snort or two before they jumped off. I wished our army did that. It was brutal to send a man into a mess like this cold sober.

The first wave seemed to be making pretty good progress. Not too much resistance yet. There was only scattered rifle and machine gun fire. The Germans were still stunned from the terrific artillery pounding they had taken.

The first wave kept sending me the fire lifts and I relayed them on to fire direction. Finally, the first wave reported back that they were at their first objective, the cemetery. The second wave got ready to go.

The wounded were now coming back from the first wave. The ones that were able to move on their own power were coming back. There weren't stretcher bearers up there yet to bring back the more seriously wounded. The abler of our wounded were bringing back a few prisoners. One kid I had been talking to, shortly before the attack, came back. He had been hit in the leg and had a nasty flesh wound but nothing really serious. He was actually grinning from ear to ear. He said to me, "I didn't last long did I?" I guess he was so happy it hadn't been worse. He also had what is called a "million dollar" wound. It's not serious enough that you will die or be crippled for life but it's one that will keep you away from the front, possibly for months. Another kid flopped down beside me. He was just a kid too, only eighteen or nineteen. He had big creases across his hand. It was hardly more than a scratch but he was as white as a sheet and he sat there with his head in his hands. He seemed so badly shaken by the whole ordeal.

Suddenly, the second wave was ready. They went up and over the top and on their way. The second wave had only been gone a few minutes when a change came over the situation.

The Germans had apparently recovered from the shock of our terrific barrage. They began to fight back hard. They began to throw in plenty of stuff. They began to shell heavily all along the canal in our sector. From the terrific scream of the shells you knew that they were 88's. Shells were landing on both sides as well as in the canal. We were really bracketed. Shrapnel was whining and singing and ripping into the ground all around. Everyone was hugging the ground. Rod and I were lying flat beside each other. Rod was just lying there with his eyes closed. I wondered what he was thinking. The way the fragments were ripping into the ground all around I expected a piece of it to rip into me any second. Two men just behind us were hit at the same time. I was lying so that I could look down the canal. I saw a couple of shells hit the bottom of the canal not far away. Mud and water went up like a geyser. Boy, was I scared.

The Sgt. in charge of the third wave told everyone to get ready to move. I took the radio down and Rod and I struggled into our pack boards. We didn't need the radio because all of our artillery fire had been lifted to beyond the railroad tracks. By the way shells were screaming in

I didn't think we would last two seconds once we were out of the canal and in the open.

It was time to go and out of the canal we went. Lady Luck was laughing hysterically again. Just as we climbed out of the canal the German artillery, at that very instance, shifted down the canal a ways. What luck!

We plodded on toward the cemetery in a crouched position. Rain began to pour down. It's funny about rain and war. It was supposed to be a fine, cloudless day and now it was raining.

All went well until we were about half way to the cemetery. Shells then suddenly began to go in on us. They were our own shells. It was easy to tell, not only from the direction they came, but the swishing sound our 105 shells made. Everyone hit the ground. Some of the boys looked our way astonished and dismayed almost as if it was our fault. Something had gone wrong and they were catching us in our own barrage. I crawled over to Rod and slipped out of my pack board. We didn't take time for Rod to get out of his. He just lay on his stomach so I could hook up the set to the battery pack. My hands were trembling so much I could hardly get the set hooked up. In my haste I forgot to put up the aerial. Fortunately though, I was able to contact our L.O. (Look Out) who relayed the information back to fire direction. Soon our shells stopped and we continued on toward the cemetery.

There was plenty of grief at the cemetery. The cemetery and the fields around it were heavily mined. Several men, including two of the Company officers, had already stepped on them and were out of action. We moved cautiously into the cemetery. We had our eyes glued to the ground trying to pick our way and trying to detect any tell-tale signs that might tell us where any mines were. Most of the mines that were giving the trouble were the large box type ones made of wood. With only the detonator being made of metal it made it hard for mine detectors to pick them up. Of course, there was no one with mine detectors with us anyway.

The medics were trying to get the wounded off the mines. They were having a rough time. Several medics had set off mines and were hurt. The mines had large charges of powder in them but being made of wood had no fragments. They were actually Italian built mines. When a man stepped on them they were blown into the air several feet.

A few prisoners were brought into the cemetery. A couple of them were taken out to try to get the wounded off the mines. They also set off mines and were blown up. Finally, a medic came into the cemetery and said it was impossible to try to get the men off of the mines until they got someone to remove the mines. There was no telling how long it would be before there would be any engineers up here to clear the minefield.

One young German prisoner was brought into the cemetery. He was a kid, not more than eighteen or nineteen. He wore thick rimmed glasses and looked more like a book worm than a soldier. He had a camouflaged suit on and even had a twig of leaves stuck in a band around his helmet. The boys stripped him of his stuff and threw it in a pile. The kid was well healed for smoking material. He had about five packs of cigarettes, a couple of cigars, pipe and two cans of tobacco. As they were about to take him away he asked for his billfold back that had his mother's picture in it. One of the wounded officers lying there in the cemetery told them to let him have it.

Those poor devils outside the wall of the cemetery were moaning and calling for help. There just didn't seem to be anything that could be done for them right now. It might be hours yet before the mines could be removed. A G.I. brought in a couple more prisoners. One of the wounded men on the mines was so mad and in such agony he grabbed his rifle and shot one of the prisoners. The other prisoner hit the ground but fast. The dead and wounded were piling up fast out there. From the cemetery we could look through a big shell hole and see everything that was going on.

The cemetery that we were in was rather small, probably no more than fifty yards square. The place had taken a terrific beating. Besides the many shell holes in the walls the one lone building in it had taken a battering. I wondered if the place was abandoned. Despite all the craters in the cemetery there didn't seem to be bones or pieces of caskets that would have been uprooted. Of course, six feet is pretty deep. Anyway the whole thing now was hardly more than a bunch of rubble.

The Germans began to throw in the shells again. They were no doubt aimed for the cemetery. They were 88's again with their horrible scream. One would hit just in front of the cemetery and we would be showered with rocks from the wall. The next one would just skim over and crash into the wall behind us, knocking a big hole in it. Then one would land to the left and one to the right. They really had this place bracketed in alright.

One medic was excited and kept yelling that we'd better get out of here. He screamed that the Germans had the cemetery zeroed in and would get us all. We knew he was right but there didn't seem much we could do about it. The shells kept crashing in. We lay there expecting to get it any second. I sort of felt sick to my stomach. I took out a cigar my wife had sent me and lit the damned thing. There was no use saving it any longer. This was the end. I never expected to get out of the cemetery alive.

I saw, in my estimation, the bravest man in the war. I never saw him after this day and never even knew his name. He probably never made it through. He was a Staff Sgt. He appeared absolutely fearless if there is such a thing. When our wave jumped out of the canal he had calmly led us over. He had been cool as a cucumber when we had been caught in our own barrage. Now, here in the midst of this terrific, shelling he was up on his knees calmly fooling with the damned field telephone. We couldn't believe our ears when he suddenly announced that the wire was out somewhere and he would have to go out and fix it. We didn't see how he could possibly live moving along in a semi-upright position. I'd have bet my last dollar that not another man in the cemetery would have just volunteered to do that himself like that. Probably any one of the rest of us would have done it if we had been ordered to go. This Sgt. though, on his own, took the combat wire in his hand and disappeared around the corner of the cemetery. I never expected to see him again. He was back a little later however with the wire repaired.

Suddenly the First Sgt. of the company told Rod and me to follow him. He was going to join the rest of the company a couple of hundred yards up ahead. Rod and I struggled into our pack boards. Before we could get going the First Sgt. disappeared out of the cemetery. The Sgt. who had just fixed the wire told us to hold up and go up with him.

The shells continued to scream in. It seemed as though they would never stop. Our uniforms were now getting pretty white from the powdered rock that sifted down on us from the wall.

Suddenly the fearless First Sgt. said, "Let's go". Rod and I were both dreading it because shells were crackling all around. We went creeping out of the cemetery. There, just around the corner, we found the First Sgt. with his guts blown out. He was already turning black. If Rod and I had gone with him no doubt we would have been lying there too. We moved slowly forward. The rain was pouring down again. The poor devils on the mines that were still alive were calling to us for help. It seemed bad to just pass them up and let them lay there.

We inched along slowly. The whole place was pitted with thousands of shell holes of all sizes. When shells started coming in we would dive into one of the larger holes and sweat it out. When we started moving forward again we would pass the large shell craters getting ready to jump into them. Rod began to fall farther and farther behind. He was reluctant to leave the safety of a large shell hole. The Sgt. and I got quite a way ahead of him. I could look back and sometimes just see a couple of white eyeballs peering out of a crater. I could see up ahead where the rest of our company was. I told the Sgt. to go on ahead and I would wait for Rod. My radio was useless if I didn't have the battery pack. Rod finally made it up to where I was and we pushed on toward the rest of the company. It wasn't that he was a coward that he had hung back, because he certainly wasn't. Just scared like the rest of us and maybe he didn't see any sense in being in a hurry.

By now we were getting up under the artillery. We could look back and see dust boiling up from the cemetery. They were giving it a pounding. I felt sorry for the wounded back there. Some of the shells were going on back to the canal where we had jumped off.

When we joined what was left of the company we found that Liggett and Smith had made it O.K. so far. In fact, they had had it easier than us. They hadn't received much artillery but had also lost men on the mines and from small arms fire. The company was without any officers. All had been knocked out of action.

Major Mitchell was now up here with us. He was the Battalion Executive and was supposed to be back at the C.P. He was a real soldier and had been with the outfit a long time and had worked his way up through the ranks. He was a pretty tough looking guy and acted tough. Someone called over the field phone and asked him how things were going. It was probably a battalion commander, but Mitchell said, "Oh, just fine. Only one fellow turned his ankle." There were guys strewn from the canal clear up to here. In fact, the company was rapidly becoming depleted.

Major Mitchell pointed out a place for Liggett and his party to make our O.P. (Observation Post). It was on a slight knoll a few yards ahead and to the left of the infantry. We made our way to the knoll. This was really open country. Not a bit of brush of any kind right around here. The ground was almost flat too. Just gently rolling knolls. There was a U shaped slit trench in the knoll where we made our O.P. From the looks of things it had been a German machine gun emplacement. We took our field glasses and began to scan the surrounding territory. A few hundred yards ahead was the railroad track, the day's objective. Beyond the tracks was a group of buildings and to the right of them a clump of trees.

Major Mitchell sent a runner up and told us to shell the buildings for they were full of Germans. We adjusted on the buildings. We got one slightly over and one a little short. A perfect bracket. We called for fire for effect. They gave us sixty rounds. They were all right in on the buildings. After that had been fired, fire direction said they were giving us another five rounds. They certainly weren't sparing the ammunition today. One hundred and twenty rounds on this one target. When the dust and smoke lifted the buildings were shattered. If there were any Germans in these buildings they weren't alive now unless they were dug down way underneath.

Soon some dive bombers came over. Twelve dove down and bombed and strafed the same buildings we had shelled. Twelve more bombed the clump of trees. It was pretty and nice but they didn't send enough. It was a little overcast. I guess that was the reason.

There were volleys of our own 155 shells landing a short distance to our left. The shells were coming in at about thirty second intervals. They were pinning down our infantry and keeping them from advancing. They were also causing casualties among our men. Every time we heard a volley of them coming we had to duck down into our trench and let the shrapnel whizz over.

Major Mitchell sent a runner up to us and told us to get the artillery stopped so that the infantry could advance. We called and checked different outfits trying to get it quieted down. No one seemed to know where it was coming from. The shells from the 155's stopped sometime later. They had done considerable damage among our own troops.

Over to our right we could see a lot of G.I.'s swarming across the fields. It was another company of the 157th, 3rd Battalion, that was just now getting up this far. They were a welcome sight. The more men the better.

Liggett and I were standing up beside our trench looking for some targets when a mortar shell crashed a few feet behind us. Neither one of us had heard it coming. That was the bad thing about mortars. You could never hear them. Shrapnel from it screamed past our ears. We both dropped into the trench. A mortar barrage was immediately laid in on us. The barrage was especially meant for us. The Germans had no doubt seen our radio and had seen us looking through field glasses. They knew we were an artillery observation party. They knew if they could get us our artillery in this sector would be stopped. The mortars crashed in all around us. The concussion from them made my head hurt and ears ring. Dirt and gravel were thrown into the trench on us. This was the end this time for sure.

The shelling suddenly stopped. I peeped out of the trench. Rod, Smitty and Liggett had been lying in the other parallel part of the U. I didn't see any movement there and was afraid they had received a direct hit. I couldn't see how so many close shells hadn't gotten someone.

Lt. Liggett slowly rose up. He had an odd look on his face. He had his helmet in his hand and a finger poked through a hole in it. The first mortar that had come in while we were standing had nearly gotten him. A chunk of fragment had gone through his helmet and helmet liner and bounced off of his head. The only thing that had probably saved him from being killed was the little metal stud that held the strap to the helmet liner on. The fragment had hit the stud and helped slow it down or he would have been killed. Even so, his head was bruised pretty badly and he felt funny. We called over the radio and asked that he be relieved as soon as it got dark. The rest of us were hoping that the rest of the party would be relieved but they would probably just send up a new officer. I noticed that I had also been hit. The knuckles on my right hand had a razor like cut on them. It was bleeding but was nothing more than a scratch. As many mortar shells that reached us it's a wonder all weren't killed. Lucky again.

Four infantry boys a few yards behind us were pecking away at some Germans in a trench a couple of hundred yards away. They probably weren't hitting anyone but they were probably keeping them pinned down pretty good.

We looked back and saw a lot of our tanks coming across the fields behind us. Some drew up nearby and started firing. German armor started throwing them in and soon a tank battle was raging. The German tanks seemed to be mostly just beyond the railroad tracks. Apparently neither of the tanks were going to do much maneuvering, just slugging it out.

The battle increased in fury. There were short, loud reports of the 75's on our tanks, the screeching of 88's fired from the Jerry tanks and the sound of steel ricocheting off steel. It made a terrific din. The Germans didn't forget us either. They laid in another barrage, especially for us. This time with 88's, probably from a tank. They were just as close as the mortars had been and our luck still held.

It was apparent that our tanks were losing the battle. Several had been knocked out and several more were wheeling around and taking off back toward our lines. A tank Lt. that had had his tank knocked out from under him came rushing up to our knoll. He told us there were two German tanks moving up towards us only a few yards away. We had to keep down the last few minutes due to the shelling we had gotten and the stuff flying from the tank battle. We had not seen the approaching tanks. We knew now that these tanks were the ones that had been shelling us. They had wanted to keep us pinned down and get up on us and really finish us off. It showed how much they respected and hated our artillery fire. They would go to no end to stop it. It had happened many times before to the different observers. When the Germans definitely knew that a group were F.O.s or located an O.P. they went all out to get rid of it.

We sprang into action and brought fire on the oncoming tanks. They turned tail and headed towards the railroad tracks. We felt pretty good about routing them although so many of our tanks were taking off in the wrong direction. We were beginning to feel deserted. It seemed all of our tanks that were still capable of moving were wheeling and going back.

Our good feeling of routing the tanks really collapsed. We watched as the two tanks approached the railroad tracks. Suddenly tanks began to pour through an underpass under the tracks. The two retreating tanks wheeled, joined them and they all came charging in our direction.

We were really excited now. We called for artillery and the boys back there sent out all they could and fast. They were mixing them up with armor piercing and H.E.s (High Explosives). We saw one tank spin around and stop and burst into flames. Our shells were pounding right in among them but they kept coming. One tank must have stopped and opened up on us. Shells screamed right in on us. We knew they were after us again because there wasn't anyone here but us. Our tanks were all gone. The infantry, seeing that our tanks had taken off and the German armor was moving, had been forced to move back. After all you cannot fight tanks with rifles. The shelling stopped and we had been lucky again but how long would it hold up? The area around our hole was pretty well churned up.

The tanks were really bearing down on us. We kept shortening the range and kept firing. We were all alone out here now. We could look back toward our lines and see the fields full of infantry going away. They were far away too.

We were in a tough spot and knew it. We kept shortening the range and firing. The boys back at the guns were giving us all they had. Another tank spun around and stopped. They were getting close. We could clearly hear their treads clanking. Lt. Liggett called Fire Direction and told them we were destroying our radio and taking off. They said to wait. The bastards. Little did they know what kind of predicament we were in . We started cutting the radio loose from the pack boards. We weren't going to take time to put those pack boards on. The radio and battery pack had suitcase like handles on them and we would try to carry them that way. We saw we weren't going to make it. One tank was mighty close. The 68 on it looked like a telephone pole sticking out. I called back and told them to bring the fire right down where we were.

That was the signal to get going. Liggett left with Rod and Smith hard on his heels. I emptied fifteen rounds from my carbine into the radio and battery pack. That was foolish and a time wasting effort. When our artillery plastered this knoll the radio would be destroyed anyway. It only took a second though and I left flying low. I found myself bringing up the rear by a considerable distance.

I've heard that anyone can run a mile without stopping when they are scared. I don't believe it anymore, not when you are really scared. It seemed as though I could only run a few yards and would poop out and I was traveling light too. No radio. I would slow down and then when I heard the tanks clanking behind me I would take off again for few yards. I threw a quick glance back. Shells were landing right on the knoll where we had our O.P.

Another tank was burning there. We had at least gotten four of them anyway.

Bullets were hissing through the grass around my heels. I practically ignored them. It didn't seem possible that a mere bullet could hurt after all that big stuff they had been throwing in.

I completely lost sight of Liggett, Rod and Smith but knew they were up ahead of me somewhere.

I saw some guys climb out of one of the burning tanks and take off. I didn't know whether they all got out or not. I only saw about three. The German tanks were still clanking behind and a couple of shells screeched over and landed in front of me. This was confusion plus.

I came to a place where there was a sign with a big red skull and crossbones painted on it. The sign read, "Actung Minen". It was a German minefield. I knew if I tried to run through my chances of making it were next to nothing and if I took time to try to find a way around it they would get me anyway. When I heard the tanks clanking behind me again I made up my mind quickly. I tore through the field that had been marked mined. Nothing happened, but I was expecting to get blown up any second. I was moving so fast that I probably would have fifty yards on it when the thing went off.

I finally reached a point where I felt that the danger of the mines had passed. I began to catch up with some of the infantry. The one thought in everyone's mind was to get somewhere out of sight of those tanks. The tanks were quite a way behind us now. No doubt our artillery had taken their toll. They also had been maneuvering and stopping to fire and had fallen behind.

A couple of our tanks stopped and started firing out at the German tanks. The Germans quickly returned the fire. Their fire was accurate and deadly. One of our tanks was out of commission and the other lumbered away.

I finally reached a canal and plunged into it. It wasn't the one we had left on the jump off but was over farther to the right of it. It seemed to run more east and west instead of north and south like the other one had.

The canal was partly filled with water. I got in it and waded waist deep toward our lines. The going was tough. Besides the water being waist deep the mud was sticky and gooey. The ditch was full of bodies, both German and American. They were lying on the sides of the banks and floating in the water. This particular stretch had been German held this morning. There were many German dugouts all along the ditch just above the water line. In front of many of the German holes were American "K" rations, rifles and other equipment. It was stuff they had captured during their big push in February.

The dead were lying in all positions. I saw where one German seemed to be just getting out of his dugout. He was still sitting at the entrance with his rifle across his lap. Most of the dead lay there with their eyes open. A lot of them had a pleasant look on their faces, almost a smile. Of course, they had been dead for several hours now. They didn't look like that when they were first killed. Their muscles were relaxed now I guess.

I spotted Rodriquez up the ditch a ways and hurried to catch up with him. He hadn't seen either Liggett or Smith for quite some time now. We figured there was nothing to do but push on.

There was complete confusion in the ditch. Everyone kept slogging along not knowing where they were or where they were going. Everyone was lost and trying to find out what to do. Some officers were trying to get their men organized. The company which had been in our reserve was trying to move up to go into the attack. It must have been pretty demoralizing to them to see that the assaulting force had been routed and were in complete confusion.

Rod and I continued down the ditch asking everyone where "K" Company C.P. (Command Post) was. No one seemed to know. We couldn't find any men from "K" Company. Everyone was lost: infantry, tankers, tank destroyers, men, engineers, medics and everyone else.

The farther we moved down the canal the worse the mess was. Dozens of bodies. All American now. This had apparently been No Man's Land before the attack. Our boys had gotten it when they attacked down the canal. The Germans really had this canal zeroed in. You could tell it had been No-Man's-Land because the banks of the ditch were heavily mined and booby trapped. Some of the booby traps were pretty cleverly set. I saw one that had a small wire leading from a hand grenade on the bank up along a small branch sticking out over the ditch. The slightest touch of that branch by a man passing would set it off. Other traps were rigged up with wires attached to guns etc. There were plenty of Lugers and other souvenirs around but no one dared touch them. No one was thinking about any souvenirs right now anyway.

There were dozens of Americans dead in the canal. Some of the bodies were in horrible shape. I stepped on something that was round at the same time I saw a headless body lying against the ditch bank. I didn't need three guesses as to what I had stepped on. Some bodies were missing an arm or a leg. Some had their guts blown clear out. It was a horrible looking mess. Rod was gagging and almost throwing up. He said he would never go forward again. He said they could take him out and shoot him if they wanted. He said there was no use going through hell and then being killed anyway. His reasoning did sort of make sense. It was amazing though that many of the dead didn't seem to have a mark on them. It was either a concussion or a small piece of fragment that pierced some vital spot that had killed them. There were plenty of both German and American wounded around. The medics were working like mad with the wounded. The dead were completely ignored for the time being. The Germans were shelling the canal heavily to add to the hell and the confusion.

Rod and I kept plodding down the canal in waist deep water wondering what to do. As we approached a bridge that ran over the ditch we noticed the men were getting along on the sides of the canal and getting passed this spot as fast as possible. We wondered what was up. As we neared the bridge we saw an American tank laying upside down in the ditch. It had run off the bridge. Under and around the bridge lay dozens of American bodies. We found out the Germans had shelled this bridge heavily all day. A mortar ammo bearer bunch had been completely wiped out and lots of other had been killed here too. We speeded it up as we went under the bridge ourselves. We were fortunate they weren't shelling it at the particular time we passed the area.

Rod and I gave up trying to find any part of "K" Company. We crawled into an abandoned dugout to rest and talk the situation over. I was sort of in favor of staying here until we could find out what the score was. It would be dark in a couple more hours and we could really get lost. Rod was in favor of pushing on and trying to find the Battery. He argued that we didn't have a radio and didn't know where Liggett and Smith were so we were useless here. I agreed that he was right.

We wondered how the German counter attack was

going. We wondered if it was a general attack all along the line or had just been in our sector. Things seemed to be getting quieter where we were now. We shuddered at the thought of having to make another attack like we had today. Having to go through that hell again. We would never make it through another one like that. We hoped the attack in general had been successful and that the only serious counter attack had been in our sector.

We took off down the canal and then men began to thin out. We passed several of our mortar positions. We kept inquiring as to our whereabouts and finally got a vague idea where to go. We talked to some lieutenant that thought that we could get out of the canal now without being seen.

We climbed out of the canal and it seemed good to be on dry land again and out of that hell on earth in the canal. We sort of got our bearings and figured out the direction to the big Mussolini Canal. We knew both Headquarters and "C" Battery were in position there not far from each other. We walked across flat shell pitted fields. Shells whined overhead, going both ways.

As we approached the Mussolini Canal we found Merv Kintish lying in the grass with a bazooka. He said they had heard about the tank break through and he had been put out here as a security guard. He had never fired a bazooka before though.

Rod and I made our way on into the canal and located our battery. We were really pooped and I felt a hundred years old. My face felt so drawn. It felt like the skin on it would break. We must have looked weird too. Fellows who even knew us well didn't say a word but just stared.

At "C' Battery we found Smith and Liggett. They had both made it back O.K. We also found out the situation. The only serious breakthrough had been in our sector and the rest of the attack was making some progress. Our forces had lost heavily. Some companies were down to a few men. They were digging in and replacements were going to be rushed up as soon as it got dark. Naturally, the Germans would have had to pick our sector to make their big counter attack.

Liggett's head was bothering him. Capt. Hurley had an ambulance come and take him to the hospital. Capt. Hurley told the rest of us that we had done a good job knocking out the tanks and helping blunt the attack. He said we would get a good rest before we had to go up again. Although we had been up there about twenty-four hours it seemed to have taken years off of our lives. Capt. Hurley called for a vehicle to take us back to Service Battery, or rather, where Service Battery had been.

It was dark and cool as I stood there waiting for the vehicle. Actually, I was the only one going back to the Service Battery area. Smith and Rod had their stuff right here at the "C" Battery position. My stuff was back at the old area. Anyway I was standing there cold because my clothes were wet. Lt. Lindsey came and started talking to me. When he noticed my teeth were chattering he lent me his field jacket, bars and all. When the driver pulled up I climbed on. In the dark the driver didn't recognize me although he knew me very well. All he could see was the First Lieutenant's bars shining. He said to me, "Where to, Sir?" For some reason that struck me as funny. It was the only thing that had been funny in the last several hours.

Back at our old area I found it pretty well deserted. All of "C" Battery had moved. Part of Service Battery was gone. All of the British and the engineers were gone. All of the extra Headquarters men were gone. Grady was gone and the dugout was deserted.

I crawled into the dugout and prepared for a good

night's sleep. I had just started to doze off when here came the German planes. They were really plastering everything with bombs of all sizes.

We had had so many raids in the past four months that I was getting a little used to them. Tonight seemed different though. I guess my nerves were so hot from the day's ordeal that I was extra scared. I never prayed before or after this night during the whole war but on this night I did. Bombs dropped close. One string of personnel bombs dropped a few feet from my dugout.

The next morning, I still felt pretty groggy. Everyone that was left around the area had heard about the deal and gathered around and asked questions. Bob Perkins came over and got the story.

I found out what had actually happened up there. The German big counter attack had been made in our sector. It had broken through our lines in our sector and had driven us back to our original positions, as I already knew. Our Battalion, the assault battalion, had suffered terrific loses. "K" Company, the company our party had been with, had thirty seven men left at the end of the day. "I" Company had lost even more. They had only sixteen left at the end of the first day. From an over strength company for an attack of about two hundred and ten men that was thinning them down pretty fast.

The attack was going pretty nicely now. "I" Company had been cut off all night but had made contact with us. The Germans in the Forty-Fifty sector were forced to give ground. The Third Division, attacking to our right and toward Littoria was gaining ground too. The British, to our left, were having trouble but gaining some ground. Elements from the Casino Front were expected to make contact with the Beachhead forces soon. All in all, things seemed to be going pretty well.

That afternoon a truck load of British came by and asked me if I wanted to go to a movie. We went over to a British hospital to see the show. The theater was a large tent that was well dug in. The movie was an American one. I found out from these boys that Ted Billings' buddy had been seriously wounded. A piece of shrapnel went into his head near his brain. I hoped he would pull through. I remembered what a big kick he had gotten out of Spike Jones' "Chloe" and "Old Black Magic".

After I got back from the show a bunch of G.I.s were going down to Anzio to take showers. I needed one badly, so went along with them. We passed an American cemetery on the way. There were row upon row of white crosses. Thousands of them. Most of these were from the two Infantry Divisions here. The Forty-Fifth and the Third. Right now a lot of G.I.s and some German prisoners were digging like mad. They were behind on their grave digging. There were stacks of corpses in mattress covers all around. Even as we went by three big trucks pulled in with their bed stacked high with bodies in mattress covers. The smell from the place was terrific. It must have been a swell place to work. One of the fellows on our jeep couldn't stand the smell and leaned over the side of the jeep and heaved.

Looking at the thousands of graves and the stacks of dead made you wonder what it was all about. Young fellows with the best years of their lives ahead of them were now gone. You wondered for what. Clear over here in Italy, thousands of miles from home. It all just didn't seem to add up.

The showers were in tents but were fixed up nicely. After a nice shower and some clean underwear we returned to our dugouts.

The night passed fairly quietly. The old Anzio Express

kept firing over all night. Those big shells were the only ones I heard. I figured the Germans had been pushed back far enough now that some of the smaller artillery pieces were out of range. I could hear big bombs being dropped up near the front. The Germans were probably after the road to hamper our movements.

The next day a few of the handful that were left, gathered and talked most of the day. We wondered how the attack was going and what we would do next. We were more or less isolated here and we didn't get much news. We began to feel like we were in the rear echelon, although the front hadn't actually moved up very far.

About noon we heard a plane sputtering. We looked up and saw one of our P-40s limping along, not too high. It was obviously in trouble and apparently trying to make it back to the landing strip that had been established here on the beachhead. Suddenly, we saw the pilot jump and his chute blossom out. The plane headed for the ground and picked up speed as it came down. We didn't see the exact spot where it hit but saw black smoke rising from that position.

We all took off at a run toward where the chute was coming down. We reached the pilot just as he touched the ground. He was one of the Negroes of the 99th Air Force. He said he had been out strafing some German positions and flak had hit his motor and conked it out. A jeep soon arrived and took him away to his base.

About dark that evening Harris came and picked me up. He said our party was to go forward with Lt. Lindsey. We went by the big canal and picked up Rod and Smith. We all dreaded this as we hadn't recovered from the other day yet. Orders were orders though. Harris told us that Lt. Liggett had been evacuated to a hospital in Naples. He must have been hit worse than we had figured.

"C" Battery was now located in a position behind a long sloping knoll. The cannoneers were busy pooping out the shells. It must have been hard on a person's ears being around these guns day after day. Most of the cannoneers had cotton stuffed in their ears. We went on into the C.P. and received a pleasant surprise. Lt. Lindsey had quickly gotten a party of soldiers together and had left so that we didn't have to go now. We would have been up only for the night anyway because the 3rd Battalion was to be relieved the next day. The 3rd Battalion had led the assault for the 157th Regiment and was pretty well battered up. They would have to draw back and reorganize.

We felt pretty good that night as we were taken back to our dugouts. Where I was staying was beginning to seem like a rear area not that the front line had moved up a few miles. The good old Anzio Express was still firing into the Anzio area though.

Just before dawn a kid by the name of Bruls woke me up. He said that Lt. Olsen's radio operator had been hit and I was to go up and replace him. Another fellow was to go along as well. His dugout was fairly near mine but I had never met the guy. His name was Floyd Percio and he hailed from Tarrytown, New York. We stumbled around sleepily getting our stuff together and onto the jeep.

When we got up the road a few miles the German planes were over thick. They were bombing the road and by passes. There was a new moon up. This weather helped them see the roads or they had bombed the beachhead so much they knew every inch of it from memory. We had to abandon the jeep twice and head out into the fields when the bombing and strafing got close.

We finally reached the Battery. It was now in another position. It had moved again when it got dark. It was now in a position along the railroad that we had been fighting so hard for a few days.

We reported to Captain Hurley. He said it would be daylight before we could get up to Lt. Olsen's so we would have to wait until the next night. Percio and I got out our blankets and planned to get a few more winks before daylight. The guns were in position in the ditch that ran under the tracks. The C.P. was set up under a trestle. We put our blankets down near the C.P. The guns were blasting away so fast and furious that sleep was impossible. The muzzle blasts of the guns echoed and reechoed down the trestle making the din actually worse. It soon began to get daylight so we gave up trying to sleep and got up.

All day long Percio and I hung around the Battery just waiting for it to get night again so we could go up to Lt. Olson's C.P. Our guns blasted away all day. I don't think they were firing much observed fire. They just seemed to be firing in the general direction of the Germans with all they had. They were probably shelling roads and German held towns. In the fields behind us there were some 155's banging away. They were just sitting out in the open and not in dugouts or anything. There were guns all over the place blazing away. There were guns of all sizes from 105's up to eight inchers.

Once during the day the Germans threw in a murderous barrage of air bursts over a battery of eight inchers. These big guns were situated about a half mile from us so we were in no danger but it was annoying. Later, the Krauts threw in a barrage over to our left. It was quite heavy and close but still not close enough to do us any damage.

At dusk I got ready to go forward and when it was dark Percio and I loaded on Lt. Olsen's jeep. Lt. Olsen's drivers name was Edwards. For a while we drove along parallel with the railroad. We then turned off and made our way by a large vineyard. We turned again and made our way across some open fields.

We stopped at the foot of a small hill and unloaded. Edwards told us that the O.P. was on the top of the hill somewhere. At least we hoped it was. It wouldn't be too healthy wandering around too much not knowing where you were going this close to the front. We met Roy Sapienza, one of Lt. Olsen's men, half way up the hill. In fact, he was the only man left with Lt. Olsen. They had been up there the night before and all day by themselves. Roy led us on up to the O.P. He was in a hurry too. He said the Germans plastered this area all the time, day and night.

Our new O.P. was under a house on top of the knoll. Rather it had been a house. It was nothing now but a pile of rubble resembling a large pile of gravel. We got under the house by following a trench that ran under it. This had been a German position before. The Krauts really fixed up their dugouts nicely. This one was all lined with boards. Overhead were railroad ties and rails and of course above that the rubble of the building. The roof of the place did have one weakness though. There was a hole about two feet square that was covered only by a light wooden trap door affair. It could easily be taken off by hand. This had probably been a German O.P. They had probably fixed it so when they wanted to do a little observing they could remove the trap door. That was the way we were using it anyway. Other than that flimsy trap door the place seemed bomb and shell proof.

This was the first time I had met Lt. Olsen. He was a fairly large, blonde fellow, a Swede no doubt. He wore glasses and seemed to be the scholarly type. He had me take over on the radio immediately. We had to do a lot of relaying for a F.O. party that couldn't get good contact with fire direction.

During the night the Germans heavily shelled the hill and the surrounding area. Most of the shells were mortars but they really threw them in. Many landed mighty close. Shrapnel sang over the place. Some came so close that the gravel rattled down on us from the cracks in the trap door We kept thinking they might put one right on the trap door. If they did it would be curtains for us. Also, during the night we could hear German planes very low overhead but no bombs dropped in our vicinity. One of the reasons the Germans were shelling this area so hard were the tanks and T.O's (Tank destroyers) dispersed around the hill

Things were a little quieter for a while, but not for long. Shells soon began to drop in around again and continue to do so all day. A lot of them were very close. We raised our trap door and tried to see something to shoot at. All we could see were a series of small hills ahead of us. We knew that there were Germans among them but they were keeping pretty low.

We stuck our B.C. scope up through the trap door to have a look around hadn't seen a B.C. scope since basic training days. This was the only time I was to see one during the war. They weren't used much in this war. They were heavy and cumbersome and hard to move around. In World War I, where things remained in the same locations for months or even years, they had been practical. The scope we were using had been captured from the Germans Peering through this thing reminded me of when I was a kid playing with a periscope. We used to look around corners or buildings and out of ditches with them. This scope we were using was on the same principle but was more elaborate.

Once during the day we spotted what we figured to be a German observer on a knoll about three hundred yards away. We tried to adjust on the poor guy but something got screwed up and we had to give up as a bad job. The closest and only shells we saw that day had landed about four hundred yards behind us.

The day dragged on with nothing much happening. They would throw a few shells in the vicinity. It was exactly every fifteen minutes. You could set your watch by them.

At dark Edwards came up with some water and "K" rations for us. He said that we were to be believed the following evening. He also said that we were no longer in support of the 157th, but now the 179th. He said the 157th had pulled out and were driving right up the highway toward Lake Albano. He said the going was pretty tough on them. Edwards departed for the battery.

At lease we were glad to find out who we were supposed to be supporting. We hadn't seen anyone or talked to anyone who knew what was going on. We felt we were just wasting our time here. We hadn't even fired a mission yet, and it was doubtful we would. .About all we were doing was sweating out the Krauts. I guess we should be glad that we were not with the 157th.

That night was almost a repetition of the one before. More shelling and Kraut planes over low. Once during the night there was a short exchange of rifle and machine gun fire. Bullets sang overhead and bounced off of the rubble over our heads. We wished to hell that we knew what was going on. We could really never get much sleep during the night. We would just be dozing off when every fifteen minutes a barrage would come on in. Another thing that didn't make things any too pleasant was the terrific stench here. There was a dead German lying there a few days and this hot weather was beginning to ripen him up.

Dawn finally came. This day was to be practically a carbon copy of the day before. It was now obvious that the Germans were just firing unobserved fire. The infantry, tanks and the T.O.s were long gone and even if they did know we were here we didn't deserve attention. The only things we couldn't figure out were how, if our infantry advanced in this sector, there should still be mortars still in range. Some must have been by passed. Once during the day Percio stepped out to relieve himself and drew small arms fire. We just sweated out the day waiting for dark. As long as we weren't doing any good here, we wanted to get out of here. We also wanted to find out what the score was and how things were going. It seemed as though we had been isolated for months.

After dark Edwards arrived on the scene. We gathered up our stuff and waited until one of the German fifteen minute shellings was over. Then we tore out of the dugout, down the knoll a hundred yards and into the jeep. We hurriedly piled on the jeep and took off down the road nearly wide open. In the dark he couldn't see and he hit every chuck hole and small crater there was. We hit one big hole and Sapienza and I bounced clear out of the jeep. We rolled head over heels but luckily neither of us were hurt.

We got to the battery and bedded down. It was a beautiful, clear night and quiet. There was a part of the moon and I lay there for a long time looking up at it and the sky full of stars.

The next day was a nice, sunny, balmy one. Sapienza, Percio and I just lounged around talking and taking it easy. We watched the cannoneers at work. They were really popping them out again today.

Late in the afternoon Captain Hurley rushed out of the C.P .and yelled for me. He said that Green, Sgt. Shoemaker's radio operator, had been hit and I was to go up and take his place. The Krauts were getting rough on our radio operators.

I was to go to Headquarters Battery and go forward with Lt. Fetzer's L.O. party. A driver took me to Headquarter sat dusk. Lt. Fetzer's L.O. party was ready to go when I arrived.

Right after dark we loaded on a jeep and took off. It seemed as though we drove for miles. I was beginning to think the driver was lost and half expected to drive right into Rome any second. We ground through fields for a while and then right onto Highway 6. A nice paved road. This was it. The Appian Way that was built by the Romans a couple of thousand years ago. All roads lead to Rome. We scooted down the road expecting to have to abandon the jeep any time for the German planes were strafing along the highway.

We arrived at the town of Velletri. This had been one of the German strongholds around the beachhead. It was a shattered place now. We had to make our way carefully through the ruins. The driver and Capt. Hayes' L.O. party had run over a mine on the edge of the road near here. It had instantly killed two and wounded one badly. Smith, the radio operator and Ward, the driver had been killed. Smith was completely blown to bits. They couldn't even find a whole piece of him. Captain Hayes hadn't been on the jeep at the time. He had gotten off to check with some officer about something and Ward had pulled off to the side to wait for him. Both Smith and Ward had come into the outfit with me.

When we reached the far outskirts of the town we stopped. The 3rd Battalion Headquarters were set up in a large house on top of a hill. We groped our way up the hill to the house. We found all the infantry hurrying around getting ready to move out.

I stuck close to the L.O. party. I didn't want to get separated in all this turmoil. Others in the L.O. party besides Lt. Fetzer were Sgt. Pulsey and a fellow named Howard.

Finally the infantry was ready to move out. Everyone assembled down on the highway and soon we were moving,

We took right off cross country. The going was pretty rough. We went up and down hills, over fences and through woods at a fast pace. It wasn't too bad for me though because I did not have heavy equipment, just my carbine, rifle belt and canteen. We took several breaks, but it was so cold I had just as soon kept moving.

Several times during the night we heard large formations of our planes passing overhead. To the north we could see them dropping flares and hear the distant rumble of the bombs. We could see the German anti-aircraft bursting in the sky. We figured they were bombing the retreating Germans somewhere up around Rome

Once during the night we passed an infantry company from the 34th Division. We hiked all night at a pretty good pace. About an hour after dawn we reached our destination. We stopped at a huge villa. At one time it must have belonged to a very wealthy Italian, There were several nice buildings here. Even the stables were like hotel rooms and the swimming pool was fancy and large enough for any city. The whole place was pretty well run down now thought. I guess during the war it had been neglected. The Germans had been using it for a Corps Headquarters.

When we arrived at the villa we found a Kraut waiting

for us. He claimed to be a Pole and not a German and was anxious to surrender. He said he was hauling ammunition for an artillery outfit. He said that last night he had taken a load to where the guns were supposed to be. All of the men and guns had pulled out and everything was in confusion. He said that he had come back here to find out what the score was and found this place abandoned. That had done it. He said, "To hell with it" and sat down to wait for our arrival. He was plenty fed up with the war and fighting.

The Germans had not left here in such a hurry that they hadn't taken time to thoroughly mine and booby trap the place. We were instructed not to touch anything or go into any of the buildings until the engineers, who were working right now, cleared the place. The Germans had even booby trapped a pile of rubbish. It was a very slyly wired up with two or three hand grenades. If we hadn't been warned about not touching anything some curious G.I. would have picked up a helmet to try it on for size.

When the engineers pronounced the place cleared we began to look for a place to settle down. Lt. Fetzer's L.O. party took up a position in one of the buildings. From where we were we could see the Germans shelling a crossroads a short distance down the road. They were shelling it with big stuff and it made a nasty crack. Dirt and debris went flying up into the air when one of the big shells hit. We hoped they didn't throw a few into the villa.

What always seemed odd to me was the Germans never seemed to shell any of their former positions like this one. At least none that I had been in. They always used the best places and positions and it seemed they would think we would use it too. A few shells in a place like this might get some of the top brass.

Things seemed to be going pretty well. The Germans were falling back rapidly now in the direction of Rome.

In the middle of the afternoon we got ready to move out again. I hadn't gotten in touch with Shoemaker yet, so I was still stuck with the L.O. party. Lt. Fetzer had called for a jeep so we were going to ride. The Germans were pulling back fast now. The big gun that had been shelling the crossroad had even stopped.

The road we traveled on was now clogged with our tanks, T.D.'s (tank destroyer), jeeps and infantry.

As we made our way along we spotted Shoemaker and his party off at the side of the road. I jumped off to join him. In his party were "Pop" Gardner, the driver. He had a very wrinkled face, gray hair and looked to be eighty years old although he was actually thirty nine. Then there was Ray Duguay. He was a Staff Sgt. He was new to the 45th having joined it only a couple of weeks before. He had been with an A.M.G. (Allied Military Government) outfit in Italy for quite a while. He was about my age, just a year or two older. Green, the radio operator, wasn't with them now. He had been hit a couple of days ago. It wasn't very serious but he had lost two or three fingers and probably would see no more combat. It was Green's place I was to take. Then of course, there was Sgt. Shoemaker. He was a big blonde, blue eyed fellow with an easy going manner. Shoemaker was up for a battlefield commission. He had been with the 45th for years although he was only about my age.

We sat there by the side of the road watching the tremendous amount of equipment going up the road toward Rome. The infantry was going by too. They were dog tired. The last few weeks, as well as the last four months, they had gone through hell. In fact, ever since the landings at Salerno about nine months before it had all been hell. There were a very, very few that had survived the whole way from Salerno. The one big object had been Rome and now finally it was within grasp. In spite of their weariness they were bright eyed and going down the road at almost a run. Everyone was a pretty sorry looking sight. Several weeks' growth of beard, clothes filthy and torn. In spite of the haggard faces, young fellows that looked fifty, everyone's spirits were high, almost jubilant.

As I sat there watching the men and equipment go by I wondered about other years. Conquering Roman legions coming back, anxious to get home, passed down this very road, passed this very spot. Our bunch must have looked more like the barbarians on their way to sack Rome.

I contacted the Battery and we were told to come in. Recon outfits reporting back from up ahead said that the Germans were apparently abandoning Rome but would have a rear-guard action at the Tiber River.

We soon reached the Battery area which was in an old farmhouse surrounded by fields. Lots of infantry boys were sprawled around in the nearby fields resting. Lt. Olsen came by and said he had to go forward. He wanted me to go along as his radio operator. Sgt. Shoemaker told Olsen I was on his party now and that he needed me. I really wanted to go. I figured that the Germans were retreating so fast that things wouldn't be very rough and we would soon be in Rome celebrating. Shoemaker said not to worry that we would beat Olsen into Rome anyway.

At dusk our F.O. party moved out with the battery. We didn't know how far we were going but we all hoped it would be all the way to Rome. We soon turned onto a secondary road. Old "Pop" Gardner's driving made us nervous. He weaved all over the road like a drunk. I don't think he could see very well in spite of his glasses. Driving black out probably didn't help him much either. Finally, Sgt. Shoemaker took over and started driving himself. At one place he hesitated wondering which way to go. Lt. Grabrisch was riding with us. He was just over from the States and had arrived in the outfit just a couple of days ago. He was to be a forward observer and had been sent right up with Shoemaker to learn the ropes. He cautioned Sgt. Shoemaker not to wander off the road too far looking for the right direction. Sgt. Shoemaker said to him, "Yeah Lt., get off and see where in the hell we are." The Lt. sort of hesitated. He didn't like being talked to that way by a non-com. I guess with a couple of enlisted men on the jeep he figured one of us should do it. Sgt. Shoemaker said again, "Hurry up Lt. We don't have all night." The Lt. got off the jeep and went out in front of us. We found our way and headed north again. We went on for a short distance and pulled up in front of a big two story house. This was supposed to be where we would spend the night. The bottom floor was already occupied by some of our battery. Sgt. Shoemaker, myself and Lt. Grabrisch went upstairs and got a room for ourselves. There was one single bed in the room. Sgt. Shoemaker made a dive for it. He took the bed for himself but gave the mattress to me leaving nothing for the Lt.

This place had been used by the Germans before us. There were candles burned low, empty bottles, magazines etc.

We looked through the magazines. Some of them were similar to our "Life" and "Look" magazines. The pictures were about the same as in our magazines. One artist had drawn several pictures showing planes in dog fights. Of course, it showed British and American planes being shot down instead of German. It showed scenes of Germans advancing past our knocked out tanks and dead infantry. There was one shot of trick photography. It showed a German soldier holding out a hand as if supporting the Leaning Tower of Pisa.

Shoemaker and I laid down and tried to go to sleep. Lt. Grabrisch kept puttering around lighting candles and fooling around. Sgt. Shoemaker finally told him, "For Christs sake Lt., go to bed, we're tired." Shoemaker didn't seem to have much respect for rank. The Lt. did blow out the candles and go to bed. He had to sleep on the floor while Sgt. Shoemaker and I had fairly comfortable beds.

During the night German planes were overhead dropping flares and bombing. They dropped some bombs along the road near us setting some trucks on fire.

The next morning, we were all up early and anxious to get going. We wanted to go on into Rome but we had to sweat out most of the day in this same area.

Late in the afternoon we moved out toward Rome. We soon reached the Tiber River. There was a nice large bridge crossing it. Here we saw a rather odd sight. Our air corps had really tried for this bridge. The riverbed, for a quarter of a mile on both sides of the bridge, was completely churned up. Thousands of bombs must have been dropped here. The amazing thing was that the bridge had been damaged very little. It had received a few hits but was far from being destroyed. We were able to cross quite easily.

After we crossed the bridge we tore up the road past knocked out German tanks and other destroyed equipment. In the dusk we could see the buildings of the city of Rome. We didn't go on into the city yet though. Just on the outskirts of the city we turned west. We still stayed just on the outskirts of the city and pulled into a large gravel pit and stopped for the night.

The next morning, June 6th, 1944, we pulled out of the gravel pit real early. We left the outskirts of Rome and sped through the country. We were moving further away from Rome all of the time. We soon pulled off the road again and made our way through some fields and stopped among a series of small rolling hills. We were told to make ourselves as comfortable as possible. We were now in Corps reserve and we would probably be here several days.

We had no more arrived at our new position when Shoemaker came around to Gardner, Duquay, Grabrisch and me and said quietly that we were going into Rome. We piled on the jeep and took off. We soon hit a nice paved, three lane highway and tore down it towards the city. The road was void of traffic. We had it all to ourselves. Along the sides there were signs of havoc though. Dead horses were thick along here. They had been drawing German artillery and had been killed by strafing from our planes. I always hate to see horses killed like that. Actually, I hated it almost more than a man. The poor damned horses had nothing to do with this war. The human was supposed to know what they were fighting for. The artillery pieces, mostly 68's, were still by the side of the road. The Germans had blown the breech block from each of them before they had left. The Germans must have been in a big hurry. They hated to leave their equipment behind unless they had to. When the horses had been killed they couldn't get anything to move their equipment with.

We breezed right into Rome. G.I.s were strangely absent in the city. It seemed odd not seeing hundreds of G.I.'s around. I guess their outfits were ordered not to let any of the troops in yet. I suppose there was some technicality, Rome being an open city and all. Actually, we had no authority to be here ourselves.

Rome was in surprisingly good repair with hardly any signs of war. Things seemed to be fairly normal. It surprised me to see street cars moving along the streets. There were no automobiles to be seen.

We buzzed on downtown. There were a few G.I.s around downtown but only a handful. We reached one part of downtown where we were the only G.I.s. We spied a nice looking bar and went in. This was one time I didn't care about getting something to drink right now. Here we were, in Rome, the Eternal City. There was history all around and so the first thing we do is go to a bar? The bar was a nice one though and was well stocked with all kinds of liquor.

We sat there looking out the door marveling at how the people looked. The people passing by looked like the citizens of any other cities in the States. There wasn't the raggedness and poverty of Naples and other cities in Southern Italy. Most of the men wore good looking suits. The girls were very snappily dressed and modern looking. The girls were good looking and shapely not the big plow horse type gals that were around the rural areas. Here, in Italy, there seemed to be a big contrast between the city dwellers and the farmers.

After a few drinks we wandered back out into the street. Our jeep had drawn a lot of attention. About a dozen people had clustered around it and they looked at it and us as if we were something from Mars. Two or three good looking girls knew what the score was though. They were all smiles and were planting kisses on us. They were no doubt after chocolate and cigarettes and they were successful.

Then Lt., Shoemaker and Duquay took off toward a nearby hotel that had been pointed out as the nearest and cleanest sporting house. Gardner and I went back into the bar and proceeded to do some pretty heavy drinking. I still wanted to see the Colosseum and other ancient things but Gardner wasn't interested and I didn't want to go alone. We were right in the section of the Rome of the old days—Caesar, Nero, etc.

A good many drinks later Gardner and I began to wonder what had happened to the others. We thought that we had better go investigate.

We went to the hotel that we figured they had gone to. We went upstairs to the second floor to look around. It was quiet without a soul in sight. I wondered if the place was abandoned. I told Gardner to go down the corridor and I would go down the other and we would see if we could find any of the guys. I walked clear to the end of the corridor but didn't hear or see anyone. As I turned to go down another corridor I was startled by a girl standing at an open door. She was naked except for a pair of black high heeled shoes. Before I knew what was going on she pulled me into the room and shut the door. The girl was a good looking one. She was young, small with black hair and blue eyes and very shapely.

Believe it or not this was the first time I had ever been in a place like this, although no virgin. For some reason I had to at least know the parties name and be acquainted for at least a couple of hours before I was too interested. Weird I guess. The army had also indoctrinated me pretty well and I was afraid of contracting something too. I wasn't particularly the noble type but I was married and that counted a lot too. I had all kinds of reasons. I called a halt to the ordeal after she had undressed me and had started that old breathing routine. I dressed, took a couple of big shots from the bottle of cognac sitting on the table, gave her three hundred lira for her troubles and took off. I was probably the first G.I. customer she had. I must have got her off to a frustrating start. She had been a pretty thing though. The place was clean and she had all kinds of certificates hanging on the wall which I gathered were medical clearing deals. Probably one was a license for business which is completely legal here. Anyway, when in Rome, do as...

I went back down the stairs and out into the sunshine. The rest of the fellows were waiting in front. No one related their experiences and I sure as hell wasn't going to tell mine. I felt like they would think I was some sort of odd ball if I told them what I had done.

We piled on the jeep and headed for the Coliseum. As we neared the Coliseum we passed the Arch of Constantine. We had a good look at the arena. It was quite a place. If only one could turn the clock back to an afternoon a couple of thousand years ago. The only thing that marred our visit to the place was the filth. Someone, in fact a lot of someone's, must have been using this place as a public restroom. There were dumps all over the place. It made it rather unpleasant trying to look at the places below where they had kept the wild animals or even humans.

We left and headed back towards town. In route we passed the old Roman Forum and the Circus Maximus. All along we passed ruins of ancient Rome. I hoped I could get back here and spend more time looking these things over. We visited the Italians Unknown Soldier Tomb. It was huge and beautiful. We also visited St. Peter's Cathedral, which was huge, fantastic and beautiful.

An Italian fellow came up to us and started talking to us in perfect English. He said he heard that our troops had disembarked on the shores of Northern France and wanted to know if this was true. We told him we didn't know but hoped it was true. Somehow we felt it was true.

After hearing this we all were anxious to get back to

the battery and find out if it had actually happened. None of us were interested in liquor, women or ruins now. We had to find out if the "Second Front" was a reality.

The town was beginning to get too crowded with G.I.s too. Our almost exclusive right to the city was now ended. Troops, on foot as well as on trucks, and other equipment, were pouring into the city. The 88th Division came marching into town like they had won the city as well as the Battle of Southern Italy all by themselves. They hadn't been on the line very long at all. They had been on the line only a few days compared with the months and months the 45th, 3rd, 34th and 36th had been there.

We hurried back to the battery where we found everyone clustered around a portable radio. The rumor was true. The invasion of France had finally come. It was about time too.

We also found out that we were definitely in Corps Reserve. We weren't to push on to the north. For the present anyway.

The news on our front was good too. The Germans were retreating rapidly to the north using only a light rear-guard action to slow down the advance. They were apparently dropping back to prepare positions quite a way to the north.

We hung around the battery the rest of the day listening to the news. That night I threw my blankets down on the ground and bedded down. I lay there for several hours looking up at the stars thinking about home and reviewing the last few months.

I thought that only a year ago I was still in basic training back at Camp Roberts. Christ, a lot had happened in the last year. I was now several thousand miles from home. I had traveled across the United States, the Atlantic, part of the Mediterranean, a thousand miles of North Africa and quite a bit of Italy. I had been in combat almost continually for about nine months. I had had plenty of close calls. The rain, mud, mountains and mules of the Casino Front. The cemetery, the miraculous escape from the shellings and the agony of the stalemate. Anzio and four months of hell and countless close calls, May 23rd, the breakout. Now that I was still alive I wondered how much longer my luck would hold out. Now that the Second Front was open and we were driving north, Rome had fallen, the Russians moving, maybe the war wouldn't last too much longer. I thought of home and wondered how Bernice was doing. I knew that she was working at a training base for fliers near home. With all the glamour boys connected with the Air Force I wondered if she was still true. I knew she was a wonderful person and thought she loved me but humans will be humans. An acquaintance, no matter how innocent at first could grow into something that people can't help. Her letters were always reassuring but anything could happen. I was sure of her as anyone could be under these circumstances. The temptations for a young girl at home must be terrific. One thing in our favor, I thought, was that ours wasn't a quickie marriage. We had known each other for several months before we were married and had spent twenty months happily married. Ours wasn't one of those deals where we only knew each other a few days, were married and then right overseas. I thought of those twenty months we had spent in San Francisco and the good times we had had together. Well, time would tell. I wished this war would get over so I could go home to her. Let's see, June 30th would be our third wedding anniversary.

    German planes came over later during the night in quite large numbers. They dropped heavy bombs in the direction of Rome and plastered all around our area with personnel bombs. Some were dropped pretty close to our area too.

The next day Gardner, Shoemaker, Duquay and I had a close call. As close a call as anyone can have and still be around to tell about it.

We noticed a small strange stream nearby and we decided to give the jeep a bath. We all piled on the jeep and headed for the stream. We tried to take the shortest way to the stream. We drove through some new mown hayfields. We were having fun. Shoemaker was driving and he would drive the jeep into the shocks of hay and was cutting capers in general. We crossed a little dirt road. On the other side of the road we noticed the hay hadn't been cut but didn't think much about it. The stream was only about a hundred yards away now so we sped toward it. About fifty yards into the unmown hay we reached a barbed wire entanglement. The thought then entered our minds that the area might be mined. We backed up, turned around and headed back. We reached the little dirt road and followed it to where it crossed the stream. While we were washing the jeep we heard a loud explosion. We didn't think too much about it thinking the engineers were detonating some shells or mines.

On the way back to the battery an ambulance passed us in a big hurry. We soon found out what the trouble was. Two other fellows on a jeep, with apparently the same idea that we had, tried to go through the same field. Both men were blown sky high. We could see the tracks in the hay just six feet to the right of the ones we had made.

Engineers came and examined the area. They said the mines were almost side by side in that field. They couldn't believe we had gone clear to the entanglement, turned around and come back to the road without hitting one of the hundreds of mines sown in such a small area. They were the large box type Italian mines. They said there were so many of them that it would take days to remove them and they weren't going to attempt it. They put a strip of white ribbon all around the place to seal it off and warn others of the presence of the minefield. Lady Luck was still smiling. For a while it made me weak kneed every time I thought of that deal. How lucky can you get?

We were in this area for the next two weeks. We didn't do much but just laid around taking it easy. There wasn't too much in the way of entertainment besides going to Rome and passes weren't any too plentiful for that.

We did have one U.S.O. show held near our area though. On the program were a few acrobats. The outstanding feature of the program was the request singing of Helen Young. She had been with the Freddie Slacks band and was plenty good. She sang favorites like, "Paper Doll" and "Cow. Cow Boogie".

We got two or three passes into Rome where we had some pretty good times. One time Ray Duquay and I went into Rome on a pass. His old A.M.G. (Allied Military Government) outfit had moved into town and we went to visit it. They were established in one of the better hotels in Rome. They really had a racket. They ate at tables and their food was served on plates and they had the best food. They even had maid service. They also had very little work to do. They just lived it up. I figured these guys would hope the war would last another five years. They were all highly rated too; Staff Sgts, and Master Sgts, were a dime a dozen.

They almost all seemed to have a racket on the side and weren't very secretive about it. They had excess government stuff and took advantage of it. They stole the stuff and would sell it to the Wops. I remember a racket one fellow had going. He had a trunk full of photograph paper he had stolen and was selling it to the Italians for a dollar apiece. There must have been thousands of sheets in that trunk. The Italian photographers were plenty busy with so many G.I.s wanting to have their picture taken in Rome. They were willing to pay a big price for the stuff. I never asked him but I wondered how come Duquay had been transferred from this soft touch to our outfit. He certainly hadn't asked for it if he had been in his right mind anyway. Maybe this bunch had caught him being honest. I thought of the time way back when I had given an extra pair of slightly worn shoes to that old fellow. I hate to think what I would have gotten if I had been caught. Also, the time the General found my .03 in the mud. Here these guys were selling government stuff for a big profit and didn't seem to be afraid of being caught. Maybe someone higher up was really behind it though.

On another trip into Rome Duquay and I visited a lot of the old places such as forts, Roman baths, etc. We visited the Basilica, the place where the Popes used to live before they moved to their present day home in the Vatican. It was a fortress looking far right on the banks of the Tiber. I don't know what those guys were afraid of but they had themselves really fortified. There was a moat all around the place with several draw bridges. Up on the thick walls of the place were many old cannons. We gave some Italian, who claimed to be a guide, a few lira to show us around the place. He showed us some trap doors where some unsuspecting victim was dropped into boiling oil. There was a tiny cell where the guide said political prisoners were kept. It was a dark hole with only one barred opening about a half foot square. The guide grinned at us and remarked that God wasn't the only one served here but also lots of politicians and lots of intrigue. Some of the rooms had pictures of naked women painted on the ceilings. Art I guess. Maye by some famous artist.

One day, Duquay and I were in Rome and doing some pretty heavy drinking. Somehow, we got separated and after looking for a while I gave up and went into a bar. I talked quite a while to a Negro Staff Sgt. From the 99th Air Force. He seemed like a pretty good fellow. He said he would give his right arm if he could sit in bars in the States with white guys. I told him in my part of the country he could. He said not always. He said he had gone into a bar in San Diego with a couple of white friends and he had been thrown out. He said all three of them were embarrassed.

When I found Duquay again we were both feeling pretty good. We decided to sit down on a bench and watch the people go by and get straightened up before we started back to our area. In about a half hour we were feeling much better and started to walk to the edge of the city to hitch hike a ride back. As we walked down the street Lt. Grabrisch and his driver Edwards, pulled up to give us a ride. Both Lt. Grabrisch and his driver Edwards were rip roaring drunk. We got on the jeep and made the round of more bars. Lt. Grabrisch was drunk and obnoxious. I have been drunk and was drunk now, but getting plastered is something and getting plastered and downright foul and as obnoxious as you can is something else. Grabrisch was really off the bean. He would have Edwards drive right up to a bunch of girls and stop. He would ask them in no uncertain words and using the foulest language, if they wanted to shack up with him. He even stopped married women out walking with their husbands and children. In the bars he was yelling what a good officer he was and how he took care of his men in combat. Hell, he had only been out once during the drive to Rome and then he had been with Sgt. Shoemaker learning the ropes. He was brand new to the outfit. Duquay and I soon got sick of this mess and took off. We had a few more drinks and headed back to camp. On the outskirts of town came Grabrisch and Edwards again. They said they were going home so we jumped on again. The way Edwards was driving I wasn't sure we would make it.

Back at camp some guy told me there was an Italian gal down in the supply tent to be had for four bits. I guess about half of the battery had gone to her. It was hot and the thought of the sweat and the smell was revolting enough. I said no thanks.

The days dragged by with nothing much happening. The outfit was all issued new carbines. I had to turn my old one in. I wished I hadn't for my new one didn't seem to be as accurate.

One day the whole outfit went into to Rome to see a stage show, "This Is the Army". It was held in the Royal Opera House. The opera house was a beautiful place although not too large. It was only for the rich and important people of Rome. There was a larger place for the common people. I guess today we were important people. We enjoyed the show immensely. Irving Berlin was there. He came out in his World War I uniform and sag "Oh, How I Hate to Get Up in the Morning".

As we walked around Rome that day I realized what an Allied Army was. There were soldiers from all over the world. There were Americans, British, Canadians, Australians, New Zealanders, French, Brazilians, Gurkas, Goons,and Jews from Jerusalem, Poles, Moroccans and few other nationalities.

The rumor that had been floating around about our leaving this area and heading south to around Salerno proved to be true.

Sure enough, fairly early in the morning of June 21st our outfit pulled out and headed south. We passed through the outskirts of Rome, hit the Appian Way and headed south.

We soon passed by the outer ring of the old beachhead battleground. We passed through Littoria, Valletri and Cisterna. Cisterna and Littoria were just piles of rubble. We continued on south. The countryside was pretty. The scenery beautiful. We passed the town of Terracina. It was situated on a little peninsula that jutted out into the sea. It was a very pretty setting. A little further down the coast we passed through Formia. It had taken a terrible battering from bombing and shelling from warships.

One area we passed through had been flooded by the Germans. There were thousands of acres under water. It had been flooded to slow down our troops driving up from the south.

All along the road were signs of fighting. There were battered buildings, shell and bomb holes, dead animals and wrecked vehicles. The Americans weren't the only ones that smashed their trucks. I saw one German truck that had run off the road and smashed into a tree. Probably had been driving black out or maybe was being strafed and had gotten into a big hurry.

We passed through the mountains where the Germans had held out so long. I hoped we would go through Casino and our old sector around Venefro but it was not to be. We passed the town of Itri that the Germans had held so long. It was badly battered from the months of pounding. We passed through a tunnel near here that had been built by the Romans and was still in use. It was like our modern day tunnels except it seemed to be arched higher and was narrower. I marveled at the things these people did and why the world had gone backward for nearly two thousand years. I had read that when they built these tunnels they built them like they did today. The engineers figured it out and they would start on both sides of the mountain and dig through and meet each other.

Beyond this tunnel we passed out into the "plain" before Naples. We reached Naples about dark. We passed on through Naples and continued south toward Salerno. We were all getting tired of riding and being hungry. We had only had cold "C" and "K" ration to eat as we rode. In Salerno we saw many British soldiers on the streets. The British seemed to have taken over the town. We saw G.I.s here. We pushed through Salerno and on down the highway.

We finally turned off the main highway and up another road for a short distance. We then turned off into an orchard of some kind. We were tired so we all threw our blankets down right beside the truck, flopped on them and were soon sound asleep.

The next morning we looked over our new bivouac area. It was located in a peach orchard. The land here was quite level and sloped gently toward the sea which was about three miles away. To the east the ground rose more swiftly and soon ran into the mountains.

The ground here was covered with a couple of inches of fine, black cinders. It was the stuff that had come from Mt. Vesuvius when it had erupted during the winter. Old Vesuvius must have been pretty active this time too. We were probably forty of fifty miles from it yet it had thrown out enough stuff to cover the ground a couple of inches thick. I wondered if this stuff had any soil enriching value.

We began preparing to make our new area as comfortable as possible. We didn't have any idea how long we would be here. It didn't take much work for us to get settled. The fellows either pitched a pop up tent by themselves or two went in together. Harris and I pitched a tent together under a peach tree on the outer fringes of the encampment. Most of the fellows pitched their tents around the outer edges of the orchard. The kitchen was set up at one edge of the orchard and the latrine about in the middle.

By the kitchen I don't mean a place where you go into a screened in room and sit at tables to eat. The "kitchen" just meant where the cook truck was parked. We still had to sit on the ground and eat our food from our mess kit. The food was also still all mixed together. No wonder they called it a mess kit. It was properly named. The latrine was also of the very simplest design. It didn't have stools, showers, wash basins, etc. It was just a straddle trench and you threw a couple of shovels full of dirt on it each time you used it. Things were so simple it took the battery only a matter of a few minutes to get settled down.

Here in rest in Southern Italy, the 45th was supposed to start some kind of training program. Our outfit made a weak attempt at some sort of training. Some mornings we took a short hike and on others we would get a soft ball game going. In the afternoon we had a class on carbines or something silly like that. Sometimes we would have a few minutes of close order drill.

One day we went up the mountain a ways and threw a few hand grenades. About the only good they did was scare us. The grenades were the concussion type. There were no fragments but the loose rocks where we were throwing them made it bad. Plenty of rocks went whistling past our ears. A couple of boys were hit by the flying rocks and hurt badly enough to go to the hospital. On another occasion we fired and zeroed in our carbines.

Life in general was pretty easy though as far as the training went. We were able to do a lot of loafing. That's what I liked about the 45th. When you were at rest that is what you did most of the time. It seemed like in those other divisions their boys had all kinds of full field inspections and all that sort of crap. Maybe a lot of the different outfits in the 45th did it too. I did know that "C" Battery of the 158TH Field Artillery didn't go in for it too strenuously.

We began to get passes into Salerno quite often. I also got one to Pompeii. I found Pompeii very interesting. It was much better preserved than I had expected. Being in such a preserved state made it more interesting to me than Rome. One could walk down the streets of Pompeii and almost see it as it was two thousand years ago. I would have given a lot to be able to turn the clock back for a day and be there in its hay day. It must have been quite a place. It was supposed to have been a city of fifteen or twenty thousand. Naturally it wasn't one of the largest cities of the Roman Empire but it had been so well preserved from being covered by the volcanic ash that it was just like it was two thousand years ago.

It had an arena or bowl similar to the one in Rome except it was smaller. It was in much better shape though. This too, of course, was where they had their games and fights. It was easy to see where our football bowls had gotten their design. This bowl even had box seats. The choice seats were down near the bottom. I judged this arena had a seating capacity of around ten or twelve thousand.

The streets of the city were paved and had sidewalks. Both the streets and sidewalks were paved with what appeared to be slabs of rocks. At the intersections there were blocks across the streets for people to step on while crossing the street. Between the stepping blocks were spaces wide enough to allow chariot and wagon wheels to go through. The wheels of the chariots and wagons had made quite deep ruts into the paving between the stepping stones.

You could walk down the streets and visualize how the people lived in those days. The guide showed us the different shops. There were bakeries, saloons, etc. One place was the shop of the importer of wine from all over the Empire. Some of the houses were still in good repair. Even in the back yards were fish ponds and sun dials. There were little flume like structures running down the walls to carry the water. It was probably a continuous small stream with the surplus running on out to keep the fish ponds etc. full.

Writing on the walls was still legible. One place I saw something written with the word Caesar in it. It was written in large red letters on one of the buildings. The guide pointed out other writings on the walls. Some were like Marcus loves so and so and the like. One was about someone losing his dog. The dog answered to the name of Rex and a reward was offered for his return.

One place was like a small glassed in museum. There was one of the citizens of old Pompeii shown there. He was mummified from the ashes and in perfect condition. You could even see how they dressed; toga, sandals and all. This guy didn't look like any kid and was balding. There was a dog there too sort of curled up like he was sleeping.

One place was a world-famous whore house in those days. Girls from all over the Empire and of all nationalities worked here. It was supposed to be a "must" when visiting Pompeii in those days.

The city had a large plaza, something like the one in Rome, and several temples. One I remember was the Temple of Apollo. All in all the place was absolutely fabulous. The guide said after the war a lot more would be uncovered. He said that there was a lot more to the city as well as a suburb called Herculaneum, to be uncovered. I thought to myself, I would like to come back in a few years and take another look. Even now I would have liked to spend more time here. It seemed, as always, when in a place like this, I was always with someone that wasn't interested in this sort of thing. The guy I was with this time wasn't impressed at all and kept wanting to go and get something to drink. I hoped I would get back here again soon and be able to spend more time. This character kept griping until he got his way and we went to the new Pompeii just a few yards from where the old one left off. The new Pompeii wasn't built by the survivors of the old one. The survivors from the volcano were supposed to be the one that started the city of Naples.

I took a few passes to Salerno. It was a fairly large city but there wasn't much to do. There was a Red Cross place that was always very over crowded. The Americans had taken over one nice theater and I saw several good movies there. One day Gill and I went to a theater that was showing an Italian picture. We sat through the whole thing hardly knowing what was going on. As our luck would have it, it was a dramatic picture where an understanding of the language needed to be known to appreciate the show. It wouldn't have made so much of a difference if it had been an action picture. The acting seemed to be very good however. The Italians seemed to go in for movies in a big way. Even many of the small miserable villages had a theater. Most of the time it was the best building in town beside the church.

BYE FOR NOW

One day I returned to camp and found posted on the bulletin board that I had made T-5. I was surprised and pleased. We knew that there were to be a few new rating given but I never expected to get one as I was new to "C" Battery and all. I looked back and remembered that Sgt. Breidenbach had been down from Headquarters a few days before. It was a few days before the time the ratings were being discussed. I think he had recommended me. He had been impressed because I had volunteered to go forward that rainy night way back when we were on the Casino Front. As it turned out I didn't have to go but I had gotten ready and was ready to go. Maybe that didn't have anything to do with the rating but I'll always think it did. Not that making T-5 was a big deal. It wasn't. The rating was considered a bastard rating. I didn't care about ratings anyway. I didn't intend to make the Army a career and wanted to get out as soon as possible. The ten dollars a month raise, from fifty to sixty dollars didn't mean much either. Oh yeah, it was a raise from fifty-five to sixty-six dollars because you got ten per cent more for being overseas. Christ, I'd have to lay awake nights trying to figure out how I was going to spend my money. Actually, now I would be getting thirty some odd dollars a month after my allotment and insurance were taken out.

I guess the biggest thing about getting a rating, no matter how small, was for the people back home. They knew all kinds of morons that were Sgts. Officers probably wondered why you didn't come up with something. They didn't understand the ratings system of the Army. For that matter, no one else did either.

Ratings in the Army are a weird thing. There was not a set pattern, just a hit and miss proposition. Education or ability had very little to do with it. If you were at the right place at the right time you might get a rating. I noticed that good soldiers that went on day after day doing their job properly and doing the best they could never got anywhere. The goof offs, the gold bricks and the screw ups got the ratings. When new ratings were in order, the commanding officer and the First Sgt. would go over the roster to see who should have the ratings. The goof offs, the trouble makers, they knew. The steady soldier they didn't know. Consequently, the goof offs were the ones that came up with the ratings.

Of course, not all officers and non-coms were yard birds. There were many thousands of fine officers and noncoms. Until shortly before the war the United States had a standing army smaller than Bulgaria. To go from that size to sixteen million, almost overnight, there were bound to be plenty of mistakes. All in all though I think the U.S. did a tremendous job in getting most of the guys in a job most suited to them.

Ratings were a funny thing in our own outfit. A replacement hardly had a chance. It didn't matter if your job called for a rating or not. As soon as we lost a man one of the old men of the outfit would get the rating whether his job called for it or not. This wasn't a National Guard outfit and most of the original fellows had come from the same area and had known each other for years. Naturally, they were going to get the ratings and understandably so.

The replacements, like myself, understood and accepted that method. What really frosted everyone was the new method they had come up with. Now that a lot of the original fellows were thinned out and a chance for some of the replacements to get a little rank they were sending rated men right over from the States to take the ratings. Some of the noncoms they were sending over hadn't even been in the Army as long as we had been overseas. How stupid can the big brass get? These replacement noncoms were supposed to be a high caliber men and had gone to noncom schools, similar, I guess, to O.C.S. (Officer Candidate School). Guys in the field and in combat a day or two knew more than these bastards would learn in a life time in school. It was a dirty rotten deal. I guess I was lucky to get any sort of rating of any kind under the circumstances. Even before my T-5 rating Capt. Hurley told me I was the senior radio operator and in charge of the other F.O. radio operators and equipment. I didn't like any responsibility no matter how small. I guess I was a better follower than a leader. That's unique anyway. Everyone fancies themselves a born leader. I guess I was a born follower.

When Lt. Liggett came back from the hospital he wanted his old party back. Shoemaker wanted me to stay with him as his radio operator. He was soon to get his Battlefield Commission and would be transferred to another battery as was the custom. I knew that I probably couldn't transfer with him so figured I better go back with Liggett. So, Rod, Smitty and I went back to Liggett's party. Harris was still to be our driver. So here we were again.

While we were in this area a couple of new fellows came to the outfit. One of the guys was Robert Murphy who was one of those rated men right from the States. He had been in the army only a short time but was a T-5. He was going to be an example of weakness of those noncom schools. One thing they didn't teach, of course, or know how a student would be was if he was going to be a coward when things got rough. The other fellow, I forget his name, was also a T-5. He had been overseas quite a while with a 155 rifle outfit. The new T.O. ruling had cut him out of his outfit and he had been sent to us as a replacement. He was also to be on a F.O. party. He would find out that being in a 105 rifle outfit and F.O.ing would be quite a change from being a truck driver for the Service Battery.

During the second week in July we moved down to Pateum a few miles on farther south. Here we moved into a rest camp that had been set up. Here we had large tents to sleep in and cots to sleep on. We also had a screened in mess hall where we could sit down at a table to eat. This was living compared to what we were used to. The only trouble was we were here only three days. A pretty short rest.

Near here were the ruins of Pateum as it was called. When I first saw it just sitting out in the field I thought it was an ancient Roman building. Instead it turned out to be a temple built by the Greeks when they were colonizing the area a thousand years before the Romans amounted to much. Seeing it made me wonder again why the world had gone backward from those days.

While in this "rest" area we saw a couple of movies. We went to a G.I. stage show that showed pretty good talent and was enjoyable.

Also while we were here our battery threw a party and dance in Salerno. A pavilion on the water's edge was rented for the occasion. A few girls, who were supposed to be checked out as to morals and character, were to be there. Most of us arrived at the party pretty early in the afternoon. There was plenty of gin and we began drinking a few, getting an early start.

The pavilion was right on the sandy beach a few yards from the sea. Beside the pavilion was a long row of bath houses. I guess they were called dressing rooms. There were quite a few girls in swimming or sunning themselves on the beach. Some of the guys were among them trying to get dates for the party.

One of the guys I had been guzzling gin with, had spotted a girl and wanted to ask her to the party. He didn't have the nerve and dared me to ask her for him. Ordinarily I would have shied away from this idea but the gin was making me brave and I agreed to try. He pointed her out and we approached her as she came toward the dressing rooms. He was right. She wasn't bad at all. She wore a tight, form revealing white bathing suit. Besides her physical charms I thought she was pretty too. Anyway, with my fine Italian vocabulary of ten words and a lot of gestures I got over what I was driving at or thought I did. Much to my surprise she accepted the invitation.

We waited on the porch of the pavilion while she dressed. She was smiling as she approached us I almost fell over when she came up and slipped her arm through mine. What I hadn't explained I guess, was that she was supposed to be the other fellow's date. She thought I had been asking for myself. The second the other fellow saw what happened he took off in a hurry so there I was.

I recovered in a second or two and invited her to have a drink. Lt. Norton was acting as a self-appointed bartender and served us the drinks. In my drink he used a jigger of mix and three-fourths a water glass of gin. I was grateful to him for with this turn of events I needed a good stiff one. Lt. Norton was looking out for the F.O.s anyway. He had been an enlisted man and was still one now since he had gotten a Battlefield Commission. He had hidden a few bottles of gin too where only the F.O.s knew where they were.

The girl with me, who said her name was Tina, was gracious and pleasant. We had a few drinks and sandwiches. We couldn't carry on much of a conversation but she seemed to be enjoying herself. I judged her to be nineteen or twenty. She hardly looked like the typical girls we were used to seeing here in this part of Italy. Much more attractive than the general run. For some reason the girls around these parts did not seem to be as attractive, streamlined, chic etc., as the ones around Rome. Don't ask me why a few miles should make so much difference. The ones here tonight seemed to be an exceptional bunch though. There were several girls here although they were badly outnumbered by the guys of the battery.

About seven o'clock a Limey orchestra showed up to play for the dance. They were all drunk, funny and having a whale of a good time. The numbers they were playing were modern ones but sometimes they were rather difficult to recognize. They sure liked their booze but everyone seemed to be having a good time. Tina and I danced a good many times. I never could dance and the rough floor, combat boots and gin didn't improve my dancing either. By now Lt. Norton was really plastered and reeling around on the floor with a bottle of gin and a water glass. Every time he passed a F.O. he would stop them and pour them out a glass full of gin. He hit me with a few slugs of the stuff.

In spite of my horrible dancing and also a little staggering, Tina seemed to enjoy every minute of it. She really snuggled up close and hummed in my ear. I guess she was humming the tune the orchestra was playing. I don't see how she knew what they were playing. It seemed to me each of the musicians was playing a different tune. It really wasn't that bad though, but not too good either.

The party was a huge success. Everyone had a good time and there was no trouble of any kind among the boys. Only one little incident marred the whole thing.

Some sailors tried to crash the party. They came strutting down to the pavilion all dressed up in their whites. They seemed to be in the habit of crashing parties. They weren't fooling with some rear echelon outfit now though. Some of the boys met them at the door and quietly asked them to leave as this was a private party. The sailors laughed at them and started to push their way on in. Then it happened. The sailors hit a hasty retreat after a few of our boys knocked them down and kicked them around in the dirt a little. Their nice white uniforms were a sorry looking mess. I didn't join in the fun for I was a lover tonight not a fighter.

The party finally broke up early in the morning. I found that Tina lived up the street a short distance so I walked her to her place. After a long goodnight kiss, thanks for everything and all I had to go. I couldn't promise to see her again for more reasons that one even if the opportunity came up again. I ran down the hill and caught the last truck as it was pulling out for camp. Everyone was in some stage of drunkenness. Some were singing, others were swearing and other lying on the floor passed out. In spite of the amount of liquor I had consumed I had stayed reasonably sober. I had had an unexpected good time that night.

The next day everyone informed us we would move to another area that evening. Liggett had gone to Naples and had left word for Rodriquez to take care of his bags. It was funny to see and hear Rod cursing about being a porter and nursemaid. When I mentioned to him he looked like a porter he knew I was referring to his color and cursed me as well. He wasn't really mad though for he liked me. I liked him too and he knew it. Several times his being black was a point of humorous incidents, at least for me.

At dusk we loaded ourselves and our equipment on our vehicles and took off. The convoy headed north towards Salerno. We passed through Salerno and on to Naples. There was a lot of war equipment on the move and the traffic in Naples was pretty congested. An accident happened behind us. A fellow fell off from a truck and the 155 Howitzer it was pulling ran over him killing him instantly.

We passed on through Naples and on north a few miles. It was plenty late when we reached our destination. We pulled down a back road and into what appeared to be a peach orchard.

The next morning we looked over our new area which sure enough turned out to be a peach orchard. The trees were loaded with nice large fruit but still a little green to eat. Nearby was a large corn field, a watermelon field and a tomato patch. About a hundred yards away was a farmhouse where we got our water. This farm was the most prosperous and productive place I had seen in all the time I had been in Italy. It almost compared to some of the farms back home. Practically all of the rural area I had been through looked pretty stricken. The land looked worn out. The olive groves and vineyards looked old and as if they hadn't had much care in years. I noticed the cows had real small bags. I thought that maybe it was the breed but a G.I. with a dairy background said it was from poor breeding. It looked as if they wouldn't produce over a quart or so to a milking.

It was around the 20th of July when we moved into this area. There were plenty of rumors flying around about us making an invasion somewhere. Even Captain Hurley seemed to think it would be soon. He even had a rumor. He said he had been told that the beach where we would hit would have a big break wall with a road running right beside it. It was probably just another rumor but there were plenty of them so a couple more didn't mean much. We figured though that we would be going back into action and probably make a landing somewhere. The hottest rumor was that we would hit Southern France.

Actually, the rumor stage about us making an invasion was past now. It was more or less official that we had moved into this area because we were training for an invasion. The biggest thing was where the invasion would be.

Some of the fellows from Headquarters Battery were going to a radio school to learn shore-fire control. They were to learn to work with the ships instead of the field artillery. They were going to school in Salerno for the preliminary schooling. Then they would be flown to Toronto, in the instep of Italy, and spend a few days on some warships to get acquainted with the crews and their firing procedures.

I was asked to go if I wanted to. After the invasion and when the ships were out of range I would be transferred back to Headquarters. It would probably mean no more F.O.ing. I declined the offer. I guess I was a sucker but I liked "C" Battery and the fellows. I even liked F.O.ing even if it was dangerous and rough. There was something exciting about it even though I did get the hell scared out of me a lot of the time. I liked being in our party and the fellows in it. We were fairly independent and did pretty well what we liked most of the time.

Many preparations were being made for the coming invasion. We began gathering our equipment into shape and water proofing it. We were informed that Liggett's F.O. party was going to be with the assault companies of the infantry. That was going to be just dandy. Maybe I should have gone to Shore Fire School. I kept telling myself that this was what I wanted.

Our F.O. party was going to be with "I" Company, 3rd Battalion of the 157th Infantry. We went over and went on several dry runs with them.

We would go down to the beach, load on Higgins boats and go out to sea a mile or two. Then we would board a L.S.T. (Landing Ship Tank). We would stay on the L.S.T. a while then climb down the nets back onto Higgins' boats and head for shore. When we reached the shore we would charge off and hit the beach just like the real thing. We would go inland a few hundred yards and the problem would be over. We did this training exercise on several occasions. We would get up early and join the infantry for the dry run. The problems would be over and we would be back at the Battery around noon.

In the afternoon our party had it easy. While the rest of the battery took hikes, had details, etc., we took it easy. We usually jumped in our jeep and went down to the sea to swim. We would spend hours in the water. The water was just right and the beach was nice and sandy. It was just right for bathing. We had a spot of beach all to ourselves and would never even see anyone. I guess that's one thing I liked about being a F.O. You had your job to do and they let you alone. None of the routine stuff to do around the Battery. There was a reason for this. F.O.ing was more or less a volunteer proposition. At least, even if you were put on a party you could be relieved if you had been on for a while and had had it pretty rough. No one wanted the job so they tried to keep the ones already in parties happy. Sometimes it was almost comical. Sometimes early in the morning a Sgt. would come around routing out guys for details. Sometimes he would wake up one of the F.O.'s by mistake. He would say, "Oh, for Christ's sake. I'm sorry. I sure hope you can go back to sleep". Can you imagine a First Sgt. looking for a detail talking to anyone like that? Generally, when new stuff came in for our P.X. (Post Exchange) we would be asked to come in and pick out what we wanted before it was put on sale to the rest of the Battery. We had first crack at cigars, certain types of popular cigarettes, an occasional watch or other hard to get items. They sure wanted to keep us happy. They weren't trying so hard though that we didn't have to pay for the stuff. I guess you can't have everything. In the evening we usually went to a movie that was set up in a field about a mile away.

One night I was awakened by a familiar sound. It was the sound of the drone of a German plane. It was a long plane and headed in the direction of Naples. The plane must have come a long way. We were now two or three hundred miles behind the lines. This was no doubt a recon plane sent over to take a few pictures of the Naples Harbor. They probably wanted to see if there was an invasion fleet being assembled there.

When the plane was almost overhead I heard a whistling sound. At first I thought it was a falling bomb. I then realized the plane was dropping an empty gas tank. It whirred down and plunked down into the cornfield a short distance away. I would have hated to have been hit with that empty tank. You might as well been hit by a bomb.

When the plane was directly overhead the anti-aircraft opened up. Plenty of flak began to drop around. I just had a mosquito net pitched, not even a tent. The mosquito netting would be no protection against falling flak. It would be ironic to get it here, three hundred miles from the front. Looking toward Naples I could see search lights sweeping the sky. I never did find out if the plane was shot down or not.

August 1st came but we hadn't moved from this area.

We figured we would hit somewhere the 1st because there would be a full moon. Almost everyone that had been with the outfit any length of time called the full moon the "Invasion Moon".

The early morning excursions of our F.O. party with the infantry gave us something to do and often proved to be interesting.

The L.S.T.s that we were making the dry runs in were the same ones we would be using for the real thing. They had just arrived from the States two weeks before. The crews on them were almost all green and most had only been in the Navy for a short time. They were friendly and seemed like a pretty nice bunch of fellows.

The sailors were always after war souvenirs. They would buy anything that was German for almost any price. Some of the infantry boys brought stuff along with them to sell. German helmets would bring from thirty-five to fifty dollars. Old beat up German rifles brought about the same. A nice Lugar or P-38 would bring as much as $200. I kicked myself for not having brought at least a couple of things from the Front with me. I had passed up many chances to pick up lots of stuff. I had always kept putting it off. It was hard enough to lug around the necessary things without having lots of excess baggage. The fellows that were able to take the best advantage of the situation were jeep drivers who would haul supplies from the rear to the line companies. They would come up at night with the supplies and ask around for some helmets, etc. They would take the stuff back to the rear where they had a place to keep it without having to cart it around.

About the only piece of German equipment I had kept for any time was a gas mask carrier. German gas mask carriers were made out of metal. They were strong, light and waterproof. They made a nice thing to carry some of your valuables in. I had it for a couple of months but it was lost with the rest of my stuff on the drive to Rome.

As near as I had come to keeping anything was to try on a helmet for size, do a couple of "Heil Hitler" salutes and throw it down again. I had seen several beautiful Lugers but they were always attached to a booby trap and I was no expert at disengaging them so I left them strictly alone. I wished now I had even gotten a couple of buttons or something. These sailors were eager to buy anything.

I couldn't help noticing what a nicer, cleaner life these sailors lived than the combat soldiers. We climbed aboard the boats, a pretty grimy bunch. It didn't help that we had to sleep on the ground all of the time. Your helmet was your only tub in which to bathe, shave and wash your clothes. It was tough to even try to keep the worst of the grim off. Washing clothes was a big problem too. Sometimes, if we found a stream, we would get a chance to wash them. Sleeping, working and sweating in them got them right back to their grimy condition in a very short time.

The sailors were always clean and had nice clean clothes. They had showers any time they wanted them. They had more and much better chow too. They had tables to sit down to eat at as well. Coffee was available at all hours. They had nice bunks to sleep in. Everything was clean. They slept under cover and out of the elements. They didn't have to sleep in the mud with the rain beating down or on the cold ground with a water soaked blanket at freezing temperatures.

They were in very little danger too. The Germans did have a few subs still operating but they seldom got a ship. They seldom lost a ship from enemy aircraft either.

It seemed they had a life of Riley with very few problems. I guess I should have joined the Navy. Even when they were in on an invasion it didn't last long. They would dump the Army and be off to distant places. Even if it was a rough invasion they didn't have to be around long. It was the army that had to hit the beaches and meet the enemy face to face and slug it out for months. Strange as it may seem, even after comparing the sailor's life and ours, if I had to do it again I would have still taken the Army. I must have been sick.

While in this vicinity I went into Naples several times. I didn't care much for the place so didn't go in as often as I could have. It was a hot and dirty hole. Everywhere were beggars and Wops trying to peddle rot gut wine or some flimsy trinket. They had a terrific price on everything too. There were many kids pimping too. Some looked to be only seven or eight years old. Most of them seemed to be working for their sisters or so they said. They would tag along behind you telling the merits of their sister or the gal they were working for. Their favorite pitch was that she had big teats, small hole and was clean. These damned Dagos didn't seem to have the morals of monkeys.

Naples was supposed to be a beautiful city. Maybe some parts of it were but I saw nothing to show me it was a beautiful place. Maybe it had been a little better before the war but I doubted if it had been much better. Downtown Naples was a crumby place. Even the main drag, Via Roma, was a filthy street. Rome was a much nicer, cleaner city than Naples. The people in Rome seemed to be a higher class than the people around here.

Most of the side streets were off limits to the G.I.s. Up these narrow streets were dives of all kinds. Whore houses at almost every door.

There were a couple of pretty theaters in downtown Naples that the Army had taken over. I saw "Show Business" with Eddie Cantor at one of them.

I soon got fed up with Naples and stayed away from the place. I got sick of fighting off the beggars and pimps for one thing.

These Dagos expected a lot and never appreciated anything that was done for them. A good example of this was that there were a couple of Wop kids working around the Battery. They helped out the cooks a little. They had been supplied with complete G.I. outfits. They were given pup tents to sleep in. They got to eat our chow all they wanted. They had lots of cigarettes and candy given to them. Every few nights they were paid off with cash. A collection was taken up among the fellows for them. They always got a lot more than they were worth. They were making a lot more money than I was.

Did these little bastards appreciate any of this? Hell no. I heard them say they liked the Germans better than they did us. They said we had lots of cigarettes and money but were poor soldiers. Even if we were all they said they still had their God Damned nerve talking like that after all we had done for them. Who in the hell were they to talk about being good soldiers anyway? The Germans or someone had dubbed the Italians as a "Nation of Cowards". If I had my way I would have had the bastards stripped and booted them out of camp.

They were typical Wops though. Once a Wop, always a Wop. I guess that's the way they are and there is nothing anyone can do about it. The longer I spent in Italy the worse I hated the bastards. I hoped the U.S. wouldn't do a damned thing for these bastard.

When one would say to me he was going to the States after the war, I would tell him that was what he thought.

I would tell him that we had too many of his kind there now and American had wised up.

I never disliked any particular nationality but I seemed to hate these Dagoes with a passion. I wasn't the only one who hated them. All the G.I.s hated their guts. The only exception was the few Dagoes in our own army. Even most of the American Italians were ashamed of them. Many of them hated to admit that they were of Italian ancestry. Even though they could speak the language lots of them wouldn't even speak to them. Too bad to feel that way but that was the way it was.

Some of the batteries had picked up Italian kids and kept them with them. Service and Headquarters both had one. The kid in Service Battery was around twelve. He was sullen and a smart aleck. Every time I got near the brat I would have liked to give him the back of my hand. The kid in Headquarters, Marty as he was called, was a little older, maybe about seventeen. He was just about as miserable though.

The Captain of Service Battery liked his kid so much he wrote home trying to adopt the brat. I understand he got a reply something to the effect that if he wanted to adopt anyone there were plenty of orphans in the States. Anyway, he wasn't going to be able to take him home and I was glad.

We knew our time in Italy, or at least this part of Italy, was running out. The rumors were flying thick and fast. The most persistent one had us hitting the beaches of Southern France.

The F.O.s were winding up the dry runs working only with the infantry. On August 9th there was to be a big dry run with all of the units taking part. It was supposed to be exactly like the real McCoy.

On our little jaunts with the infantry everything had

been working smoothly. There hadn't been any accidents or anything.

Several amusing things happened though. One time Lt. Liggett couldn't make it for one reason or another so Smitty, next in rank, was supposed to be in charge. The assault boats we went to the shore on would drop the fronts anywhere from twenty to seventy-five yards out according to how soon it got hung up on the sand bar. We would go charging off into the water and towards the beach. The time Smith was in charge, I guess he wanted to inspire us. As we plunged out of the boat and towards the beach Smith turned toward Rod and me and yelled, "Come on men. Let's go". About that time he stepped into a deep hole and disappeared. He came up spouting water and floundering around for his rifle. Rod and I laughed so hard that we could hardly make it to the beach.

After we hit the beach we would go inland a few hundred yards and the problem would be over. When we went inland one day another rather amusing thing happened. Lt. Liggett was in charge that day. We came to a ditch several feet wide and full of water. A small log was the only way across it. Liggett, also trying to inspire us, was going to show us how to cross the ditch properly and rapidly. He started running across the log. Half way across he missed his footing and in he went, belly flop fashion.

Another time Rod and I pulled a rather mean one on Smith. We had orders to go over to "I" Company one night and we would be ready to go on the dry run with them early in the morning. It was very late when we arrived where "I" Company was bedded down. It was pitch black too. You couldn't see your hand before your face. In fact, the only thing that you could see was a faint red glow coming from Mt, Vesuvius. I was carrying Smith's blanket while he went to check up on something somewhere. Meantime, Rod and I flopped down under an apple tree to sleep. It was very quiet. All you could hear was the deep breathing of the infantry boys sleeping on all sides.

Suddenly, we heard Smith approaching. He was a big man with a heavy walk. It being so quiet it seemed like he made the earth tremble as he walked. He walked right up to us, stepped over us and continued on. We just let him go on past. We lay there listening to his crashing around in the brush looking for us. He sounded like a bull in a china shop. We could hardly keep from bursting out laughing. Smitty was still crashing around and calling our names softly a half hour when we dozed off to sleep. Sometime during the night he must have found us for he was curled up by us the next morning. Rod and I never let on that we had heard him at all.

An amusing thing happened to Rod and Smith one day after one of the dry runs. After we got back to the Battery we usually went swimming. On this particular occasion I didn't go with them. Anyway, after their swim they had wrapped towels around their heads and were walking back toward the battery on some dirt road. A guy came by in a jeep and was apparently lost. He spotted Rod and Smith. Seeing them, especially Rod with some sort of turbans he figured they were some sort of Indian or other Colonial Troops. He was desperate to find the main road and decided to see if he could find the way from them. He went through all sorts of sign language and Pig Latin. I guess he nearly fell over when they answered him in American. It must have been funny even though Rod didn't seem to think it was too funny.

On August 4th we had the big dry run. All units took part. The guns, trucks and other equipment were included. The F.O.s went in with the assault infantry as usual. The guns were brought in on "ducks". The 105's on the "ducks" were set up so they could fire. They would be used that way in the invasion if necessary. I imagined that would be quite a stunt, firing a field artillery piece from a moving "duck". (A duck was a six-wheel-drive amphibious truck that was used for transporting goods and troops over land and water or for use approaching and crossing beaches and amphibious attacks).

On this big dry run we hit the beach of Salerno. The terrain here was supposed to be similar to what we would encounter on the invasion. They had even constructed a concrete wall like the one that was on the invasion beach.

We had one last big dry run. This was on August 9th. They shot the works on this one. Everyone was in on it; artillery, tanks, tank destroyers, engineers and even the quartermasters. As soon as the problem was over we were to load back on the boats and wait for sailing orders.

Another thing that was different on this dry run was that the infantry took a long hike. Of course we F.O.s went with them. After we hit the beach we kept going inland. We walked twenty-eight miles that day and with that old August sun beating down it made it a day to remember. We went up and down hills. Forded streams, over fences, through underbrush and had a lot of tough going.

Another thing that made it tough on the F.O.s was not having any relief in carrying the radio set and battery pack. Ordinarily the three of us would change around some in carrying the equipment. We weren't able to do that on this day however because we had to carry part of the Shore-Fire Control Party's radio.

A Shore-Fire Party was supposed to be with us. Sgt. Kuza was in charge of this bunch. Kuza was the only veteran among them. The rest had come right from the States. Someway, two of the fellows had gotten fouled up and didn't get off the boat with Kuza. The one fellow that had come with him wasn't very robust and soon pooped out so we had to carry his stuff. It made someone in our party, with the exception of Liggett, carry something heavy all the time. Liggett did spell Rod with the battery pack every once in a while. I carried that seventy five pound radio the whole twenty-eight miles without relief.

We finally reached our objective about fourteen miles inland and to the north. Our "objective" was a small village. A few hundred yards beyond the village we stopped to eat our "K" rations. We were at the half way point now. All we had to do now was to make our way back to the starting point.

The only humorous thing on the whole trip happened just outside the village. We were hot and tired and trying to save all the steps we could. We came to a high stone fence that seemed to reach a good distance in both directions. It was too high to climb over and we didn't know how far we would have to walk to find a gate or some way around it.

We discovered that the wall was thin and flimsy so we began to kick at it to knock a hole in it. We were making pretty good progress on the wall when a couple of Italians approached. We thought they might own the property and were going to squawk about us knocking a hole in the fence. Liggett growled, "If those guys give us a bad time, shoot the bastards." He meant it too. I didn't dislike Italians that much to do something that rash. The fellows didn't say anything about the fence but just wished us luck. We didn't know whether they wished us luck in knocking down the fence or what. We finally made a hole and continued on to our destination. After our lunch of "K" rations and a short rest we started back to the ships.

BYE FOR NOW

The road back was tough. Although we traveled on road most of the time the pace was killing. It grew hotter in the afternoon and the radio got heavier and heavier. I became so tired with the old radio bearing down I began to walk pigeon toed. The straps around my shoulders cut way in.

Even the infantry boys felt sorry for me. Most of them were traveling light with just their rifle and canteen. Even when they had a full pack it wasn't as bad as this damned radio. An infantry pack fit to your back better. The radio on a pack board just hung there lie dead weight. I heard one of the infantry officers ask Liggett if I had carried the radio all the way by myself. Liggett told him that I had carried it every step. The infantry officer said, "Christ, what a tough son-of-a-bitch he must be". Hell, it made me feel good to hear him say that. Maybe here was something I could do better than most of the men. That was it. A strong back and a weak mind. I was lucky to have been blessed with strong legs and a back that never gave me any trouble. I seemed to have good endurance too. I had never been bothered with my feet either. In all the hiking and marching back in Basic Training and over here I had never had a hint of a blister or sore feet. I knew I was going to have to be tough today if I ever wanted to make it back to the ships. I was getting pooped. If only I had someone to relive me for even a mile. Liggett spelled Smith and Rod once in a while but never me. I guess he thought I was as tough as the infantry officer had thought.

We finally got down to the sea, where we could now see the ships but they were still several miles away. One of the infantry officers figured if we went down by the water's edge we would find the sand packed down hard and we could follow it right on down the beach to the ships. It sounded like a good idea.

We wallowed around in ankle deep sand but the hard packed sand at the water's edge never materialized. We had to walk back through the soft sand to the road. That little trek into the sand just about finished us off. When we reached the road again I was staggering. By now many had dropped out from exhaustion and blisters. I didn't know if I could make it or not without dropping out.

Finally, those of us still capable of walking made it back to the ships. I was never so glad to get to any place in my life. We walked in waist deep water and up the ramp of our L.S.T. (Landing Ship Tank). On this day, August 9th, 1944, when I stepped off of the beach it was the last time I was going to be in Italy for quite a while.

We were so pooped that after a "K" ration supper we rolled out our blankets and turned in. Rod and I made our bed under a half track. During the night I sensed that we were moving.

The next morning, we were at anchor a few miles farther down the coast. We were still in the Gulf of Salerno however. We weren't very far from the shore either. Maybe a mile or two.

Looking toward the mainland we could see the town of Sorrento. Farther on Mt. Vesuvius rose skyward. The old volcano was pretty quiet at the moment. A little smoke rolled off it and at night we could see a dull red glow from it. That night Rod and I again bedded down under the halftrack.

The next morning we were still in the same place. There was no way of telling how long we would be here. Time passed pretty slowly aboard the L.S.T. There was very little to do but talk and stare in at the shore. There was plenty of activity of ships in the gulf. The gulf was so big and the ships spread around so much that it was impossible to make out if a convoy was taking shape or not.

Rod, Smitty and I spent most of the time talking and playing Casino. We didn't see much of Liggett. He had a room for himself and ate with the Navy Officers. These officers really had it pretty good at that.

The three of us talked a lot about everything from politics, religion, war and home. I was surprised to find out that Smith was part Jewish. He said his mother was a Jew. Once Smith and I got into an argument about religion. He accused Bernice and me of running off to get married just because we had been married in Reno. He said that maybe we were married in the eyes of the law but not in the eyes of God because we had not been married in the church. Of course I blew up at him but it was nothing serious.

Smith was still unmarried although he had gone with the same girl for fifteen years. I gathered he was one of those guys who believed in having his first million made before he got married. He showed me the picture of his girlfriend. She was a very attractive person. She must have thought a lot of him to wait that long. Smith hadn't had much education but you wouldn't know it. The way he talked and appeared he could have passed for a college graduate. Apparently his father had died when he was pretty young and he had gone to work. He had gone to work for the finest jewelry firm in Philadelphia at the age of fifteen. I guess he had worked his way up pretty well. I figured he got his more or less refined ways form the type of clientele he was used to serving. In fact, I could imagine Smith in an exclusive jewelry store, all dressed up in pin stripes and a swallow tailed jacket, showing some rich gal some $50,000 earrings. He wasn't the least bit on the sissy side though. In fact, he was just the opposite. He was a big guy and rugged looking. He was tough too. He could keep up with any of us even if he was thirty nine. Apparently he had saved his money because just before he was drafted into the Army he and a partner had opened a store of their own. About the time he had come overseas the Army had started releasing draftees thirty-eight and older. Being with an outfit already to go he had been stuck. He didn't complain about if much though.

Charley Smith did seem a little on the stuffy side though. He seemed to hold Rod a little in contempt. Not much but I seemed to sense it somehow. It could have been my imagination. It also seemed to me that he thought I should be a little closer to him than Rod. Maybe it was because we were both noncoms and Rod was a Private. I don't know. Maybe he was a little miffed that I seemed to like Rod's company better than his. It wasn't that I liked Rod so much more but we seemed to have more in common and I guess I felt a little more at ease with him. Smith was a great guy though and I liked him a whole lot.

Ruppert John Joseph Rodriguez. I was amused when he would tell me he was Spanish. He was about as much Spanish as I was. He might have had a couple of drops of Spanish blood in him but it couldn't have been much. About the only thing about him that was Spanish was his name. He bragged that his name was different than the run of the mill Rodriquez because he spelled it with a "g" instead of a "q". He was probably the only G.I. in the whole army that didn't have a picture of his wife or family. Everyone carried a picture of their wife, sweetheart, or even a casual female acquaintance to show. Not Rod though. He had five or six kids though and no pictures of them either. I was sure it was because they were as black as or blacker than he was. He claimed his wife was French and had been the daughter of some diplomat to Puerto Rico. I imagined she was as much French as he was Spanish. I often wondered how Rod had gotten into a white man's unit. Probably the only colored guy in any white man's outfit and I was with him and his buddy. It could have been sort of tough on him at that. He kept saying his wife was going to have some nice pictures of herself and the kids taken and send him some. None ever came however.

Rod was born in Puerto Rico and had gone to high school in San Juan. He had come to New York City and worked for a law firm that had a large Puerto Rican clientele as an interpreter. He was just my age, twenty-four. He had several kids already. He said his people believed in having their children while they were young. They would be fairly young when their families were grown and they could take it easy then. Maybe they had something there at that. Rod didn't seem too happy with the way the United States was handling affairs in Puerto Rico. He said the old timers said that they had been a lot better off under the Spanish. It seemed he thought that the U.S. was skimming off the cream and not leaving enough for the natives of the island. I wasn't up on Puerto Rican politics so had no argument.

Rod of course was a Catholic but didn't seem to worry too much about it. He didn't seem to take it as seriously as Smith.

Rod must have noticed the double looks guys would give him when they saw him. Everyone was so surprised to see a colored guy in a white man's outfit. Sometimes they would stare for several seconds.

He was a good fellow though. He seemed sincere and he seemed to like me a lot. He wasn't too large of a fellow.

He probably didn't weigh over one hundred and twenty-five pounds, but he was pretty wiry.

The three of us speculated on where we were going. We all were positive it would be Southern France. It seemed so obvious. I couldn't help think that it might be somewhere else. Some way it didn't seem logical to hit France when we already had troops there. I couldn't get the idea out of my mind that we might sail around the end of Italy, up the Adriatic and hit somewhere in Yugoslavia. We could drive east, meet the Russians and cut off the lower Balkans. I was sure that it would be Southern France.

All kinds of rumors floated around the ship. The one about Southern France was the strongest. Some of the rumors had it that we were to make an "end around" and hit Northern Italy. Another was in western France near Spain. Others were Yugoslavia, Holland and even Norway. Well, time would tell.

Of course, "I" Company, 3rd Battalion, 157th Infantry was aboard with us. They were the ones we had practiced with and they were the ones we would make the landing with.

We knew some of the infantry boys pretty well. There was one fellow with "I" Company that was quite a character. His name was Miller and everyone called him "88 Miller". He could imitate 88's so well you almost hit the ground. He also imitated rifle fire, machine guns, mortars, tanks and almost any other kind of war equipment. He made them sound like the real McCoy. He even imitated battle. He was always cracking some sort of joke. Miller never had a serious moment. He was always carrying on some sort of nonsense. Sometimes I wondered if he wasn't cracked. He was well liked by the whole outfit.

A couple of more days passed without anything of

interest happening. We were getting tired of looking at Mr. Vesuvius. We were getting anxious to get going. We knew it had to come sometime so we might as well get it over one way or another. We were sort of beginning to sweat out this coming invasion wherever it might be.

Finally, on the evening of August 13th, we began to move. We weighed anchor and started sailing just after dark. A thrill of excitement ran over me. It wouldn't be long now. The sailors were really in a sweat. They were all excited and nervous for this was to be their first action.

As soon as we were out a few miles the sealed order was opened. We were going to hit southern France alright. Well, that settled one question anyway.

Soon Liggett came around and gathered up his F.O. party and we retired to his stateroom. There we opened a bunch of maps, drawings, air photos and relief maps of the place where we were to hit.

The spot was on the southern coast between Marseilles and Nice at St. Tropez Bay. The 36th Division was to land on our left, the 3rd on the right and the 45th in the middle. We were to hit what was called "Yellow Beach". The maps showed the big wall and all.

"I" Company was to land just to the right of a small peninsula, drive inland, cut left and take the town of St. Maxine. "K" Company was to land on the point of the peninsula and drive up the bay shore and contact us in St. Maxine.

Some of the maps even showed where the gun emplacements and minefields were. We looked over the maps and photos for about an hour and then turned in. I didn't feel much better now that I knew exactly where we would hit. I began to sweat out the invasion now and wondered how rough it would be. It looked like they had plenty of mines and artillery there waiting for us.

The night passed without event and we were still sailing right along the next morning. It was the 14th of August. Of course we knew the invasion was to be at 8:00 A.M. on the 15th. There were quite a few ships in our convoy but it didn't look like near enough for a full scale invasion. A drop in the bucket from what we had heard about the Normandy Invasion.

Three assault divisions didn't seem like too many either. A French Corps was supposed to relieve us as soon as things were rolling well. The good old 45th, 36th and 3rd were going to take it on the chin again.

Eight o'clock in the morning seemed rather late for the "It" hours. All of the other invasions had been at dawn. The Americans almost always attacked at dawn, at least major attacks. Eight o'clock seemed like an odd time.

During the day we passed Sardinia and Corsica. I was surprised to find that you could see both islands very plainly from the straits between them. I had always imagined that there was much more water separating them.

As night drew near, we began to say "H" minus the hours it was before eight o'clock the next day. Everyone was in a sweat now .Most of the infantry boys had some combat experience. One or two had been lucky enough to last through the campaign in Sicily, the invasion of Italy, the battles around Casino, the Anzio beachhead and the fall of Rome. Most of the fellows had come in as replacements on the drive to Rome.

I don't know who was sweating out the invasion most, the veterans or the men who hadn't seen any combat yet. The veterans knew pretty well what it was all about and sort of what to expect. That didn't help much knowing what can happen to you. Some of us had been lucky enough to last through several months of combat and knew that we were due. The law of averages was catching up with us.

Even though a replacement imagined the worst he couldn't comprehend, as a civilian, how awful those shells sound, the gruesome sights and that horrible gnawing fear. You had to go through it to ever even understand what it was all about.

About dark slips of paper were passed among us. On them were messages from the British General and Admiral in charge of the operation. It said something to the effect: "we were doing a wonderful thing and would strike the enemy a crushing blow. Good luck and God's speed".

Although we dreaded "H" hour we all wanted to get it over with. This waiting was driving me nuts. All day they had been playing two pieces on the phonograph over the loud speaker. One was "Paper Doll" and the other was "A Prayer for My Daddy Over There". I guess they were the only records they had. The one, "A Prayer for My Daddy Over There", was sung by a kid or someone that sounded like one. It couldn't have been very morale boosting for any fathers in the bunch.

The sailors got really excited at dark. They said they all had been alerted and not one of them was to sleep until "D" Day. Not getting any sleep would be their toughest deal.

The infantry boys limbered up their throwing arms by pitching a few hand grenades overboard. When the first one exploded against the side of the L.S.T. the sailors thought we had hit a mine or been torpedoed. You could hardly hear the grenades much less feel them against the boat. We made remarks to the sailors. We said we hoped we didn't get strafed by a German plane or something because they would really go to pieces. They were all young kids and this was their first action. In fact, it was the first time overseas for the biggest part of them.

After dark Rod and I carried the radio and battery pack up and put it into the assault boat in which we would be in in the morning. Rod, Smitty and I lay down and tried to get some sleep. We talked a while and wondered what lay in store for us. Everything was ready. All we waited for now was "H" hour. Final preparations had been made. We had even sewed American flags on our sleeves. I slept several hours that night although was pretty restless.

The next morning, "D" Day, we were up and getting ready to go at 5:30. Only two and a half hours before "H" hour.

About six of our bombers began to come over and bomb the shore. We could see the shoreline quite plainly. There is was, France. It was going to be a nice day although there was a kind of high haze.

Soon the assault boats were lowered into the water and we climbed rope ladders and got into them. We began to circle around and around.

The Navy began to open up. Salvo after salvo pounded the shore. We could see the shells hitting and churning up the earth. Some of the ships were turning hoses on their guns to keep them cool but they still kept firing. The big guns from the battleships and cruisers made a terrific blast when they went off. They had a peculiar sound. First there would be a sharp report followed by a deeper, heavier blast. That second blast actually rocked you.

The first wave headed for the beach. It was several miles to the shore. The Navy kept pounding away until the first wave was well on its way.

Soon the second wave, our wave, was ready to go. The assault boats were pointed toward the shore and opened up wide. It would take a half hour to reach the shore. The Navy was still bombarding the shore and we could plainly see the shells tearing at the earth.

We approached some L.S.T.s, British version, about half way to the beach. These L.S.T.s had been made into special ships. On their decks, rows of racks had been constructed to launch rockets. Just as we approached they let fly with the rockets. They whizzed shoreward in a big cloud of white smoke. They sounded like huge sky rockets taking off. The barrage was supposed to pound the shore just before the first wave was to hit it.

We roared on in toward the beach. We were almost there now. The Navy bombardment had stopped now. This was it. We had been ordered to keep our heads below the gun wales but I just had to take a look so I peeked out. We were only a few yards from the shore now and things looked pretty rugged out there. There were shell holes, twisted wire and all sorts of debris. A haze of smoke and dust hung over the whole scene and added to its eerie look. I figured I wouldn't last two minutes on the beach. I glanced back toward the ships. I saw water go gysering up some distance behind us. It looked like a salvo of shells hitting the water. I didn't know whether they were German or some shorts from one of our own ships.

Everyone was tense and poised. Even "88" Miller was quiet. He was standing in the front of the boat, head down, thinking.

We felt the boat slow a bit as we skimmed over the sandbar. We were free again and almost to the shoe. The sailor driving the damned thing got so excited that he dropped the front of the boat and was yelling at us to get off. If he hadn't gotten so excited we could have gone right up to the shore and could have stepped off without even getting damp. We began piling off in waist deep water.

In a second we were on dry land. The sailor turned the boat around and was gone in a flash. I wished I was going with him. He was going back to safety but where were we going? Maybe I should have joined the Navy at that. Here on the beach the smoke was plenty thick and the smell of gun powder filled our nostrils. There was the big concrete break wall just like they said it would be.

We had no more gotten on the beach when an officer said to "hit the dirt". I figured this was it. I thought it was just like at Anzio and that the Germans had recovered and were fighting back. I expected a terrific barrage or to be rushed. Instead the wall was going to be blown up. However, after a moment's deliberation it was decided to let the following wave blow the wall. We went over the wall on the ladders that the first wave had brought. There was a lot of rifle and machine gun fire over to our right.

I felt a little easier when we jumped down on the other side of the wall onto a black topped road that ran beside it. A few small arms bullets were flying in our direction but nothing big yet. The Navy was again lobbing big shells over our heads. They made a horrible sound as they passed over.

We moved up between a small orchard and a vineyard. We had only gone inland about fifty yards when we came up on a house with a white flag waving out of one of the windows. We figured it was some Germans the first wave had passed and they wanted to give up. Instead of Germans coming our when we yelled, a Frenchman and his wife came towards us. They were so scared they hardly knew what they were doing. I guess they didn't know who was landing; Americans. Germans, Japs, Fuzzie Wuzzies or who.

It was no wonder that they were scared to death. There were dozens of big shell holes all around their neat little home. Only a miracle had saved it from being hit. The woman grabbed onto my arm. She was jabbering something to me in French. She was so scared she was shaking and half-crazy with fear. Even as frightened as she was she was trying to tell us about some German guns somewhere. I thought that showed real guts. They both kept saying thanks over and over. I suppose it was for "liberating" them. They were both so nervous that every time a salvo or shell whined over they ducked and almost broke into a run. They certainly had been through a hell of an experience.

We passed on through their neat little farm and their well-kept vineyard. Soon sniper fire was coming over from our left. One platoon was sent over to mop them up.

We started moving up hill now and through some pines. We made it to the top of the first ridge safely. From the top of this ridge it seemed that the shells from the big Navy guns were just skimming over us. We would hear the ships fire a salvo and then hear the horrible rush of the shells as they passed over us. With four big shells tearing through the air it made the sound of a dozen trains passing over. Everyone would hit the ground as they roared over. We could look toward the next ridge and see them bursting. They weren't landing so far away at that. They probably weren't clearing our ridge by much. They made a nasty crack when they hit and I would have hated to be in the impact area of one of them. The Navy was just firing blind. At least at the moment. They were firing by maps, probably trying for crossroads or some reported German stronghold.

We continued along this ridge to its highest part. We were harasses by some sniper fire. One man was wounded but not too badly. At the summit of this ridge stood a high tower. The Germans had no doubt used this tower for observation. From this point you could see far up and down the beach and miles of the sea. Here we caught the first wave. They had waited for us before pushing into St. Maxine.

Sniper bullets were kicking up dust here and there. No one was hit but it was annoying and we had to keep pretty low. The tower was searched but the Germans had already left. A German officer was routed out of some nearby trees. He said he had been an observer for a battery of big coastal guns. He said our bombers had knocked them all out.

Kuza went out a little ways to set up an O.P. so he could fire the Navy if a target presented itself. Shortly we heard shots from the direction he had gone. Soon he came rushing back saying he had run into a couple of Germans. They had been lying on the ground and he almost fell over them. He had fired six quick shots at them with his carbine and took off. He was afraid there might be more of them around. In his haste he had dropped his map case. Later when he went back to get it he found one of the Germans dead.

Now that the two waves had joined we now started pushing down the ravine toward St. Maxine. We crashed down through the brush meeting no resistance. We knew that we would find St. Maxine in good shape. These French towns weren't to be shelled unless it was absolutely necessary.

We were in beautiful country now. Tall pine trees and from the ridge we could look down on the very blue Mediterranean. We passed a couple of nice big homes. I would have liked to live around here on the Riviera. The country was beautiful and the climate wonderful.

We soon entered the town of St. Maxine. It wasn't a large town but very pretty. I noticed some of the streets were even paved in pastel shades. A gas station looked like something out of a lavish movie. I noticed a sign above one business place. It said "American Bar".

There wasn't too much trouble in taking the town. Some Germans had holed up in some of the buildings and the infantry boys were digging them out. They used bazookas and hand grenades as well as their rifles doing this. I was getting a kick out of firing my carbine through windows of one of the buildings where some Germans were holed up.

Of course we were the first American troops in the town. We were supposed to contact "K" Company here before pushing on up along the bay road. "K" Company seemed to be having trouble. We could hear plenty of rifle and machine gun fire from the beach where "K" Company was located.

While we were here in St. Maxine an odd thing happened. We were more or less milling around the main corner of the town. I even had my gun at sling and wasn't expecting much. All of a sudden three Germans on bicycles rode around the corner and right into the midst of us. We were as probably surprised as the Germans. They had no doubt opposed "K" Company down the line. They didn't have any idea American troops were already in the town. Two of them just kept coming, in fact almost running over us. The third slammed on his brakes, drug his feet, everything to stop. He turned his bike around and headed the other way. I yelled at the two to halt but they just put their heads down and kept peddling. I jerked the carbine off my back and started firing. I emptied a whole clip at them. About the time I started firing several infantry boys had recovered and started firing. The poor devils didn't have a chance. The bikes wavered and went over. It was amazing the distance they went with all of that lead being thrown at them. I fired sixteen rounds at them myself. I was pretty excited. Maybe I never hit them at all. I hoped not I kept telling myself. The poor bastards. Why didn't they stop? They could have and would still be alive. The third guy apparently got away. There weren't many places he could hide. We figured he was holed up in a pedestrian tunnel that ran under the main street and out to the beach.

Just after the wild firing at the Krauts I noticed Kuza limping toward us. He was as pale as a sheet and said he had been hit in the leg. He had apparently gotten in the way of one of our own bullets. He had a nasty looking wound in the meaty part of his leg just below his butt. It was really a "million dollar wound". One of those that would put you in the hospital for a long time yet not too serious. No bones had been hit. He would probably be sent back to Italy and spend a lot of time in the hospital taking it easy. At first it didn't hurt too much but when the shock wore off the old pain began to set in. He gave me a little tube of morphine all of the assault troops carried and I injected it into his arm. I was surprised I did it so easily without using him for a pin cushion. Soon the dope took affect and the pained look went from his face. The last thing I remember about Kuza was he was sort of dozing with a pleasant look on his face.

When things quieted down a little the French started sticking their heads out of doors and windows. Soon they began coming out and looking us over. One woman brought out a large pitcher full of ice cold lemonade. It really hit the spot. Another passed around some nice large peaches. They were as big as the ones grown at home in California. Of course, there was some wine too. It was good wine too, not the kind we got down in Italy. Rod and I got a big bottle of it and started drinking it

BYE FOR NOW

pretty fast. Sgt. Cote, the First Sgt., of "I" Company told us to take it easy on the stuff as we had lots of walking and fighting ahead of us.

We also had our first chance to take a look at the French. Already we could see that they were so far ahead of the Italians in every respect. There wasn't any comparison. They were cleaner and much nicer looking. They seemed to be very glad we were here. One guy could speak good English. He had lived in Cleveland, Ohio for years. In fact, I think he was born there and had come back to France and became a French citizen. He enjoyed talking to us. We asked him if there were many Germans around here. He said that there had been plenty until the Normandy Invasion. Most of them and the heavy equipment had pulled out then. That made us feel a little better. He said at one time the Germans had plenty here. They had expected the "Second Front" to open up here.

We had been in St. Maxine about two hours. "K" Company hadn't contacted us yet. They were still meeting heavy resistance in their drive on the town. It was decided that we would push on without them.

Just as we started moving out a man, a Jewish looking fellow, came up and said, "France and the world thank you for what you are doing".

We passed a group of girls who had ventured out when things quieted down. One gal ran out and threw her arms around a G.I. and tried to kiss him. The G.I. was a bashful one, probably the only one in the whole outfit. He pushed her away and said, "I haven't got time for this kind of stuff". What a character. It wouldn't have taken all day for a couple of kisses and might have been morale building.

We moved on out of town. We passed the two Germans we had shot down. One was by the edge of the street and the other had dragged himself into an alley. Both were sprawled in big pools of blood.

I thought to myself. "What the Hell?" Here were a couple of poor guys dead. Shot down like dogs. No one had anything against them. They just happened to have a different colored uniform on. Maybe their big shots had different ideas than our big shots, but individually these fellow probably thought about the same way we did. They were in uniform because they had to be, just like we did. You were a big hero the more enemy you killed. Here you shot someone down you didn't know or who had never done anything to you. Back home if you even beat up some bastard that deserved it and had really done something to you, you would get thrown in jail for assault or something.

Somehow it worked out that we were fighting this war so that the rich could get richer. In the comfort of your home or in some bar back in the States, the reasons they told us we were fighting seemed to make sense. Here, in the stark reality of the horror of it all, it was hard to remember what you were supposed to be fighting for.

We passed on out of town and on down a black topped highway. We were followed along pretty close to the shore of St. Tropez Bay. Our objective now was to contact the 3rd Division that was pushing around the bay to meet us.

We moved down the road about two miles before anything happened. Suddenly, mortar shells began to drop around us. We all hit the ground and crept off the road and into an open field. We were right out in the open with nothing to take cover in or behind.

Most of the first shells dropped at the water's edge about seventy-five yards to our left. The Germans evidently had that part of the beach zeroed in. They soon began to move the shelling over toward us and they began dropping in on us. They also began heavily shelling a ditch up ahead of us. The shells were really cracking around.

It was pretty obvious where the shells were coming from, at least the general direction. A little ways ahead of us was a heavily wooded hill. The Germans probably had a strong point somewhere on it.

Suddenly there was the order. "O.K. men, let's take that hill". We got up and started running forward. Shells were cracking all around and some of the men were going down. Shrapnel was whizzing pass my ears and I was expecting to get it any second. I noticed sweat was pouring off me and I don't think it was entirely from the weather, although it was a pretty warm day. I got a glimpse of a Sgt. running a short distance in front of us. A mortar shell almost made a direct hit on him. When the dust cleared I expected to see him lying there in pieces. Instead, he just kept running like nothing had happened. I could hardly believe my eyes. A miracle? It was the law of averages. It just wasn't his time.

Just as I reached the ditch a G.I. went down and I stumbled over him and fell head over heels into the ditch. This was the ditch the Germans were shelling so heavily. My radio got tangled up in some barbed wire and I was really fighting to get it loose. Although I got loose and out of the ditch in a matter of seconds it seemed like hours. I had just gotten out of the ditch and a few yards away when shells began to drop in again. I was lucky again.

We were in the woods now and going slightly up hill. The shells were now all dropping behind us. I caught up with the Sgt. that had almost received the direct hit. He said he felt pretty good but had a terrific headache and could hardly hear a thing. He was lucky he even had a head left to have a headache with.

An infantry officer wanted our F.O. party to go up and see if we could place some fire on those mortars. Of course we had to find their exact location first. Our F.O. party and the shore fire control party, minus Kuza, sneaked up onto a house where we could get good observation on the hill where we figured the mortars were located. The house we entered was brand new. It wasn't even finished yet.

We called our artillery and tried to get some fire on the top of the hill. The guns told us they were out of range. We knew that couldn't be because we could almost see the invasion beach from here. That's what they said though and they told us to try the Navy.

With Kuza gone the shore fire control party was useless. The other three didn't know anything about firing. Liggett decided to try to get the Navy to fire. I contacted a ship. It was the French cruiser, The Terrible. It was manned by mostly French sailors and some English. The radio operator I talked to was, of course, English.

When we had them fire the first salvo we got down in the basement of the house and peeked out a basement window. Never having fired anything like this, we weren't sure where the shells would go. After all these big guns weren't 105s. Actually, the hill we were going to try to shell wasn't too far ahead of us. I had always heard that these big naval guns were very accurate. Firing ships was new to us and our sensing's might be a little off or something. Also, these guys didn't fool around with a round of smoke to adjust on. When you gave them the target they let loose with a salvo of four guns the first thing. The ship being a heavy cruiser, the guns were ten or twelve inch or possibly larger.

They fired the first salvo and we were relieved and pleased that they landed at least in the vicinity where we wanted them. They landed to the left of the hill but not too far from what we thought was the target. Liggett made his adjustments and they fired another salvo. They seemed to land in the same place. We kept making adjustments and they fired another salvo. After several salvos we hadn't gotten the shells exactly where they wanted them. We had heard that if you didn't make your target with a couple of salvos the ships would give up. After shooting all four big guns at one time they could soon use up a lot of ammunition. They were giving us all we wanted today. We could see the shells landing and see dirt, smoke and debris geysering up. We were hitting something and at least scaring the hell out of someone. Suddenly a salvo hit exactly where we had wanted it to. It looked like dirt, pieces of buildings and everything went up. We figured if that was a German stronghold we had certainly done a lot to help neutralize it so I called to the ship to cease fire. I spread it on pretty thick telling them what fine shooting they had done and thanked them. The English operator on the other end came back with, "Thank you old man. Let us know if you have any more targets for us. Good luck and cheerio". It was an Allied effort at that. American observers. A French warship with part of an English crew.

We soon began advancing up the hill. Rifle and machine gun bullets splattered among the trees. The boys set up a mortar and began lobbing them up on the hill. The infantry went charging up the hill with fixed bayonets. They seemed to ignore the bullets zipping through the trees. They reached the top of the hill and started throwing hand grenades. They jumped right into the trenches with the Germans. A few more shots and a couple more hand grenades and it was all over. The Germans gave up. Our F.O. party reached the scene just as the last shots were being fired. Coming up the hill we hadn't exactly relished the idea of hand to hand combat but we were ready. We, as well as the infantry with us, weren't needed. The first surge of men had been enough.

The German installation was an elaborate one. It was well dug in, reinforced with logs and there were several large dugouts. Like one infantry boy said, "Hell, if we had known they were this dug in it might have taken a couple of days to take the hill." The Germans had more men here than anyone had anticipated. We noticed our naval shelling hadn't hit this hill. It had hit the one toward the bay. Even if we hadn't knocked out the installation like we had hoped it could have done some good morale wise. Those big shells had no doubt shaken up the Krauts. They knew what we had when we had shelled the wrong place. We could easily shell this hill when we found out their location. It was probably a big factor in them giving up so easily. It had also given confidence to our own men. The Infantry had a lot of faith in the artillery. They knew how our barrages softened up the enemy positions and made them so much easier to take. Sometimes the artillery would completely drive the Germans away and the infantry could often take a position without hardly firing a shot. We felt a little bad about not hitting this hill and hoped it wouldn't shake their confidence in us.

Our causalities had been light in taking an elaborate place like this. Two men had been hit, one quite seriously and one officer, Lt. Smith, had been killed. Lt. Smith had been hit by a bullet, knocked down and fell on a trip wire to a booby trap.

Lt. Baerfoot, one of "I" Company's officers, was quite a character. He seemed to like to mix it up like this. He was all excited now. He had been shooting and throwing hand grenades like a mad man. He also had a nice big bullet hole through his helmet. A pretty close call.

The Germans were rounded up and searched. They were made to throw their stuff in a pile. There was quite a pile of guns, map cases and all kinds of personal belongings.

The Infantry boys didn't exactly handle the Jerrys with kid gloves. They seemed to be upset by the loss of Lt. Smith. I didn't know the man but he seemed to have been highly thought of by the Infantry boys. They made the Krauts really step around and if one didn't understand exactly what he was to do he got a swift kick in the butt to help him savvy. It did seem too bad to strip them of their medals and things that were useless to anyone but them.

Soon the Germans were headed down the hill carrying their wounded with them. In fact, they must have had a racket being here in this beautiful country and climate. There had been no fighting here and they weren't bombed in this particular area until a couple of days ago. Their clothes were in good shape and clean. Their equipment seemed new and shiny. They looked like strictly occupational troops but may have seen action on one of the other fronts.

From the pile of equipment I got myself a dandy map case. It was real leather and had plenty of room for maps, message books, the code cards and pencils. I needed something like this badly. I usually carried the code cards in my pocket and that wasn't a good idea. Having no place to carry a message book I usually didn't even have one. I usually just wrote the message down on a "K" ration box or something. Strictly no S.O.P. (Standing Operating Procedure).

The guy that owned the map case which I "liberated"

wasn't here just to fight either. In the case, among other things I found, was a good supply of rubbers.

The good old "I" Company had done a good job in taking this hill. There had been about seventy-five Krauts here. That's a lot of troops for one company to have to charge a well-fortified position and take it. The boys had taken it easily without many casualties. "I" Company was probably the best Infantry Company in the Army anyway.

We soon started moving again. We pushed on down the hill. We began passing some big beautiful houses. One was supposed to belong to some ambassador from some South American country. The Germans had been using it for a P.X. (Post Exchange).

Every once in a while we would corner some Germans in a house and blast them out. Finally the tanks began to come up the road. When we cornered some Germans in a house we would have the tanks fire into the house providing it was near enough to the road for them.

We combed the landscape with the Infantry looking for Germans. Up and down hills, over fences, through houses and garages. Hour after hour, mile after mile we walked. We were soaked with sweat and worn down to a frazzle. By now the Infantry boys had thrown away things that they didn't think was absolutely necessary. I wished I could throw away the damned radio. Rod was doing a lot of bitching and I couldn't blame him. It was a grueling day. One of the shore fire control boys pooped out and had to drop out. One thing that kept everyone going at this terrific pace was the specter of Anzio. Everyone wanted to get inland as far as possible before the Germans got organized.

Just at dusk we passed through the grounds of a beautiful estate. Two elderly ladies came out with a couple of big pitchers of wine. They poured us drinks as we plodded by. Rod and I were lucky enough to get a glassful. It was good and gave us a lift.

Just at dark we took about a half an hour break. We opened our "K" rations and ate a few bites. This was the first time we had eaten anything to speak of all day.

Too soon we were on our way again. We hit a road and headed down it. This road had been bombed and shelled heavily and had huge holes torn in it. It was dark now and the craters made walking difficult. We kept falling into the craters. This road had certainly taken a pounding.

We kept plunging down the road at a terrific pace, getting no breaks. We didn't meet any resistance and were really covering ground. About two o'clock in the morning we made contact with the 3rd Division. It looked like the beachhead was secure.

Our outfit turned inland and made our way up another road. About three o'clock they told us to fall out for the rest of the night. I really felt like falling out. Every muscle was tired.

The Company Headquarters was set up in a school house. The rest of the company distributed themselves around it. All of the windows had been blown out of the school from the shelling and bombing. There were several large craters in the vicinity.

Our first day in France had been a long one. Nineteen hours ago we had hit the beach. "H" hour seemed like days ago now. The invasion hadn't been as bad as we had expected. Our company had lost eighteen men. Not bad for an invasion but tough on the eighteen. The percentage between the killed and the wounded was high though. Twelve killed and six wounded. Usually it was the other way around. I guess the sniper fire made it that way. All of our medics had gotten it. I doubt if the Germans had fired on them deliberately but with us all having

American flags on our sleeves it may have been hard to tell a medic arm band from a distance. I think the mortars had gotten some of the boys too. I knew several who had gone down.

Eighteen was almost ten percent of the company. We considered it light casualties. I heard that the Normandy "D" Day had been ten per cent.

It had been a strenuous day as far as the hiking had gone. I figured that we had hiked at least thirty-two miles. Coupled with the fighting and the other excitement of an invasion it had been a pretty strenuous day.

Rod and I lay down in the vineyard to sleep. We were dog tired. Our clothes were soaking wet from the sweat caused by so much walking. The nights here were plenty cool even in August. With the weather cool and the sweat soaked clothing we were miserable and sleep was almost out of the question. We didn't have any blankets with us so there was no way to get warm. We huddled together trying to get a little warmer. We only got a few winks of sleep and that was from sheer exhaustion.

We were glad to see dawn breaking again. As soon as it was light enough, we built a tiny fire of twigs to warm up over and to heat our "K" rations.

I put up the radio and got in touch with the Battery. I had them send up Harris to meet us. From all reports the Germans had taken off from the coastal areas and would probably set up a line inland somewhere. It figured that we wouldn't run into much resistance for a few miles.

When the Infantry was ready to move out again Liggett insisted that we go with them. The rest of us wanted to wait for Harris but Liggett had the rank and the last word so we got ready to go. We were cursing Liggett under our breath but knew he was right. We wished he wouldn't be so conscientious.

We hit the road and the old grind started again. Mile after mile we went. It looked like we would make another thirty-five miles or more today. The pace was fast and the old sun began to beat down again. Sweat rolled off us in streams.

All along the road stuff began to appear. The Infantry was beginning to throw equipment away. There were gas masks, bandoliers of ammunition, mortar shells, "K" rations and other equipment along the way. I expected to see rifles, bazookas and mortars dumped any minute. I guessed that trucks followed up later and salvaged most of this stuff. Some of the men were dropping out with blisters. I even saw some of the fellow's feet bleeding. I was lucky as I never got even as much as a little blister in my whole Army career.

The idea that the modern Army rode everywhere and didn't walk was as far wrong as you can get. In World War I trench warfare had made the lines stable for years. An advance of four hundred yards to take some enemy trenches was a big push. Probably to hike back a few miles out of artillery range to a rest area was a big deal. In that war, the fronts had been static for days, month and even years. This war was a war of movement. Miles of ground was gained and lost in a matter of weeks. Naturally, twenty-five years later, the Army was a lot more mobile, but not that much. We didn't have any horse drawn equipment but the artillery still had to walk. North Africa and Sicily had been walking campaigns. Casino and Anzio had been static battles, a throwback to World War I. As far as walking, my own belief was that the modern Doggie did a whole lot more than his Dad had ever dreamed of.

We plodded on down the road hoping Harris (the F.O's driver) would hurry up and catch up with us. We didn't expect him soon for there weren't any vehicles on the road yet.

We kept plugging along at a grueling pace. When we would get ten, everyone would just drop in their tracks. Once we stopped right by a vineyard. Just ten yards away from us were some delicious looking grapes. Rod, Smitty and I lay there looking at them and trying to decide whether to get up and get some or not. We decided that we were too tired and we could get some grapes later.

We were up again and on down the road. I remembered a Bill Mauldin cartoon showing Willy saying to Joe, "Throw away that extra joker out of the deck of cards to make the load lighter" or something to that effect. That is exactly how I felt. To get rid of one percent of one ounce would help a lot.

A few light vehicles began to appear on the road and our hopes began to rise that Harris might catch up with us.

Sometime later Harris did show up. We cursed him for quite a while for taking so long but we were glad to see him. He had gotten lost and had been lucky to find us at all.

Our ride turned out to be pretty short. We soon passed through a small town called Plan-de-la-Tour. The town seemed to be deserted. A short distance on the other sided of Plan-de-la-Tour we stopped. Here was to be an assembly area for the 3rd Battalion. We had ridden only about a mile but it helped.

In the assembly area, an open field, we loafed and waited for the truck to come up and shuttle the Infantry farther up. We had a chance to get a little rest and eat a bit of "K" rations.

Quite late in the afternoon we pulled out again. Most of the Infantry was now riding. The ones that were walking would have to walk only until the trucks dumped their men at the new assembly area and came back for them.

We moved through a heavily wooded area. It was quite a pretty place. The roads here in southern France were good so far. All were black topped and in good shape.

We noticed that in most of the fields the Germans had planted poles. They were several inches in diameter and about twelve feet high. These were planted to wreck the gliders of air borne troops if they tried to land in the open spots. They must have spent a good many hours filling these fields with poles.

Our new assembly area was soon reached. This one was in the woods. Up ahead we could hear the rumble of war. About two miles up the road was the town of Vidaban. The 2nd Battalion was attacking it. They seemed to be meeting some pretty stiff opposition. There was plenty of firing and noise going on in that direction. Tanks and T.D.s (Tank Destroyers) were clanking up the road toward the action. Ambulances were streaming back with the wounded.

Towards evening Harris, Smitty, Rod and I jumped into the jeep and headed for a river a short distance up ahead. We wanted a refreshing dip and to get cleaned up a little. On the road were many German vehicles buzzing around with G.I. drivers, of course. The fellows who were driving them had painted big white stars on them so they wouldn't be mistaken for the enemy. Most of the stars were very crude. Most were almost comical.

Seeing all of this captured German equipment proved that they had really been overwhelmed and had taken off in a hurry. You seldom found German equipment intact. If they did have to abandon anything, they always destroyed it first.

We reached a bridge by the stream and turned off to

the left. A short distance later we pulled up into a glen. It was a beautiful spot, shaded and cool. An old vine covered house was set back a ways. It seemed abandoned but I suspected an old couple lived there. The whole scene looked like a picture from a calendar. The water here was a beautiful green. Not the green of stagnation for we could clearly see to the bottom. I guess the color came from the surrounding foliage. I could picture the place as a resting spot through the centuries. Maybe Roman soldiers on their way to the battles on up in Gaul, The Rhineland or England had stopped here to rest.

We found a wide spot that was ideal for swimming. We peeled off our clothes and dove in. We had fun diving off a log near the edge of the stream. It seemed sort of odd to be swimming so near the Front. There was a battery of American artillery set up just across the river from us and they were firing quite a bit. We also heard a couple of German shells whine but never heard them hit.

At dark we jumped into the jeep and headed back to the woods. We found everyone there in good spirits. The beachhead seemed very secure now. The fighting hadn't been too bad yet and it looked like the Germans were on the run. Maybe they were. We all thought the war would soon be over. Our morale was higher than it had been in months.

We heard German planes over head on their way to bomb the beaches where the supplies and invasion ships were. Up ahead, several fires were burning bright and we could smell the smoke from them. The sound of the guns became more distant as the battle rolled on.

It was a beautiful night, balmy and millions of stars twinkled down through the trees. Everyone laid down in small groups talking in low tones until quite late.

The next morning trucks began to show up to shuttle

the Infantry on up. It was completely quiet now with the only reminders of the war being the equipment sounds.

Our F.O. party climbed in the jeep and took off up the road. We passed through Vidaban. It showed some signs of fighting. There was quite a lot of debris lying around in the streets. On the edge of town the trees, grass and buildings had been burned. They had been burned from the Germans burning piles of ammunition. We understood that this was an important dump that helped supply the Italian Front.

We pulled into where Headquarters was setting up a few miles out of Vidaban. They knew that this would only be a temporary stop and so we treated it accordingly. The Germans still seemed to be a good distance away.

Everyone was in good spirits. So far, the Southern France Campaign had been pretty successful. This was what everyone liked, traveling fast and little opposition. Surely the Germans were done and they would fold up now.

We got back in our jeep and tore down the road. There was plenty of traffic on the road. There were all sorts of heavy and light American equipment. We also noticed some large groups of German prisoners.

Harris drove like mad and finally we were out ahead of the traffic. We were beginning to wonder if we weren't getting too far ahead of the traffic. We might run into the Germans before we had planned. These roads weren't swept of mines yet and we were hoping the Germans had taken off so fast they hadn't had time to plant them.

After we had gone about two miles and hadn't seen an American vehicle, we decided we had better stop and wait for someone to show up.

Finally, two jeeps came up the road. Sgt. Shoemaker's party was on one of them. They pulled up and we talked the situation over. As far as they knew only armed recon cars had gone up this road. We decided to push on together though. Our jeeps weren't going to make very good armored cars.

We soon reached the town of Tavernes. We stopped here, got a couple of drinks and a bottle of wine. Shoemaker took off for the next town which was Salernes a few miles farther on. Shoemaker didn't give a damned about anything. He was about as near fearless as they came. His battlefield commission hadn't changed him either. He was just as easy going as before.

We soon took off for Salernes ourselves. Just outside the town several Frenchmen flagged us down. They had dozens of large cans of something with them. It looked to us like large cans of beer. They were German ration cans and we naturally supposed that it was beer. The Frenchmen wanted us to take a bunch of the cans. The cans were scorched as though they had been in a fire. One thing we didn't need was scorched beer. The Frenchmen kept insisting we take some of the cans. We took a few cans to keep from hurting their feelings. We later kicked ourselves for not taking more. Instead of being beer it turned out to be cans of beef and pork. The stuff was delicious. The best rations that I had ever eaten overseas.

We soon reached the town of Salernes. The only vehicles in town, besides a couple of jeeps, were a couple of recon cars and a couple of light tanks. We decided that this was as far as we should go. Even the recon cars were apparently waiting for more stuff to come up before they pushed on.

We soon found a local bar, went in and began to have a few drinks. The place seemed to be run by a couple of girls. The French in the place were celebrating their liberation or something. Anyway they treated us like kings and our money was no good. They insisted in buying our drinks and the liquor was flowing freely. Most of the drinks seemed to be on the house at that. The stuff we were drinking was good stuff too, not just wine.

Even Liggett seemed to be having a good time. Usually when we were out to have a good time like this, he was always so worried about what some higher ranked officer might say. He could never relax and enjoy himself.

Smitty was the one that surprised us all. He was always the dignified type and everything he did was proper. He drank very little and was often griping at Rod and I, for in his opinion, we occasionally drank too much. He was in the right mood today though for he drank drink for drink with us. He got to feeling pretty high and was having a real swell time. We each had a French gal draped on us and we were getting kissed between each swallow of booze. Not Smith though, he had one on each side of him and was going to town with both of them. We couldn't believe our eyes. That couldn't be Smith. This France must be a wonderful place. Even Smith had gotten into the spirit of the country. We often kidded Smitty about how he had acted that day. He said he couldn't imagine what had gotten into him but he admitted that he had had a good time.

Rodriguez got to talking to some Spaniards that were in the place. They could also speak French. Using three different languages some of the conversation with the girls was translated. Actually, there was more action than talking. We had a very enjoyable time.

Harris had stayed outside to watch the jeep and radio. He didn't drink anyway so he didn't mind staying outside with his vehicle. The rest of us were glad he didn't drink being the driver in the party.

After a couple of hours in the tavern we got on the jeep and headed back down the road looking for the battery. We soon found it off to the side of the road in an open field.

We were feeling pretty high when we reached the battery. We were still nipping at bottles of wine that we had been given back at Salernes. We seemed to have trouble getting our Coleman stove going and were having quite a time trying to get something cooked to eat. We took turns kicking the stove over.

Some of the boys in the battery envied us a lot. They liked the way we were on our own so much without too much interference from the brass. They liked the way we got into town first, etc. Also, they disliked the routine and the discipline of the battery and wished they had more variety like ours. We never heard anyone volunteer though until today. One fellow, a truck driver, staggered up to us and said he wanted to join our party. He was obviously drunker than we were. We found out that he had just received a "Dear John" letter from his wife. I guess he wanted to do something desperate or commit suicide. It could be just that, suicide, if he was on a F.O. party very long. We acted like we were interested and would take him up with us on our next job. We knew when he sobered up he would realize that he wasn't that broken up. That's exactly what happened too for we never heard a peep out of him again about volunteering.

We hung around this area for most of the rest of the day. Harris, Rod and I wanted to go back to Salernes and take up where we had left off. Liggett wouldn't go for it however. We were pretty sore at him and muttered curses at him under our breath.

Toward evening our party jumped on the jeep and went up to join "I" Company. We found them getting ready to bed down at the foot of a wooded hill. They hadn't made contact with the Germans yet.

Just at dark, five German planes came down strafing low over the road. Nothing near us was damaged and no one was hurt.

We finally got bedded down for the night. Just as I was dozing off a shot rang out from up the hill and a bullet sang by, I figured there were snipers up in the trees and they would harass us all night. That was the only shot however and the night passed quietly.

Early the next morning we moved out. We moved a few miles and took up a position on the side of a hill overlooking the Durance River. There was a house nearby. An old Frenchman came out and talked to us. He said he had been in the last war and showed us pictures of himself taken in his uniform.

The Germans began to shell a little town to our left that was a half mile or so from our position. They were pouring the shells into the town in a steady stream. They didn't seem to be from very large guns, probably 75's.

A little later we learned that our own "C" Company was in that town and had gotten some of the shells. Two fellows had been killed and a couple of others weren't expected to live. I never knew how they made it out. Duguay had received a pretty bad wound. The two fellows that were killed were Shuck and Charmo.

I had known Sgt. Shuck very well. He had done a lot of F.O.ing in Sicily and Italy. Just before we came to France he had been assigned to the C.P. Battery. He told me that now that he never had to go on F.O. again he figured his chances of living through the war were very god. I guess when your number is up you are going to get it regardless.

A little later we moved out again. We sent Harris and

the Jeep back to the battery. We didn't know what was up ahead but it was obvious that we were catching up with the Germans. From now on, for a while at least, we would go on foot with the infantry.

We soon reached the river. There was a nice large bridge spanning it. The bridge was intact except for a section in the middle of it that had been blown. The section destroyed was only a few feet, perhaps ten. A hastily constructed wooden section had been built across the destroyed area. The structure was flimsy and only substantial enough to allow foot troops to pass over. No vehicles, even jeeps, could get over it. We could see engineers beginning to make a Bailey bridge across the river a short distance away.

Soon, we were all across the river and continued up the road. The foot soldiers were on their own now. No heavy equipment across the river of any kind yet.

Just across the river we noticed a lone plane circling slowly above us. We couldn't see any markings on the plane and couldn't make out whether it was German or one of ours. It did look like a British Spitfire but it was acting so strangely we were suspicious. Everyone kept an eye peeled towards the sky. We were in a bad place if a plane did strafe us. On one side of us a cliff rose perpendicular from the road. On the other side of the road it was just as bad. From the edge of the road it was a sheer drop straight down. If we were strafed we would just have to lie in the road and hope for the best. Fortunately we weren't strafed. The plane circled around a couple of more times and then headed toward the German lines. We decided that it was a captured Spitfire and the Germans were using it for recon work. Being a Spitfire and with no markings would confuse the anti-aircraft boys long enough for it to come in and take a look. A few pictures and he would be gone before anyone could figure what to do. It had probably come over here to see if anything was across the river yet.

We continued on down the road meeting no resistance or even hearing anything that sounded like the Germans were anywhere around. We soon reached a small town and took a short break. There was a large fountain and pond in the middle of the town. We washed up a bit here.

Again we hit the road and took off on what was apparently going to be another marathon. We moved down the road at a grueling pace. We started going up a long fairly steep hill. It was a long three miles. Poor old Rod began to fall farther and farther behind. Although he was losing ground he kept plugging along. He was a wiry little guy at that. He was small and weighed one hundred and twenty-five pounds. He had done mostly office work before getting into the army so wasn't too used to this sort of thing. He could carry a big load with the best of them.

The Infantry boys that I felt sorry for were the mortar crews. That base plated gun was heavy and dead weight. The ammo carriers had a tough load to pack too. This hill sapped all of us.

Finally we reached the top and pulled off the road into a pear orchard. It was just dusk and we were to spend the night here. Harris soon arrived and joined us. The bridge across the Durance had been fixed enough to let light vehicles cross.

The night passed quietly. Again it seemed that the war must be thousands of miles away. Surely the way the Germans were falling back the war couldn't last much longer. You couldn't shake the idea that they would make a stand somewhere soon and lash out at us.

Early in the morning we set out again. We traveled

down a black topped road that was absolutely deserted. We met nothing and nothing passed us.

About five miles down the road we came to a tiny village called Gambois. We were told that we might stay here a day or two. We had to wait here for definite orders. Things had moved so fast and the lines were so fluid I guess the big brass wanted some of the outfits to stay put for a while so they would know where they were, then they would be able to make some sensible plans for the future.

This little village of Gambois was in an out of the way place. No other G.I.s came here while we were here. I doubt seriously if any ever came after we left. There were no main roads or important ones that passed near the place.

As soon as "I" Company moved into town the Frenchmen began to gather around. We passed out a few cigarettes and soon were busy chatting with them. They said that these were the first cigarettes they had had in four years. They had been using leaves of some kind for tobacco.

At first the place seemed to be deserted of women. We thought maybe they were afraid of us and were hiding out. What apparently happened was that the women and kids had gone in to doll up before they came out to meet us. Soon the women and kids came out and gathered around. The women were dressed in their best and the kids were neat and clean. It was a real treat after seeing those ragged, crummy people in Italy.

The people of this village treated us nicely. They gave us wine, grapes, eggs and fresh vegetables. In return we gave the kids chocolate, the men cigarettes and the women some rations and coffee. We had been traveling light and didn't have much to offer.

A couple of the men could speak pretty good English. We spent hours talking to them. We asked them how the French Underground got their weapons and ammunition. Several fellows of this village carried British rifles. They said that they had pre-arranged places for the stuff to be dropped. At night, British planes would come over and drop the guns and ammunition. The English were clever at that sort of thing. I wondered how they knew the stuff would drop into the right hands.

We asked how the Germans had treated them. They said that they hadn't seen too much of the Germans because their village was small, unimportant and off the beaten path. They hadn't been overlooked entirely though. A German big shot had come to the village and had gotten hold of the mayor. The mayor had to promise that this town would furnish so many eggs, chickens, potatoes, etc. to the Germans each week or else. Trucks would come to pick up the stuff every few days. That was about the only time they had seen any Germans with the exception of an occasional armored car passing through on routine patrol.

They said that living in a small farming community like this, the local people had been able to get enough food to get along pretty well. What was very scarce though were chocolate, cigarettes and things like that. They had not been available for five years.

One of the men had seen the bombing of Marseilles. He said three thousand Frenchmen had died in that one raid. He said they had been caught flat footed when our bombers hit the town. He said everyone was out watching our formations of the bombers. Always before they had passed on over on their way to bomb the great naval base at Toulon. This time though they dropped them on Marseilles instead. They had been trying for the railroad station and freight yards. Many of the bombs had gone astray and had flattened everything for blocks around. He had owned property in the bombed area and it was all completely destroyed. He felt lucky though that he had escaped and was thankful that his wife and child had been here at this village and were also spared.

We asked if the French had hard feelings towards the Americans about the bombings. He said that some of the mothers that had lost children were pretty bitter at first. However, they realized that it was necessary and knew that the time for their liberation was coming nearer. He said the people of Southern France had been looking and praying for the Americans to come for a long time.

Later Rod and I got to talking to a couple of elderly old maid sisters. They both spoke perfect English. After graduation from college here in France they had studied in England. They were very intelligent and well-traveled people. They had a home on the Riviera at Menton, near the Italian border. They told us that when the French Army was defeated and the Wops began coming over into their city they were forbidden to speak French. The Italians told them they must speak German or Italian. They said they were conquered and there would never be a France again. They were here in Gambois visiting some relatives. They told us if we ever got to Menton after the war to come to their place and we would be welcome to stay as long as we wanted.

Of course there is always a beautiful girl. Harris spotted her on a porch of one of the houses. She stood there quite a while eyeing us curiously. We tried to talk to her but couldn't make much headway. Not that she was giving us the brush-off but it was the old language barrier. We wished that everyone spoke a universal language.

We always kept a few extra "D" chocolate bars for such occasions. The girl became much friendlier when we offered her the chocolate and didn't point toward a bed. We were probably the only Americans she had seen in her life but she had probably heard stories of Americans of the other war. Probably stories like the ones we had heard about the French girls.

Her name was Simone something or other. We got out our little French books that were given to us on the boat when we were coming up here for the invasion. Simone, Rod, Harris and I had our head together over the book and tried to make a little conversation. The book had an American word with the French translation and showed how to pronounce the French. We made very little progress with any intelligent conversation. Rod, being able to speak Spanish fluently, could sometimes carry on a fairly good conversation with some of the French. I guess in this particular area the dialect must have been quite different for he seemed as lost as the rest of us. Anyway, we laughed a lot and enjoyed ourselves. It was something to watch Simone eat the chocolate. It was the first she had eaten in five years. She would take a bar, break off a tiny piece and put it in her mouth. She seemed to savor every little morsel. These Frenchmen sure loved their chocolate.

At dusk, Harris went down and got the jeep and brought it back and parked it in front of Simone's house. We got out the little Coleman stove and began to prepare something to eat. We made coffee and fried Spam and potatoes. Simone got a loaf of bread and a jug of good wine from the house. We stood around the jeep's hood for a table and ate the Spam sandwiches and drank the wine and coffee. Simone enjoyed the Spam almost as much as she had the chocolate.

We sat on her porch for a long time talking to her. The conversation wasn't too much but we enjoyed ourselves. Simone seemed relaxed and at ease with us now. She knew that we just wanted to be friendly and had no ideas about dragging her out in the brush or something. This was a clean cut girl and would have made some G.I. a nice wife to take back to the States. Some difference from those bags that some of the G.I.s had married in Italy. I'd have been ashamed to be seen in public with most of those bags. Those guys must have been pretty hard up or dead drunk when they were married. I don't think Simone had any ideas about leaving France though. She said she was engaged to someone that was in the French Army.

Later we went back to find Smitty and Liggett. They wanted to know where we had been. I guess they were afraid they might have missed something. Liggett gave us hell and said to hang around close for we might have to pull out at any time.

We had noticed a pathetic little procession passing through the streets several times a day. It was the kids from a school for handicapped children that was here in the village. The kids were either deaf and dumb or blind. The deaf and dumb children would walk along ahead with a blind one hanging on to them. The whole procession was escorted by a Sister. I guessed they were taking them out for a little fresh air and some exercise. We felt sorry for these kids and wanted to do something for them. We rounded up the last of our candy and canned goods and got a few things from the infantry boys. We went over and knocked on the door and presented the stuff to a Nun. She was so pleased she invited us in. Other Nuns gathered around and they thanked us over and over. They brought us a couple of bottles of wine. I don't care for wine as a rule but this stuff was the best I had ever had. On the bottle it stated it was vintage 1923. I don't know what the alcoholic content of the stuff was but I seemed to start getting a buzz after a few swallows. A priest showed up and invited us to dinner. I was a little leery of this. I was afraid that these people, being Catholic, might go through some ritual and I'd be lost, like bowing down three times in the direction of Rome or something. I didn't want to embarrass anyone, especially myself. It was alright for Rod and Smith for they were both Catholic.

The dinner was served in a large room. To my relief there were no complicated rituals like beating yourself in the head with a hammer or something. We just sat down and began to eat. The priest as well as the Nuns seemed to enjoy the Spam immensely. Besides the Spam we had potatoes, a salad, bread, wine and coffee. Our hosts enjoyed the coffee to no end. It was the first they had had in years.

Later we sat there drinking wine and talking. One of the Nuns came in and said that the kids wanted to meet the American soldiers. They were brought in and each one came up to shake our hands. We had to reach out and grab the hand of the little blind kids. They each thanked us for the candy. They seemed tickled to meet us. We felt happy that we could do something to brighten the lives of these poor little devils a little.

We went back to Liggett and found that he had gotten a call from the battery. We were supposed to go there immediately. We jumped into the jeep and took off for the battery. When we got to that location we found out they were going to move up again soon. They told us to go back to the infantry and stay with them and to keep our radio on and be ready to move at a moment's notice.

We returned to Gambois and spent another peaceful night there. The next day we stuck around pretty close waiting for orders. I kept in contact with Headquarters all day. Simone came down to where we were, and we talked with her awhile.

I was proud of the way the fellows of "I" Company had behaved the two or three days we were here in Gambois. Everyone had behaved themselves. No wild drunks quarrelling with civilians or trying to shack up with some of the women. In fact, the boys, for the most part, had stayed right in their little area and did little moving around the village. I wondered how come? One thing I was sure of was that the boys respected these people. Almost everyone had been in Italy and had been in contact with those ragged, dirty, begging, sniveling Wops. Here the people were clean, polite and had pride. They were sincerely glad we were here and trying to help them get their country back. They wanted to do something for you and not just expect you to give them everything and gripe because it wasn't more. The G.I.s wanted these people to like them but in Italy they didn't give a damn.

This little village was old, very old and there really was not too much crap and debris laying around. The whole atmosphere here was completely different than it had been in Southern Italy. I think what I heard one veteran say mirrored, more or less, what most of us thought. He said, "I hope to Hell I don't have to go back to Italy. I might have a hard time containing myself around those Dagoes as well as I did when I was there." We all realized that the people over here in Europe weren't like those we met in Italy, especially now that we had come to France.

Maybe we berated the Italians too much. Their poverty couldn't be helped, but it does seem like they could have been a little cleaner. That begging and whining couldn't have just come during the war. It must have taken years of practice. I had heard stories of travelers in past years telling of the begging and all in Sicily and Southern Italy. We had only seen a small part of Italy and maybe "up north" was much better as the Italians kept telling us. The poor souls seemed to realize they were living in sub-standard conditions and some even seemed to be ashamed of it. I hoped things up north were better. I'll admit that even Rome, which is not very far north, wasn't too bad, but Naples and that area was rough. I guess the poor bastards in Southern Italy, after living miserably for generations, having nothing, owning nothing, just gave up and didn't give a damn anymore. Oh well, we were in France now and that was all behind us.

Late in the afternoon trucks began to arrive to pick up the infantry. I got a coded message from the Battery that seemed pretty hazy. It told us to go in the opposite direction from where we were sure we supposed to go. We started out anyway to see what would happen. Just as we were leaving the town we almost had a wreck. We met Simone and another girl walking into the town. We all, including Harris, had to yell and wave good bye. Harris failed to see a bend in the road and we went off the road and narrowly missed a telephone pole.

After traveling a short distance, we decided that something was wrong and we were definitely traveling in the wrong direction. I called the Battery again and they sent another coded message. This one made even less sense than the last one. I called in again and asked for the new code key. They changed it often and we hadn't been to the Battery in several days and knew it must have been changed. They sent the new key and then the message made more sense. We got squared away and headed in the right direction.

The code system we used was a simple thing but it seemed clever and seemed to me it would be hard to break. I carried a small aluminum plate with quite a few messages typed on paper and glued onto it. On the left side of the plate was a thin strip of paper with double letters like Aa, Bb, etc. This thin strip was not glued and could be moved. A certain place on the plate was more or less the starting point. The messages were simple, like "return to your unit", "or "advance with the infantry", or "remain in your present position until further instructions" and things on that order. The next day the key set of double letters would be moved and then an ensuing set of double letters in a message would line up on different messages. It seemed to me that the code would be hard to decode unless, of course, one of these plates fell into the hands of the Germans. When one of the plates fell into the hands of the Germans the whole thing was changed. Of course, our messages weren't the type that even if intercepted could change the whole course of the war. One decoded message might make it rough on some individual outfit or something. Of course, the top secret stuff and important things were sent by a very complicated system I suppose. Our little system fit our purposes well though.

We started up the road hoping to catch up with the infantry. The road on which we were traveling seemed to be deserted. It was hot, and we were getting thirsty. We stopped at a farm house to get water. The farmer there insisted that we fill our canteen with wine. We begged him to just let us have some water but he would have none of it. I think the French think water is to be used for washing and not for drinking. He had his wife come out and fill our canteens with wine. We thanked him and took off again. We drank the wine as we rode. We still wished we had water but this stuff helped some.

A little later as we rounded a bend and our way was blocked by a bunch of black soldiers. They were some kind of French Colonial troops, Senegalese maybe. They were very black, a shiny black. They wore bright red and blue uniforms and all had huge bolo looking knives hanging from them. I kidded Rod about his countrymen and to talk them out of eating us. Rod cursed me but he was getting a kick out of my kidding. I wasn't alarmed myself because these guys were grinning and laughing. We stopped as they flagged us down. We saw a few more rolling a big wooden barrel of wine down a hill. These guys just wanted to buy us a drink. We got out our canteen cups and they filled them up two or three times. I got a good look at these guys. They were all coal black and shiny. Their skin seemed very clean. They all had ridges on their faces. I understood it was some kind of ceremony when they were young. Gashes would be made in their faces and then filled with mud. When the skin healed the mud left the ridges. That's the story I heard. True or not they all had these ridged scars on their faces created by man. Their teeth were filed off to sharp points too. I wondered how this was done without ruining their teeth. These were the jokers that took those big knives and wandered around behind the lines at night. They would slit the throats of sentries etc. One of their favorite tricks was to come upon, say, three Germans sleeping together. They would slit the throat of one of them, maybe the middle guy, and leave the other two untouched. It would be rather morale shaking in the morning to wake up to something like that. I imagine a whole outfit's morale could be shaken and a lot of sleepless nights for all.

In spite of these fellows' appearance with the scarred faces and filed teeth, to me they didn't look that ferocious. In fact, they seemed to have a pleasant look on their faces and acted the same way. Of course, it probably wouldn't have been a good idea to belt one in the mouth to see if he would get mad or not. We drank wine with them and grinned at one another. We moved on down the road and they were grinning and waving as far as we could see before we made another bend.

We continued up the road a considerable distance and finally caught up with the infantry. They were just dismounting at the small town of Rains. From here everyone would go on foot. The people of Rains were giving us a royal welcome. They were all out cheering and yelling at us.

Finally, "I" Company was organized and we moved out of town. We marched on down at a fast clip. We knew that the Germans were out there somewhere and not too far away. Our artillery was firing over our heads and landing a considerable distance ahead of us. The Germans were answering with their own artillery. We heard a few shells smash in but not too close. As darkness closed in the artillery from both sides became almost silent.

We plodded on for miles and finally came to a halt early in the morning. We were to spend what was left of the night here. We flopped down on the hard rocky ground to try to get a little sleep. The days here in Southern France were plenty warm but the nights were miserably cold. When we moved like this we didn't carry any blankets and it was miserable trying to keep warm.

The next morning finally began to dawn. Everyone tried to get the kinks out. There is almost always someone funny under the most adverse conditions. This morning was no exception. Here we were all cold stiff and feeling pretty grim. But this one guy soon had most of us laughing. He kept a steady stream going about what a wonderful night's sleep he had had etc. He said that when he had awakened this morning his legs were so cold and stiff they were numb and he had put one of his leggings on the trunk of a small tree beside him thinking it was his leg. I even like to joke under rough conditions but I always say things with such a poker face and not laughing. Hardly anyone got my sense of humor. It is a dry sense of humor I guess you would call it. Even most of the guys that knew me well couldn't get me. I hated it too because I thought I came up with some pretty funny stuff sometimes. Oh well.

When we arrived in this area I had radioed the Battery and asked to have Harris sent up to us. Sure enough, bright and early in the morning he showed up. We hung around this area with the infantry waiting for orders. Finally we got the orders and a little information. The Germans (as we already knew) had really taken off during the night. We were to move several more miles to a rendezvous and wait for further orders. It seemed that the Germans were taking off to the Fatherland as fast as they could.

We jumped on the jeep and took off for the rendezvous. We soon came to a town called Forcalquier. All the people of the town were out to welcome the Americans. They were yelling and screaming at us. The whole place was going wild. They were clustering around our jeep so thick that we could hardly move. Some were poking wine at us, others had some kind of soda pop. We happened to have a good supply of cigarettes and were handing them out generously.

A French car with a man and a woman drove up. They said they were FFI members (French Fighters of the

Interior). That was what the French Underground was called at the later stages of the war. They were under the direction of Charles DeGaulle. They asked us if we could spare some gasoline. We dumped our spare five gallons into their car. They may have been F.F.I. or they may have been Sally and George. We were in too good of spirits to ask too many questions. Several girls were climbing on the jeep and throwing their arms around us and kissing us. Who said war is Hell? I remember one girl in particular. She was a good looking blonde and wore a bare mid drift dress. She climbed on the jeep threw her arms around me and kissed me for about five minutes. Her chest was shoved against me and she smelled good too. Here was the place to spend the duration. All of the girls who were here seemed to be well dressed and had cosmetics. Lt. Liggett was anxious to get to the rendezvous much to my disgust.

We moved slowly out of town and soon the cheering died away. We went down the road only a couple of miles from Forcalquier. We turned off the road and started driving up a steep bank. We went as far as the jeep would take us and then went on foot to the top of the hill. From this high hill we could look out over a valley for miles. What an observation post this would make. We almost wished that we could spot some Germans and equipment to fire at.

The view from here was beautiful. The valley below looked green and peaceful. The only activity we could see was a couple of women working in a field below us. They appeared to be digging potatoes. We figured some nice spuds would fry up well with the German rations. Rod and I gathered up our remaining "K" rations and prepared to climb the cliff. I had my gas mask carrier on the jeep. I took out the mask and threw it away. I was going to use the carrier to put the potatoes in. I hoped I would never need it. I was very confident that it would never be needed. If the Germans hadn't used gas yet in the war they weren't going to now. Allied Forces were pushing closer to their homeland and our planes controlled the skies. They knew that we had dumps of gas and the means of delivering it. Of course you never knew what they might do as a last resort. Hitler might demand that it be used or something.

The cliff was very steep, and Rod and I had to make our way carefully. We finally made it to the bottom by falling head over heels the last fifty feet.

Sure enough, the field turned out to be a potato patch. There was a girl and two older women working in it. We asked the girl, who seemed to be the owner, if we could trade for some of her potatoes. Plum de terre or something like that the French called them. The girls said to help ourselves and take all we wanted. I filled my gas mask carrier full of them. We gave the girl the "K" rations and took off back up the hill. The cliff was higher and steeper than we had thought and we had quite a struggle making it back to the top.

When we arrived at the top of the hill, we found that the infantry was arriving in the area. We got out our Coleman stove and made a nice meal on potatoes and beef from the German rations.

The night here passed quickly. We got a good night's sleep although a heavy dew settled, and it was pretty cold.

The next morning was a bright sunny affair. The weather here in France had been beautiful. The days nice and clear. The nights seemed to get a trifle cool but not too bad. We hung around this area until afternoon.

We saw a bunch of our planes dropping propaganda leaflets to the north. Rather than propaganda leaflets it was instructions to the F.F.I. on what to do and how they could cooperate with the Allies the best. It didn't seem as though they were dropping them behind our lines.

In the afternoon we got orders to report back to the Battery. We jumped on the jeep and headed for the outfit to see what was up. At the Battery we were told that the outfit was going to make a big jump. We were going to the Rhone Valley toward Lyons. It would be a move of about a hundred and twenty-five miles.

As soon as darkness fell our convoy moved out. Driving mile after mile began to get tiresome. Five of us and all our equipment made quite a jeep load. We were really crammed and cramped. Things weren't too bad until we began to get sleepy. Harris and Liggett didn't have it so bad. Harris was in the driver's seat and Liggett had the other front seat. They had enough room to be comfortable. Rod, Smitty and I, with the radios, batteries, guns, rations and other equipment, were all crammed in the back. The three of us got entangled with one another trying to stretch a little to get a few winks. The convoy stopped seldom but when it did, we could jump off and try to wake ourselves up a little. We kept hoping we would reach our destination soon.

In one little village we almost had a wreck. I was sitting on the battery pack dozing when Harris made a sharp bend at a pretty fast clip. I was almost thrown from the jeep. As I started to go out I started grabbing. I grabbed the nearest thing to me and that happened to be Harris. He lost control of the jeep momentarily and we almost cracked up. Somehow he righted the damn thing and got back onto the road.

The convoy ground on for miles. We passed through several small towns. Nothing very large. We finally arrived at a town called Crest. It seemed to be the largest town that we had come through yet, although it wasn't very large. We were now at our destination. We pulled on through the town and stopped at its outskirts. Dawn was breaking when we tumbled from the jeep onto the ground to try to get a few winks.

We had gotten only a few winks when we were awakened by the banging of our guns. Apparently we had caught up with the Germans. We were supposed to be in support of the 36th Division. Only part of the 45th had come this way. The rest of the division had gone toward the French Alps. Our outfit and the 2nd Battalion of the 157th were the only 45th Division troops here.

We figured that this would be a good deal as far as our F.O. party went. As long as the 2nd Battalion was on the line, "B" Battery was supposed to furnish the F.O.s. We worked when the 3rd Battalion was on the line.

Our new position was in and around a dry creek bed. From here we could investigate the town of Crest. The north end of the town was pretty badly shattered from bombing.

From the position of our guns the Germans must have been on three sides of us. Every gun of our battery was pointed in a different direction. They were pooping them out too. It was the most firing they had done since we had hit France.

We hung around the guns all morning watching the gun crews at work. Although I had been in the artillery all of the time I had been in the Army, I knew very little about the firing of the pieces. I had always been in communications. The boys were pretty handy around the guns. Most of the fellows should knew what they were doing. I imagine these men had fired more 105 shells than any other outfit in World War I or II. That was no idle chatter either. They had fired thousands in Sicily, tens of thousands in Italy and now here in France. They were to fire thousands more before the war was over.

In the middle of the afternoon the battery moved about a mile. We moved in and around a big old house that was set back form the road quite a way and in among some trees.

Murphy was around. What a yellow bastard he was. In this new area there was a large outdoor place. He sat in there for hours with the hunted look in his eyes. He had only been in combat since Southern France so he couldn't have "combat fatigue" already. He hadn't seen much either and here he was scared to death. He had been in only one shelling that amounted to much. It was that one back at Peyrolles where Shuck and Charmo had been killed.

He had been sent up on F.O. a couple of times but had always gotten "sick" and had to be sent back. I didn't have any sympathy for the guy. Some might have a good excuse to get "sick" or something if they had been through a lot of hell. This bastard was just plain gutless.

Everyone is scared when the going is tough, and I don't give a damn who it is or what they say. Some guys appear pretty calm and brave but deep down in they are really scared.

You admire a guy even if he openly shows he is scared but goes ahead and does what he supposed to do. I know that no one could have been more scared than myself in some spots. Several told me that things didn't seem to bother me much and they wished that they could have some of that ice water in their veins. They were wrong. I was afraid as anyone but I did my best to hide my feelings. I would have almost rather died than to let anyone know I was scared. A lot of the fellows were like that too. What else did we really have? You had to keep going and show you were some sort of a man.

Our Army was too easy on this "mental fatigue". Many would put on an act when they had to go on an attack or do something they thought might be dangerous. Doctors and headshrinkers had a lot to do with the fear attitude with this type. They claimed that some men could take a lot more than others. Your background and upbringing were supposed to play a part too. To me, that was a lot of crap. Everyone's prime objective was to stay alive. The men that went ahead through hell and did what they were supposed to do wanted to live just as badly as the ones that feinted "battle fatigue". We would have had a hell of an army if everyone had complained of being the kind that weren't able to take it and were excused from doing anything that might be dangerous. I don't believe there was one true case of "battle fatigue" out of fifty. Some bastards just didn't have any guts at all and it was just that simple. I know I wanted to get home and had as much to go home to as most of them. I felt it was my duty to do what I was supposed to even if there was a good chance of being hurt or even killed. After all, war is hell and not a kid's game. Lots of fellows saw a hell of a lot more than I did but those guys weren't the ones doing all the complaining either.

Some of the guys in Headquarters and the firing batteries did most of the complaining. I imagine there was almost as much "battle fatigue" in the artillery as there was in the infantry. The guys in the artillery thought they had a tough time. Of course they were bombed and shelled quite often but it was an easy lot compared to the infantry. I figured I could qualify as a competent judge of that because I stayed with both the artillery and infantry at times.

The infantry sees more in a week of tough going than the artillery sees in a whole war. When I tried to tell the artillerymen that they scoffed at me. Like Gill said, "Well, the infantry is trained differently". All the training in the world didn't build a guy's guts. The infantry had to take it and that was it. The infantry was the Queen of Battle alright. They really won the war and the rest of the branches just helped out a little. I was proud that I had been able to say I had worked with them so closely and to have been associated with them.

I even noticed a difference back in the rest areas. When the artillery boys did a little work or took a little hike they bitched like hell. On those mornings of the dry runs the infantry would be routed out at three in the morning with real work ahead of them. The bitching would be at a minimum and there would even be lots of laughing and wise cracking.

The infantry boys appreciated any little thing that was done for them too. I remember one simple little thing that happened right here in France to prove my point. A few days after landing here our F.O. party had gone back to the battery for one thing or another. The battery had just finished chow so we had gone down to the kitchen truck to find out if there was anything left to eat. We found the cook very despondent. He said he had gone to a lot of trouble to make the battery a bunch of hot biscuits. His supplies were rather limited and he had trouble raking up the necessary ingredients. Instead, a pleasant surprise for the men they had just turned up their noses at the biscuits. He had a lot of them left. We decided to take them back to the boys of the infantry. We got back to the company after dark but passed the word around that we had some biscuits in case anyone wanted any. Damned if they didn't line up like a bunch of guys going to get a steak or something. They enjoyed them even if they were cold and there was nothing to put on them. For days after that many would mention to us the night we had brought them the biscuits and how much they had enjoyed them. A simple thing like that had been appreciated. It showed how little it took to please a guy with a miserable lot such as these guys had.

Decorations came hard in the infantry too. In the Air Corps they got a medal just for flying over enemy territory a few times. Infantry didn't even get thanked for the hundreds of patrols and months of hell. When some of the guys in other branches received a Bronze Star every infantryman should have gotten half a dozen Congressional Medals. There was that much difference.

Anyway, there should have been something done with Murphy and his kind. Playing sick all of the time and making someone else have to go in his place. It's bad enough to have to get killed, but to get killed for some coward so that he can go home in one piece is out of the question. Those kind of guys should be made to carry on with their jobs like the rest or face the firing squad. The British Army didn't tolerate much of that "battle fatigue" crap. In a lot of their cases a slacker or coward was disgraced for life as bad as a criminal if they weren't shot. If our army had been tougher on "Fatigue" cases the number of them would have probably been smaller. They could have found out the true cases and the fakers if they had consulted the men of a guy's outfit rather than letting some crack pot doctor decide.

Murphy was one of those rated men right from the States. He had only been in the army a short time and had gone to some non-com school and sent right over to fill a rating in our outfit. Instead of giving it to some man that was a good man and had been with the outfit a long time this was what they were doing. Look what we got. He had probably been sharp in school where it had been nice and safe but here it was a different story. They couldn't build courage into a man in school. I wondered what little gem the big wheels would come up with next to ruin the morale of the Army.

I guess Murphy was the smart one though. I guess he believed in being a live coward instead of a dead hero. He could go home, probably soon too. He would be a hero there. He would be one of those poor boys that was "shelled shocked" as the civilians called it. That sounded romantic. Yep, lot of those guys became big heroes, and hell, no telling he might be elected governor or something on the strength of it. It's too bad people didn't know the real truth about this kind.

The guys that did carry on sure as hell didn't want to be dead and no one was trying to be a hero. They were here where the fighting was and it looked like they wouldn't go home until the damned war was over so that was what they were trying to do. They were doing their job the best they could hoping it would help shorten the war.

I think medals to most of the guys were a pretty hollow thing. If they had been given out right and to the deserving they would have meant something. I don't mean to say that every guy that got a medal didn't deserve it. Most of them did. There were cases that soured everyone. Some guy would just have a routine thing happen but just happen to be in the right place at the right time. Some officer would get wind of something he thought was great and put in for a Silver Star for the guy. Maybe some unit commander figured a few medals in his outfit would make it look like they were a top outfit and be a feather in his cap.

In our own 158th, especially Headquarters, fellows

received medals that no one could see what for. A couple of guys had received the Bronze Star mainly because a ranking officer had liked them and nothing more. Of course, the Bronze Star isn't a real big decoration like the Silver Star, but it is at least something. I wasn't sourballed because I hadn't received anything. I didn't care but at least we F.O.s were doing more than carrying chow to some major. Oh, well, war is hell anyway. Change the subject and quit bitching.

We spent the day around this area. There was a potato patch nearby. Smith and I dug a few and with some tomatoes and meat we made a fairly good tasting stew.

About dark Smitty, Rod, Harris, Lt Liggett, Lt. Olsen, Lt, Grabriesch and I were all out by the road talking. Suddenly two M.E. 105s came roaring down the road just a few feet off the ground. They had all guns blasting. We hardly had time to hit the ground. One of the planes let loose with a burst of 20's. Fragments from the shells whizzed in all directions. I glanced up as the planes zoomed over. They were so low I could see the pilots very plainly. One had a cigarette in his mouth. If they had been much lower I could have been able to see what brand it was. In a flash they were out of sight. No one had been hit except Lt. Grabriesch. He was hit in the butt with a small piece of fragment but it didn't hurt him that much.

Night fell and we had a pretty quiet evening. A short distance ahead the sounds of battle could plainly be heard. The Germans seemed to be making some kind of a stand here.

The next day was August 26th, 1944. It is a day I will never completely forget. It was another beautiful day and our party figured on staying around here and taking it easy. The 2nd Battalion was on the line and we never dreamed F.O.s from our Battery would have to work. "B"

Battery was supposed to furnish the F.O.s for them. That wasn't to be the case today however.

About eleven o'clock in the morning Captain Hurley sent for Liggett's party. He said that the 2nd Battalion was going to jump off on an attack from Allex at noon. Allex was a town three or four miles up ahead. The F.O. party that was to go with them were sick or something and they wanted to borrow us. That was just dandy. With four parties to pick from they had to pick us. Orders are orders though and we got ready to go.

We jumped on the jeep and headed for Allex. In Allex we found the 2nd Battalion Headquarters and tried to find out the situation. The situation was something like this. Part of the German Eighteenth Army was supposed to be cornered up on the forks of the Rhone and Drone Rivers. We were to attack at noon and put the pressure on them and draw their attention. Later the 141st Battalion of the 36th Division was to try to get in around behind them and cut them off completely.

Final preparations for the attack were being made. We were to jump off with "E" Company. Three tanks were to be on the attack with us. We watched the tankers getting ready. When the tanks were ready to crank up one of the tank officers told us we had better take cover. He said when the tanks started moving around the Jerrys threw plenty of stuff into the town.

We didn't have time to take cover because the "E" Company was starting to move out of town. We stopped by a large walled cemetery at the edge of town and waited for the tanks to move out. Soon the tanks clanked out of town in our direction. Even before the tanks reached us they opened up with machine gun fire. The Germans returned the fire of the machine and rifle fire. The Krauts were closer and thicker than I had expected.

Suddenly big shells began to swish by, at least 170's or bigger. These shells didn't scream like the 88's but made a more horrible sound. They just sounded big and when they hit they seemed even bigger. Even the first one got several men. The place was already splattered with blood. They kept throwing those big shells in around us and back into the town. Shrapnel seemed in all directions. We lay as close as possible to the cemetery wall for protection. It seemed something like this always happened around cemeteries. The big shells continued to crash in. One dud hit nearby and it even made the ground tremble.

Harris was anxious to get out of here. I didn't blame him a bit and only wished that I was going back to the battery with him. Once there was a moment's lull Harris jumped into the jeep and took off like a wild man.

More shells crashed in. The medics and stretcher bearers were trying to get the wounded back into the town. They were handling some awful bloody messes.

Finally, the tanks started moving again and we moved up with them. The Infantry was already thinned out quite a bit and the attack had hardly started.

We went around the corner of the cemetery wall and started up a small dirt toad. Shells of all sizes were coming in now. There were 170's, 88's and mortars as well as rifle and machine gun fire. Several men went down and this little road was already blood splattered. I broke out sweating for all I was worth. It wasn't just the heat either. I was scared. We all were scared. Liggett, Smith and Rod all looked drawn and older. They looked pale, even Rod and I knew I must look like them.

This is it. This is the kind of ordeal where you have to muster every ounce of courage to keep going. This separated the men from the boys. I guess I must have been a man but I sure as hell didn't feel like it. There were some cowering and not going forward. We were going forward to die, no doubt about it this time. This was the end.

Despite the terrific fire we kept advancing up the road. We were driving the German Infantry back. They were losing men too and a few prisoners were being taken.

The tanks kept clanking along with us. I wished I had the thick steel those guys had around them.

We would hit the ground awhile, then get up and made a dash forward. Shells were crashing all around. Rod saw a big piece of shrapnel skim pass my head and embed in a tree. This shrapnel that was flying around would go through you like you were a piece of paper. You wouldn't even slow it down.

We finally reached a point less than a mile out of Allex. There was a big cave there and what was left of the company crowded into it. A German tank was firing direct fire down the road. The shells screamed by.

The Company Commander of "E" Company, a First Lt., asked us if we would go up ahead and try to knock out the tanks. He said that the way things were it was almost impossible for the Infantry to advance any further. We must have been dumber than we thought for we agreed to try. It is a wonder it wasn't the last thing we ever tried.

We left the cave, crossed the road and started sneaking up along a fringe of small trees that grew along the edge of the road. We soon reached the top of a rise and passed to survey the situation. While we were there our three tanks rumbled by.

We saw two German tanks sitting there in a field a short distance away. We thought of setting up our radio and firing at them. We saw our tanks headed toward them so we waited to see what would happen. Our tanks rushed at them with their guns blasting. One of our tanks made a direct hit on one of the German tanks. The shell just glanced off and nothing happened. The German tank fired just one shot and the Sherman burst into flames.

We could have fired from here but wanted to get closer. We decided to try to make it to a barn about two hundred yards away. There was a house about half way there but we picked the barn. We started running towards the barn trying to keep both the house and the barn between us and the German tanks. We looked in the field and saw another of our tanks knocked out. The third one was hiding behind the house and wisely so. It was apparent they were no match for those Tiger Tanks. We passed the house and tore on toward the barn.

We found the barn unoccupied, although we were damned lucky not to find it full of Krauts. We climbed up in the loft of the barn and took a look. One of the German tanks was sitting in a field a few yards away. The turret was open and a German was studying our building intently. That gave us the willies. We were peeping out of small crevices and were sure we couldn't be seen but we were afraid the tank would put a few rounds in here for luck. We decided we had better get some fire on the tank before it did us in. We couldn't see the other but figured it had moved into a clump of trees a short distance back.

I called fire direction and in a matter of a couple of minutes we had shells coming into the area of the tank. The turret of the tank dropped down and the big steal monster began to move slowly. It began to back toward the trees. German tanks always backed away if they possibly could. They had lots of steel on the front of them, several inches more than ours but were very lightly armored in the back. With the heavily armored part toward the line of fire they could almost withstand any ordinary artillery. The tank looked huge, even bigger than the Tiger.

I understood that they had some larger ones but this was probably a Tiger. The tank slowly backed away with our shells crashing around it. Our shelling seemed to be pretty ineffectual but at least we were making it move. The tank soon moved into some trees and out of our vision.

The terrain out in front of us was quite flat and open. A couple of hundred yards away was a line of trees that appeared to follow a stream bed of some kinds. The trees ran to our right and left as far as we could see. The belt of trees wasn't wide though for a few yards beyond them we could see open country again. The ground beyond the trees sloped gradually.

One thing we knew. The Germans that were opposing us in this immediate vicinity were in that belt of trees. We could easily spot any sort of movement beyond the trees. We plastered the area quite heavily where we had seen the tank disappear.

We discovered that our barn wasn't just a barn. It was a barn with living quarters attached. The living quarters weren't too bad either and had several rooms. It was probably where the hired man and his family stayed but it was empty now.

From our lookout in the loft we spotted some mortars firing over to our right. We plastered the spot with three rounds. The mortars never fired again.

The German artillery was very active. They were still using those big guns. They crashed in all around our building shaking it violently. They could drop a few in around us and then send a few over us a few miles into Allex. We couldn't tell where the guns were firing from but guessed they were beyond the next hill. We didn't really have any idea so we didn't fire out there blindly as badly as we wanted to stop that big stuff. It was scaring the Hell out of us.

A little later our infantry came advancing past our building. When they were about half way between our position and the trees all hell broke loose. The Infantry was caught out in the open and had no place to take cover. The Germans blasted away with their tanks hidden in the trees. They also opened up with machine gun and rifle fire. There was nothing the Infantry could do but withdraw and they came streaming back past our place.

We again shelled along the whole line of trees where the most of the fire seemed to be coming from. We hoped to neutralize the area so the infantry could advance. Probably the Germans there were pretty well dug in with those tanks. It might be rough to dislodge them.

We fired into a clump of trees to our right near where we had seen the mortars firing from. We had seen tracers coming from there so we knew there were enemy there and probably at least one machine gun. Sure enough, as soon as the first shells started hitting there about twenty-five Germans came running out. They wore black uniforms of tank men. They came running, crouched and heading for another clump of trees. We had fired into the clump where they were heading so we had a contraction number on it. I quickly called for this number. Our shells and the Germans got to the trees at about the same time. We fired five rounds into that small area. Some of the shells hit up in the trees causing high bursts. I would be willing to bet we got everyone of those guys. We never saw any activity from there again. We shelled it a couple more times to make sure but I'm sure that first barrage got them all. In calling that concentration number it was the same as if I had held a pistol at each of their heads and pulled the trigger. I guess it made you not so guilty when it is a team effort. We find them and the guns fire. At least the guys back of the guns hardly know what they were firing at from back there five or six miles. They never see the results of their efforts. Well, those Krauts could do the same to us. This game is to kill and try to keep from getting killed if you can. It's still a lovely thing for recreation.

The Germans were keeping their big guns hot too. They dropped plenty of shells all around. Once we were peeping through a very small opening. A shell hit close in from our building. A piece of shrapnel zipped through the opening, glanced off Liggett's helmet and embedded in the masonry wall. The old helmet had saved Liggett again. It was lucky for him that the fragment had hit the rounding part of his helmet. If it had hit a little lower it would have gone through both his helmet and head. Our helmets didn't seem to be too much protection. The metal in them seemed to be too soft. I suppose they did save some lives such as in this case. I often wondered why they hadn't been made of harder steel. You could dent the hell out of them by just trying to drive a tent peg into comparatively soft ground. The German helmets were made of very hard metal. You could shoot one a few yards away with a pistol and not phase it. I had never heard a good explanation why ours were so soft. Maybe there was a good reason but I doubt it. Probably the American helmet maker got an order to make ten million of them on the recommendation of some lame brain so this was it and it was what we had to wear.

I found a real honest to goodness toilet in the place. I thought it would be nice to take advantage of it. You didn't get an opportunity like this very often over here. I was just getting ready to do my duty when a shell hit close. It blew the window out of the place and showered the room, as well as myself, with rocks, glass, dirt and pieces of grapevine. I hurriedly pulled up my pants and got out of there. I didn't have to go as bad as I figured.

The Infantry had orders to attack again. They came out of their holes and passed our building again. They had just passed our place when the same thing happened again. The Germans hit them with everything they had. The Infantry was forced to withdraw again.

We were sore and plastered the whole line with plenty of artillery. We knew we had done some good but there still seemed to be plenty of them in there. They must have been pretty well holed up in there.

While we were firing out there something happened that went haywire in fire direction or the guns. It couldn't have been our fault because we had used the same sensing as before and the shells had gone where we had wanted them to go. In fact, we used a concentration number they had given us. It absolutely couldn't have been our mistake. Anyway, we almost got it from our own shells. They crashed in mighty close, splattering shrapnel against the building, scaring the hell out of us. It was a miracle we escaped. Most of the shells landed only a few feet from our barn. They started on the right side of the place and worked their way right around the corner. A few feet to the left and we would have all been killed. It was also lucky that the Infantry wasn't near here or it would have played havoc with them.

I grabbed the mike and screamed at Fire Direction to for Christ's sake level the bubble, get on the ball and take it easy. Major Scheaffers must not have liked this. He evidently grabbed the mike away from the radio operator. He had yanked it away from me a couple of times when I worked at Fire Direction. He yelled back to shut up and never mind the asinine instructions. He told us to sense them and they would fire them. Why, that lousy son of a bitch. It was damned easy for that fat slob to sit way back there on his fat fanny and give us a bunch of B.S. like that. I wished the bastard could be up here with us for five minutes and he might understand what we were up against. That bastard hadn't been two feet away from that C.P. during the whole war.

Liggett also picked up the mike and started doing a little chewing. Scheaffers shut him up quickly too. What were you going to do with a bastard like that?

For the third time the Infantry tried to advance. Their ranks were really thinned out now. It was the same story. They were blasted back. They couldn't advance and that was all there was to it. They really had shown guts taking the beating they had. It wasn't their fault. It was a case if the enemy having too much and having the advantage of being on defense. It is the age old story of the attacking group having to have a lot more men and equipment to be successful.

The artillery duel continued. The Germans kept throwing in lots of stuff around us and back toward Allex. We kept plastering everything that looked like it might be hiding Germans. We were lucky not to have received a direct hit. Some landed mighty close and fragments, rocks, dirt and debris rained off the house. I think the Germans figured our building was empty. The Infantry was dug in quite a way behind us and they didn't figure anyone would be crazy enough to be that far ahead by themselves. I'm sure if they thought something was in our building, especially F.O.s, they would have made a real effort to destroy it. They would have even brought their tanks up to it and blasted it. I guess they figured even the Americans were smarter than to do some fool thing like this. If their tanks had left the woods and come toward our building we sure could have raised hell with them I think.

When it was dark we got out of the building and headed back to the Infantry. What was left of them were dug in along a little ridge about three hundred yards back from our building. We looked up the Company Commander. He was a pretty worried man. He didn't have many men left and was afraid the Germans might try to counter-attack through us. He wanted us to go back up to the house we had been in, stay on alert and start firing if we head them coming.

We told him we would if he gave us some infantry boys to go with us. We wanted a few men at least to help out if the Germans started attacking. The C.O. said he would give us the largest squad left. That squad had five men in it. If what was left of the company had all gone with us it wouldn't have made much of a group.

The nine of us started toward our building. We were all dreading going back up there to spend the night. We had only gone a few yards when we heard our tank which had been hiding behind the house start up. We knew the Germans could hear it too and expected them to start laying them in again. We all ducked into a ditch and waited. The tank moved off and was soon almost out of hearing distance. The Germans hadn't opened up on it so we figured they didn't want to give their position away.

We started out for our building again. We were about half way there when a runner caught up with us and said we had been relieved. In fact, the whole battalion had been relieved. We couldn't figure out what had happened. The Germans must have really gotten the hell out of there as soon as it got dark. Maybe we had given them a good shellacking. We sure had tried to and had used up a lot of shells. I know we were relieved in more ways than one. We didn't ask questions but turned and started back at almost a run. When we got back to the Infantry we found them preparing to move out in great haste. Everyone was in such a hurry to get going that the C.O. cautioned the fellows not to forget shovels and other equipment. I didn't blame them for wanting to get going. I was ready myself.

It had been a rough day. Very rough. They don't come much rougher. Probably the Battle of Allex as we called it, couldn't have been rougher on our little bunch. Poor old "E" Company would have a lot of new faces in a day or two.

We hiked back to the outskirts of Allex. I set up the radio and called for Harris to come and pick us up. He showed up in pretty short order and we were soon back at the Battery. It seemed like we were safe now. Almost like being back in the States.

When we reached the Battery, we all flopped on the ground on our blankets and talked over the day's events. One thing we agreed on was that this had been one of our toughest days. One of the very toughest days.

In spite of the ordeal we began to relax and laugh a little. We talked about little things that had happened that now seemed funny. At the time they were happening they hadn't seemed very funny at all. Of late we had picked up a new saying. "C'est la guerre" or "It's the war". When things were tough or something had gone haywire or we were tired we would pass it off with c'est la guerre. It was silly but we seemed to get a kick out of it. I guess we were beginning to get a little silly anyway.

We didn't know it but Murphy had been lying near us taking in every word. He said something to us and his voice quavered. You'd have thought he had been with us or on even a rougher deal. He said he hoped he wouldn't have to go through anything like that. Of course he'd think of something like that but I personally hoped I wouldn't have to do it again either.

The next morning everything seemed quiet and peaceful. There didn't seem to be any fighting up ahead. We wondered what had happened.

We found out that our efforts had not been in vain. We had given the Germans a bad time. The 36th had attacked them from the flank and nearly cut them off. They had taken off so fast they had left lots of heavy equipment. They also left many dead and many prisoners were taken. Our all-out frontal attack had been rough but it had kept the pressure on them and kept them busy to help the 36th. We guessed that in our sector they had fought like hell to hold us off until dark. As soon as it had gotten dark they had tried to pull out and had only been partially successful in getting away. That's why it had quieted down so quickly right after dark in our sector. We were glad to hear our efforts had not been wasted.

We stayed in this area all day. That evening a few of us were out near the road talking. Two planes, just like the other evening, came down the road strafing. We all hit the ground quickly. I felt my right leg stinging and my first thought was that I had been wounded slightly. Apparently, a pretty well spent piece of fragment had hit me. It didn't break the skin but it did sting a little. We decided we had better keep away from the road before someone got hurt.

We spent the night here and most of the next day. In the afternoon of the next day, August 30th, we were informed that we were to take another long motor march. We were going to swing east now into the French Alps and join the rest of the 45th up in that direction. We were going to the vicinity of the town of Grenoble.

All day long parts of the 36th Division passed by our position. Infantry, trucks and guns. Just as we were ready to pull onto the road we had to hold up to let some 36th

Division vehicles go by. A truck load of guys went by. They asked us if we were the 45th Division's Quartermasters. They had spotted Rod and had taken him for a Negro. It seemed like most quartermasters outfits were Negro outfits. It really griped Rod to be taken for a Negro. I don't know what else he could have been taken for though. When I said to these guys, "Yeah man, de is the quartermasters". Rod really blew up. He cursed me like he always did when I needled him a little. He acted sore but really wasn't. He always said, "All right Borthwick, all right, all right. God damn it." I never overdid the teasing though. I don't know why he didn't like being mistaken for a person with Negro blood anyway. I never heard anyone give him a bad time. There were lots of Southerners in our outfit too.

Our convoy was off down the road. We headed away south and then headed east. It was going to be another one of those grueling rides.

We went on through really beautiful country. Hill and dells and beautiful little wooded lots. We passed through several quaint little villages. The country was beautiful. France was a beautiful country. "Le Belle France" was right.

One thing I noticed here in France was that the land was so neat. The meadows were so neat they looked as if they had been mowed with a lawn mower. The woods were clean, free of underbrush and fallen dead limbs and other debris.

The roads here were good too. Even little out of the way roads and mountain roads were paved. They were much better than the roads in Italy. In fact, they were very comparable to the roads in the States. Perhaps better than the roads in some parts of our country.

We passed along mountain roads that we were awed

at the engineering job that had been done to build them. The roads followed narrow ravines yet were smooth and had few bad corners. To construct these roads without making turns in them they had made many tunnels. Also, instead of even making a slight turn they had hewn into solid rock. Some of these places were like driving under huge man-made ledges.

If the Germans had blown a few of these tunnels and overhangs down onto the roads it would have taken months to clear them. Probably the reason they hadn't done it was because of their own forces in southern France were so spread out and confused. They could have blocked their escape route through this area if they had sealed off the roads. It was lucky for the Allies that they had left this route open. If they had blown up these tunnels and over hangs driving toward Germany through these mountains would have had to be forgotten.

It soon became dark but the convoy ground on. It was too bad that we couldn't pass through this area during the daylight. I imagined the beauty of these mountains was something to behold. It had to be from what I had seem already. Higher in the mountains we began to climb long, steep grades. We began traveling on roads that seemed to be paved with some sort of crushed rock. The convoy stirred up a terrific fog of choking dust.

When we would pass through a little mountain village the people would all be out cheering and yelling at us. Even the tiny kids were out by the road cheering. Even though we passed through some of these villages in the wee hours of the morning the people were there cheering and yelling. Their enthusiasm never seemed to diminish. Although there must have been hundreds of vehicles in the convoy and we were at no means near the head of it, they cheered and applauded every vehicle.

Again I could see the great contrast in the attitudes between the French and the Italian people. Here the people showed a little pride in their country. They were glad the Germans were being driven out and that they were getting their country back again. They were trying to show a little gratitude. In Italy the Wops had shown a lot of indifference. They didn't seem to give a damn who was in their country just so they were taken care of and got the handouts.

I wondered what had really happened back in 1940 when France had been overrun and conquered so easily. The scoop had it that the French had no stomach for fighting, were sold out by the government etc. After being in contact with these people for even a short time that was hard to believe. I was more inclined to believe and wanted to believe differently. I believed that the main reason for their miserable showing was that they were just not prepared for modern warfare. Even before the war had started the Germans had scoffed at the armies of France and Britain. They said they were still building them on World War I standards and ideals. A few months later it was a proven fact. Then too, maybe the French had too much confidence in the Maginot Line.

Anyway, after seeing these people and their enthusiasm and apparent sincere love for their country I couldn't believe they had not wanted to fight. It must have been unpreparedness plus a couple of military blunders and perhaps a couple of traitors in key positions. The average Frenchman surly must have been ready and willing.

We ground on and on without stopping. We were sick of riding. We went up and down treacherous grades and around mean curves.

Just before dawn we passed Grenoble. It seemed like a pretty large town. It was probably the largest I had seen in France. It was still dark but from what we could see it looked like it might be a nice place. We knew that we were now near our destination and everyone was glad.

A short way out of Grenoble we turned off the highway and into an orchard. The five of us toppled out of the jeep and were asleep as soon as we hit the ground.

The next morning we looked over our new area. We were in an apple orchard and the ground was covered with long, bright grass. It was a beautiful spot. There had been some fighting here a few days ago but it had now passed on further north.

A Forty-Fifth Division news reporter came to our Battalion Headquarters and asked if here were any good stories. Colonel Funk sent him down to see our party and get a good story on our part of the Battle of Allex. Maybe Col. Funk did recognize the fun we had had on some of our capers at that. It's a wonder that guy hadn't gotten a story of how some characters had beaten their way through the chow line and carried food to one of the officers.

The weather here, around the first of September, took a definite change. I guessed it was the altitude. I had no idea at what altitude we were but it must have been thousands of feet higher than where we had been in the Rhone Valley. One night, to start out with, we had thunderstorms. Everyone was sleeping out and not prepared for rain. Naturally, everyone and everything was drenched. There was a lot of swearing and scrambling around.

It also began to get pretty chilly. The natives said it wouldn't be too long before the first snow began up here. Grenoble was supposed to be a famous winter resort. It had also been a resting place for American soldiers in World War I. In fact, I think I had heard my brother-in-law mention coming to this place.

The eating at the "kitchen" was pretty slim. We had been moving so fast our supply lines had a hard time keeping up with us. About all we had were warmed "K" rations and not much of that. We would also have a little corned beef once in a while. I guess I was one G.I. in a hundred. I enjoyed corned beef and could eat pounds of the stuff. We didn't have bread anymore, just crackers. This was still better than eating cold "K" rations.

We got a little back mail while we were in this area. I didn't get any letters from anyone knowing that I was in France yet. The mail had all been forwarded from Italy. Bernice sent me a small camera. It was something I had wanted for months. I could have gotten some dandy pictures. The trouble with pictures was getting them home. If I took any of combat or some of the carnage the censors would destroy them. They would probably destroy even a picture of one of your buddies. A lot of our censorship was corny anyway. I figured on taking a lot of pictures and having LaCrosse develop them and take them home with me when the war ended. I hoped the war would end before I had a chance to take any action pictures. It didn't seem that it could last much longer. Allies on all fronts were advancing and the Krauts were being pushed right back into their Fatherland. Actually, we weren't a great distance from the German border ourselves.

We stayed around this area for a couple of days. We didn't have anything to do but try and keep dry. It rained most of the time that we were here.

Around the second of September we moved out of this area. We moved on down the road several miles. The terrain soon began to get a little more level as we seemed to be getting out of the high mountains. It still wasn't exactly plains but more the gentle rolling type of country.

BYE FOR NOW

In the middle of the afternoon we pulled off the road and up a small hill and stopped in an apple orchard. We were to wait here for further orders. We wondered where the Front was and what would happen next.

Liggett must have decided to give the boys of his F.O. party a little surprise and a treat. He bought some rabbits from a farmer. He spent most of the night killing, cleaning and trying to cook the damned things. Sometime during the night he came and woke Rod, Smitty, Harris and I and proudly led us to where he had been cooking them. The rabbit was about half cooked and didn't taste too good. We all choked the damned stuff down and pretended it was the best food we had eaten. We didn't want to disappoint him after all his trouble. Liggett was sort of funny in his relations with his party. I think he always wanted to be sort of a buddy but never knew exactly how to go about it. I guess he didn't know where to stop being an officer and a superior and being a comrade. I guess it could be tough at that. Liggett was a good guy though. He was a pretty good officer and the Army could have used a few more of his caliber. Anyway, we gulped down the rabbit and after telling him again how good it was we went back to try to sleep out what was left of the night. We were all glad we had put on a good act. We figured Liggett had gone to sleep happy with the thought he had pleased us and with the feeling he had done something for his "boys".

The next day we moved on further. The rain had quit and the sun was beating down again. We finally stopped again near a farm house. We just lolled around wondering what would happen next. There was a stream nearby and Rod, Smitty and I tried to wash a few clothes.

That night we moved out again and headed on toward the Front. It began to drizzle again and it was pretty chilly. Later on our F.O. party was told to go up and join the Infantry. This sounded like the complexion of things were changing.

After the miserable night of being cold and wet and with the frustration of trying to locate the infantry, we finally found them just at dawn. It had quit raining now but it was still threatening and it was plenty cold. We tried to catch a little sleep sitting in the jeep.

We found "I" Company alright. If we had stayed with the Battery until daylight instead of trying to find them during the night it would have taken us only five minutes instead of half the night. In fact, the Infantry was right along the different firing batteries.

At dawn the Infantry was stirring around and getting ready to move out. Apparently we had caught up with the Germans and from here on anything could happen. We started getting ourselves some breakfast as the infantry moved out. I had a nice can of cold corned beef.

A little later we moved out and went slowly up the road. We soon caught up with and passed the Infantry.

A little later we arrived at a small ravine where our Battery was set up. We were getting close to the enemy, no question about that. Our battery was already doing some firing. We didn't know who they were supporting.

It began to drizzle again, and it was a miserable day. The Infantry passed our position and continued on up the road. It looked as though they were going to be back in action in a few minutes.

Later our F.O. party got orders to go up and join the Infantry. Although no vehicle had gone up this road, yet we decided to take a chance. It was drizzling and there were low hanging clouds making visibility pretty poor.

We took off up the road hoping for the best. Harris was really lead footed today. The Krauts were throwing some shells onto a ridge across a little ravine to our right.

We could hear them crack and see black smoke swirl up. We were tearing down the road so fast I guessed the Germans would have had trouble bringing fire on us even if they had wanted to. It's a wonder we didn't skid off the road on this wet pavement.

We finally caught up with "I" Company. They were dug in around a group of buildings. These buildings apparently belonged to a large farm. We set up our O.P. in the loft of the barn.

We couldn't see much out ahead of us. A couple of hundred yards ahead of us were some woods. There were Germans in those woods and apparently in quite some strength. The Krauts had been skirmishing with our boys already.

We immediately raked the outer fringe of the woods with artillery, hoping to make the Krauts draw back. They were evidently well dug in and had armor with them. They didn't have any intention of pulling out.

The Germans had plenty of artillery back there with them to go along with the guns of their tanks. They were throwing plenty back. They were using their artillery differently today than I had even seen them use it before. Instead of concentrating on any one particular target they were throwing shells all over the landscape. You never knew where the next one was going to hit. A lot of them were landing mighty close too.

I was feeling pretty low. I seemed to feel that something not pleasant was going to happen. I sensed that the rest of our party felt something like that too. Maybe it was the gloomy weather. I didn't know. I started to scribble a few lines to Bernice but found it was hard to write. I just couldn't seem to be cheerful and optimistic. Some way I had the feeling I wasn't going to make it through this man's war. Maybe this was my last day. There seemed to be a chance that the war would end any day but that didn't seem to cheer me much. I had a strange feeling I wasn't going to make it. Maybe I was cracking up. I had noticed lately, and so had Smith and Rod, something about Liggett. Once in a while we would catch that hunted look on his face. That was a sign. A sign that you were getting weary. I hoped I didn't have that look. I decided to forget the whole thing. The war was going to be over soon now. I had a strange feeling though it was going to be over for me one way or the other. Oh well.

A French family was still in the house here. They were the poorest class of French I had ever seen. They must have been the tenant farmers of the place. Most of the family wore wooden shoes. This sort of surprised me. I thought that wooden shoes were worn only by Hollanders. I guess wooden shoes wore well but I couldn't imagine them being very comfortable. The little ones for the kids were sure cute though.

Rifle and machine gun fire came singing past. Others splattered against the buildings and bounced around the stone walls. All of this fire was coming from the woods just up ahead.

Just before dark we zeroed in on the woods and on the little dirt road that ran right along the edge of it.

At dark Harris and I tried to find a place to bed down. We wanted to get in one of the buildings because it was cold and rain was threatening any minute. We also felt we would be safer behind a stone wall of a building from flying bullets and shrapnel.

About the only place we found that was at all suitable was in a stall in one of the barns. There were several stalls in the barn but all but one was occupied with cows or horses. Even at that we had to shoo a bunch of chickens out of our stall. We got some hay and piled it over the manure on the floor. Another thing that bothered us was a couple of loose cows in the barn. We figured we might get walked on by them during the night. To prevent this we lined some wooden boxes and boards in front of our stall. We still maintained our O.P. in the loft where activity from the woods and road could best be seen and heard.

Harris and I had just dozed off when Liggett came in and woke us up. He said the whole party had better stay awake and in the loft of our O.P. in case of any eventuality. The loft turned out to be a better place than where we were trying to sleep anyway.

We talked Liggett out of having us all stay awake. We convinced him that one of us on the alert at a time was enough. With us all right there it would only take seconds to get us alerted. Liggett seemed to be getting awfully nervous alright.

We took shifts on the radio and listening. There wasn't a chance of seeing anything. It was an inky black night. The Germans were still in the woods. Their artillery had died down but they sent spasmodic rifle fire into our buildings.

While I was on my watch apparently some of the boys from our outpost sent up a green flare. We never found out what it was for. It was probably a mistake. The Germans sprang into action though. They probably thought it was an attack or something was coming. Their tanks in the woods opened up and they also sent lots of rifle and machine gun fire in our direction. It died down again in a few minutes.

When my time on the radio was up I woke up Harris to take his turn. At least I thought I woke him up. When I shook him he said, "O.K. I'm getting up". I dropped down on the hay and was asleep in a matter of seconds. I naturally supposed that Harris had gotten up and taken over on the set.

The next morning Liggett was storming and raving in his quiet sort of way. He had awakened to find the radio unattended and no one on watch. Instead of getting up Harris had turned over and went back to sleep. Consequently no one had been on watch since about 2:00 a.m. Harris said he just remembered me shaking him and that was all. We had been so tired he had never gotten fully awake and had dropped off again. Liggett told him he could have him shot for sleeping on duty. Of course I got a good chewing out too for not making sure that the radio was attended before I went to sleep.

We wouldn't blame Liggett for being sore this time. To make things even worse, the Krauts in the woods had sneaked off during the night. It had to happen while we were all snoozing. Had anyone been awake we could have surly heard their tanks and vehicles starting up because we were that close to them. Earlier when we shelled them we could hear them calling for the medic, "doctor", as they called the medics. We had fouled up alright. Had we heard them stirring around we could have shelled the hell out of them. Shelling them while they were up and moving around and getting out of there could have been pretty effective. It could have been a lot more effective than when they were stationary and all dug in.

We had made another mistake too. We were working too independently and had not been in touch with the infantry close enough. Although we were right in among them we hadn't notified any of the Infantry Officers where we had our O.P. If things had been a little better organized the Germans couldn't have sneaked away so easily. Even if we were asleep the Infantry could have awakened us if they had known where we were. Oh well, it was one of those things.

It was good Headquarters didn't know about our goof off. I could imagine what Col. Funk or Capt. Scheaffer would say. That was our lot anyway. We could kill all kinds of Krauts and destroy all sorts of equipment etc. and we never even got as much as a "thanks" for it. If we made a little mistake or not do enough in the Brass's estimation we got hell. I could imagine Capt. Schaeffer telling us we probably had prolonged the war a couple of months by letting them get away so easily.

The day was another cold, miserable affair. It rained off and on all day. We hung around this area all morning waiting for orders.

I took the radio out of the loft and connected it up in the jeep. I turned it on to see what was going on. Generally we kept the set up unless we were firing a mission or something. Even when we were waiting for orders I would just turn it on once in a while to check in to see if there were any orders for us. In other words, we contacted Headquarters instead of leaving the set on for hours waiting for them to contact us. This, of course, was mostly to conserve our batteries. When the radio was on in the jeep though it could be connected to the jeep battery and it didn't matter how long we had it on. Anyway, on this morning I sat in the jeep with the radio on listening to the traffic going on over it. It was lucky I decided to do it too.

I pricked up my ears when I heard some F.O. scream, "Fire Mission". It was going to be nice to hear someone else work. This F.O. continued, "Enemy troops and equipment". He gave the map coordinates and requested a heavy concentration. My hair stood on end for the position he had plotted was ours. I grabbed the mike and yelled at Fire Direction to for Christ's sake not fire that mission. I told them that the "enemy troops" were us. Fire Direction immediately canceled the mission. The damned jerk that called that mission must have been way back somewhere. Probably some characters on static O.P. back almost as far as the guns. We never found out who tried to fire on us. If we had we certainly would have given them a bad time. I was glad that I had just happened to be listening to the radio at this particular time. It would have been hell to get killed by your own artillery. I guess it just wasn't our time yet.

Shortly after noon we had orders to move. It was raining spasmodically. Everyone was wet, cold and miserable.

We started moving down the road. We rode on the jeep but went along slowly with the Infantry. Our Battery passed us moving up with the guns. They looked worried when they passed us. The way they looked they likely were going up pretty near to the Front.

Suddenly, we began to see high bursts up a head. These high bursts were the adjusting kind. It looked like the Krauts were getting ready for us. We reached the place where the artillery was going into position. The artillery boys were digging for all they were worth. The guns were really up on the front lines alright. Beyond them was nothing friendly. This was as far as Harris was to go with the jeep. From here on we would be jumping off into what was anybody's guess. I envied Harris. He could stay here, dig a hole while the rest of the party had to go on. I guess I should have been a jeep driver.

We started walking up a little dirt road that ran parallel with the gun positions. This was the jumping off point. Suddenly, Liggett said he was sick and couldn't make the attack. He said he was going back to the Battery and would get another officer to take his place. When he left the rest of us looked at each other knowingly. No one said anything but we understood. We knew Liggett wasn't any sicker than any of us. The old "battle fatigue" was certainly catching up with him. I felt sick myself. So did Rod and Smith. Sick with fear and apprehension of what lay ahead. Soon another Second Lt. came up and joined us. He introduced himself to us as Lt. Veach. He had come to the outfit at Anzio. He was friendly and seemed to be a nice guy. Although I had never seen him before I had heard of him. He even had a little article written in the Stars and Stripes about him. It wasn't from anything heroic he had done but rather a human interest story I guess you could call it. There is the old saying, particularly from World War I, that there is a bullet or shell with your name on it. Back at Anzio during a shelling, a rather large piece of shrapnel had narrowly missed Veach and embedded in a sandbag or something. He had dug it out and on it was the three initials of his first, middle and last names. I suppose it was the lot marking of the shells or something, but it was a rather odd little happening. I never asked him if he felt immune to getting killed now that the shell with his name on it had missed him. I don't imagine he felt any safer than any of us

We continued on up the road. Friendly shells were whining over our heads. Just as we were about to reach a wooded area mortar shells began to drop in there. There was another company in the woods. We were told to hold up so everyone laid down in the road.

We could hear the mortars firing. Mortars don't make too loud of a report when they are fired so we knew they weren't very far away. It sounded like there were about eight or ten of them. They were really laying the shells into the woods. "K" Company was in the woods and they were catching hell. They must have been losing plenty of men.

The observer with them must have spotted the place where the shells were coming from. Volley after volley of artillery crashed in the area where the mortars seemed to be coming from. After a couple of volleys of artillery the mortars would stop. When the artillery ceased fire the mortars would open up again. This process went on for quite some time. Those mortars must have been well dug in. The mortar, artillery duel went on for an hour or two. Finally, the mortars were quiet. They had either been knocked out or had taken off.

We began to move again. It was getting quite dark when we entered the woods. We crashed through the thick underbrush of the woods. The farther we went the faster we went. We didn't meet any resistance for which we were thankful. We were setting a terrific pace though. The heavy loads Rod and I were carrying made it hard for us to keep up. It was pitch dark and we stumbled and fell many times.

We kept plunging ahead for hours and took no breaks. Everyone seemed anxious to catch up with the Krauts. I could tell I was getting pretty pooped because I noticed when I crawled through a fence or something I would stagger a little. Lt. Veach spelled Rod and I once in a while. It was a good thing he did or we never would have been able to keep up the pace.

Over to our right the sky suddenly lit up followed by a terrific blast. Then there was another flash and another blast. This continued for some time. Apparently our artillery had found a German ammo dump. When the explosions died down a little we would hear more shells crash in that area and again the sky would light up.

We plunged on and on, never stopping. We were almost catching up with the Germans too. They were pulling out just ahead of us. We could hear their trucks and motorcycles start up and go down the road.

Some of our 155 rifles, Long Toms, were firing over our heads. No doubt they were shelling the roads and harassing the retreating Germans. Even though the Long Toms were probably miles behind us the report from them was loud and sharp. They sounded like they were in position just a few yards behind us. That 155 rifle was quite a gun. It carried a real wallop and had a maximum range of something over twenty miles.

Some of the Infantry boys had found some bicycles abandoned by the fleeing Germans. Those characters were riding them up and down the road.

We had been following down a railroad track awhile then down a paved road and now we were making our way down a narrow dirt road again.

Early in the morning our pace began to slow considerably. I didn't know what the deal was but we would go only a few miles and stop. It hadn't rained any since about noon but it was plenty cold. We had worked up a good sweat from the rapid pace we had been making and our clothes were soaked with sweat. When we would stop we all would start shivering. We were really suffering from the cold. You could almost feel frost in the air.

Patrols reported back that the Germans had abandoned a tiny village a short distance up ahead. It was decided that we would stop for the rest of the night in the village.

When we reached the village, I set up the radio and tried to get a hold of Harris. We wanted him to come up with some blankets. The C.P. was moving and he was with them so he couldn't be contacted.

We found a barn and climbed into the hay loft. I had

never before noticed how soft and comfortable a bed of hay could be. We burrowed down in the hay and soon began to feel warm and cozy. We were all fagged out and went to sleep immediately.

The next morning was a clear one with the sun shining down brightly. It was Monday, September 4th, Labor Day. Outside the barn we found Lt. Veach busy cooking us some breakfast. Veach had gotten some bacon out of the jeep and had bought some eggs from a local farmer. We had a nice breakfast of bacon, eggs and coffee.

We decided that there wasn't any use in waiting to go into the next town of Bourg with the Infantry. It had been reported the Germans had pulled out of the town during the night. We were anxious to look the town over.

We jumped in the jeep and took off for Bourg. It was only a short ride to the town. We were among the first into the place. In fact, there were only a handful of G.I.s in the place.

The town of Bourg was going wild. All of the townspeople were out cheering and shouting at us. I was still amazed at the wild enthusiasm these French people showed when one of their towns was liberated. It was sort of hard to tell how large the town was. I guessed a place of maybe twenty-five thousand. They must have all been out in the streets too. We soon had our jeep half filled with bottles of booze, most of it champagne. We were also given several loaves of bread. One poor guy came running towards us to give us a bottle of champagne. He got excited and ran in front of us. We hit him and knocked him for a loop. We were barely moving so he wasn't hurt. All that he had left of the bottle was the neck. It didn't dampen his spirits either. He jumped up and kept on cheering.

Lt. Veach had other things on his mind besides champagne. He asked one of the men where the nearest whore house was. The guy jumped on the jeep and directed us to one. We stopped at the place that had a sign out in front saying, "Establishment". We traipsed into the place. They seemed to run their sporting differently here in France. Inside the place there was a nice bar, some tables and a nice hardwood floor that could be used for dancing. In this place you could apparently find some other forms of entertainment than just taking on a gal.

There were a couple of girls there and we invited them to sit at the bar with us. We bought a quart of whiskey and set it on the bar. We fixed our own drinks when we pleased. One of the gals was pretty good looking but the other was a real beast. These gals had made an American Flag of which they were very proud. It was made out of velvet and was a beautiful thing. We kidded them that they had probably had a German Flag on display last night. I wouldn't have been surprised either. The girls didn't proposition us but we just sat there drinking and talking. I guess they were satisfied as long as we were buying something. We bought three quarts of booze.

Finally, Lt Veach went upstairs with one of the girls. Rod and I were surprised when he picked the one we considered downright ugly. Oh well, everyone to his own taste. The rest of us waited downstairs for him. Rod and I continued to drink while we waited.

When Veach came down again we loaded on the jeep and headed back downtown. Downtown we ran into a lot of people who wanted to be a big help. Everyone seemed happy and were very friendly.

Veach spotted a good looking girl walking along the street. He had Harris pull over to the curb and Veach asked the girl for a kiss. What a character. He got the kiss though. She then started on down the street again. We again pulled up alongside her and Veach asked for another kiss. He got this one too. This process repeated itself several times for the next two blocks.

We finally stopped completely and took the girl into a bar for a few drinks. Veach was doing some real high powered necking with the girl. Right in the middle of all this some guy came up and tapped him on the shoulder. He said he was the girl's husband. Rod, Smith and I began looking for the nearest exit. Veach had been having all the fun, let him get out of this himself. The guy just beamed and told Veach to go right ahead and have a good time with her. Broad minded these French. It seemed to take the edge off a little though and we decided to get to hell out of there. I found out that this girl had relatives in Mountain View, California. I took their address but soon lost it though. Although Veach had unwrapped himself from the girl he seemed to want to talk to her. The rest of us left them and went back outside. We found a bunch of girls clustered around the jeep. We loaded six of the best looking ones on the jeep and started driving around town. This was the life. A wiggly, good looking, friendly girl in one hand and a bottle of good champagne in the other. Sometimes war wasn't hell. I kept wishing it was dark though.

Later a few other American vehicles began to come into town. Some Lt. Colonel stopped us and asked us if we knew it was against regulations to give civilians rides on our vehicles. We said, "Yes Sir", and kept right on going. To hell with him. He was just sourballed because he didn't have a load of girls with him.

A couple of hours later we decided that we had better get back to the Battery. We were supposed to have reported there early in the morning. There were a lot of G.I.s coming into town now and the place was getting too crowded anyway. When there were too many around it wasn't so much fun. I guess we didn't like competition.

We took Lt. Veach back to Headquarters and then showed up at the Battery. Captain Hurley wanted to know where we had been all this time. We told him we had been out doing a little recon work. Of course he knew this was a lie. All he said was that in our recon work we must have come in contact with a barrel of whiskey. I guess we reeked of booze and were a little tight. Pretty good guy, Captain Hurley.

We looked up Lt. Liggett. He said he had backed down from the attack not because he was sick but because he was scared. He said he had felt so nervous that he had just felt he couldn't make it. He was man enough to admit it and we admired him for it. It was catching up with all of us anyway. When we told him that there hadn't been anything to it but a hell of a lot of hiking he was sorry he hadn't stuck it out.

That afternoon we got some of the new ten-in-one rations. These rations had cans of bacon, butter, jam and other goodies. We put several cans of different food in our jeep. We also picked up a couple of loaves of bread from the kitchen truck.

Late in the afternoon we moved out with the Battery. We passed through Bourg. The people were still cheering and celebrating.

We moved on down the road several miles before we pulled off into a green field that was situated on the slope of a hill. As we dismounted, the rain began to fall again. Most of us put up pup tents getting ready for the night.

Up ahead we could hear the booming of artillery. Both "A" and "B" Batteries were up there. They were in position in a narrow pass and there wasn't room for our battery just yet. It rained steady but not hard all night. For once we were able to keep fairly dry in our tents.

The next morning it was still raining and plenty

chilly. Rod and I found an abandoned house nearby and moved in. The house was a pretty place. It seemed above average for houses around this particular area. It looked as though it had been abandoned for quite some time however. Whoever had lived here had apparently been in the bee business. There was all kinds of bee supplies in the house as well as scattered around outside.

We persuaded the rest of the F.O. party to move in with us. For a couple of days we had it pretty nice. We had a nice dry place to sleep and could keep our equipment dry. We had a nice place to cook too. There were plenty of potatoes in the cellar and we spent hours making French fries. We had a couple of candles and spent nights playing Casino by the light of the candles and from the fireplace.

The couple of mornings we were here, German planes strafed the area. They were raiding in spite of the bad weather. They roared past our house going mostly for the roads. The house we were in was several yards from the road so nothing came too close to us.

On September 8th we went out for what was to be our last F.O.ing job. Of course we didn't know it at the time. There was always the chance when we went out we wouldn't come back but we always hoped for the best.

The First Sgt. of the Battery asked Murphy to go in place of Rod. He hadn't been doing a damned thing lately anyway. He came out with that old crap saying he was "sick". I felt like popping him one. I did curse him up one side and down the other. I was also sore at the First Sgt. for not making him go and tell him in no uncertain words. He should have given Murphy the choice of either going or being court martialed for disobeying orders in combat. The yellow bastard. He would get home safe and sound alright unless he got it in a barrage or air raid.

Our party started out for the Front late in the

afternoon. We had our raincoats on trying to keep dry from the driving rain.

We first stopped at Headquarters Battery to pick up maps and the late dope on the situation. At Headquarters I saw Perkins. I tried to persuade him to go along on this trip. I told him he might get a real story. Boy! What a story he would have gotten. I almost talked him into it, but he declined saying the weather was too bad.

We were informed that if we needed artillery support, we would receive it from the 160th F.A. The 158th was at the moment in support of another outfit and would be until morning at least.

We left Headquarters and started up the road towards the Front. The road we were on wound around through the woods. From here it was supposed to be only a few miles from the Swiss border. We joked about heading for the border and getting interned for the duration. If we had known what was going to happen in about seventy-two hours we might have done just that.

Just after dark we reached a small bombed and shelled town. The town was situated on the banks of a small river. The Danube River I think it was called. Anyway, this river divided the lines. On this side were the American Lines and on the other were the Germans. No one knew how far across the river one would have to go before they ran into the enemy. A platoon of Infantry was going over into the enemy lines to find out what the score was.

The bridge across the river in the town had been blown as well as the others in this area that crossed the river. No vehicles or heavy equipment were across the river yet. A Bailey bridge was being built downstream a way but it would be at least daylight before it would be completed.

As the situation shaped up it looked like the best thing

for our F.O. party to do was to find a good O.P., probably in one of the tallest buildings in the town and wait. The platoon of Infantry that was going across the river would find out if the Krauts were close or not.

The plans for our F.O. party never materialized. Our Liaison Officer had other ideas. He decided that we should go over the river with the platoon. He was a brave fellow. Of course he was going to stay on this side in the town. He assured us that the bridge would be done by morning and then we would have tanks and other heavy equipment. That wasn't going to help us much tonight.

We cautiously made our way across the blown out bridge. On the very fringe of the town we stopped in front of a building. It was evidently a F.F.I. (French Forces of the Interior) Headquarters. Liggett and Lt. Barfoot, the officer in charge of the Infantry, went inside to get some additional information. Our party and the Infantry boys sat outside and waited. Some of us leaned our rifles against the building while we waited.

Soon the officers came out and we got ready to move out. Smith got a surprise when he reached for his rifle. Where his carbine had been leaning he now found a sniper's rifle with telescopic sight and all. Apparently some Infantry boy had decided that a carbine would be lighter and easier to carry instead of his .03. Maybe he didn't like the idea of being a sniper either. Whatever it was, Smith was the owner of an old bolt action .03.

We passed out of town and down the open road. It was pitch dark. We moved cautiously and as quietly as possible. We expected to run into trouble any second.

A mile or two out of town we came to a fork in the road. We took the road that turned to the left. We went up this road only a couple of hundred yards when bullets began to whine past our ears. We moved back toward the way we had come. It was obvious that we had run into a German roadblock. Just before we got back to the fork in the road we moved off the road a few yards.

I set up the radio and contacted the 160th. I requested fire in the vicinity of the road block. They came back with, "Are you sure it was the enemy?" I told them we were sure because we had been fired on. They again came back with, "Does that necessarily mean that it was the enemy?" I just about blew a fuse. No one can mistake a German zip pistol as friendly. Their information probably was that there were friendly troops across the river. They were right and the "friendly" troops were us. There were also enemy troops here too. One did realize though that the artillery must be careful and not fire on their own troops. Sometimes some hair brained F.O. would get excited and fire before he found out what it was. Something like a deer hunter firing at brush that moves before he sees whether it was a deer or his partner.

I knew they were clearing everything through Division Artillery from the pauses between their answers. We wished that we were firing the 158th. They knew us and knew that we generally knew what we were doing. If we had been firing the 158th I doubt we would have even been questioned.

We would hear the German vehicles moving around down in the vicinity of the road block. We could hear them come down the road and turn off and kill their engines. It was apparently a rendezvous area and from the sounds many vehicles were congregating there.

I kept calling for fire but not getting any results. I called our L.O. (Look Out) and told him to for Christ' sake get some artillery out here for us. Both our L.O. and the 160the seemed to be doing their best but still no artillery. This was a heck of a note. The place crawling with Krauts and no artillery.

Finally, after begging for three hours they began to give us a little artillery. We were firing blind and more or less guessing as to where the German's exact location was. The Germans were up against a hill and we had trouble getting the fire in where we wanted it. Many of the shells were hitting the top of the hill.

We were getting some of them in there anyway. When we would get some shells in close to them, we could hear them start up their vehicles and stir around. It sounded like a bunch of angry bees.

The night dragged on. It was clear now and bitterly cold. We didn't have blankets and coats and were miserable. We wouldn't have dared sleep even if we could have. We didn't know what might happen next.

We knew the Germans knew that there were Americans on this side of the river because they had fired on us. They probably just thought it was a patrol out snooping. We figured that they might send a patrol or larger force in our direction to investigate so we had to be very alert.

All night we could hear their vehicles coming down the road and turning off. We figured we had the road between us and them pretty well zeroed in. Now if we could just get some artillery. The 160th was just halfheartedly trying to help us.

Just at dawn we heard the sound of many motors. They sounded like they were getting closer. I called quickly for artillery but by the time the shells were pounding in the road the Germans were almost to our position and the shells were landing behind them.

The German column was led by three Tiger tanks followed by several armored cars and about twenty trucks loaded down with troops. An awful sight to behold. We were so near the road we could have almost reached out and touched them.

Our hearts really started to pound when the convoy stopped right in front of us. Everyone just crouched there with their guns leveled at the Germans. A squad of men wouldn't have had a chance against three Tiger tanks plus armored cars and twenty truckloads of troops. We intended to take as many of them with us as we could.

It seemed unbelievable that the Germans could be so close and not spot us. It was almost broad daylight now. You could tell they didn't have any idea anyone was so close. Some had climbed out of the trucks and were nonchalantly walking around talking and smoking. It was a real miracle they didn't see us. We had been pretty well caught flat footed and no one had had time to try to conceal themselves. Most of us were out in plain sight. We were only about ten yards from the road and up on a knoll only a few feet high. There were a few trees and some underbrush around us but not enough to really hide us if they had been looking. Even German soldiers can make mistakes.

No one got excited and opened up. If they had it would have been all over for us in a couple of seconds. All those tanks would have to do was turn their turrets and lay a few rounds into our hillside and that would be all. If we had opened up on the troops in the trucks no doubt we could have gotten a lot of them before they had gotten organized. Maybe that is what we should have done. No one gave the command though and no one fired. I think the suddenness of the way the situation developed had stunned everyone. I couldn't imagine Lt. Barfoot throwing away a chance to kill a few Krauts no matter what the odds were.

It was a fantastic spot to be in. In spite of the tense

situation I could hardly keep from laughing. Situations like this only happened in fantasy stories.

Just as the Krauts were getting back on their trucks my radio blurted out. The artillery said, "Is that artillery falling in there O.K.?" I just about crapped. It seemed so loud and clear I was sure the Krauts could hear it. Still, to my amazement, they paid no attention. They just piled on the trucks and got ready to move. I didn't even try to answer but just turned the damned thing off. There was another thing that happened that was comical in spite of the situation. Smith made signs to me that he didn't have any ammunition. The guy that had exchanged the .05 for his carbine hadn't been thoughtful enough to leave any ammunition for it. It struck me as funny that here we were face to face with the enemy and some joker didn't have any ammunition for his gun. I must have been cracking up to find something humorous at a time like this.

The three German tanks pulled off to the edge of the road and let the trucks with their troops pass them. The armored cars pulled on ahead too with the tanks bringing up the rear.

As soon as the Germans started moving I called the 160th and told them that the Germans were passing us. Everyone in the rear area began to get excited now. Our L.O. back across the river heard my message to the 160th. He got on the radio and wanted to know how many tanks there were and which way they were going. I was so damn mad I doubled everything. I told them there were six tanks and forty truckloads of troops and several armored cars. It made me mad to think about the way we had to beg for artillery and got mostly nothing but a lot of silly questions and answers. If we had gotten more cooperation and received the artillery we wanted this situation probably would have never happened. We could have made it so hot for the Germans in their rendezvous area we could have made them withdraw as well as causing casualties among them. If we had plenty of artillery to interdict the road between them and our position the chances are that they would have never come down our road. It is also possible that our way was their only escape route. Maybe they couldn't have come the other direction if they had wanted to. This would have been good. If we had had the artillery they would have had to stay put. When our troops had the bridge across the river repaired we would have soon had plenty of troops and tanks on this side. Possibly the whole German outfit here could have been captured or wiped out. That wasn't to be the story however.

Even though the German convoy was turning to the north at the fork I reported that they were heading in the direction of town. After the bulk of the convoy turned to the north the tanks stayed a minute or two at the fork in the road and pumped a few rounds into the town. With what I had told them and some shells dropping into the town, our people there thought for sure that the Germans were starting a counterattack towards them. Everyone back in the town and farther back were in a real lather. I got everyone but General Patton on the radio. Captains and Majors were a dime a dozen. I let them get in a state of confusion and then checked out.

We didn't check out purely for meanness though. We knew by running to the top of our hill that we could probably get sight of the convoy again and be able to fire on them.

When we got to the top of the hill most of the convoy was out of sight in the woods a mile or two away. The three tanks were fairly close though and seemed to be loafing along. We were about to fire on them when we saw a strange thing happen. Three of our own trucks drove into view. They were loaded with troops. They were rapidly gaining on the Germans. It was obvious they didn't know who they were catching up with. Probably what had happened was that the bridge was repaired below the town and these were the first vehicles across the river. They must have seen the tail end of the German convoy going around a corner or something. They must have figured it was part of their own convoy and had hurried to catch up with them. Three shots from the German tanks were all it took. Three trucks were knocked out and it must have rained havoc with the troops on them. The Tigers took a few more shots toward town and took off.

We started throwing shells after them for all we were worth. We weren't having any trouble getting artillery now. We were able to fire a couple of volleys at them before they disappeared into the woods. We didn't stop any of them. We watched the woods closely for quite some time to see if they stopped there and did a little shooting. They didn't however and were probably long gone. They knew for sure now that there were American troops and equipment on this side of the river. They were probably heading for a defensive position some place back a way. They had probably gotten away unscathed. We might have gotten some of their troops riding on the tanks for they all disappeared into the woods. Our shells were pounding those woods now.

Soon more Infantry boys began to come into our position. Also, more trucks and tanks appeared. If we could have held the Krauts for a few minutes more we could have gotten them all one way or the other. Things will happen like this in a fast moving situation like most of our campaigns in France had been. Things moved fast and often things were fouled up. Both sides made some awful booboos from time to time.

World War II was a war of movement for the most part. Of course, there were times, like in Italy at Casino and Anzio, where it was more or less a throwback to World War I. The same positions for months and more or less trench warfare. For the most part though it was a war of movement. Thousands of miles involved in North Africa, in Russia and here in France. And look at the thousands and thousands of miles in the Pacific Theater. It seemed odd, despite the millions of men involved in so many battles and skirmishes. The thing was spread over too much of the world to have too many men concentrated in one place. This was surely a war like the Civil War.

The bunch of Infantry that moved into our position set up mortars in firing position. We figured it was a little late for that now. A little later they did prove to be useful. Later a group of Germans that had been left behind tried to infiltrate through our position. A few mortar shells got them going back the way they had come.

Our F.O. party stayed on top of the knoll for most of the rest of the day. We didn't see anything to fire at. One of our observation planes kept flitting around over our heads. We tried to keep hidden from it. Sometimes these guys didn't seem to be able to see very well and would fire on their own troops.

In the afternoon the Infantry wanted us to go down and zero a crossroads just in case something came up like the night before. Zeroing this crossroads sounded easier than it was. We had to go down in the direction of where the Germans had been trying to infiltrate earlier in the day. There were many thickets of evergreens along the route and we were afraid of being ambushed from one of them.

We sneaked, crawled and worked our way down near enough to the crossroads to zero in on it. We made tracks back to the Infantry making it safely without event.

Our party was getting to spend the night here in the same position. Things seemed to have moved on north and we were anticipating a quiet night and a good night's sleep. Late in the afternoon another F.O. party came up and told us that they were taking our place and that we were to go up and join "I" Company in a tiny village about three miles up the road. They were preparing to spend the night here. Rod, Smitty and I found a place in a barn that seemed to be a nice spot. We would be in out of the cold and have hay to sleep on. We had no more than lain down when Lt. Liggett decided that we had better get out to the outpost and stay on the alert. Instead of sleeping in a nice warm hayloft we had to stretch out and try to sleep on the cold ground. We had no blankets so this was going to be another lovely night. We muttered curses under our breath all the way to the outpost although we knew Liggett was right.

However, we felt that there would not be a situation like last night. There were quite a lot of our troops and equipment on this side of the river now. We were sure all of the Germans in this area were ahead of us now. The ones that had been left behind this morning must have been captured by now. There had only been a few stragglers so they didn't really matter too much. Still, we didn't know how far to our left it was before there were friendly troops so it was just as well that we were on the alert.

We took turns on the radio and were pretty watchful. It was too cold to get much sleep anyway. Even when we did get a chance to lie down it was miserable. Another thing that bothered us were some of our tanks were moving around a short distance from us. Some of them were passing close to us and we were half afraid one would loom up out of the dark and run over us.

Early in the morning we went back to the village. We got ready to move out with the Infantry. Actually, we were going to attack out of this town. No one seemed to know where the Germans were exactly but they were supposed to be up ahead of us somewhere.

"I" Company moved out of the village with our F.O. party leading the column. This was great. The F.O.s at the point.

Our artillery was now passing over our heads and crashing out ahead of us. About a mile down the road we approached another little village. Suddenly machine gun and rifle fire greeted us. There were also a few small caliber artillery shells popping around. A few of the men were hit. We all scattered off the road and took cover.

We began to advance on the town in skirmish formation. The bunch we were with pushed through a thicket that came up on the right side of the village.

Machine gun and rifle fire were raking our thicket. We crept and crawled along with the Infantry to the edge of the thicket. From the edge of the thicket to the rear of the buildings on the street running though the village was only a few yards. The Germans were firing out of windows and doorways. Everyone started banging away at the openings. I started having more fun shooting when the returning fire grew less and finally stopped. We figured the Krauts had got the hell out of there.

We cautiously approached the village. We entered the first few buildings on the very edge. The Germans had abandoned these alright. We now held this end of the village and the Krauts held the other. The Germans seemed to have one thought in mind and that was to get the hell out of there before they got trapped. They were sending plenty of machine gun and rifle fire into our part of the village. They were still shelling us with the small artillery. I guessed it was 40mm.

A couple of tanks were supposed to come and help run the Germans out and we were to hold up and wait for them. Our F.O. party took cover in a house/barn affair that was on into the village three or four buildings. A German prisoner was shoved into our building. No one was going to the rear yet and someone told us to keep an eye on him. We had problems of our own without watching a prisoner. Whoever shoved him in here was gone before we could protest.

"Our prisoner" really jumped when we spoke to him. He said he had been a truck driver up around Dijon for some supply outfit. He said that a couple of days ago he had been handed a rifle and informed that he was now in the Infantry. He had been sent down here yesterday.

In a side room of our barn we found more or less living quarters. The Germans had been using it to cook and eat in. They had taken off so fast that they had left potatoes boiling on the stove. They had also left a big bottle of clear looking liquid sitting on the table. We were sure it was liquor of some kind but we were a little suspicious. The Krauts could be pretty tricky. There was a remote possibility they had left us a mickey of acid or something. We didn't want to take the chance of tasting it ourselves. We asked the prisoner what the stuff was. He said it was schnapps and indicated that it was good. I poked the bottle at him and he took a drink of it. Rod and I then took a slug of the stuff. A big snort of the stuff made us stagger back a few steps. It seemed to be pretty potent. We continued to nip at the bottle taking turns. We handed the prisoner the bottle and insisted that he drink. We just wanted to be friendly. After all we didn't really have anything against this guy. He was a little reluctant. He made us understand that he hadn't had much to eat for the last couple of days and the liquor would make him drunk quick. Hell, we were all in the same boat. We had hardly eaten in several days either. We insisted that he drink with us. He took the bottle and took a big gulp. He was probably afraid not to.

A Frenchman sneaked out of a nearby house and made his way to our barn, braving the rain of bullets and flying fragments. He had a loaf of bread and a big chunk of cheese he wanted to give us. He congratulated us on driving the Germans back. He then tore back to the house amid a hail of bullets. We divided the bread up giving the prisoner some too. The bread was good but I hated the Swiss like cheese. The prisoner amazed us all by reaching in his pocket and pulling out about a half pound of creamery butter. It was still in its wrapping and in perfect condition. How he had kept this it was a mystery to us. He must have picked it up somewhere just before he was captured. We spread the butter a quarter of an inch thick on the bread. It was the best butter I had ever tasted.

The tanks that were supposed to come up and help us out never showed to no one's surprise. They had some lame excuse about being low on fuel or faulty radios or something. The Krauts seemed to have pulled out of the town although small artillery continued to harass us. We had spotted a church up the street at the other edge of the village and we thought we would try to make our way to it. It was the biggest building in the village and we figured the bell tower would make a good place for an O.P.

Still, no one was going to the rear so we were going

to have to take our prisoner with us. He wanted to be helpful. He helped us get our packs on our backs and handed us our rifles. I guess we trusted the guy, letting him handle our guns. It seemed pretty obvious the guy was no fanatic and would shoot us with our own guns. We hadn't treated him roughly or anything and he was probably glad that he was a prisoner. I guess if he figured we were typical Americans and he had it made.

On our way through the village we came upon on a wounded German lying in the street. Our boy knelt over him and talked to him and lit a cigarette and put it in his mouth. The wounded German looked like a young kid of nineteen or twenty. He had been hit pretty badly and seemed to be suffering a great deal.

We continued on until we reached the edge of the village. We went up to the church steeple to set up our O.P. Liggett and I took a look around. We weren't able to see much. There were woods and hills directly in front of us. We went back down to the ground floor.

An Infantry boy brought another prisoner into the church. He said he was going to the rear and would take our man with him. The prisoner with the Infantry man kept insisting he was a Pole and not a German. He even sang the Polish National Anthem to prove it. He probably was a Pole. There were lots of them that had been forced into the German Army. German prisoners we had gotten in the past often would say they were Regular Army and not S.S. (Shultzstaffel, the armed wing of the Nazi Party). I guess the whole world hated the SS Troops and the regular Army knew it. I guess they felt it would go easier with them if their capturers didn't mistake them for SS.

We were about to push on out of town when a rather peculiar thing happened. The boys had rounded up a couple of German Officers. One was a Captain and the other a Lt. The enlisted prisoners that were being rounded up really snapped to attention and saluted when they saw them. Even as prisoners they didn't forget the discipline they had been accustomed to. The German Captain had been hit. One of his arms hung limply at his side and he was bleeding quite a bit. He still carried himself erect and was poker faced, showing no emotion whatever.

The younger officer was a different story however. He was yelling and cursing. He threw his cap on the ground and kicked at it. One of our men who could understand German said he was mad because they had been left behind when the rest had retreated from the village. He was yelling that the war was almost over and he was glad. He said he would be home in a month. That was the only time I ever saw a German Officer show any emotion at all. They were always very placid regardless of what happened.

By the time we left the village Rod and I were feeling pretty good. We had brought the bottle of schnapps along with us and had been nipping at it when we got a chance. We took a few more nips as we plodded along.

We soon entered the woods and started making our way up a ravine. Suddenly 88mm high bursts began to pop in around close. They weren't the high adjusting kind either. They were bursting just off the ground a few feet and they meant business. Everyone hit the ground and took cover. A couple of the boys were hit. Road and I just stood there looking around as if nothing had happened. The liquor had really made us brave. I decided I was going to always the stuff with us. Smith and Liggett were yelling at us to get down.

BEVERLY RICHARD BORTHWICK

Front row, left to right: Beverly "Dick" Borthwick and Marty Martinovich
Second row, left to right: "Rod" Rodriquez and two unidentified friends.

When the shelling stopped Smith, for the first time that I could remember, pulled his rank. He gave us hell. He also took our bottle and dashed it against a rock. That was the end of that but no matter, the liquor was almost gone. It was a damned wonder we didn't get it. How stupid can you get? Actually I didn't feel drunk but I must have been something.

We moved out of the woods and onto a flat open field on top of the hill. More 88 shells crashed in around getting some more of the fellows. This time Rod and I were flat on the ground with everyone else. From here we spotted some German horse drawn artillery moving along on a hill a good distance away. We tried to fire on them but couldn't tell if our shells were landing near them or not. We had to keep pretty low because of the incoming mail. Later in the afternoon things quieted down.

Just at dusk we started to move forward. A short time later we stopped on a wooded hillside. Patrols reported that there were plenty of Germans and equipment in the next little village which was about a mile away. It was decided to stay put here for the rest of the night and attack the village in the morning.

We prepared to spend the night on this rocky, root filled hillside. It was bitterly cold and with no blankets or coats made sleep impossible. I was hungry too. Eating had been pretty slim the last few days. We hadn't been able to get even enough "K" rations. Everyone was grimy and tired.

The company commander of "I" Company, Lt. Barfoot, was quite a character. He had earned the Congressional Medal of Honor at Anzio while still an enlisted man. If anyone deserved one he certainly did. He seemed to love combat and was apparently always looking for trouble. He spent a lot of time out with his radio operator wandering around. Tonight was no exception. He had gone sneaking up to the village to see what the Germans were up to and to try to find out in what force.

He came back and wanted the F.O.s to go close to the village with him. He wanted us to be there at the crack of down so we could start shelling the place. We didn't think much of the idea but went with him.

We stopped on a slope of a wooded hill right above the village. The village was situated in a little valley. We were plenty close to the Krauts too. We could hear the German sentries challenging and hear vehicles moving around. We stayed awake through the long night. We had to be alert if a patrol should happen our way. It was so cold that sleep would have been impossible anyway. I really didn't have much fear of the Germans discovering us as long as we were quiet. They were retreating and this didn't seem the time or place for a stand. I imagined they were strictly on the defensive here. They were using road blocks and outposts to keep the Americans from surprising them. We weren't going to shell the village tonight even though we knew they were there. French towns weren't to be shelled if we could keep from it. The Germans would probably pull out under the cover of darkness anyway. We had to stay alert though. A German Patrol might come snooping around to find out where our troops were. Even if they did it was a very remote chance that they would stumble on us. As far as we knew we were just on a wooded hillside not close to a road or even a trail. If we were discovered it would be purely by accident.

At dawn the Germans were still in the village. To our surprise they had not withdrawn. Maybe they were going to make some kind of stand here after all. As soon as it was light enough to see we began to shell the village. That stirred up the Krauts. They didn't seem to have expected artillery. I guess they knew the main part of our troops were back a mile or two and hadn't expected anything quite yet. Our shelling sent them into great confusion. They were scrambling around and trying to get out of the village. Our view of the town and a short stretch of the road leaving it were pretty good.

Some of the German field pieces were sitting out in the open. When one of their vehicles would pull out from around a building and try to hook on to one of them we would let them have it and they would disappear behind a building again. We were causing casualties. Some ambulances with their red crosses on them came into town and started picking up the dead and wounded. When these ambulances came in we would shell another part of the town and leave them alone. Two big tanks tore out from behind a building and headed out of town. They were down that short stretch of open road and out of sight before we could bring enough artillery on them to stop them.

Several vehicles with red crosses came into town and we held up from firing on them as usual. The bastards were tricky though. They wheeled over to the artillery pieces and started hooking on to them. We knew we should fire but held up. We told fire direction what was going on. We were told if the vehicles were hooking on to guns disregard the red crosses and fire on them. This we did. The hesitation had given the Krauts an advantage though. By the time we started firing on them some had managed to get out of town.

We had really given the Krauts a bad time. In the middle of the afternoon, what was left of them and their equipment, finally got out of the village. They had no doubt lost heavily. Now the town was cleared of the enemy and the infantry that had moved up started to move in.

We took down our radio and went toward the town with them.

We found the town abandoned by the Germans and it seemed to be empty of French also. There was not a joyous welcome here. The French were probably still holed up and waiting for us to leave. They were probably afraid of a German counterattack or that they would start shelling the town. They were probably holed up in a reasonably safe spot and were going to wait awhile to see what developed.

However, there was a big bell tower ringing away. Someone was welcoming us and telling the villagers of their liberation. We all wished the bell would stop ringing. We seemed to think it could draw German artillery. Of course, the bell wouldn't have anything to do with the German artillery. They knew we were in the village and would shell it if and when they saw fit.

Thinking like that showed in what state of mind everyone was in. The way we had been going the last few days, the lack of sleep, being keyed up, hungry, tired, etc. made us jumpy. We were expecting German artillery on the town at any moment.

We moved on out of the village and started across open fields. Suddenly we were called back to the village. Lt. Mathis, the Company Commander, had us group around the barn. He gave us a little talk. He said the word came down from the big brass that we had to go faster and push harder. They promised that as soon as we took the next little town and on further to the outskirts of a larger town called Villersexal, we would be relieved. It was the same old crap. Take that next hill or town and you would be relieved. I had been hearing that same old thing for months. Even when the next hill or town was taken you were never relieved.

I didn't know what the big brass sitting way back there fighting the war over a map and a drink expected us to do. We had been covering a lot of ground. Everyone was dog tired. Our clothes were grimy and caked with mud. We all had a week's growth of beard and accumulated grime on us. We hadn't had enough to eat lately either.

Those bastards with the razor sharp creases and the polished boots and eagles and stars on their shoulders could do a lot of talking. When they drove the hell out of us they got all the glory and credit. Headlines were what those bastards wanted. Things like General Joe Doaks umpteenth Corps taking so and so or General Fartheads juggernauts driving the Nazi's back to the Fatherland etc. They should be here with us and see what the war was really like.

Articles and books would be written on general so and so about how smart, brave and clever he had been beating the enemy. Any moron could win battles if he had more men and equipment. I didn't give any general an ounce of credit for winning any battles or campaigns in this war.

The Italian Campaign had been a good example of the "big brains" running this war. The Anzio Beachhead had been their masterpiece. Any experienced infantryman, a private at that, could have done better. Had some ordinary Doggie been running the show we would have been in Rome in a few days instead of taking four months of hell. It had even come out that during the Anzio fiasco an old incompetent general had been in charge. It was politics. Some joker had been in the army a hundred years or something and they wanted him to have a little glory. He was relieved soon but by then the damage had been done. The stupid bastards running this show didn't know what the hell the score was. If the American morale was low it was because of lack of confidence in the stupid characters running things. No one had any confidence in them. It was obvious that we were winning the war because of the superior amount of equipment. It certainly wasn't from the wonderful strategy of our generals. Quit bitching. Anyway, this was the fateful day of September 11th, 1944.

Again we left the town and headed up a small dirt road. Major Mitchell, the Regimental Executive Officer, had joined us. We had gotten a short distance out of town when bullets began to rain in all around. The Germans were really pouring the rifle and machine gun fire our way. It was obvious it was coming from a woods a short distance away.

Two of our tanks had ben cautiously creeping along behind us. They were asked to go up toward the woods and blast the machine gun nest. The tanks made some lame excuse about being low on fuel or something and wouldn't come up. Seemed like our tanks were just about next to nothing.

The word passed down the line. F.O.s forward. That was a lovely sound. We wondered if we were to go up and beat the Krauts to death with our aerials. Major Mitchell was yelling at us to get up there and knock those machine guns out. This was fine for him to say lying there flat on the ground with everyone else.

We got up and made a dash forward. Bullets were whistling all around and kicking up the dirt everywhere. It was a miracle we didn't get it. Lt. Mathis, near the head of the column, was up on one knee watching us. As we neared where he was a bullet plunked through his head. The poor devil had finally gotten the relief he wanted for us all. His was final and permanent.

We got a few yards ahead of the Infantry, dove through

a barbed wire fence and into a ditch. I hurriedly set up the radio and called for fire on the woods. We were soon giving the edge of the woods a good plastering. The artillery apparently did the trick. The firing from the woods tapered off and finally stopped. Good old artillery. The Infantry began coming on up the road toward us.

The two tanks way back there decided that it must be pretty safe now and began to come up our way. I guess they suddenly found that they had a little gas left after all. The tanks came on up and began to fire into the woods. They fired into them for about half an hour, sending a good many rounds in there. They also raked the woods with 50 caliber machine gun fire.

It looked like the Krauts in the woods had either retired or had been killed. A couple of scouts were sent out to walk right by the edge of the woods and back. Christ what a job a scout had. If they were shot down we would know the Germans were still there. If a scout wasn't a suicide troop I don't know what the hell it was.

Although things seemed to have quieted down in the woods right in front of us there were still Krauts in the vicinity. Artillery landed behind us about halfway back to the village. A short distance ahead mortars were crashing in.

We laid by the road waiting for further orders. Reports came to us that "L" Company had been contacted. In fact, we could see them straggling across a field over to our left. Our spirits began to rise. Maybe the Germans were dropping back and covering their retreat with artillery. Maybe we could take the next little town up ahead and reach the outskirts of Villersexal during the night. Maybe we would be relieved the next day.

I took out a can of "K" ration meat I had been saving.

This seemed like a good time to eat. We hadn't gotten orders to move up yet and I was hungry. I had just taken a bite when Major Mitchell called to us. With the major was a French Sgt. named Paul. He was a liaison man with our outfit. Perhaps he had lived around this part of France before the war and knew the lay of the land.

Major Mitchell said that there was a road a short distance over to our left. The company was to find it and advance on the next village that was up the road two or three miles.

We started moving toward where the road was supposed to be. The two tanks followed along cautiously behind. Instead of going ahead like they did in any other army and the way they were supposed to be used, they crept along behind the Infantry. That was a hell of a note. The Infantry was having to go ahead and make it safe for the tanks.

Our F.O. party was a little ahead and to the right of the main body of the company. This may have been the only thing that saved our lives. We started crossing a big open field. There were woods on our right and behind us now and we approached another thicket along a stone wall. Beyond this thicket and wall was supposed to be the road we were looking for.

We were right in the middle of the open field when all hell broke loose. The Germans were lying in ambush behind the wall. They opened up with all they had, and they had plenty of rifles and machine guns.

Fortunately for our F.O. party, they seemed to concentrate their fire. They started to our left and moved to the right. Major Mitchell, the French Sgt. Paul and many Infantry boys were almost cut in half with the first volley. We hit the ground as the fire swept our way. Still we were lucky. There was a hole right beside us. It was a natural depression in the ground, almost like a fox hole. It was about six feet deep and cone shaped. There was room for us all and we rolled into it in great haste. An infantry boy rolled in with us. I never knew where he came from.

Thousands of bullets were whizzing overhead and tearing the air. There were a couple of little saplings growing out of our hole. Their branches that stuck out beyond the ground level were rapidly being picked clean of leaves.

You could look up and see thousands of German white tracers going past. A few red tracers were going the other way. There were damned few though and in a few minutes none at all. We heard our tanks turn and shag ass. Those dirty bastards were letting small arms and machine gun fire drive them off. If they had held their ground and fired a few rounds at the Krauts they may have been able to rout them. They were only buttoned up with a few inches of steel to protect them. Not only did they take off and leave us when they got back a couple of hundred yards away they turned and began to throw shells right in on us. We were expecting to get it from our own tanks any second.

I set up the radio and we began to plaster the landscape toward the road and the woods over to our right. We had them use both H.E. (High Explosive) and phosphorus. Our own shells were landing mighty close. Shrapnel from both the tank shells and our own artillery was whining overhead. We expected a shell from either our tanks or our artillery to drop in our hole any second. It didn't make any difference. We were goners anyway.

We kept firing out in front of us and in the woods to our right continually. We were firing blind. We couldn't stick our heads out of the hole to see where our shells were hitting. A fraction of a second above the ground level and no head.

Suddenly, the firing from the Krauts quieted down a little and we heard screaming and yelling. Liggett peeked one eyeball over the top in their direction. He said he thought they were giving up. The rest of us wanted to know who? Us or them?

What the racket turned out to be was actually the Germans coming on the attack. I didn't know whether that screaming was to shatter the enemy's morale or to bolster theirs. It didn't do mine any good. We just waited in our hole with our guns pointed at the top. We were going to take a few of them with us anyway. For some reason they never looked in our hole but just swept by us. The bulk of them passed over to our left a ways.

The Infantryman with us had a small intercompany radio on his back. It was somewhat larger than the walkie-talkie. He kept trying to contact any of the four sets in the company. He didn't have any luck. We knew Major Mitchell and his radio operator had been killed. No doubt that was the fate of the rest of them too. The Germans had really caught us flat footed and had mowed down a lot before they even had a chance to hit the ground. The company must have been hurt badly.

Right in the midst of the worst of things the Fire Direction asked me if we were receiving an attack. Of course he had known it because they could hear all the racket coming over the set. The operator said it so calmly it made me sore. I answered him and it was the last time I ever said anything over the radio. I said, "You're God damned right". Famous last words I guess.

Just about dusk things seemed to quiet down a bit and we wondered what was up. We decided to wait until dark and try to make our way back to our lines wherever they were.

Just at dusk the Germans opened up with some kind of gun that I had never heard before. It made a horrible sound when it went off. To me it sounded like a huge rusty barn door swinging shut. It was set up somewhere in the woods not far from us. The projectile from it moved so slowly that we could see it passing over. The shells from it seemed to have the appearance of a big potato masher grenade. We figured it must be some kind of new rocket gun the Krauts had come up with. We were scared enough as it was yet something new, something we were not accustomed to, was added to our fear.

The shells from this "new" weapon were landing behind us on back toward the village. From where we were we couldn't see the impact area. We heard Lt. Olsen talking to fire direction over the radio. He evidently was in a position to see the projectile hitting the ground. He said they appeared to have gasoline or something in them and that they burst into a huge flame when they hit. That would be nice. To have one of those land near our hole.

It was almost dark and things quieted down some again. We could hear the murmur of voices in the woods a hundred yards or so behind us. It sounded like a bunch of G.I.s talking. We were sure that it was and our hopes began to rise. We should have known better but we weren't thinking too clearly right then. We figured the remnants of the Infantry must have held there and the Germans must have veered off into the woods to our left. We should have talked the situation over a little better.

Lt. Liggett was anxious to get going. He suddenly announced that he was going to try to make it. He jumped out of the hole and started running toward the woods.

He had no more than got going when a hail of bullets began to whiz around.

In spite of the firing we still thought it was our men in those woods. We figured they were still trigger happy for this afternoon skirmish and fired at anything that moved.

In a minute or two the rifle fire died down again. We knew either Liggett had made it or been killed. We knew that if he made it, he would tell them that we were out there.

In a few minutes the rest of us tried to make our way towards the woods. We crawled out of the hole but only got a few feet when a rain of bullets began to kick up dirt in our faces. We yelled at them to for Christ's sake cut it out, it was the F.O.s. We then heard machine pistols open up. We heard a German say Achtung and it didn't mean attention in English.

We crouched in the hole wondering what to do. Smith asked me what I thought we should do. I told him I didn't have the slightest idea. Besides he was the ranking non-com now so it was up to him. We knew for sure that we were in one hell of a spot. It would be an understatement to say that we were scared. So this was the way it was going to end. Here in a hole in an open field surrounded on all sides by woods somewhere in eastern France.

We could hear voices on all sides now closing in. We had our guns pointed toward the top of the hole. It was so dark now we wouldn't be able to see anyone if they looked in. I was expecting a potato masher to drop in our hole any second. It's a miracle it didn't happen too. Suddenly a dozen voices yelled, "Hans up, hans up". They were right at the edge of the hole on all sides. I vaguely wondered why they had come right up to the hole like that instead of tossing a few grenades first. It didn't matter anyway now.

Smitty crawled out of the hole first. Rod and I and the Infantry boy lagged back. We still had our guns pointed at the outer rim of the hole. We hadn't decided it but I knew that if they shot Smith down we were coming out blasting.

I was carrying a German map case with the code and a few things in it. I didn't have time to destroy it. For some reason I hung it up in the branches of one of the saplings. I guess in the back of my mind I thought they might overlook it in the dark and might withdraw or something before daylight and never find it. It didn't really make that much difference anyway.

They yelled again for us to come out and this time the rest of us did. They hadn't shot Smith yet. We were pretty shaky though, and wondered if they were going to shoot us.

We were taken over to the woods and searched. They found the radio mike I was carrying in my pocket. One said "telephone" and threw it away. I felt a little better after the Germans searched us. They apparently weren't going to shoot us right away anyway. We found Liggett here lying on the ground. At first I thought he had been hit but he was O.K. He said, "Boy!!! Am I glad to see you guys".

One German that could speak a little English asked me what I was. I didn't know whether he wanted to know what rank or what nationality. I guessed at rank and told him what I was. Surly they knew we were Americans but you never know.

The area was alive with Krauts. They were milling all over the place. From what little I could see and from the noises around there must have been a couple or three companies, maybe more. No wonder they had had so much fire power. Some were walking around nonchalantly, others were digging holes. Some were smoking, keeping the glow of the cigarettes hidden in a cupped hand.

We were taken over to where a German that had been wounded lay. They told us that we were going to have to carry him back to the aid station. There wasn't a stretcher but just a shelter half and a couple of sticks ran through it for handles. This wasn't going to be easy.

Liggett and the Infantry boy, whose name was Kaiser, got at the wounded man's head. Smith and I got at his middle and Rod put his feet over his shoulder.

We started back toward the German rear lines. We followed along a power line. The ground was rough and full of stumps making the going tough. It was pitch black and we stumbled and staggered. The wounded man had been hit badly and he was just dead weight. The fellow seemed to be in a lot of pain and moaned from time to time. He had been hit in the stomach and his guts seemed to be oozing out. Blood from him soaked through my field jacket and shirt and clear to my skin. We were giving the wounded man a bad time although we were doing our best. First Liggett and Kaiser would stumble and almost drop him. When they would get righted Smith and I seemed to start stumbling. We had to set him down several times and get reorganized.

There were four Germans besides the wounded man with us. One led the way and the other three brought up the rear. The ones behind us kept their guns leveled at us all the time. They weren't taking any chances that we would make a break for it. The only one of them that said anything was the one in the lead. When we would come to a bad place he would say, "Achtung, Achtung". This "Achtung" in the German language seemed to cover a multitude of things, like attention, watch it, be alive, look out, danger, etc. Sometimes the wounded man would say something to the lead Kraut and then the leader would say something to us about "der mittel" meaning to take it easy on this guy's stomach.

We passed an area that had been torn up by our shelling. There were shell holes and ripped trees. We had done something anyway. I wondered if one of our fragments had gotten the guy we were carrying.

I still couldn't get over the predicament that I was in. I had always thought that I might be killed, maimed or flip my lid, but becoming a prisoner had never once entered my mind. I still could hardly grasp the situation. Maybe if we had talked over the situation back at the hole a little more we wouldn't have been caught. If we had only had sense enough to know that those were Krauts in the woods instead of our own men. If we had done a little reasoning we might have gotten away with it. If we had known what the situation was for sure and just stayed put we might have made it. The Germans would have had to withdraw during the night though. If they had still been there in the morning we would have been discovered anyway. From the amount of them that seemed to be here they might be here for several days. Oh well, too late to think about things like that now.

We continued on down the power line. The going got tougher and tougher. I was working up a good sweat. The warm blood from the German kept slowly sinking through my uniform. The smell was bad too. I guess the poor bastard's bowels had been ripped open. We were all getting pretty tired struggling with the guy but didn't know how we would be taken if we asked for a short breather.

We were challenged several times by German guards. We passed big trucks and other equipment.

Even in a spot like this there can be something humorous, if that is possible. Rod was carrying the wounded man's feet over his shoulder, actually the easiest job. Anyway, he suddenly quipped, "Christ. This guy's feet stink". I thought to myself, "He better be careful what he says for a lot of these guys can understand English. They might not think it is so funny. A prisoner making some wise crack about one of their boys, especially a badly hurt one".

After about three miles we came to a little village. We carried our man to an aid station. We were then taken to a building and taken upstairs. There were Germans swarming all over the place. A German officer started screaming at us about what we didn't know. He used a sharp, high pitched voice that sort of made your hair stand on end. These guys must have taken special courses in speech. From the screaming he was doing I still wondered if they were going to take us out and shoot us. Maybe all they had kept us for was to bring the wounded man in.

Upstairs in this building we entered a large room. There were several other 45th boys sitting on the floor. We were surprised at seeing them. For some reason we figured that we were the only ones captured in that skirmish. They all sat there silent and wide-eyed. I guess we looked pretty wide-eyed too.

Here we were searched again. The thing that surprised me was that they didn't take anything from us other than weapons or things that could be used for weapons. I had a little box of four cigarettes from a box of "K" rations for instance. They merely looked at them and put them back in my pocket. Many of our boys had watches too but I never saw them taken from them.

A German Officer came in and looked us over. He

asked if anyone was wounded. One of our boys was wounded pretty badly. He saw the blood on me and came over and asked if I was hurt. I said no and then he said, "One of your comrade's blood?" I still said no. He looked at me oddly for a second and then left.

A little later we were taken downstairs and loaded on a truck. There were about a dozen of us now. As we were sitting in the truck Germans began to climb up on the side of the truck and look at us. It was dark and they couldn't see much. We wondered why we were such an attraction. The only think I could figure out was that we were the first Americans they had seen. They must have either been a new outfit on the line or had been fighting in Russia or some other front.

We were asked if any of us could speak German. One kid said he could. He was then told to get our wounded man out of the truck and they would take him to the hospital. When the Germans hanging on the side of the truck heard that they said, "Good, good". They climbed down and carried our wounded man away themselves. Maybe these Krauts weren't so bad after all.

Just as we were getting ready to pull out one of the Germans climbed up on the cab of the truck. He rattled his machine pistol and said in very broken English, "If you fly, you are dead." He got the message over to us.

The truck started up and we bounced along through the village. As we sat there in the darkness Kaiser handed me a piece of paper and whispered, "chew". I crammed the paper in my mouth and began to chew it. I supposed it was a code he had that the Germans hadn't discovered. As I chewed the thing I thought how actually silly it was. This simple code Kaiser was carrying wasn't going to make any difference on the outcome of anything. Even if the Germans did try to use it it wouldn't make sense now anyway. The minute it was even suspected a code might have fallen into enemy hands the whole code was changed. I guess it didn't do any harm to destroy it though. That is what we had been taught in training to do.

We only rode a short distance and then stopped again. We dismounted and went into a large building. We wondered what was up now.

The building turned out to be a large farmhouse and it seemed that the Germans were using it for some kind of C.P. (Command Post) or headquarters. Although it appeared to be some sort of a headquarters we didn't see any commissioned officers around. An old Sgt. seemed to be in charge of the twelve or fifteen men there.

Several of the Germans here could speak good English. We weren't searched or asked any questions. This bunch seemed ready to move on out and seemed to be just killing time.

The Germans here seemed to want to be friendly. In fact, they were so friendly that we soon relaxed and were talking to them like long lost buddies. They offered us cigarettes and gave us each a glass of wine. Some of our boys had chocolate "D" bars and gave them to the Germans. This seemed to please them immensely. I was beginning to wonder what kind of a war this was anyway. Here a few minutes ago we were trying like hell to slaughter one another and now we were acting like brothers. Our propaganda had led us to believe that all German soldiers, right down to the lowest private, were mean, tricky, miserable, sadistic monsters. They had undoubtedly been told the same crap about us. Now that we had met face to face and not shooting at one another we both found out that the other was a human after all and O.K.

The old Sgt. in charge of the place seemed like a pretty good guy. He said that he had been in the last war and had been a prisoner himself. He had been taken prisoner by the British just two weeks before the war ended. We asked him how much longer he thought this war would last. He just laughed and said it would be over sometime next year. We all figured he was joking. The Allies were moving so fast on all fronts they would soon be in Germany. We were sure it would be like the last war. The Germans would not want to fight on their own soil. We all figured the war would be over in a few days. After all, we were only a few miles from the German border ourselves and some of the outfits on the northern front were even closer.

It struck me rather odd that a bunch of prisoners should be talking to their captors like this. Speculating when the war would be over and telling them that it was going to last only a few more days. The G.I.s seemed to be like that though. If anyone was friendly and treated them half way decent and got their confidence, they weren't bashful about saying what they thought, no matter what. This particular bunch of Germans didn't seem to mind though.

When we started to leave the old Sgt. said that we were starting on the first leg of our trip to the Fatherland although we would have only about a twenty minute ride tonight. Another told us to take a good look at what our bombers had done to Germany for it was pretty much a mess. No one said, "Who in the hell started this war anyway?" It was just as well too for I'm sure it wouldn't have gone over too well.

Outside we began to climb back on the truck. Germans were running around with a kind of flashlight I had never seen before. They had a little lever on them and when it was squeezed it started a little generator and made the thing light up. It was pretty clever and did away with the worry of batteries going dead.

We took off on the truck and down a narrow road with tall trees growing on either side. As we moved along a shot rang out and a bullet zipped by close to our heads. We figured it was a Frenchman doing a little harassing. This was new though. It would be nice to get ambushed by the French Marquis rural guerilla bands of the French Resistance or the F.F.I.

After a few jolting miles we came to the town of Villersexal. This had been our objective. We had made it alright but not quite in the way we had planned. Our brass must have been optimistic anyway. From where we had been picked up and to this point we had seen plenty of Krauts and equipment. To take the little village we had just come from and to the outskirts of this place would have been quite a chore. Well, here we were anyway.

We were taken into a nice large building. The place was very nice inside. It had big marble pillars and a marble floor. I couldn't imagine what it had been used for. It wasn't a church, I was sure of that. It was probably some building that was used for the administrative works of the town maybe like town hall or something.

We were lined up against a wall but not close enough to be able to lean against it. We just tried to stand there. We were a rough looking bunch. Dirty, unshaven and our eyes were bloodshot from lack of sleep.

A German officer paced up and down in front of us saying nothing and practically ignoring us. Two German soldiers leaned against a table across the room from us watching us which was their job. They took turns going over to another table and whacking off hunks from a big baloney. The meat sure looked good. Boy was I hungry!

Once in a while some gal would walk into the room and then soon leave again. We wondered who she was. Must have been one of the guard's girlfriend but what an old bag.

I was really dead on my feet. The lack of sleep the last few nights was catching up with me. I would go to sleep standing there and my knees would buckle. Finally, the officer told us we could sit down. Everyone just sat there without making a sound. The only sound was the pacing officer. The guards looked sleepy but they kept a steady eye on us and their machine pistols ready for action. The old bag kept flitting in and out.

Later we were herded into a small windowless room and locked in. No one cared what happened now. All we wanted was a little sleep. We all flopped on the hard marble floor and were soon sawing logs. Boy, what a day this September 11th, 1944 had been!

We were up early in the morning wondering what would happen next. During the night a couple more prisoners had been brought in. They were both from the 3rd Division.

Everyone was hungry but we weren't given anything to eat. I hoped we would get something soon. My big guts were beginning to eat the little ones now.

We were taken out of the building and across the street and loaded into a bus that had a camouflage draped over it. We sat there in the bus quite a while before it moved. We didn't know where we were going but we wanted to get out of this town before our artillery started dropping in.

Finally, we started moving. Just at the outskirts of town we crossed over a bridge the Germans were getting ready to blow. They had dug a large hole beside the bridge and were planting a large bomb in there.

We traveled on down the open road. It was a nice

sunny day and we were hoping that some of our planes wouldn't swoop down on us. All along the road German soldiers were patrolling. I guessed they had to patrol the roads carefully so that the French wouldn't plant mines in them or blow up bridges to hamper their movements. There were a few Frenchmen moving along the road on foot. The character that was driving our bus seemed to be trying to see how close he could come to them. In fact, he seemed to be deliberately trying to run over them. Several Frenchmen were nearly hit.

After a trip of several miles we reached the town of Lure. There were plenty of Germans and equipment around this town. We stopped in front of a place that seemed to be some sort of Headquarters. There were lots of Germans going in and out of the buildings. They were all clean shaven and their clothes were neat and clean. Some even carried brief cases. These were typical rear echelon troops. I never saw so much saluting and heal clicking in my life. The old Nazi salute.

Although we stopped here for quite some time we didn't get off the bus. Later we moved on and went to the other edge of the town. We pulled into a place that appeared to have been a ritzy riding academy at one time. A sign over the entrance to the place had Von Mackensie something or other on it. I guessed it was the name of the general in charge of the troops on this front and this was Army Headquarters.

We dismounted from the bus and were taken upstairs in one of the buildings. We were all crowded into one fairly small room. We wondered what would happen now and when they were going to feed us, if ever. I was half starved. It had been most of a week since I had had anything to eat to speak of. I knew the rest of our party was in the same boat and, no doubt, so were most of the other fellows.

They began taking us out one at a time for questioning. Liggett and the Infantry Officers were taken first. From this time on the officers were kept separated from the rest of us.

I was the last of the enlisted men to be taken out to be questioned. I was ushered into a small room where the interrogator greeted me with a friendly "hello". He offered me a cigarette and then fired questions like: How long had I been in the Army? How long had I been overseas? Had I been in the Southern France Invasion? To all these questions I said I didn't know. This didn't seem to make him mad or discourage him and he kept right on. He even got out maps and air photos and asked me if I could pick out the spot where I had been captured. I still answered that I didn't know. His question of what outfits were on the right and left and who was in our support got the same answer.

I got a big surprise though. He picked up a piece of paper on his desk to fold. I was amazed to see Captain Hurley, our Battery Commander's, name on it. As the interrogator folded the piece of paper he said, "Your Battery Commander's name is Captain Hurley, isn't it?" I was so surprised that I said, "Yes". I immediately felt like kicking myself but I guess it didn't make any difference anyway as he already knew it. I wondered how he had found out. Either Rod, Smith or Liggett had to have told him.

I made another slight error. He told me that the Forty-Fifth had been at Anzio and asked me if I had been with it there. For some reason instead of the usual, "I don't know", I said, "Yes". I couldn't see any difference that would make anyway. He ginned at me and said, "Pretty rough wasn't it?" I didn't even answer that one at all.

Actually, if I had been trying to answer all of his

questions to the best of my knowledge he wouldn't have gotten much information. A combat man knew very little of the situation. He seldom knew exactly where he was, especially in a rather fast moving situation. At least not near enough to pinpoint the spot on a map or air photo. He seldom knew who was on his flanks either. About all he knew was to take the next town or next hill. Few line officers knew anymore of the situation than the enlisted men. I suppose though, by questioning dozens of prisoners, if some of them talked even a little, they might derive a vague picture of some sort.

It seemed to me they were now just wasting their time questioning us. The war must surely be almost over so what possible good could it do now. I supposed they had been making a routine out of it for so many years now that it was just a habit.

Finally, the fellow pushed his chair back and seemed to relax. He said that was all and offered me a cigarette. He began to ask me questions about myself. He asked me if I was married, had kids and what part of the United States I had some from. He showed me pictures of his wife and kids. I showed him pictures of Bernice. Finally, he said I could go. He shook my hand and said he hoped that we could meet again under better circumstances. From asking me just a personal question he had found out more than from the formal questioning. He could just about tell how long I had been in the Army and that the U.S. was drafting married men, childless men and a few other things. Pretty tricky these Krauts. Again I thought, "What the hell. Maybe the guy was really interested in my personal life." Anyway what did it matter now?

When I left the room a guard took me to a table on which there were several chunks of bread and baloney. On each piece of bread was a hunk of margarine. To my surprise I saw Smith sitting in the hall nearby all by himself. He was sitting there bent over and his arms folded. His face was flushed and he looked mad. I wondered what the heck had happened. He just stared at the floor and didn't even look my way. I loaded down with as much of the bread and baloney I could carry and went back to the room where the prisoners were. Others went after the rest of the food.

There was exactly one piece of bread for everyone. There wasn't a piece too much or too little, but exactly right. The portions weren't too large but we were all starving and the stuff tasted good. I could have eaten much more though.

Finally, Smith came into the room. Rod and I wanted to know what in the hell had happened to him. He said when they had asked him how old he was he had refused to tell them. He said they insisted for some reason but he wouldn't tell. He said the guy got rather upset and had done a little threatening. They had put him out in the hall to think it over a while. When they brought him back in he still refused to tell so they let him go. I wondered why they insisted on finding out how old he was. I supposed the reason that he was fifteen years, or more, older than any of the rest of us had aroused their curiosity. They hadn't even asked any of the rest of us our ages. I was also surprised that they had threatened him a little. The rest had been treated the same as I had. When a question was asked and the answer was either name, rank and serial number or I don't know, they just went on with the questions. I hoped to hell they didn't have suspicions that Smith was half Jew. The stories we had been hearing of the gassing and baking of the Jews didn't make very pleasant listening. Even though Smith was an American soldier it might not make any difference. The Krauts seemed bent on exterminating the Jews regardless of where they were from.

At dark we lay down on the floor to try to get a little sleep. It must have been around midnight when we were routed out and taken downstairs.

Out in the court we were loaded into a couple of ambulances. The ambulances were a long sort of semi affair. Stretchers were rigged up along each side. I was lucky enough to be one of the first ones in the ambulance so I had a stretcher to lie on. The whole thing reeked of the dead that it must have carried from time to time.

Our ambulance soon pulled out. I was tired and fell to sleep almost immediately. This bed on the stretcher made the best sleeping I had had in a long time.

A couple of hours later we stopped again. We were now in the city of Belfort. We were taken to the upstairs of a building beside the railroad tracks that seemed to be a railroad station. We flopped on the floor for the rest of the night.

We were stirring around early the next morning wondering what our next move would be when we moved out again. We hung around in the building all day. From the windows of the place we could look down on the railroad tracks and a large street that ran parallel with the tracks.

There was plenty of activity on both the street and the railroad. Hundreds of German soldiers moved up and down the street. There were also many trucks and cars. Most of the traffic seemed to be heading toward the Front. The German Army was using lots of civilian cars painted to look camouflaged. Most of the trucks and cars had tree branches on them. This, of course, was to help camouflage them. The German Infantry that was moving toward the Front were really loaded down with their packs. They must have carried everything they owned with them.

A couple of hospital trains stopped here. They unloaded a good many wounded men. There must have been a German hospital in Belfort. Other trains passed through loaded with all sorts of war equipment.

The air raid sirens blew and we saw many of the Germans head for the shelters. We hoped that our planes didn't have Belfort for target practice today. It didn't make us feel too comfortable locked in a railroad station. When our planes hit a town one of the main things they went for were the train stations and yards. The alert ended about an hour later. We hadn't even heard our planes. They were bombing elsewhere today.

In the past, I had often wondered how things were on the Germans side of the lines. One thing for sure now was that I was going to get a chance to observe what went on behind enemy lines.

In the afternoon a German came up to see us. He spoke perfect English and said that he had lived in America for a long time. He was in the German Army now and worked in some office nearby. We asked him why he had come back to Germany and joined the army. He said that in 1939 he had come back to visit relatives. The war had broken out and he was forced to join the German Army. We didn't think too much of his story. If he had lived in the United States as long as he said he had he should have been an American citizen. If he had been a citizen of the U.S. I don't believe they could have made him fight. He probably figured the Germans were going to win the war and had come home to get on the gravy train. He talked about the war. He said if the plot to kill Hitler in July had been successful the war would have been over by now. He almost came right out and admitted that Germany didn't have a chance to win now. We asked him what he had thought about the Italians when they had been Germany's ally. He just laughed and said that they were wish-washy.

At dark we were taken down into the railroad yards and loaded onto a car. It seemed to be a baggage or express car of some kind. We wondered where we were going next. Besides the G.I.s there were several guards in our car. Everyone felt low, miserable and hungry.

A couple of the guards were singing softly to themselves. We got the idea to sing ourselves to boost our morale. We began to sing old familiar tunes that everyone knew the words to. The guards seemed to approve and one even asked us in very broken English to sing Old Black Joe. Our singing went along fine until we started singing God Bless America. The guards blew their tops then. They screamed at us, cocked their rifles and nearly had a fit. We got the idea that they wanted us to stop singing patriotic songs.

Soon the train began to move. We gradually picked up speed and soon were moving at a pretty good clip. We sidetracked often to let other trains go by. I imagined a bunch of prisoners had a pretty low priority rating on the German Railroad these days.

We weren't in Germany proper quite yet. We were in the Alsace-Lorraine area that the Germans had taken over or something about ten years ago. All night we jolted along, sidetracking often.

Once during the night we stopped in some town and were ordered off the train. We were taken down into a subway under the tracks. The place was crammed with both soldiers and civilians. There must have been an air raid alert on. There were a couple of nurses sitting near us. They had been riding on our train too.

It was pitch dark in the subway. Everyone just sat there quietly. The only noise was made by farts. There were long high pitched ones and low juicy ones. The Germans were the ones that were doing it. One thing that an American, no matter how crude or ignorant about anything else won't do was to fart in the presence of ladies, unless of course it was absolutely necessary. I figured here in Germany it might be some sort of economic status. Maybe it proved you had plenty of sauerkraut and wieners to eat today. I had heard that in some places to let out a big belch after a meal at someone's house was supposed to be correct. It showed the host that you had had plenty to eat and had enjoyed your meal. I wondered what the nurses thought about the situation but I suspected they were used to this type of entertainment. I didn't care much what they thought. I was too sleepy. Nothing happened in the way of an air raid so I guess our bombers were working elsewhere.

Finally we loaded back on the express car and the train took off again. The rest of the night we jolted along, stopping often. Sometime early in the morning we sidetracked for the rest of the night. We were able to get some sleep on the hard floor of the car.

At dawn the train started moving again. We didn't travel far before we reached the town of Mulhouse. Here we stopped and dismounted from the train. The railroad station and the immediate area around it were pretty well battered up from bombings.

We were lined up and marched through the city. Although the city had been German for quite some time before the war, much of the population was French. As we walked through the streets we watched the civilians to see what their reactions would be. Most of them stared at us showing no outward emotion. A few just gave us a short stony smile.

After we had passed through the main part of town and were again reaching the outskirts, a civilian called out to us in English. He said the war was over for us now but the war would soon be over and we all could go home. The guards screamed at him, telling him to shut up and not to talk to the prisoners. No doubt the guy was a Frenchman.

Soon we reached a group of buildings on the outskirts of town. It was an army camp of some kind. It turned out to be a training center. As we moved through the place we could see soldiers being instructed on war equipment. Some were having classes in wire and communications while others were working with mortars. Still others were having classes on machine guns and rifles.

We were taken to a huge galvanized iron building and locked inside. This big building seemed to have been a place to store hay. There were still a few bales at one end.

There were plenty of guards surrounding the building. A couple of them were standing by the door talking. One of the 3rd Division boys was peeping through a crack in the door at them. One of the guards spotted him and figured he was listening to them. He really blew his top. He opened the door and came in screaming at the kid. He shoved the kid around and took his bayonet out of its carrier. We all held our breath wondering if he was going to use it on the kid or not. He was just bluffing I guess because after about ten more minutes of yelling he slipped the bayonet back and stalked out. This was the kind of Germans we were used to seeing in movies and had heard about.

In this place we got the first food we had had in thirty-six hours. They brought in three large buckets of stuff. One bucket contained some sort of greens. There were two kinds of soup in the others. The greens and the soup were plenty good. The big problem was how to eat the stuff. No one had a spoon or anything to eat with. This didn't hold us back long though. We knelt down beside the buckets and began to scoop the soup with cupped hands. Having thirty guys going after the soup with hands that hadn't been washed in a couple of weeks didn't make the meal sanitary. We cleaned up every bit of the food and felt much better.

In the middle of the afternoon we were routed out of the building and lined up. We were told we were going to have a three day trip and we were going to get our rations for the trip now. We each received a third of a loaf of bread, a small square of margarine and a small hunk of baloney. This was supposed to last for nine meals, ten counting this evening. We thought they were kidding. This was about enough food for a between meal snack. We figured that his was surely only one days rations. We found out though that they weren't kidding. This was three days rations and then some.

As we moved out to the road we saw another bunch of American soldiers moving in. It was a much larger bunch than our group, probably about sixty. We didn't get close enough to talk to them or be able to see if we recognized anyone.

We retraced our route back down to the railroad station. This time I noticed something on the outside wall of the station. I was to see it many times while I was in Germany. On the side of the building a large shadow of a man in an over coat and hat had been painted. Across the shadow was printed, "Psst" and nothing more. It was of course a warning to not talk to strangers about anything concerning the war such as troop movements, production figures, new equipment being worked on etc. It was like the posters back home about "A slip of the lips can sink a ship" etc. Our stuff like this was usually more complicated and sometimes corny. This shadow thing was simple and was the best of this sort of thing I had seen. I was to see this everywhere. Lots of times there would just be "Psst" on a wall beside a door or in some conspicuous place. Even book matches had "Psst" on the covers of them.

We loaded onto a train. We got a day coach. I would have rather been in a boxcar. It would have been easier to stretch out in the boxcar. Liggett and the couple of other officers with our bunch were put on a car ahead of us. The other cars in the train were filled with German soldiers.

Soon a bunch of young German soldiers came down to the station and got ready to get on the train. They looked fresh, had a full pack and brand new uniforms, rifles and other equipment. They were no doubt replacements for the training camp we had just been to. Their mothers and relatives were down to see them off. The mothers were kissing their sons and there was a lot of crying among them. I guess the German mothers had the same feelings seeing their sons go off to war as the mothers back in the States. You would think that with the amount of wars these people had been in through the years that they would be used to it. I guess that's why they have to wait another generation to start another war. The same generation wouldn't go through it twice.

About dark our train began to move. The night passed much the same as the one before. A lot of jolting along and sidetracking. We passed through a few towns but weren't able to catch the names of any of them. We were so crowded in our car that sleep was next to impossible. Some were trying to sleep in the baggage rack above the seats. Others were in the aisles and others, including myself, tried sleeping sitting in the seat. The guards had a small compartment in front of us and took turns watching us.

Early the next morning we crossed the Rhine River. What amazed us all was that the huge railroad bridge across the river was in perfect condition. There weren't any bomb craters around. It appeared that they had never tried for this bridge. I just couldn't understand that at all. A big important bridge like this and it had never even been tried for. If a bridge like this had been knocked out it would hamper the Germans' movements to no end. No doubt the bridge was well protected by anti-aircraft guns and maybe even fighter planes. Maybe our brass didn't think it was that important but I could hardly believe that. There may have been other reasons they left the bridge but off hand I couldn't think of any.

We got glimpses of the fortifications here. There were lots of trenches, pill boxes, tank traps and guns. There were lots of big guns sitting on the railroad sidings waiting to be unloaded. The defenses here looked pretty formidable alright. The Rhine itself was a wide river so cracking it would be a tough job.

Our train plugged along all day sidetracking often, sometimes for hours. It had been pretty foggy and overcast for the last few days for which we were thankful. Weather like this kept our Air Force from being so active. We didn't relish the idea of being locked in these cars and being bombed and strafed.

A thing that did surprise me was the condition of the German railroads. We had been led to believe that our bombers had completely paralyzed their railroad system. I had never expected to travel by train in Germany. I expected to see every station, yard, bridge and stretch of track blown out. About all that seemed to be hit were the stations and the yards around them.

The Germans had a system to get the railroads going quickly again. Near every town of any size or an important railroad junction they would have a forced labor camp. As soon as the place was hit they would have hundreds of men working on it before the dust had hardly settled. It seemed as though if our planes had gone for the open stretches of tracks away from towns and the forced labor camps they would have done a lot more to wreck the rail transportation. I guess a double row of tracks makes a pretty small target but they surely could have gotten some hits. Even so, it must have kept the Germans pretty busy keeping their trains rolling. Train after train rushed past us as if they had a schedule to keep.

Once during the afternoon, the Sgt. in charge of the guards came in and talked to us. He couldn't speak any English but tried to carry on a conversation. He was an older fellow and could have easily been in World War I. He was the typical tough looking Sgt. but seemed to be a pretty good guy. Once he pointed to a little town quite a distance from the tracks. He proudly announced that it was Baden-Baden, the famous winter resort. I had never even heard of it before.

There was only one guard that gave us any trouble. It was that miserable bastard that had pulled the bayonet on the guy back in Mulhouse. We called him "Laughing Boy". Every once in a while he would stalk among us and do a little yelling. What a character. There are some of his kind in every army I guess. He also fancied himself as a ladies man. Every time he saw a bunch of girls he would yell at them and was no doubt making cute remarks. I got the impression he thought they were all swooning over him.

BYE FOR NOW

The old Sgt. told us we were going to a town called Limburg and would get there the day after tomorrow. We hoped we would get there sooner for our food was getting low. In fact, some of the fellows had eaten theirs already. Some of us had a little of the bread and baloney left only by making a big effort to conserve it. It was hard to try to stretch the food. We were all hungry and could have gobbled it down in seconds.

That night the guards got some schnapps and got pretty high. They did a lot of laughing and singing. They didn't get tight enough to keep an eye on us though.

We didn't do any traveling that night but just sat on a sidetrack somewhere out in the sticks. We were glad that we weren't sitting in some big railroad yard. We were in constant fear of our own Air Force.

The next morning, we moved on. It was another gray, gloomy day which we were thankful for. We hoped the weather would stay like this while we were traveling on the railroads in Germany.

I thought to myself that these guys were just wasting their time taking us into Germany to a P.O.W. (Prisoner of War) Camp. I figured the war would end any day. I couldn't see how the war could last any longer than the end of September. I figured that we would be back with the Americans in a few days.

Thinking that the war would end any minute kept us from being quite so willing to try to escape. I had thought about it though but it would be a tough proposition. When we were in France I would have had a reasonable chance of making it. There, if you could have gotten away, probably ninety-five per cent of the French would help you. They would hide you and give you directions. There, in France, you wouldn't have had to go far to get to your lines. Of course, the Germans knew all this too and they really watched you very closely. It seemed that someone had a gun in your back every second.

Now that we were getting into Germany a ways it would be rough. Not being able to speak the language would be one obstacle. Being in an American uniform you would stick out like a sore thumb. You would have to travel only by night and that would be tough too. It would even be hard to tell which direction to start out in. A thing like getting across the Rhine River would be a task. You would have to cross on a bridge and they would all be guarded. The more one thought about it the more of an unsurmountable task it seemed. Anyway, the war would end any second.

You heard stories and saw movies of someone escaping and all the fantastic things they did and how clever they were. Those were just stories and movies though. It just wouldn't happen that way. I doubt if anyone, and not more than a handful at most, ever got away once they were well into Germany like we were.

Had I known the war was going to last as long as it did and all the crap I was going to have to put up with I believe I would have made an attempt. I almost tried anyway. Once I went to the toilet at the end of the car. Usually a guard went with you but this was my golden opportunity, or not. The train at this particular moment was barely moving. I studied the window and saw it was unlocked. In seconds I could be out and disappear in the darkness. I was about to reach for the window when "Laughing Boy" flung open the door. He must have known what I had in mind. He did his usual yelling and screaming only this time a little longer and louder, Maybe it was all for the best. No doubt if I had acted quickly enough I could have gotten off the train but how far I would have gotten would be another story.

Once, during the day, we passed a woods that had had a factory blown out of existence. Pieces of it were scattered for almost a mile. What a terrific blast that must have been. The factory had been so well hidden in the woods that I wondered if maybe it had been an inside job. It would have been hard for the Air Force to spot such a well-hidden place. It must have been the work of the saboteurs or maybe just an accident. Whatever it was it must have been working on some high powered ammunition there from the blast it had made.

Later that day we passed though the outskirts of Stuttgart. It was a large city with a large factory area. We passed right through the factory area. The place had been given a terrific going over. Factory after factory was just piles of rubble. The homes and apartment buildings near the area were also nothing but piles of rubble and skeletons. The whole place was quiet and seemed deserted. It was a sad looking mess to behold.

We stopped at Stuttgart and were taken to a German Red Cross place near the tracks. Here we got two bowls of macaroni soup. We were half starved and the stuff tasted good. Just as we were leaving some prisoners from another train came down the tracks. They were carrying big buckets to get the soup. They said there were about sixty people in their bunch.

Back on the train it was the same old story. We would go a short distance and sidetrack.

Now when we saw planes we would ask one another. "Are they ours?" It now meant the German planes. It was a big relief to see the big black crosses on them. One time about eight American planes came down the tracks strafing. The guards locked the cars and headed for cover. Luckily, just before the planes reached us they veered off down some other tracks. Another time we saw them dive bombing and strafing back down the tracks from us. They were circling and swooping down like a bunch of vultures.

One time when we were locked in and the Krauts headed for cover I saw something which showed the discipline these guys had. After the danger had passed the Germans came slowly back toward the train. We were out on an open stretch of the tracks in farmland. There was a lone apple tree growing alongside the tracks. It no doubt belonged to the farmer whose house we could see a short distance away. This tree was outside his fence, probably actually on the railroad right of way. The tree was loaded with beautiful looking apples. The Germans soldiers passed by the tree and never touched an apple from the tree. They found a few that had fallen off and picked those up but no one took one that was on the tree. A simple thing like this convinced me that there was a great national obedience here. It may have been fear but whatever it was it was something to behold. I couldn't imagine a bunch of G.I.s passing up something like that. That tree would have been stripped of its fruit in a matter of seconds.

Another night came and passed. We were hoping that we would reach our destination soon. We were cramped, cold, hungry and tired. We figured a camp couldn't be much worse than this car.

Someone wondered what the folks back home would think when they got the "Missing in Action" notice. It hadn't dawned on me that way. For some reason I just figured they would receive word that I was a prisoner. Naturally, the first word would be "missing in action". That sounded pretty ominous and I hoped they wouldn't be too worried. I wondered how soon they would hear that I was a prisoner and still alive.

The next morning one of the guards told us we were almost to our destination. We were now passing through hills. There were lots of fine hotels sprinkled around through these hills. This must have been some sort of a resort area in peacetime. It was now used for hospitals, rest centers and convalescent homes for the German soldiers. We could see lots of them strolling around and others sticking their heads out of windows of the hotels.

Soon we were down on flat country again. In about an hour we reached the town of Limberg. At last we were at our destination. We unloaded from the train and hiked through town. This was our first real contact with German civilians. We wondered what their reactions would be. We wondered if they would stone us or what. However, the people practically ignored us and went about their business. We got an occasional glance but that was all. I guess they were used to seeing prisoners of all kinds.

We moved through town and on out about a mile or less. We arrived at our camp. It had a big German flag flying in front of it. Inside several thicknesses of barbed wire surrounded several rows of low green barracks. There also were several large tents inside the wire.

Inside the gate we were stopped and searched again. Our helmets were taken away from us. From here we were led down to a barracks where we had to give our name, rank and serial number. Then we were given a dog tag with our prison serial number on it. My number was 86037. I guess I was a real prisoner now with a number and all.

We were each given a tin bowl and an old blanket. My bowl was cracked and obviously hadn't been washed in some time. It was cruddy and there were still pieces of old cabbage in it. The blanket I got was so thin I could see through it. It was small too. Only about half size,

The tent that Rod, Smith and I were assigned to was really crowded. There were five or six hundred of us in it. It may have been able to accommodate a hundred or a hundred and fifty comfortably at most. Everyone was just stacked on top of one another. There was a thin layer of excelsior on the ground floor of the tent. You were supposed to lie on it I guess. I couldn't even get near the stuff.

By the time we had been issued our blanket and bowl we had missed the soup they gave out here. I was so hungry I could have eaten the tent poles. I felt that I would gladly give my right arm for a few bites of food. It was the 18th of September and I had been a prisoner for a week. The food I had during this week wouldn't have even made one decent meal. A week before my capture the eating had been mighty slim so the old hunger pangs were rally having fun.

At dark, Rod, Smith and I wandered into the tent we had been assigned to. It was impossible to get a place on the excelsior. We divided up and tried to find the best place there was to sleep. I finally had to settle trying to sleep on the ground in the aisle. I lay down and put my ragged blanket over me and tried to get some sleep. The ground was hard and the night cold. I could hardly get a wink of sleep at all. I kept getting a foot in the face or stomach or somewhere as the boys groped down the aisle trying to get out of the tent and to the latrine. What a cold miserable night. I couldn't have felt much lower.

The next morning we were up early for roll call. Our names weren't called of course, we were just counted. We were divided up into companies of about a hundred men. There was a G.I. first three grader in charge of each group. It was his job to know exactly how many were in his group. It took the Germans an hour or more to count us. They would check and recheck. In all, there were about five companies or a thousand Americans here. There were also about five companies of the same size of British here with us.

After roll call we were given part of a bowl of soup. The soup was made of purple cabbage which we called "purple passion". It was thin with no seasoning whatsoever. When one is starving to death you don't notice whether it was seasoned just right or not. You just gobble it down. Also, after the morning roll call we were given a small piece of bread with some kind of strong molasses on it. In this camp we were given soup twice a day after morning and evening roll call. Both meals wouldn't have made a small cup of decent nourishing soup.

After the morning roll call that first morning, our bunch was taken in for questioning. We were taken to a building and seated. Then, we went into the interrogation room one at a time. In the outer room there was a black board with some names on it. On it was written so many Englanders, so many North Americans (as they called us) and one African. I poked Rod and said, "Look at all the special attention you are getting". He said, "Damn it. I am not an African". Maybe they didn't mean him. There might have been a British African around somewhere but I hadn't seen any. I think they meant him. I doubt if there were any other American Negroes captured. Most of them were in the Quartermasters and rear line outfits. The exception might have been some that flew planes.

When it was my turn to be questioned I was surprised to see three Navy Officers sitting at the table. Their questions were, "How many ships in your convoy? Where did you leave from? Were there barrage balloons anchored to them? Did you come on a ship that the front let down (meaning a L.S.T.)?" There were other questions too. To all I answered that I didn't know. Wouldn't these guys ever give up? One final question they asked me was, "Were the bridges blown out in front of your advance?" For some reason I blurted out, "Hell no." I was surprised at myself. I guessed it was from being hungry and disgusted.

In the afternoon of our first full day at Stalag 12-A, some of our bombers came over and bombed Limberg. The town was only a few hundred yards away from the camp. The bombs made the ground tremble and knocked dust from the tents. We were hoping the bombardiers would keep on the target and not let a few drop on us. We also hoped they knew this was a prisoner of war camp and not just a camp full of Krauts. The bombing scared the daylights out of us. We just lay in the tents sweating it out. There weren't any holes or shelters to get into and this tent wouldn't give much protection. It was the first time Limberg had been bombed.

On this day, the 19th of September 1944, I was allowed to send word home. We were given a postcard sized card on which we had to put a check mark by the sentence we wanted to use. One said, "I am a prisoner of the Germans and in good health". The other was, "I am a prisoner and am slightly wounded." Some of the boys that had lost arms, legs and eyes were only "slightly wounded"? There was no use worrying the folks back home anyway. Another sentence we checked said, "Don't write me here. I will soon be transferred and will write you at a later date."

This camp was just sort of a "reception" center. From here all the different nationalities would be separated. Also, the officers would go to one camp, the non-coms to another and the privates still another.

I noticed quite a difference between the fellows captured on the northern front than those of the 45th, 36th and 3rd. The guys from the northern front seemed like a bunch of wild eyed kids. They seemed a lot younger, not so tired and very optimistic.

After I talked to them I came to the conclusion why they seemed different than our bunch. Most of them had come right over from the States and had only seen a few days of combat at most before being captured. They hadn't experienced the sleeping in the mud, being shelled and bombed day after day and being hungry most of the time. They hadn't suffered the disappointment of being stopped cold for month after month and getting nowhere. In other words, these guys just hadn't seen it. Lots weren't even in the Army when some of our guys had already seen action. On the whole they were no doubt a little younger but not that much younger. In my experience I had noticed that the G.I., in the age bracket from say twenty-one to thirty, for the most part, were much better soldiers than the eighteen and nineteen year old kids. The fellows that were a little older weren't as excitable or as apt to get hysterical. They were tougher too. They generally could walk those kids to death.

Rod and I would sit there and look at a fellow walking some distance away. We would guess whether he had been in Italy and Southern France or on the Northern Front. We never missed. We could just tell by the shuffle of our bunch and the live step of the Normandy bunch. This war did make an old man out of you fast, no doubt about that. I had had 252 days of actual combat myself. I felt pretty old too and I was only twenty-four.

These guys were so optimistic too. They knew the war was in its last hours. A few days ago I had felt the same way but now I began to wonder. Our bunch had known the frustration of things not going the way it looked like it would. I very well remember that in October of 1943 we had been so sure we would be in Rome way before Christmas. That was before the stalemate at the Gustav Line and Anzio. Instead of Christmas it had taken six months longer beyond that date. It had taken about nine months to get around a hundred miles. In spite of all of that, these kids were so optimistic we began to get infected with their enthusiasm. We had expected to see Patton's tanks rolling across the fields any minute.

The fellows that had been here in the camp about a week were a little better off in the way of food than our bunch. They had each received a Red Cross Box. It made my mouth water to see the goodies in their boxes. It would be another week before another box would be issued. I couldn't think of anything else.

The fellows from the Northern Front always spoke of "D Day" and dated everything from it although very few of them had been in on "D Day". They seemed to think the war had started on June 4th, 1944. It griped some of the boys from "Our Front" to hear these guys talk about their one and only wonderful "D Day".

When one of these fellows mentioned "D Day" one of the fellows from our front would say, "Which D Day?" The guy would look surprised and say, "Why in Normandy of course". Then our guy would say, "Oh yes, it does seem I heard something about a small landing in Normandy. Guess it didn't amount to much though." The Normandy G. I. would blow his top.

It was disgusting to hear about "D Day" in Normandy though. Even the people back in the States seemed to think the war started then. All they seemed to know was the "D Day" in Normandy, the hedgerows, St. Lo, and the Bulge. Sicily, Salerno, the Volturno, Casino and Anzio didn't seem to amount to much. "D Day" in Normandy had been publicized so much for months, even years, it had to be a big show.

No doubt the "D Day" in Normandy had been on a larger scale than Salerno but I doubt if it was actually as bloody and as many killed in proportion. The Normandy Invasion had been talked about for so long and so many more American G.I.s were in that area it was naturally on the minds of more people in the States.

I had the opportunity to talk to paratroopers and others that had fought as infantry in both Italy and Northern France. They said that in Italy it was much tougher. In northern France there were so many outfits you were getting cut out every few days. In Italy you stayed on the Front for months without even enough replacements.

And sure as hell if Patton and his tanks weren't cutting such a pig in the ass by racing through France like they had been lately. It was because they weren't getting much opposition. The Germans were dropping back to the Maginot and Siegfried Lines. Not trying to hold on to those tanks they certainly wouldn't have moved like they did. It sounded good of him though that Patton and his tanks were making miles a day and "glorious" victories. If the Germans had been trying to hold at all it would have been the Infantry slugging away and clearing the road for the tanks.

Everyone was pretty pepped up about the war ending though. Something told me not to be too optimistic but I couldn't help it. The enthusiasm of these Normandy kids was one of the main reasons. We had been moving rapidly on our Front too. Just a day or two ago, American fighter planes with their comparatively short range, were working behind the lines. Surely the Front must not be far away. We began to make predictions as to when the war would end. Many guessed it would end in less than a week. Others ranged from the last of September to the middle of October. Very few figured it would go beyond the middle of October if that long. I thought I was pretty conservative. I picked Armistices Day. I remember all the disappointments in Italy. I hoped it would end sooner and the enthusiasm of the majority infected me too. I half expected to see Patton's tanks rolling across the fields outside the camp any minute.

We probably had the wars biggest bastard at this camp. He was an American Master Sgt. named Keating. He was supposed to be in charge of the Americans in this camp. When we arrived at the camp he said, "Now I don't want any of you guys to give me any of your troubles. After all, I'm a D Day prisoner myself". What a silly bastard. What in the hell was so wonderful about being a D Day prisoner?

I would say that this bastard was definitely collaborating with the Germans. He was always hanging around them. Instead of trying to help us and go to bat for us he did just the opposite. He forced us to go down to Limberg and work on the bombed town and railroads. Doing this is of course against International Law. I believe if he had told the Germans that absolutely, under no circumstances would we work on the railroad, we wouldn't have had to do it. This Keating though was making a big hit with the Krauts through this. We even suspected he was behind it all anyway. The Germans had plenty of "forced labor" around and probably didn't actually even need us. It paid off for him though. He had a nice warm room for himself and plenty of good food.

Evans, our tent Sgt. had gone down to see him on business. He said he found him eating a cake with chocolate frosting on it. The Germans had baked it for him and used the chocolate out of the Red Cross Boxes to make the frosting. There was no question that he was giving the Germans Red Cross Boxes. Lots of them had also been robbed of the chocolate and cigarettes they contained. Chocolate and cigarettes were two valuable things to the Germans as well as ourselves. He was making it right for the Germans and for himself at the expense of the rest of us. We all hoped we would get an opportunity to meet this bastard if we ever got out of this place and back to the States.

When our bunch had been in this camp for about a week everyone was issued a Red Cross Box. When a fellow got his box he would put it under his arm and walk away with a big grin on his face. We were just like a bunch of kids on Christmas morning. I hadn't had anything to eat in weeks and was damned near starving to death.

We eagerly opened our boxes and examined the contents. All of the boxes contained almost the same things with only slight differences. Mine contained a can of Spam, a can of corned beef, a pound can of powdered milk, a small box of cheese, a box of raisins, six packages of cigarettes, two Hersey bars, a small can of jam, a dozen crackers and some vitamin pills. It was a nice selection of food for one small box.

After everyone had lit up a cigarette and sampled most of their stuff the trading commenced. Some were trading food for cigarettes and vice versa. Some traded prunes for raisins, others cheese for jam, Spam for corned beef and all sorts of combinations. I decided that meat would do me the most good. I traded my can of milk and box of cheese for a can of Spam and a can of corned beef.

It seemed good to have a little good food and

cigarettes again. In spite of the cold and the crowded, miserable conditions everyone's morale was a good deal higher that night. It seemed that we weren't completely forgotten. That night dozens of cigarettes glowed in the darkness of the tent. Everyone stayed up later than usual talking.

You couldn't let go of your Red Cross Box for a second or it would be gone. We carried them with us every place we went; to the latrines, roll call and everywhere. You had to sleep with your head on them or fastened to you some way. Even then some of the boxes were stolen. One guy sleeping next to me had the contents of his box stolen even though he was sleeping with his head on it. Some son-of-a-bitch took a knife, cut a hole in the side of the box and swiped the food. I couldn't imagine what kind of a fiend would steal from another at a time like this. We were all hungry and needed the food. We all got the same amount of stuff. Some seemed to want theirs and then some. It sort of made you wonder about your fellow countrymen. I honestly believe that if I had caught someone trying to steal my box I would have killed him without remorse. We all took off our belts and put them around the boxes to make a handle so that carrying them around would be easier.

The sanitary conditions around the camp were horrible. There was a latrine but it was in terrible shape. Of the dozen stools there were only two in working condition. The rest were plugged up and running over. The crap, slime and muck was ankle deep in the place. Many men had diarrhea and couldn't possibly wait for their turn at one of the workable toilets consequently the muck got deeper. Also, there was no toilet paper or paper of any kind. We would scrape with a little excelsior off the floor of the tent but that was pretty rough. It was a horrible mess at any rate. Approximately fifteen hundred men trying to use such facilities made the situation almost beyond belief.

The water situation wasn't much better. There was only one faucet in the place. Even at that the water was only turned on for two hours in the morning and two hours in the afternoon. There was no excuse for that either. The overcrowded conditions of the latrines might have been one thing but having only one place to get water and for only four hours a day was unreasonable. The Krauts must have been trying to make us miserable. Fifteen hundred men trying to get water from one faucet in such a short time had its problems. Even if you were lucky enough to finally get to the faucet all you could do was partly fill your tin bowl and move on. You didn't have a second to try to wash it out or even think of washing yourself. You took the water and usually there was only about enough to quench your thirst. You kept letting your bowl go and the crust of old cabbage and water cress built up.

One time the Germans got peeved at us for one thing or another and turned the water off for three days. Things were really rough then and everyone really suffered. Luckily, it rained a little one day and I was lucky enough to catch a little water that ran off the tent to help quench my thirst. It was lucky too that the weather now was quite cool. Had it been hot there would have been some real suffering.

That bastard Keating had a work detail go to Limberg every day and work on the town and railroad. Our planes had bombed for the second time in about ten days. Naturally, the whole camp didn't go every day but details of about two or three hundred went daily. I was pretty lucky hiding out in the tents when he was around and wasn't chosen to go. However, one morning Keating caught me and I was put on work detail.

We were marched to Limberg. It had been badly battered in the business section as well as around the railroad yards. We hoped our planes wouldn't hit the place while we were here.

I was put to digging with about thirty others on a bombed out house near the railroad station. The German guards told us there was a German woman and her young daughter buried in the rubble. I don't know whether it was true or if the Krauts just wanted us to feel bad. They wanted to make us think how terrible we were that our Air Force bombed and killed civilians just for the hell of it. They also told us that our planes had bombed the hospital on the outskirts of town and had killed many. I never saw the hospital so I didn't know whether they were telling the truth or not. Anyway, before we reached the "bodies" nine of us were pulled off the job. Before we left I got some priceless paper to use as toilet paper. The paper I got were old German Mark notes. The Marks had been printed after World War I when Germany had so much inflation. All of the bills were of large figures ranging from 10,000 to 1,000,000. That was going to be something. Wiping my behind with a million dollars. I had millions of marks in my pocket when I left the place.

The nine of us were taken down the tracks about a quarter of a mile. Here we were instructed to start digging beside the tracks. We were digging for either a water or gas main. We took it as easy as we could and tried to do as little work as possible. To take it easy wasn't so easy to do. When you would try to let up a little you would have a guard pointing a gun at you and telling you to work faster.

About noon the air raid whistles began to blow. People

went racing by heading for the shelters. They were in cars, on trucks, bicycles and on foot. There were the old with canes to the babes in arms. You couldn't help feel kind of sorry for these people. Probably for the most of them this damned war had been pushed on them, just as it had been for us prisoners. You could just picture your own mother, wife or kids in their position.

The people were dressed amazingly well. They had nice looking clothes, coats and shoes. We had been led to believe that the Germans were starving to death and going around in rags. The only ones that were hungry and ragged in Germany were the prisoners.

We had to keep working while the alert was on. There was a high fog and we couldn't see our planes, but we could hear them passing way up there. We hoped Limberg wasn't one of their targets today.

The alert had no more ended and the people returned to their homes and businesses when the sirens began to blow again. Again, the people headed for the shelters. This happened four times during the day. At this rate they couldn't be getting much done in terms of work. During one of the alerts the guards took us down the tracks a way to a shelter. This particular shelter was under a small underpass under the tracks. It was closed in and looked pretty safe. It was crammed with people. We didn't enter the shelter but remained outside with the guards. I wondered if bombs did start falling here if we would be allowed into the shelter. It was possible the guards had come down here to be near a shelter in the event of bombing. They may have gone into the shelter if a raid started and made us stay outside. I hoped we wouldn't have the opportunity to find out.

We worked all day on the pipe line. We found it and dug up several sections of it. We didn't eat all that day.

Of course we had carried our Red Cross Boxes with us but didn't get a chance to eat anything out of them. We didn't have much left in them to eat anyway.

At about four thirty we knocked off and walked back into the town square. Here they brought out soup to feed the whole bunch.

I noticed a statue of a bomb in the park. I asked one of the fellows that knew German what was inscribed on it. He said that it said that this place will never be bombed. I wondered what the people here now thought when they saw that statue.

There were a bunch of little bastards hanging around. None of them appeared to be over twelve years old. They were a sullen looking bunch and some spit at us. We guessed they were some kind of Hitler Youth bunch. They wore tan uniforms and each had a Swastika on their arm. You wanted to take these snotty little bastards and shake them out of their shoes.

After we ate we headed back to the camp. At the gate we noticed a bunch of American Officers lined up ready to move out. They were going to be transferred to another camp. I spotted Liggett among them. It was the first time I had seen him since we had arrived here as they kept the enlisted men and the officers separated. I waved to Liggett as they moved out. This was the last time I ever saw him.

The days dragged on here at Stalag 12 A. Some prisoners were shipped out and more came in. Lots of British and American paratroopers and lots of American Air Borne troops were being brought in. We tried to find out from them what the score was. They couldn't tell us a thing as to how the war was going. They had come over from England for the drop and only knew where they were supposed to land. Most of them were supposed to have been dropped by a river on the Holland-German Frontier. They were to take and hold some large bridges for the ground forces coming up. Some had been dropped miles off their target and never had a chance to get organized. Although, they all seemed to think that the Allied drive had been slowed up. We had already surmised this and were afraid that was the case.

The weather here in western Germany was definitely beginning to feel like fall in the latter part of September and the first of October. Almost every morning was damp and foggy. It would clear up toward noon and would get fairly warm during the afternoon. The nights were plenty chilly however. It also rained some during this period.

Almost every day now men were leaving our camp. Bunches were taken down to the railroad and loaded up for destinations unknown. We knew that we would all move in a matter of time.

Stalag 12 A was sort of a "reception center". Here the officers, non-coms and privates were separated and sent to different camps. The British and the Americans were also separated and sent to different places. Here we could mingle with the British but they were kept in different tents. This camp was apparently the first camp where all American and British prisoners from the Western Front hit first. A lot of both had been pouring through this camp in the last few days. Maybe we weren't winning the war after all. It was now apparent it wasn't going to end by the end of September anyway.

There were Russian prisoners in this camp too. They were kept completely separated from us. They were in the permanent barracks and had probably been here for a long time. I never saw any of them being moved out for shipment. There were also some British Indian troops here. Although they were British troops they were kept separated from the rest of us.

One time when a fresh bunch of British paratroopers were brought in, Rod and I made a good deal with a couple of them. We traded cigarettes for their jump jackets and berets. The jump jacket was a thick sort of canvas like thing and of course colored camouflage. The beret was red or maroon and had a big silver badge on it saying something about "the Queen's own Scots". The jacket made us much warmer. The beret was a novelty and they were rather attractive at that. Smith had also gotten the same sort of outfit. It did seem odd that out of all the American prisoners, the three of us were the only ones that got the outfits.

An amusing thing came out of our having the British clothes. Naturally Rod, Smith and I, knowing each other well, hung around together a lot. Especially Rod and I. Once when Rod and I were sitting together talking a G.I. came over to us and said, "Say, what nationality are you fellows anyway?" I guess it was puzzling. Here we had half American uniforms and half British. We stayed with the Americans but then there was Rod an apparent Negro. I guess it was rather confusing. Of course, Rod stood out like a sore thumb, but I was pretty international myself. It seemed that I could pass for many nationalities. In the past, when fellows would try to guess each other's national origin, I always had a field day. They always guessed almost everything but what I actually was. French, Greek, Italian, Armenian, Syrian, Arab, Hungarian, German, Slav, almost anything.

Even my name didn't seem to give a hint like it should. The last name is a giveaway to most nationalities. Borthwick is a very uncommon name in America so no one had ever heard of it before and didn't connect it to any country. In fact, the name is so uncommon you can't find it in most telephone books of large cities. A relative in New York State once looked up the history of the name in the United States. At that time, in about 1930, there were only 150 Borthwicks in the United States and Canada. That's not many and there are probably fewer now.

The name is definitely Scottish though. Although it is quite uncommon in the States I understand that it is fairly well known in Scotland and England. I have always been rather proud of my Scottish blood. I must be mostly Scots. My father was a Borthwick and my mother was a Campbell. I guess you can't get much more Scottish than that. If my last name had been Campbell I wouldn't have had any fun with the fellows trying to guess. It would have been a cinch.

The damned Germans could be stinking sometimes. Just plain ornery for no reason at all. Sometimes they would keep us standing in formation for hours for no apparent reason. Sometimes they would hint it was something the British had done. I would see the British standing in formation for long periods of time too. They had probably been told they were being punished for something the Americans had done. I guess they wanted to create distrust between us even though we were prisoners and out of the war. Why didn't these bastards give up trying crap like this? The war must be almost over and they ought to start trying to create a little good will for themselves. We might help them out some time.

I was expecting to get shipped out of this camp any day. Most of us were looking forward to it too. We couldn't see how we could get in a place with much worse conditions than this. We were willing to take the chance anyway.

We finally received another Red Cross Box. This time we weren't so fortunate. Two men had to share a box.

This seemed stinking too. Sgt. Evans said he had seen a large warehouse full of the boxes. I had no reason to doubt Evans either. He was a good guy and had he been in Keating's place I'm sure things would have been a little better. As least I know he would have gone to bat for us and would have tried. That bastard Keating probably wanted to save as many of the boxes as he could for his own use. I figured that asshole wanted the war to go on indefinitely.

The fellow I shared a box with wanted to divide everything equally. I was more in favor of dividing up the cans of meat. I figured we might be able to make the stuff stretch a little farther if we didn't have to open them all up at once. He couldn't see it that way so we cut everything in two, including the Spam and corned beef. The only thing we didn't cut was the can of tuna and the box of cheese. He took the cheese and I took the tuna.

One day a bunch of privates were called out for shipment. Rod was among them. Just as they were leaving we shook hands and said we hoped we could meet again someday in New York or California under better circumstances. This was the last time I ever saw Rod. Now just Smith and I were the only ones of the old F.O. party left together.

Finally, after three miserable weeks in Stalag 12 A, I got my shipping orders. Some other non-coms and I, including Smith, were on this shipment. I was glad that Smitty was still going to be with me. The day before our shipment our planes bombed Limberg again. I was glad we weren't down at the station loading on when the planes hit. I wondered if any of our boys had been killed in any of those raids. Work details had gone down there almost every day. I had been lucky and had had to go only that one time.

The afternoon of the 9th of October we marched down to the railroad yards of Limberg. After the bombing of the day before we weren't sure whether we would ride or walk. We thought maybe all of the tracks would be out.

The Germans wouldn't tell us where we were going or how long the trip would take. They didn't give us any rations either. All we had was what we had left in our Red Cross Boxes and that wasn't much because we had only had half a box in two weeks. In fact, all I had left was a can of tuna and a pack and a half of cigarettes. All Smith had left was a can of pate, which was some kind of sandwich spread. Some of the fellows didn't have a thing. I had had to really stretch my food to even have the tuna left.

Just before we boarded the boxcars, we were told that there would only be twenty five men to the car. At first we thought this was going to be a good deal until we found out how we were to be situated on the cars.

These European cars are much smaller than those in the States. The door is about the same size though, taking about a third or more of the wall space. We found out, to our dismay that the twenty five of us were to occupy only one third of the car. Barbed wire was stretched across the end of the car from the door. In other words, one third of the car was for the prisoners and two thirds for the three guards that would be with us. I had heard about the stories of the forty and eights and thought that must have been pretty crowded. At this rate seventy five men could have been crowded into this car. I guess we call this deal the seventy five and eight.

This was an absolutely impossible situation. We couldn't all sit down at once, to say nothing about lying down. You could hardly take a breath. We finally solved the problem of at least sitting down. We would sit in between the legs of the guy behind you. We were packed solid and any movement was almost impossible. To top it off several of the guys had diarrhea and were crapping their pants. Another was vomiting all over the back of the fellow in front of him. I was glad the guy in back of me was holding everything in. This was going to be a lovely trip wherever we were going. Animals going to the slaughter house got better treatment than this.

We knew that this situation was impossible and decided to try to do something about it. We took a collection of our last remaining cigarettes and offered them to the guards. They finally agreed to let four men get just outside the wire. It didn't do too much good but it didn't hurt either.

There wasn't much danger to the guards letting a few men out. They were heavily armed with automatic weapons and had one machine gun set up for action. If the guys had tried to rush them or something they would have been mowed down in seconds as well as the rest of us behind the wire. These guards were Poles too and probably a little more easily bribed. However, they had no intention of letting us escape or over power them or anything like that. They knew it would be their old butt if we did.

At dark we tried to get a little sleep. We just sat there in rows not even being able to lean back a little to relax. Sleep was impossible. We would nod occasionally from sheer exhaustion. The only redeeming thing about the whole situation was that we were so tightly packed in that we could keep warm. I envied the guys that had been lucky enough to get on the outside of the wire. At least they could stretch out a little. I also envied the guards, having most of the car to themselves. They had a couple of kerosene lanterns burning and seemed comfortable and content. My mouth watered when they started eating their bread and baloney. The stench in this place had taken my appetite away though.

Sometime during the night we began to move. No doubt this was going to be a wonderful trip wherever we were going. I hoped we would soon reach our destination no matter where it was or what was going to happen to us. I was beginning to feel like I didn't care what happened now.

The next day we were still plugging along. It was an overcast day and we figured it would keep our planes down some. We all had a horror of being locked in some freight yard during one of our big plane raids.

We were surprised to see the number of railroads in Germany. Surely, for the size of the country they must have more miles of tracks than even the States. We were traveling along a nice double track road. Every so often there were large switch yards. The trains here seemed to be running regularly almost as if they were keeping schedule. We had expected to see the railroad in Germany completely destroyed. I still wondered why our planes didn't go more for these open stretches of track if they wanted to paralyze the railroads. It seemed as if a double set of tracks like this would be a fairly easy target. Perhaps it was done a lot but I never saw any evidence of it. Of course, I didn't travel on all the tracks in Germany. The Air Force knew what they were doing though, I guess.

In the middle of the afternoon we reached the city of Kassel. It seemed to be quite a large city. It had been visited by our bombers several times. The place was pretty well battered up but we could see several large factories that seemed to be going full blast. I guess the Germans had a knack for getting things going again quickly. Besides that, there is a lot of Germany. It is small compared to the States but still there were thousands of square miles in it. It would be impossible to flatten everything in a short time and keep it that way no matter how may planes you had. Also, there were just twenty four hours in a day. As industrialized as Germany is there must have been hundreds of places with important factories. On the outskirts of Kassel we could see bomb craters for a considerable distance. They had really tried for this place alright.

The second night out we didn't travel as far as we sidetracked and stopped often. On this night the guards let me out of the barbed wire. I was surprised and grateful. I didn't even have any cigarettes to offer either. I guess they felt sorry for us poor bastards. That made five of us on the outside of the wire. I was lucky to have been the first one sitting next to the gate of the wire. When they had decided to let one more out I was in line and the lucky one.

Outside the wire I could stretch out and get the kinks out. The drawback now was that I almost froze to death. It was almost hard to decide whether it was better to be back inside the wire crowded but warm or out here with more room but freezing. I was miserable and doubted if I would ever be warm again.

I lay down beside a fellow that had been let out here the night before. He had a little better spot than I did. He was situated so that I lay between him and the door. It helped to keep the cold wind from him that whistled through the cracks of the door. I was practically an icicle.

I got to talking to this fellow lying beside me. He seemed like a nice fellow. His name was Wallace Graves and he had lived in Fort Worth, Texas before the war. He was a well-educated fellow having graduated from the

University of Oklahoma in 1943. He had been married a short while. He had been a Forward Observer with the 30th Division and in combat about six weeks when he had been captured around the Moselle River.

We soon became good friends. He seemed to be a very intelligent fellow and was nice to talk to. He flattered me by saying it was nice to talk to someone who could carry on a descent conversation and not like most of the G.I.s. He wasn't stuffy or conceited though. He wasn't bitter that at the last minute he hadn't gotten his commission. He was another victim of our army already getting too many officers. He wasn't the type that just because he had a little better education than most, thought he was doing a job too dangerous or beneath him. He had evidently come from a family with some money. His father had come to Fort Worth years ago and started the Retail Merchants Association there. They had their choice of colleges to go to and his brother had chosen Texas and he had chosen U of Oklahoma. He got more money just to go to school on than I even made. He didn't tell about himself in a bragging way and I knew he was telling the truth and just not bulling. A real nice fellow.

The night passed slowly and miserably. We were cold and hungry. All that there was to go to the toilet in was a big bucket. This can wasn't our toilet but was also for our drinking water. I don't imagine they were too careful how they cleaned it up before putting drinking water in it. It's a wonder we all didn't get sick and die. Again, it was good that the weather here was cool so we didn't get quite so thirsty.

We didn't get any food and my stomach and whole body was racking for the want of food. I could have eaten horse manure and liked it. Smith and I agreed to share our food to try to make it go a little farther. We decided to eat his pate first. To our great disappointment the whole can of stuff was as green as grass with whiskers growing on it. We reluctantly threw it away. All we had left was my can of tuna. Our tuna didn't last long. It was just a couple of mouthfuls apiece.

Our second night out from Stalag 12 A we didn't travel much. We would go for a short distance and sidetrack for long periods.

Graves and I talked earnestly of trying to escape. We knew it would be tough. We were now in the heart of Germany and the chance of success was practically nil. We wouldn't even know which direction to strike out. We were getting weak from the lack of food and would have to have some soon. We were getting to the point where it might be a relief to be shot trying to escape. We figured if the conditions of the trip we were now on was any indication of what we were in for at our next camp, shooting might be the easy way out. I think the only thing that kept us going was the hope that the war would soon be over. By now our hopes for the war ending in a few days after we were captured was gone. I had been captured a month ago today and the war was still going on. I still hoped my predictions of Armistices Day would hold up.

Through the cold miserable night, we speculated where we might be going and what lay in store for us. We knew that under the present conditions and getting no food we would soon be dropping like flies.

The next day we did get a little break. We stopped and were taken off the tracks and to a German Red Cross place. We were each given a bowl of macaroni soup. There wasn't much of it but it tasted good and helped some. This was the only food I had had in three days besides a half can of tuna. Here we also were taken in small groups to some wash room where we could go to the toilet and wash up a bit.

Our train had pulled up beside another. On the other train were a couple of gondola cars full of potatoes. We tried to talk to the guards into going over and bringing us a few of the spuds. They said they would like to but the German railroad police were tough. They said if anyone even looked like they would take one lousy potato they would shoot and ask questions later. They said they wouldn't hesitate to shoot anyone either, a civilian or one of their own soldiers. I guess the "police state" we had heard about was true. I began to believe that what I had taken for just plain national discipline, as in the apple tree incident, was instead fear of being spied on and reprisal.

This day was October 12th, 1944. It was Bernice's birthday. I wondered what she was doing and it she was O.K. I wondered if the folks back home had received the "Missing in Action" notice yet.

Also on October 12th we passed through the city of Berlin. The city showed plenty signs of being bombed and was pretty battered up. Huge apartment houses had been hit. Factories, stores and homes had also been hit. In some places only a wall or two stood. In other words they were in rubble. I don't know whether we passed right through the heart of Berlin or more or less through the suburbs. I remember passing one station that had a sign saying Charlotteberg. We were in Berlin alright and it was a big place.

Our train followed along an inter-urban electric train track. As these inter-urban trains passed we could see well-dressed men and women riding in them. They were dressed and acted as if they were going downtown to a movie or coming home from a day at the office. The electric trains reminded me of the Key System Trains between San Francisco and Oakland. It sort of make me homesick to see them. Berlin seemed to have plenty of electric power yet. Lights twinkled from apartments and homes.

We stopped near a big factory and side tracked. The factory was going at full blast and as it worked the sky would light up with red flashes. It must have been some kind of steel mill. It was a perfectly clear night and we were afraid that Berlin might be visited by our bombers or the British. It would be hell to be locked in a box car, especially beside a big factory, during a thousand plane raids.

The train side tracked here for a couple of hours. We sat there cold and miserable, talking to keep up morale. We wondered how the war was coming and when it would be over. The thing we were thinking about right now more than the war was food. We tortured ourselves talking about what we could do to a nice juicy steak.

In a couple of hours, much to our relief, the train started to move. We were sure that on a night as clear as this, Berlin had a good chance of a visit from our planes. We jolted along pretty steadily the rest of the night. It was bitterly cold and sleep was impossible. Graves and I lay there just shivering and talking.

We got to talking to the guards quite a bit. One of them could speak a little English. It was obvious that they were Poles that had been forced to serve in the German Army. We asked them if they had been in any combat. One said that he had been in the big bombing around St. Lo. He said it was hell beyond comprehension and he hoped he wouldn't have to go through anything like that again. The one that could speak English said he hadn't seen any action. He laughed and said that they were afraid to take him near the Front. He said they knew he would head for the Allied Lines as soon as he got a chance.

The next morning we were passing through a thick wooded area. We wondered where we were. It was hard to determine which direction we had taken out of Berlin. The land here was pretty level and the trees, for the most part, seemed to have been hand set. The woods were mostly pine, fir and some kind of evergreen trees. Once we saw a deer standing at the edge of the woods watching us go by. We wished we had it to eat.

One of the guards told us we weren't too far from the Polish Border now. We figured that we had come due east from Berlin. We wondered if we were going to a prison camp in Poland to work or something.

We stopped for a minute or two beside another train that was side tracked. That train had a couple of box cars full of American prisoners. We found out from them that they were what the Germans called "Kommando" or working party. They were on their way to Poland to work. They said that we were probably going to a large American P.O.W. camp near the town of Frankfurt on the Oder.

At first their prediction seemed true enough. We continued on and passed through the city of Frankfort. A short distance on the other side of town we stopped in front of a camp that was situated near the tracks. We could see lots of French inside the barbed wire enclosure. We figured that this was the place and prepared to get off.

Just as we were about to dismount a couple of official looking Germans came up along the box cars. There was a lot of shouting from them and by the tone of their voice a lot of it was swearing. They were apparently giving the boys hell for bringing us to this camp.

Our engine went down a switch track and hooked

onto the other end of our train. We were soon going back from where we had come. As we passed over a trestle in Frankfort, we noticed a column of German soldiers marching through the streets singing. The officer leading them was riding a beautiful white horse. The Krauts sure went in for that sort of thing.

We passed on through Frankfort and continued on. We figured that now we were probably headed back to the Berlin area to some camp. We didn't think much of this now that Berlin was starting to get bombed so much.

After traveling quite some time we arrived at the town of Krustin. This was apparently going to be the place of our permanent camp.*

We dismounted from the train and started marching down the streets. We didn't do much marching, just more of a shuffle. We were all so hungry and weak from the lack of food we could just about make it. We passed on through Krustin and on out into the country about three miles.

The camp we arrived at was the typical looking prison camp with rows of low green barracks, guard towers and miles of barbed wire.

Inside the gate of the camp we were searched again.

---

* Stalag III-C was a World War II POW camp for Allied soldiers. It was located in north eastern Germany about 50 miles from Berlin. It is now in Poland. Originally it was for several thousand soldiers from Poland, France, Britain, Yugoslavia and Belgium. From 1944 soldiers from the United States were also held there. The majority of Soviet prisoners (up to 12,000) were killed or starved to death. In September 1944 the first Americans arrived, taken prisoner as a result of the failure of Operation Market Garden and the advance of the U.S. Army toward Germany. In December 1944 the roster showed that there were 2, 036 Americans, 631 Belgians, 416 British, 17,568 French, 1,046 Italians, 2 Polish, 1,591 Serbian and 13,727 Soviet prisoners. (Source: Wikipedia 2016)

Our prison dog tags were also checked. Anyone that had any money with them had it taken away. As a matter of formality they gave us a receipt for the American and British money. Of course no one expected to see any of it again. The invasion money was torn up. They didn't recognize it at all.

As we were standing there a rather interesting thing happened although somewhat gruesome. Two Germans immerged from the nearby barracks. Between them they carried the body of a man. The fellow was naked and as stiff as a board. One guy had him by the head and the other by the feet. The stiff was white-white and was practically nothing but bones. A short distance from the building was a small four wheeled cart. They tossed the stiff into the cart and he plunked on the bottom with a thud that sounded just like a stick of wood hitting the bottom. The little wagon we quickly named the "apple cart".

So this was to be our new home. That little deal had made a nice little reception and we all wondered to ourselves if we would be tossed into that "apple cart". We were all losing weight rapidly and getting down to that dead man's size. The camp looked pretty formidable alright. An officer gave us a little talk. He said we would get along alright if everyone behaved themselves. He also told us that the drinking water in the camp was "poison", as he called it, and none of us could drink it unless it was boiled first.

We were taken to some barracks and were assigned one hundred men to the building. The barracks were small, about the size of a good sized garage. Each barrack was divided into three rooms which meant there would be about thirty-three men to a room. This was going to make things cozy. Graves, Smith and I stuck together and got assigned to the same room.

The room, needless to say, was way too small to accommodate thirty-three men. A shelf like deal had been constructed along two walls of the room. The shelf was about six feet wide and about four feet from the floor and on the shelf there was just enough for everyone to lie down. In the middle of the room was a table running the length of the room. Benches were attached to the table. In other words it was sort of the picnic type set-up. There was only one door to the place and on one end there were a couple of windows. There were nails in the wall by the door from which we were to hang our soup bowls.

Most of the fellows wanted to get up on the shelf. Graves, Smitty and I picked a spot on the floor near the door. It was just the floor too. Here we were issued two blankets and a mattress cover. There was nothing in the mattress cover, not even one piece of straw. Even the cover was almost paper thin. They issued each of us two blankets. I got a couple of lousy blankets again although no one got any to write home about. One of mine was small, only about four feet square. The other was so thin and ragged it looked like something like a tablecloth. I could hold it up and see daylight and even objects through it. A mosquito netting would probably have kept me warmer. Graves and I decided to pool our blankets and sleep together. Our blankets weren't going to make the floor softer or keep us much warmer either for that matter.

Of course, everyone was starved but we wouldn't get any food today either. We had arrived too late to get any food today. They served soup once a day in this place.

On this first day they did take us to have a shower and get deloused though. The shower consisted of water running on us for about two minutes. The place wasn't heated and several windows of the place were broken out letting the cold wind whistle in. We got miserably cold standing around several minutes waiting for our clothes to come out of the delouser. The delouser was a big oven affair in which our clothes were placed, sprayed with disinfectant and subjected to intense heat.

We were so hungry we could hardly make it over to the showers. In fact, one guy named Sanders keeled over.

Our bunch was in a part of the camp called Block 3. Across a double barbed wire fence was Block 1. Block 1 also held American prisoners. There were about a thousand of them and they had been the first Americans and had been here about two months. In our block there were only about three hundred prisoners so far.

This camp, Stalag 3C, had been occupied by French soldiers up to now. We heard that before the war it had been a Hitler Youth Camp. There were a few paved streets in the place. Even a cement segment of street ran through our compound. It certainly wasn't for the P.O.W's (Prisoners of War) or would do them any good. Probably when this place had been a youth Camp things had looked considerably different.

Our new home, Block 3, Stalag 3C, looked something like this: It was situated in a barbed wire enclosure about two hundred yards long and a hundred yards wide. For living quarters there were ten of the small three roomed barracks. One side of the compound was a building that was supposed to have had plumbing or something. A few yards to the rear of the barracks were two latrines. They were strictly the mountain boy type. They were neither very comfortable nor sanitary. Up near the gate of the block were two more buildings. One was sort of a Headquarters for the block and the other was a storehouse. The whole area was surrounded by a double fence of barbed wire. Guards walked between the wires twenty-four hours a day. There was a guard tower with a search light at the latrine end of the compound. It was set over the Block 1 side a few yards. Our compound was situated between the other blocks. One was Block 1 that held the other Americans and the other held Russians and later on Italians.

In front of the American compounds and outside our wire but enclosed in more wire was the "mess hall". This "mess hall" was for only making soup. It was never meant to go inside and eat. Inside the "mess hall" were the vats for making soup. The soup was brought outside in tubs to be given to us. Beyond the "mess hall" was the hospital and the delouser. Still beyond that were some buildings that were used as Camp Headquarters and then of course the road. At the rear of our compound and beyond there were wide open fields. There were woods about a half mile beyond the fields.

Across a drive to the left of the Headquarters were a couple of large warehouses. A little farther on were the barracks for the German Officers and enlisted men. Near the hospital were the barracks for the Russians and near the warehouses were the French quarters. Of course, everything was surrounded by scads of barbed wire.

Our block had only one pump in the place. We had been warned that we had to boil the water before we drank it. The catch to that was that we never had enough fuel to boil it on the small stove in our room. Everyone drank the water just as it came from the well. No one ever seemed to get sick from drinking it. The pump was a busy place with the thousand men that eventually came into our compound.

The fellows crammed into the tiny room with me and were to share this "cell" for the next few months were from all parts of the States. To start with there was a guy named Cecil Robatille. He came from Detroit, Michigan. He always had some wild tale to tell and was always getting into heated arguments with someone. He wouldn't get sore during the arguments but was just stubborn. He wouldn't admit he was wrong even if the rest of the guys in the room told him he was. He had been with the 45th Division and had been captured in Allex, France.

Raymond Gagnon was another of the boys. He hailed from somewhere in New Hampshire. He was a big guy but just a kid. He spent most of his time sleeping and never entered into the conversation much. He had been in the 45th Division and had been captured at Allex, France along with Robatille.

Another of the boys was Charley Smejkal. He had come from Little Ferry, New Jersey. He had been with the 30th Division recon outfit. He had been captured when out on a recon and had run into a bunch of German tanks. His recon car had been knocked out from under him. He was a very nervous, fidgety fellow. He was about twenty three years old.

Then there was Ernest Lusk. He had lived in San Antonio, Texas before getting into the Army. Since then his folks had moved to Porterville, California. He was a quiet sort of a fellow who also spent a lot of time sleeping. He had actually never been in combat. He was just taking a joy ride into Nancy, France. He heard that it had been taken by the Americans but it hadn't.

Another one of the "boys" was a fellow named Rex Badder. He had lived in some small town in Michigan. He had been with the 35th Division combat Engineers. He had been captured when his outfit was cut off and surrounded in a small town in France. Badder was about my age and a clean cut looking fellow. He seemed to be a nice sort of a guy but had a quick temper. He got involved in a couple of fights while we were here.

A fellow that had been in the same outfit and had been captured at the same time as Badder was Bill Jones. He had also lived somewhere in Michigan. He was a big, quiet, nice guy.

Still another from that outfit was Rocco Rich. He came from somewhere in Pennsylvania. He was also a nice, quiet, likeable guy. Both Rich and Jones were about twenty-five.

There were a couple of paratroopers in the room. One was named Bill Mahan. He went by the nickname "Red" for obvious reasons. He had originally come from Massachusetts but had kicked around a lot. He was about thirty and had been in the army since 1937.

The other paratrooper was an Italian named Camelo Verga. He had lived in St. Louis, Missouri before the war.

Then there was Nick Alfred. He was a big, rugged, barrel chested Dago. He was really a pretty good guy but didn't take any crap off of anyone. He told anyone what he thought of them. He hailed form New Castel, Pennsylvania.

One of the nicest kids of the whole bunch was a kid by the name of Nichols. He had such a funny first name he wouldn't tell anyone, even his closest buddy. He was called Nick by everyone. He had been a forward observer with the 36th Division He had been captured shortly before I had. He lived on a farm near Fort Worth, Texas before getting into the Army.

One of Nichols' closest buddies was a fellow named Roy Sanders. He was a tall, homely cuss but a heck of a nice guy. He was very quiet and seldom talked to anyone except Nichols. He had been an infantryman with the

36th Division. He had lived on a farm near Harrodsburg, Kentucky before the war.

The fellow that chummed with Nichols and Sanders was a guy named Lawrence. I never knew his first name. He always went by the nickname of "Buckshot". He was an old army man being in since 1937. He held a Tec Sgt. Rating. He seemed to be a lazy cuss and Nichols and Sanders waited on him hand and foot. He was the type that was an authority on everything and wrong half the time. He was a pretty modest about himself though. He had gotten the Silver Star and Bronze Star and the Purple Heart. I just happened to find it out in a casual conversation with Nichols one time. No one heard him bragging about it.

There was Frances Progin. He was the homeliest fellow I had ever seen. He had a huge nose with a big wart on it. His teeth were yellow fangs and his eyes were set close together. He had a disposition to almost match his looks too. He argued all of the time and was stubborn and couldn't be reasoned with. He came from Massachusetts.

Another weird character was a guy named Neil Shea. We all came to the conclusion he was cracked. When he talked he rambled on so that no one could get heads nor tails what he was talking about. He had been with a 45th Division Service Company. He also came from some place in Massachusetts.

Another one of the boys was a kid named Junior Haworth. He was really a kid too, only nineteen. He had been in the army some time however, joining when he was sixteen. He was a tall, clean cut looking kid. He didn't seem the type to deliberately join the army and seemed sort of out of place with the rest of us roughnecks. He wasn't the sissy type or anything. I guess being younger than the rest made him seem misplaced. He had been with the 45th Division Service and recon outfit. He had been captured a couple of days before Smith and I had. Haworth's home town was Hartford Connecticut.

James Scott was another of the group. We naturally called him "Scotty". He was a big, good looking man. He was pleasant to talk to. He hailed from Vanceburg, Kentucky.

A fellow by the name of Parmenter was another of the "big happy family". He was sort of the "lone wolf" type. He seldom mingled with the rest of us. He was weird and seemed girlish acting. We suspected he was a queer but as far as I knew never made any funny moves toward anyone. He came from somewhere in Ohio.

Then there was Herb "Pop" Cunningham. He was about Smitty's age but looked much older, at least fifty. He was partly bald and pretty wrinkled. He had been a squad leader with some infantry outfit on the Normandy Front. His hometown was Chicago, Illinois. He had been a bartender in civilian life.

Another fellow from Chicago was a guy named Stanly Bruch. He was one of the Chicago Poles. He reminded me of some of the Poles from Chicago that I had gone to basic training with. He was a pretty crude individual. He had been a Staff Sgt. in the 30th Division machine gun section.

Still another one of the boys was a fellow named Dan Vlad. He was a thin faced fellow and spoke so low you had to get very close to him to hear what he was saying. He was quiet and minded his own business. His hometown was Youngstown, Ohio.

Vlad's closest buddy was a completely different personality. His name was Jimmy Orton. He was a silly little bastard and talked a whole lot. He was a little guy and spent a lot of his time giggling. He had been in the

35th Division. His home town had been near Pine Bluff, Arkansas.

Then there was a Slav by the name of Mihilak. He was a tall, gaunt fellow. He dropped off fast in the prison camp. He showed me a picture taken before he was captured. He was actually fat then. He had been with the 36th Division. Before getting into the Army he had lived on Long Island, New York and had been a fisherman.

Andrew J. Mooney had been an Air Borne "glider rider". An odd fellow who hailed form Jasper, Alabama.

Then there was Jack Leura. He had been captured along with Badder, Jones and Rich. A day before they had been captured he had been shot. The bullet went clear through him and tore a hell of a looking hole in his back. He was lucky that it didn't seem to have hit any vital parts or that he didn't bleed to death. He was of Spanish-French extraction and had lived around Monrovia, California before the war. He had been a boxer and a good one. He was a feather weight. He was really on his way up when the war came along.

Then Smith, Graves and I made up the rest of the bunch. Quite a bunch, from all over the States, all walks of like, different religions, different national origins, different political beliefs, different economic levels, etc. It would be interesting to see how this many men as different individuals would get along crammed into such a small space and under such adverse conditions. Time would tell.

After being in 3-C for a couple of days, Jack Leura sort of fell in with the group of Smith, Graves and me. He was a likeable fellow and at least he had something in common with both of us being from California. He had had twenty five pro fights and had won twenty one, drew one and lost one so he was plenty good.

We had only been here at Stalag 3-C for a few days when we each received a Red Cross Box. This was a most welcome sight. We had hardly any food in weeks and were starving to death. The food they served in this camp wouldn't keep you going very long by itself.

From the Germans we received one bowl of watery, unseasoned soup and one loaf of bread a day for six men. Our soup was usually rutabaga and all it really was lukewarm water with a few pieces of rutabaga floating around in it. It had no seasoning or anything and was tasteless. About once a week we got potato soup and that was equally weak and tasteless.

On Sunday, the Krauts must have thought they were overfeeding us. We usually got some kind of pea soup with a little horsemeat in it. The peas were as hard as rocks and tasted like rocks. The horsemeat was so rotten it stunk so much we could hardly get it down. The horse meat smelled so bad we could smell it clear from the "kitchen" the minute we stepped outside our barracks to go get the stuff. The soup tasted sour and almost unbearable. I guess they were feeding us horses that were battlefield casualties. I imagined they brought them in on flat cars or something and they were pretty ripe when they arrived. They must have just cut them up and dumped the pieces in a vat to cook a little. Even rotten teeth were found in the soup and one guy found an eyeball in his. This was really living. In spite of the horrible stuff no one ever threw any of it away. We even licked the bowls. I would just have soon had the regular soup on Sunday. At least it didn't stink so much.

The 19th of October brought my 25th birthday. In October 1943, I had been on the line in Italy and now October 19th, 1944 in a prison camp in Eastern Germany.

I wondered what October 19th 1945 would bring. There would be only one step worse and that would to be dead.

By the end of October, the last of our Red Cross Boxes were gone. We hadn't gotten much from the one box to build us up much. Our foodless time prior to and including Limberg and our trip here had weakened us a lot.

November was the most miserable month I have ever spent and had to bear as food went. We were already down because of the lack of food and as soon as our Red Cross Box was gone we dropped off even faster. Each day that passed we got weaker and weaker. You just had to drag yourself around. Your feet felt like they were big chunks of lead and it seemed hard to pick them up.

All that our diet actually amounted to was about a gallon of very weak soup and a loaf of bread a week each. If anyone can last very long on that diet I'd have to see it. If the soup had been really honest to goodness soup, like say Campbell's or something, it would have been a lot better. This stuff we were trying to survive on was next to nothing.

We got our soup about noon and our bread around three thirty in the afternoon. It was rather interesting to see peoples' reactions in a spot like this. From around 7:30 A.M. until around 11:30, when we went to get our soup, there was practically no conversation. In fact, so little, that in spite of around thirty men in one small room there would often be dead silence for long intervals. Almost an hour before it was time to get our soup we would get our tin bowls and wait by the door to be called out.

We would get our soup and bring it back to our room to eat it. While we were eating our soup things would liven up a bit. Almost everyone would talk and there might even be a little laughter. As soon as the soup was gone the conversation would die down to nothing in a few minutes. Then again around 3:30 or 4:00, when the bread was brought in, things would again liven up a bit.

Dividing the bread was one of the day's big events. We divided into groups of six to get the bread. Each group of six would get a loaf to be divided among them. Jack Leura always cut the bread for the group of six I was in. Jack, Graves, Smith, me and two others always shared the same loaf. Poor Luera broke out in a sweat trying to divide the bread equally. No one will ever know how important his job seemed to us. There would be six pairs of eyes glued on his every motion. Of course, he always tried his very best to cut the bread into six equal parts. It seemed like someone always thought that some of the pieces were a little larger than some of the others. To keep everyone happy, we cut cards to see who would have the first pick. Your turn to pick your hunk of bread depended on how large the card you got was. Even an eighth of an inch of bread seemed like a great deal. The bread was actually more important than the soup. It seemed as though there was a little something filling to the bread.

Speaking of cards, I was the only one in our barracks and very possibly the whole camp, who had a deck of cards. I never was much of a gambler but always liked to have cards to play some simple games. I had been carrying this deck when I was captured. Those cards got so much use that the spots were nearly worn off. It was hard to distinguish what they were.

When I would get my chunk of bread I would try to figure out how to eat it and make it last the longest. Sometimes I would dice it, other times scrape it into crumbs or try to slice it really thin. Most of the time I was so hungry I would gobble it down in a second or two. Most of the others did the same.

It was obvious what this kind of diet was going to lead to. We saw what shape the Russians were in. They were getting the same thing we were but of course they had been here longer. Everyday a Russian seemed to be hauled away in the "apple cart". Many others were in the hospital with T.B. and other diseases. Even the ones that were still able to get around were in bad shape.

A couple of times small groups of American prisoners were brought into the camp for a few days. Most of these groups had been working in nearby fields and had been brought here for food and shelter. We learned from these fellows, some of which had been prisoners from North Africa that this camp was the bunk. They said that they had been to many American prison camps in Germany but this was by far the worst. They said that the one at Frankfort on the Oder (the one we had gone to first and turned back) had a lot of G.I. prisoners and things there were fairly bearable. The camp was a lot more organized and they got Red Cross Boxes quite regularly. I wished to hell we had gotten in that camp. We figured that this camp was never meant to hold Americans but some of the other camps were getting overcrowded and this one still had some space left in it.

Beside November being a month of short rations it also began to get colder. That added to the miseries we already had to put up with. The lack of fats and sugar in our diets made us more susceptible to the cold weather. It seemed as though the cold wind would cut right through you. There was no way to heat the barracks to amount to anything. Each room received about six pieces of coal to last three days. That wasn't even enough to warm up the room for a short time. The coal was a very low grade too. We had to keep blowing on it or fanning it just to make it smolder.

No one even wanted out of the barracks only when it was necessary, like for roll call, to get the soup and go to the latrines. We didn't have to go to the can very often as far as bowel movements went. About once a week was enough. The cold weather or something made a lot of the fellows go a lot. Maybe it had something to do with their kidneys. Some went as high as seven or eight times a night. I guess I had strong kidneys for once a night was all I had to go and some nights not at all. No one drank much water and I couldn't see why they had to go so much. It had something to do with the cold weather and the starvation diet somehow.

It was tough to keep warm. All I had, besides my regular uniform, was the British jump jacket I had gotten back in Limberg. Several would pool their blankets and huddle together.

Someone got desperate and ripped a few boards off the latrine to burn. It wasn't anyone from our room or even in our barracks that took the wood but we were all in for it. When the boards were discovered missing by the Germans they raised all kinds of hell. Sgt. Becker, the German non-com in charge of our compound, took personal charge of our punishment. He had everyone fall out and march around the compound. He had several guards with him, gun in hand, and they looked like they might not hesitated to use them.

We marched around the compound for quite some time. We yelled at Becker calling him a son of a bitch, bastard, pig and other choice names. He took all this but when we started singing "God Bless America" and other patriotic songs it made him mad. We had to double time and the shape we were in made it rugged. We were all ready to drop when the deal was called off. I guess Becker got his point over though. No more boards were taken from the latrine. No one was in condition to do much double timing if they could get out of it.

The boys in our room got a bright idea for getting a little wood. We discovered that our floor had a subfloor. We found that we could pry up a section of the top floor. We took turns getting underneath and prying off places of the subfloor. We had to be careful because guards would burst in every so often to check on us. We would place a couple of guys outside near the barracks. They would try to act nonchalant as if they were getting some exercise or something. They would keep a sharp look out for any guards that might be anywhere near our area. If they spotted one they would rap on the side of the barracks and the section of the top floor would be put down. We needed some time to get the section of the top flooring back in place.

One time Sander sand I were underneath when the signal of a guard approaching came. The boys above quickly put the top down. Sanders and I lay there and waited. Sure enough the guard came to our room. We could tell by the deathly silence from above. We could hear the clumping around of one man and knew it was the guard. Sanders and I grabbed hands to bolster our courage. We didn't want to get panicky. I could hear my heart pounding and it seemed so loud it seemed like the guard above, in the silent room, might hear it. After a little more clumping around the guard left. He had probably only been there two or three minutes but it seemed like an eternity. I often thought afterward what a hell of a feeling it would have been if the top floor had lifted up and a gun was shoved down and we had heard "Rous mit you". The whole room would have suffered but I hated to think what might have been in store for Sanders and me.

We were afraid to bring up more than a few small pieces at a time. A guard might pop in and recognize the sources of the wood. Also, if they saw a lot of smoke coming from the chimney they might get suspicious and make a thorough investigation to find out where we were getting our fuel.

Food was constantly on our minds. We tortured ourselves talking about it. Everyone would talk about their favorite foods and dishes. Instead of talking about some peach of a girl they had met in some town back in the States they would talk about some dandy restaurant they had eaten in. Almost everyone said they were going to get a job as a cook if they ever got home. I wasn't going to be a cook but I had plans. I was going to have plates of sandwiches and packs of cigarettes all over the house. If I woke up in the night all I would have to do is reach out any place and get a sandwich or cigarette. I'd have them placed in route to the bathroom and on the way to the kitchen. I was going to have the refrigerator full of hams, chicken and all kinds of things to make a quick meal.

Women or sex were seldom, if ever, mentioned. One guy had carried a picture of Linda Darnell on him. He hung it up on the wall. It was a typical pin up picture with the sultry look and the scanty, form revealing attire. He asked the question, "If we had rather sleep with this a night or have one "K" ration". The vote was completely one-sided. Poor old Linda didn't even get one vote.

We thought if we could just get one "K" ration a day we might make it. I would have gladly traded the soup and bread we got here for just one "K" ration or "C" ration. I now wished I had all that I had thrown or given away. Most would have signed up if we could have one "K" ration a day but would have to give all the money they made for the rest of their life. If we didn't start getting more food soon our lives weren't going to be very long anyway.

A couple of nights a rat would come up through the floor and race around the room. I don't know what he was looking for. There was no food for him here. The third night several stayed up waiting for him but he didn't show up. It's a good thing for him he didn't or he would have been killed and eaten. I wondered if someone in another barracks had gotten the idea and had gotten him first. Sometimes crows would land in the compound. Guys would try to sneak up on them too. Cold crow didn't sound bad at all.

We heard reports from the other rooms that food was being stolen from one another. There couldn't have been much stolen though because most gobbled it down as soon as they got it. I guess a few would hold back a bite or two of bread to have before they went to sleep. I always ate mine in a few seconds after I got it even if I was trying to take it easy.

Graves was about the only man in our room that held his bread back. He got sick and couldn't seem to eat anything. I couldn't see how he could be that sick to not eat that little hunk of bread. He finally had five or six pieces of his bread left over. The stuff was drying out and shrinking up. When he went to the latrine or out of the room I would stare at his bread and wonder if he would notice if I took a little of it. It seemed as though a thin slice of it would help a lot. I never took any of it but it was about all I could not to. When Graves got to feeling a little better he began to augment the daily ration with the old pieces. I envied him having what seemed to be a lot of food. I hated to see him eat the extra bread in front of me. It just made my stomach gnaw all the more.

We got so desperate for food we began to try to find things to trade the Germans for food. Some of us were lucky enough not to have our watches, rings and other personal things taken from us. Everyone began to trade in their school rings, wedding rings, watches, fountain pens or anything of any value that they might have. Some even took the gold bands from their tooth bridges. I was lucky enough to still have my wristwatch. It was practically new, only about four months old. Smith had a bunch of them sent over by his business partner. I had bought it while we were still in Italy, just before we made the Southern France Invasion. In fact, I had only paid ten dollars for it. I had planned to make the remaining fifty dollars I owed in installments. It was a good serviceman's watch, stainless steel, shock proof, dust proof, etc. It had a sweeping second hand and a luminous dial.

We couldn't get much for our things which was understandable. We were glad that we had anything at all left to trade. The stuff could have been taken from us without any trouble. Many had had their things taken in one of the many searches they had gone through.

The Germans went for anything that was gold or looked like gold. A thing like a fountain pen with a gold plated tip was a much better trading item than a much more expensive pen if it just had a steel tip. Lusk had a much cheaper watch than mine but it looked gold and had a gold plated elastic band. He got fourteen loaves of bread for his watch while I was able to get nine for mine. My loaves cost about $7 each. I still felt that this was the best deal I had ever make or ever would make in my whole life. I was so hungry that the cost meant nothing. Actually, if I had only gotten one loaf for the watch I would have been happy and eager to make the deal. I felt very fortunate to even still have the watch so I had really nothing to lose.

I did have to make a tough decision though. Graves wanted to buy half the watch. Of course he didn't have any money and would have to pay me if and when we got back to the States. The money didn't mean a thing of course, it was just getting the food. I really didn't want to make any kind of deal like this but I knew he was as hungry as I was so I said O.K.

You made your deals with the Germans through "traders". The "traders" were G.I.s of German decent and could speak the language. The trader who did the trading for me in fact had relatives right here in this part of Germany. The "trader" took my watch up to have it appraised. Whoever wanted it would tell the trader how much he would give. I imagined the trader got a good deal out of the trade. He might have gotten twenty loaves of bread for my watch for all I know. When he told me he could get nine loaves for my watch I was happy enough. I only hoped that I would get the bread. There was nothing to keep them from keeping my watch and sending no bread.

I wondered who was behind this operation. I wondered if it was some high officer in charge of the camp getting his hands on all this stuff. It was possibly civilians. Someone seemed to have a source of quite a bit of bread. I was pretty sure that everything couldn't have been on the up and up on the German end of it. Someone had to be stealing from someone someway. I didn't care if they were taking Hitler's own food just as long as I got my bread.

The first installment on my watch was two loaves, one civilian and one army loaf. Graves wasn't feeling too good so he told me to take the first loaves and he would take the next two. I sat down and started cutting big slices off from the civilian loaf. I ate three quarters of it before I even took a deep breath. Boy, was it good. I had never tasted anything so good in my life. The civilian bread is much different and better than the army loaf. It is white bread and lighter and tastier than the army loaf. The army loaf was a brown color, heavy and tasted almost like it might have a little sawdust in it to make it go farther. Of course, the army loaf was the one that we received for regular rations.

While I was feasting on my bread, Jimmy Orton just sat there watching me. He never said anything and was man enough not to ask for any of it. The look in the poor bastard's eyes got me though. He was hungry and was torturing himself watching me eat. I didn't care too much for the silly little "Arky" but we were all in the same boat. I gave him the other fourth of the loaf of bread. He didn't say anything and for him that was unusual. I guess he was so surprised. I could see in his eyes though how much he appreciated it and what a wonderful guy he thought I must be. He and his buddy Vlad had a pretty good bedtime snack themselves. I went to sleep that night fuller and feeling better than I had in weeks.

The days dragged on slowly. We wondered what had happened to the drive that was on in the first part of September when most of us here had been captured. We knew it had either been stopped cold or at least slowed down to a walk. If it had kept going like it was then the Allies would have been clear through Germany to where we were by now.

The only outside news we got at all was from a little paper published especially for American prisoners. It was called the O.K. Kid (Overseas Kid). Of course, for the most part, it was strictly propaganda as far as the war news went. It did give the results of the World Series and football scores which were no doubt accurate. I almost wondered if that wasn't propaganda. It said the St. Louis Browns had won the pennant. As long as I could remember the Browns had always been in the cellar so deep without even a chance of even getting to seventh place.

As far as the war news went, of course, we were pretty skeptical as to how true it was. Although it never said that the Germans were scoring great victories it hinted that they were doing alright. It mentioned quite a bit about the V2 rockets bombarding London and Antwerp. We tried to read between the lines and figure out what was really going on.

We were supposed to receive the paper once a week, but we only got a couple while we were here. The paper was a small paged high school sized paper. There was only one paper to the room so we had to take turns reading it. It took quite a while for it to get around to everyone. When a person got it he would read every word in it for reading material was scarce here.

Here in Eastern Germany the actual war did seem far away. We never saw any planes except German ones flying over. We could see Berlin being bombed however. On several different nights we saw flares over Berlin and could hear the bombing. Although we were approximately forty miles due east of Berlin the bombings would rattle the barracks. When the bombings were going on the barracks would have a constant rattle punctuated by occasional sharper jolts. We figured the heavier jolts were from the "block buster" bombs the R. A. F. (British Royal Air Force) carried on their raids. We could also see the night bombings of Stettin to the north although it wasn't too plain so I supposed it was a further distance away.

Apparently, there was a training airfield near us. Almost every day German planes flew over going through all sorts of maneuvers. Sometimes they flew over the camp just missing the tops of the barracks. There also was an artillery range nearby. Day after day we would hear the pieces firing.

November dragged into December with the days getting colder and colder. When I did get up courage to take a sponge bath in that icy water I was aghast how thin my arms and legs were getting. I wasn't the only one losing a lot though. Everyone was falling off badly. Graves seemed to be dropping off more than anyone in our room. He also started developing a nasty cough. I was worried about him and afraid he might be getting T.B. or something.

Some of the fellows were getting some sort of infection. It seemed to come from scratching louse bites. The barracks were crawling with lice. Most of the fellows were covered with them. A few of us didn't seem to be bothered by them. I happened to be one of the lucky ones. I found a couple of big juicy varmints of some kind in my socks once but that was the only time. The lice seemed to be worse on the blond and light skinned fellows. Guys like Dick Adams for instance. They were thick on them, even in the seams of their pants. Some of the guys that were getting the infection were getting crippled up. Cunningham, from our room, got crippled up in his knees so badly he had to go to the hospital and his legs were cut on.

There was one thing that we all feared. That was getting something seriously wrong with us that might require surgery. We knew that the Germans were low on medical supplies and they weren't going to use what they did have on a bunch of prisoners. We knew that if we had to go to the hospital for anything serious our chances of coming back would be just about nil. Even a simple operation like taking out your appendix would be a touch and go matter. Everyone hoped that they wouldn't get seriously ill. There would be no drugs, dope or even decent bandages. The bandages they were using were made of paper.

The boys were holding up pretty well so far though. Only two or three had died. No one from our room or our barracks and no one I knew. I felt amazingly well myself. I hadn't been sick a day since I had been a prisoner. I hadn't even had the G.I.s (diarrhea). I was only one of the few to escape that. Some had had it several times.

I saw one fellow die though. He didn't starve but starving was the cause of it. One day we were dragging up after our soup when a semi-truck loaded with potatoes came through. I don't know who the potatoes were for, certainly not for the prisoners. They were probably for the German garrison here. A French "trustee" was driving the truck. He drove it very slowly through us and by the grin on his face we knew he was doing it deliberately. He knew a lot of us would manage to get a few potatoes.

Of course, there was a mad scramble for the spuds. Everyone was trying to grab as many as possible. I was about in the middle of the column and a huge wave of humanity swept back with the truck towards me. By the time the truck had reached me there was a big fighting human mountain. I fought my way in and managed to grab three potatoes and then was swept along with the tide. Fellows were pushing, shoving and climbing over one another. Several were knocked down and trampled on. Suddenly, there was a noise like a pumpkin being run over. One poor devil had got knocked under the wheels of the truck and had his head run over. There was blood and brains all over the driveway. A hell of a looking sight. Of course, the accident sobered everyone immediately. Everyone began to hide their potatoes figuring the Germans might shake us down to find offenders. They would, of course, investigate the accident and would want to know how it happened. I put my spuds by the edge of the driveway and put a little sand over them. When I came back after getting my soup I found that some bastard had discovered them and stolen them. A whole day of good eating right there.

During this miserable stretch of fasting here at Stalag 3-C, a Red Cross representative from Geneva came to inspect the camp. He was horrified with the conditions of the camp. He said we weren't getting enough food to keep us alive. He wasn't telling us anything. He didn't like the sanitary conditions of the place or the way the barracks were heated. In short, the place was way below the absolute minimum. The day he visited we ate a little better than usual too. The Germans were trying to make things look a little better.

A thing that struck me as rather funny was a sign the Germans had down near where we got our soup. On a blackboard they showed how many calories we were getting each day. So many calories, so much fat, sugar etc. I wondered who they thought they were fooling. They had down a grand total of 800 calories for the day's meals. Hell, if we got 800 calories a week from that crap we were eating we were doing great.

Another time something else struck me as rather funny. There was a giant of a man from one of the barracks. I didn't know him or even what his name was but I would always see him on the way to get the soup. He was red headed and had a huge red beard. He must have been growing it for some time. One day a German Officer jumped him. The officer yelled at him, "I want you to shave that beard off. We are humans here, not animals". If the world wasn't acting like a bunch of animals now I don't know what they were doing. On second thought, we were worse than animals. Animals are much kinder and more sensible than humans.

Nerves were frayed to about the breaking point now. Guys growled at one another over nothing, although the bunch in our particular room got along pretty well. Badder and Adams had had sort of a feud going for a long time. It finally broke down into a fist fight. We let them fight it out knowing it would stop the bickering once and for all. It had been accumulating for a long time. Badder beat up Adams pretty badly, giving him a black eye and cutting his lip and face up pretty badly. Sure enough though it was the end of their growling at one another. Adams didn't quit though. He fought until he was knocked down four or five times.

I almost got in to a fight with Nick Alfredo. I always got along with everyone really well but my "dry" sense of humor almost got me into it with Nick. He came in the door one day and left it open a little. I said jokingly, I thought, "Shut the damned door". He walked up to me and said, "Listen you, I'm not used to being talked to like that." Instead of apologizing and telling him I was only fooling, like I should have, I said, "Well, there is always a first time isn't there?" I expected that would do it and he would come in flailing. Instead he just looked me in the eye for a second, smiled that cold, thin smile of his and walked away. I had figured that I could hold my own with anyone in the room if the occasion ever arose. Old Nick I figured might be the only exception. I probably outweighed him some (I weighed 198 when I had come overseas). Now, of course, I was way down from that but he was down from the top of his torso. I was taller than he was. I was six foot even while he wasn't more than five foot ten at the most. Still, he was a ruggedly built guy and looked rugged. I don't know why he backed down. He probably thought the same as I did. This wasn't the time or the place to fight and a fight never settled much. It's just as well we didn't fight, for the nose that was saved could have very well been mine. Neither of us ever mentioned the incident again.

I got along with all the fellows though. I tried not to get carried away in any argument. Most of the fellows got along well under the circumstances.

In the first part of December we each received a Red Cross Box. This was a welcome sight and our salvation. I don't know how much longer we could have kept going on the food we were getting here. Now that we each had a Red Cross Box again spirits picked up considerably. Everyone was more friendly to one another now and there was very little growling at one another. The fellows began to talk to each other more now. Before, it seemed an effort to carry on a conversation and it seemed there was nothing to talk about.

Everyone divided up into pairs and pooled their boxes. Graves and I went together on our boxes. One advantage in going together on the boxes was that we seemed to be able to make the food go further. Instead of us each opening a can we would open just one and make it do. If a person opened a can of say corned beef, it was almost impossible to keep from gobbling it right down. Making one can do for two people made the food go a lot farther.

Soon after we received our boxes the trading began. The trading was done much more carefully than it had been back in Limberg. I guess we figured we had more time now and it might be the last box we ever got so wanted to make the best deal we thought possible. Sometimes just to trade a box of raisins for a box of prunes took half a day. Trading was like an immense business transaction. It seemed that cigarettes were the medium of exchange and all of the other things in the boxes had a price of cigarettes on them. It was amazing how valuable cigarettes were. I guess the thing that made them valuable was that you could trade them to the Germans for things. They would even give a box of prunes some consideration. Cigarettes could be traded over the fence to the Russians too. They worked out of the camp and were sometimes able to come up with something to trade. They usually had a little brown sugar, some bread or little bundles of wood to trade. We had to make our trades with the Russians in a hurry as the Germans didn't like it. With practically no bartering we would throw over some cigarettes for what they had to offer. Some of the guards would take the stuff away from us if they caught us. Some of the guards didn't give a damn and would turn their backs if they knew we wanted to make a trade.

For trading with the other fellows in our room Graves and I put both cans of powdered milk on the block. Nichols and Sanders gave us five packs of cigarettes a piece for them. We were pleased with this deal for we knew we could trade with the Germans and Russians. With our own cigarettes we now had quite a lot of buying power.

When the boxes first arrived, the Germans, as well as the Russians, knew that cigarettes were plentiful for a few days. In a week or so, when the cigarettes were about gone, you could get much more for them. Graves and I saved our cigarettes for this period. Even though when I had been able to get plenty of cigarettes I had practically been a chain smoker.

I never craved the things. If I didn't have them it didn't seem to bother me. I guess it was because I never inhaled. Guys made fun of me and wondered why I even smoked. I wondered myself. Just a nervous habit I guess. It came in handy now for I just smoked a few of the cigarettes and saved the rest to trade for food from the boys, Germans and Russians. Graves hardly smoked at all either.

We tried to use the food from our boxes very sparingly. We were never sure when or if we would ever get another one. The Germans demanded that we eat the stuff up right away but they never seemed to check on how fast the stuff was going. I supposed they didn't want anyone hording anything to take along with them in an escape try. They seemed to open boxes at random and punch holes in the cans of meat. They did it to about half of the boxes. Naturally, if your cans of meat had holes punched in them you had to eat it fairly soon or it would spoil.

Some of the fellows that got their boxes intact did try to hide some of the food. The food would be hidden under the barracks or buried in a hole somewhere. One time the Germans gave us a shakedown and discovered a lot of food. They confiscated it too. A lousy trick. Graves and I didn't have to worry about having food found. It never lasted very long with us and we never had much held back.

Also, in the first part of December, we received a shipment of clothing through the Red Cross. The stuff was all clothing. We each received a new pair of pants, shirt, coat, scarf, and gloves. We each got an Army blanket. This was going to help keep us much warmer and if we could now get a box of food anywhere near regularly we would make out fairly well. Smith almost got in it with Germans when we got our clothing. He and I had to give up our British jump jackets and berets. I didn't think anything of it and gladly turned my stuff in to get the new clothes. Not Smith though. I guess he wanted to keep his beret as a souvenir or something. The German Supply Sgt., a miserable, cigar smoking character, took the beret off of Smith's head. I saw old Smitty flush with rage and wrenched the things out of the German's hands. The Kraut screamed, yelled and swore but he didn't try to get it back. Smith had plenty of guts alright. To me, the damned thing wasn't worth the chance of getting knocked on the head. I would have at least had the silver badge to keep though. Smith had better take it easy or he was going to wind up in a gas chamber or oven yet.

One day along in the middle of December something happened that made us think for a minute that the war was over. The guards were acting strangely. They seemed extremely happy and were tossing their guns up in the air and firing them. They were shouting happily to one another. We were sure this was it. The war was over. Another thing that convinced us this was it was that all of the Room Sgts. were called up to 'Headquarters" for a meeting. We figured the Germans wanted to give them the word and instructions on what to do. We were very disappointed when the Sgts came back. The only thing the meeting was for was to get a chewing out for something we were doing that didn't please the Germans.

We found out a little later what the Germans were so happy about. They told us that the Germans were making a great drive on the Western Front. They said the drive was going well and that they were almost back to Paris. They were going to split the Americans and the British forces and drive them back into the sea. We figured they were overdoing the thing but figured something pretty big must be going on. We were afraid that whatever it was would prolong the war and keep us here just that much longer. It was pretty demoralizing. Later we found out that they did make a drive that was called the "Battle of the Bulge".

It showed the Germans still thought they had a chance to win the war. They were happy and encouraged when the new front first came to them. I guess these guys never gave up.

As the month of December dragged on, the weather became colder and colder. We had snow on several occasions. The snow got to several inches thick a couple of times.

Christmas was drawing near and we heard the rumor that we were going to get a special Christmas box. We hoped so for our food was low. On the 20th of December, it was pretty official that we would get a special Christmas box for Christmas. I hoped we would get any box, special or not.

We could hardly wait for Christmas Eve to come. We planned to have the best time on Christmas we could under the circumstances. We tried to save all the food we could and tried to accumulate a little firewood. We really wanted to have a big blow out.

Finally, Christmas Eve arrived. We were like a bunch of little kids waiting for their presents. We could hardly wait to get our hands on that Christmas box and see what was inside.

I figured by now that the folks at home surely knew I was a prisoner of war. I wouldn't have felt in such a good mood if I had known the truth. They hadn't received any word about me other than the "missing in action" notice. I probably enjoyed this Christmas much more than my wife.

Finally we got our boxes. We eagerly tore them open to see what they contained. They had quite a variety and were nice. They were quite different than the regular boxes. They contained: a can of boned turkey, plum pudding, a can of jam, a can of deviled meat, a can of Vienna sausages, cigarettes, coffee, sugar, powdered milk, a box of dates, a box of assorted Christmas candies, a can of honey and a couple of packs of gum. There was a small present of some kind in each box. The presents were tiny chess and checker sets, cribbage games and horse race games. Almost every box contained a deck of cards.

I wondered if the people who packed these boxes knew what joy they were bringing to a bunch of G.I.s in these miserable conditions. I had hardly ever met anyone who had a good word about the Red Cross. They were called crooks, big time promoters, grafters and everything else. I could remember, as a kid, older people and Veterans of World War I telling about how lousy the Red Cross had been. I remember my own experiences of the cigarettes in North Africa and how in Naples they charged a price for a cup of cold chocolate and a stale cookie. I wondered what they did with all of the money. Most defense plants at home were taking a good sized hunk out of the help's pay for the Red Cross. They were raising millions by drives and other means, yet it seemed anything they had they sold and gave nothing away. I even understood that the boxes we got here were paid for by our government. The Red Cross was only supposed to pay for the boxing and distributing. I didn't know if this was true for sure or not though. Tonight, no one was doing any wondering about the Red Cross. We didn't care how much in graft etc. these boxes had cost. We were just thankful that there was such a thing as the Red Cross no matter what.

Everyone was in quite a merry mood this Christmas Eve. The Germans had been kind enough not to punch any holes in any of the cans. They also said they would leave the lights on all night, a decent thing for them to do.

We built up a good roaring fire from the wood we had been hoarding and had a big can of coffee going. Everyone lit up cigarettes and smoked them completely without butting them. Usually we butted a cigarette at least three or four times. There was no trading or anything like that. Everyone had his box and was enjoying it. All of the goodies in the boxes were sampled. As long as the lights were going to be on most of us decided to stay up all night.

My poor old cards could be retired now for almost everyone had a new deck. There was a big poker game going on with cigarettes for stakes. I went to the well several times during the night to get water to make more coffee.

Leura and I took a big cup of coffee out to one of the German guards. He leaned his rifle against the barbed wire and drank the stuff. He said he hoped by next Christmas the war would be over and he would be home. We told him we hoped so too. He slipped us a small bottle of brandy he had been carrying under his tunic. He had probably figured on drinking it himself or at least getting more than a lousy cup of coffee for it. I guess because it was Christmas Eve and we had shown him a friendly gesture he had decided to give it to us. We had quite a chat with the guy and again it made me wonder what the damned war was all about.

There was one thing that put a damper on the night's festivities. Practically everyone began to get sick. The rich food in the boxes was too much for us. Although no one had gone overboard and gorged themselves, just nibbling at the stuff had been too much of a shock to our systems. A lot of the fellows were throwing up and having a hell of a time. Fellows from the other barracks were having the same trouble. When you went outside it seemed like a wild orgy of drunken men on New Year's Eve. There were plenty of guys outside heaving their guts out. It was too bad to get a little good food and not to be able to enjoy it and get any good out of it. Some of the fellows were affected in another way. Their legs gave out on them and they couldn't walk. Smejkal was one of them in our room affected this way. He went out to the latrine and his legs gave out and he had to crawl back to the barracks. I was lucky. I felt dizzy a couple of times but didn't get sick.

The German guards didn't know what in the hell was the matter with us. They thought that we were drunk. One asked me if we had gotten some liquor from the Russians someway. When I told him no I don't think he believed me and I couldn't blame him. Half of the guys seemed to be on a terrific drunk. The only difference was that no one was loud. Everyone was just throwing up and crawling and staggering around.

I turned in about five in the morning and of course had to get up again soon for the eight o'clock roll call. Christmas Day we all ate more of our boxes than we should have. We should have taken it a little easier. It was no telling when we would get another box. We figured that Christmas came but once a year and if we were going to starve to death this would be a good day as any to be full once. On Christmas Day the Germans gave us a few potatoes and so everyone was really feeling full. Our stomachs had shrunken so much it didn't take too much to fill them up. The ones that had been sick the night before made a rapid recovery and felt fine. Everyone was in a good mood and we sat around and talked over other Christmases under better circumstances.

The remaining days of December dragged on. It was bitterly cold now and snowed quite often. Frost would form on the inside of our room. We didn't have enough fuel to keep the place warm. We stuck close inside the barracks only going out for roll call, our soup and to the latrine. We seldom washed. It was hard enough to keep warm without touching any icy water. We didn't shave very often either. I usually washed and shaved about once a week or ten days. We had one razor for all of us in our room. We each received one razor blade a month. With no soap, warm water and a dull blade it made shaving rather difficult and a dreaded task.

New Year's came and went. I had spent more pleasant New Year's than this. We didn't have a big New Year's Eve even though the Germans left the lights on all night. By now our food and cigarettes were beginning to start getting low again and we wanted to take it easy on them.

New Year's Day 1943. We hoped we wouldn't have to spend another New Year's in this place. We were all positive we wouldn't one way or another. If the war wasn't over by then probably some of us wouldn't be around by then anyway. We were positive that the war would be over long before another year.

Again we began to speculate on how much longer the war would last. The fellows weren't as optimistic as they had been back in September at Limberg. Some guessed along in March or April. Some even guessed the latter part of February. I was pretty conservative, guessing around the first of July. I may have been conservative but I had also been conservative back in Limberg when I guessed November 11th. Everyone at that time had picked a much earlier date than I had. Even my conservative guess was now way off. It was already off a couple of months and the war was still going on. I figured that the

Germans with their lines shortened could make a pretty good stand at well prepared defenses at their border. The winter weather would have an effect on the thing too. The Germans said they had made a push and according to them it had been very successful. I figured that by May, the spring rains would be over and equipment could be used better. It would take a couple of months of pounding on the German lines before they collapsed. So, I picked around the first of July. I hoped with all my heart that it would be over much sooner.

We wondered why the Allies had been stopped in September when things had been going well. We guessed that the shortened German lines must have been the biggest reason. Instead of having their western front armies scattered all over France and Italy they could have them concentrated on one front. Maybe they were fighting even harder now that their homeland was about to be invaded. The drive they talked about might have been a lot more successful than we figured. Whatever it was the war was still going on. The paper, the O.K. Kid, admitted fighting on the borders of Germany but said the Allies were being held there. We wondered if any of our troops were well into Germany or not.

We also kicked around the question of whether Germany might still be able to win the war. Most of us agreed it just wasn't possible. The Western Allies and the Russians now had an overwhelming superiority in men and equipment. The German war industry had almost been shattered to nothing.

Still, one couldn't help thinking that they might still have an ace up their sleeve. The Germans had a knack for coming up with some new weapon or method to kill people. I visualized them coming up with something that might make a huge electric arc and burn everything for miles. Or maybe something that shot out huge bolts of lightning. I took some razzing for my Buck Rogers ideas but it seemed that wars produced strange and new weapons.

It was also possible that as long as they were going to lose the war they might as well take the rest of the world with them. Maybe they had developed a new and fantastic gas that they had been saving in case they saw all was lost. They could deliver it anywhere in Europe, and maybe further, with their V2 Rockets. They may have perfected germ warfare and that could also be delivered by the V2s. I had read articles that both had been worked on by both sides. Some scientists said they had been perfected, other said they had not. It was a sobering thought anyway. You never could tell what that nut Hitler might use if he had it at his disposal.

The Salvation Army had had some sporting equipment sent to the camp. There were footballs, baseball and bats, basket balls and even boxing gloves. The stuff was used very sparingly. No one had any extra energy to use playing strenuous games. Once in a great while a few of us would get out and toss a football or a baseball around a few minutes. Sgt. Evans put out a call for anyone that had any experience in boxing. They said the boxers would be given a little more food.

Jack Leura, from our room, being a pro, volunteered to fight. The guys were divided up into weight groups and the matches were arranged. The ring was just the dirt of the compound. A line had been drawn in the dirt the approximate size of a ring. The Germans seemed interested in the fights. It seemed as though most of the guards who were not on duty would watch. There were several officers there too. A make-shift stand was made for them to sit on. Everyone else stood up to watch. It was pretty rough on these guys trying to fight in their run down condition. They went at it with a lot of enthusiasm though and there were several good bouts. Surprisingly enough two or three besides Jack showed that they knew something about the game. Evans was one of them. He was a heavyweight but could move and looked good. He must have had considerable experience at some time. No one cheered much or bet or anything. I think they felt sorry for the poor guys trying to fight to get a little food. A couple were mismatched and took awful drubbings. Jack took it easy on his man but the guy he was fighting was willing and put up a real scrap. I watched the German officers while the fights were in progress. They sat there intently, apparently interested, but showing no emotion. The Krauts held true to their words and gave the boys some extra rations. After the fight Jack came back to the barracks with about six or seven boiled potatoes. I was glad I was his buddy for I got a couple of spuds. Fights were held two different times.

There was another way that some of us could have gotten food. If we volunteered to work outside the camp we were promised more food, even fresh milk. Apparently, according to International Law, non-coms couldn't be forced to work but could volunteer. You weren't supposed to have to work at anything that would help the war effort. In this area the work was to be in the sugar beet fields. No one from our room or barracks volunteered. As far as I know no one in our compound did either.

It was pretty inviting though. The thought of more food and possibly some meat, fresh vegetables and milk did make you at least give it a thought. Everyone thought like I did. To hell with them. It seemed to me that no matter what you did in the way of work would help their war effort. The "trader" that came to our room trying to recruit volunteers was almost thrown out the door. I wondered where poor Rodriguez was and what he was doing. He was a private and would have to work. I was sure glad I had a couple of lousy stripes.

The first part of January was routine and monotonous. We passed a lot of time playing with the games we had gotten from our Christmas box. Playing cards was the most popular but we played a lot of checkers and chess too. All kinds of card games were played: Bridge, Casino, Rummy, Hearts, Euchre, 500, cribbage and poker. The game I played the most was Rummy, mainly because Smitty loved it so much. Leura and I usually played partners against Smith and Graves.

I played a little chess but the game made me nervous. About one game a day was all I could stand. It seemed so slow and nerve wracking I could about blow my top trying to concentrate. How those big chess players could sit there a couple of hours before making a move was more than I could understand.

We also passed a lot of time in friendly arguments, although they sometimes became pretty heated. Everything imaginable, big and small, was discussed. Politics, religion, sports, the Civil War, almost anything. Once there was a two day argument on whether a small can of Underwood's Deviled Ham had cost seven or sixteen cents before the war. Many such trivial things such as that were argued. We talked about why girls screamed, hollered and fainted when they went to see Frank Sinatra sing. Graves and I got in an argument about when the song, "Lullaby of Broadway" came out. I said either in or before 1939 and he insisted it didn't come out until later. We even bet a case of beer on it.

Some of the more intellectual members of the camp decided to try to have some classes. There were a few school teachers and some fairly well educated fellows among us. There were to be classes in English, Math, French and German. Of course, there were no textbooks and there would be no homework. A German Officer offered to try to teach a class in German. Graves, Smith Leura and I decided to take the German class.

The German class met in a room in the "headquarters" building. There were about twenty five of us in it. The German Captain was a man probably in his fifties. He looked and acted like an officer. He wore campaign ribbons of the Crimea and other Russian Fronts. He had a pretty rugged looking scar across his face. It was completely healed and must have happened years ago. He seemed like an intelligent fellow and was also quite humorous. He made a few jokes about the Jews. I went to a couple of classes but lost interest. There weren't many classes anyway.

The Officers of the German Army were something to behold. They seemed to be soldiers through and through and you couldn't help but admire them. They looked and acted like you visualize an officer to be. They didn't seem to let their personal feelings stand in the way of their duty. There were only four or five officers in this camp, a Colonel was in charge. One day he inspected our barracks. A German Sgt. threw open the door and screamed "Actung". Everyone jumped and froze. The Colonel entered with plenty of poise and dignity in his rank. He looked around and when his eyes rested on you they seemed to bore through you and it seemed he could read your mind. I hadn't been impressed with an officer like this since Basic Training days at Camp Roberts.

High ranking German non-coms usually acted like soldiers who knew the score. They generally seemed pretty much on the ball but not as stuffy as the

Commissioned Officers. Sgt. Becker, the Kraut in charge of our compound, was one that no one cared about. We felt he was sort of a sneaky individual. Although we never came in contact with him much we all despised that cigar smoking, snarling son of a bitch of a Supply Sgt.

There was one older fat Corporal that everyone liked. He was the typical looking Kraut that they depicted in the movies. When he was taking roll call we would toss snowballs at him. He didn't seem to mind and would chuckle and say, "Ya, Ya". When he was assigned to check our barracks he didn't burst into the room as if trying to catch us red handed doing something wrong. When he checked our room he would first knock on the door! The guy seemed to really like Americans. He was finally transferred from our camp. Before he left he came around and told everyone good bye and shook most of our hands. He looked like he was going to cry any minute. We wondered if he was sorry about leaving us or being sent to the Front. We hoped it wasn't because he was friendly to us that he was being sent somewhere else.

The Privates in the German Army were about the same as in any other army. They get all the crap and are the most down to earth people. When you tried to trade over the fence with the Russians they would usually turn their backs so you could. Of course if there happened to be an officer or noncom in the area they raised all kinds of hell.

One night I made a trade with one of the guards. I don't think this was done too often or at least I hadn't heard of anyone doing it. It was pretty risky, especially for them. It was just like the set up on our side I suppose. I went to the latrine in the middle of the night and a guard hailed me and wanted to know if I had any cigarettes that I wanted to trade. This was a period when cigarettes were scarce but I had a few left. He had a loaf of bread to trade for a few cigarettes. It was a good deal so I went to the barracks to get the cigarettes and he went to the light tower to get the bread. Ordinarily the searchlight swept continually all over the compound. It was hand operated and never set to any one pattern. I noticed that when the guard and I were making the transaction the light conveniently shone in some other direction.

There was a "barber shop" set up at the headquarter building. It consisted of a couple of straight backed chairs and that was it. The "barbers" were a couple of G.I.s with only scissors and clippers to work with. They didn't know anything about cutting hair but would chop it down a little shorter. It had only recently been set up and two thousand guys wanted a haircut. You had to get an appointment to get your hair cut. My turn finally came and I went up to the shop. It was warm in the place and a few hung around there including a few Germans. The conversation was something like that in a shop in the States. The talk was a little different here I suppose. It was mostly about when the war would be over, what would happen after the war, etc. Someone asked one of the Germans why they didn't feed us more. He said they had nine million prisoners in Germany. He claimed the German soldiers were eating the same as we were. I had no doubt that they weren't eating too well but they had to be eating better than we were. They all looked pretty healthy and none looked half starved.

There was a young Frenchman in the French compound who was good on the accordion. Where he had gotten the instrument no one knew. Of course, he like the rest of the French, had been here for a long time. This fellow was allowed to come to the American Compound and entertain us. He would play different nights in different rooms. He had a price he charged in cigarettes and it was pretty high. He was in demand though and it was hard to get him. We contacted him through the "Trader". The Frenchman, the "trader" and the Germans must have all gotten a cut out of the cigarettes. It would have been impossible for him to get into our compound without the German guards letting him in so they were in on it some way. He played in a couple of rooms a night. There were thirty rooms in our compound and thirty three in the other American Compound so it was going to be tough to get hold of him. Our room decided we wanted some entertainment and we were willing to pay for it. We upped his regular price of cigarettes quite a bit and told the "trader" of our proposition. It was arranged for him to come to our room the next night.

The guy was good too. He was supposed to have been a professional in France before the war and it was easy to believe it. He must have started young because he seemed pretty young and he had been a prisoner for over four years. He played anything we wanted. He knew all the numbers it seemed and no one could stump him on anything. He played everything using all of the instruments, not just picking out a tune. Of course he played all the tunes like, "Beer Barrel Polka", "You Are My Sunshine", "Star Dust" "St. Louis Blues" and everything. He wound up his concert by playing the French and American National Anthems. We just sat there in the dark enjoying the music. The evening had been well worth the cigarettes.

It was a funny thing about American cigarettes and their value. I couldn't figure out why they were in such demand. You could get almost anything if you had enough of them. I honestly believe you could have bought your way out of the camp with them. If some way you could have insured the Germans of so many cartons of cigarettes they would have let you out and taken you back to your lines. The Germans seemed to have plenty of their own cigarettes but they wanted ours. I can't see anything so complicated in making cigarettes that they couldn't have their own made just like ours.

Toward the end of January rumors came through the grape vine that the Russians were getting close. Even though the rumors were strong we weren't sure of them but hoped they were true. We weren't thinking about being liberated by the Russians for we knew the Germans would move us before they reached us. However, it would mean that if the Russians were getting close they must have penetrated into German territory. It would mean that the war was getting close to being over. We figured the Germans wouldn't fight on their own soil very long. After all, we were only about forty miles east of Berlin where we were now.

One thing that made us doubt the Russians were very close was the lack of air activity. We figured if the Russians were very close they would have their planes out in droves attacking German towns, road and communications. We hadn't even seen or heard a Russian plane. The only air activity was from the west where Berlin and Stettin were being bombed.

A thing that made us think the Russians might be fairly close was the fact that the German guards were now walking their posts with full packs, helmets and all. Another thing was we didn't have any light in our barracks at night. The Germans said they had to save power for a few days.

At night we strained our ears for sounds of artillery. Occasionally a rumble of artillery seemed to come in faintly. Some thought it was thunder off in the distance. Even though it was hardly more than a faint whisper of a sound I was convinced that it was artillery. I had heard too much of it in the past to be mistaken. They didn't have thunderstorms this time of year anyway. I was sure it was artillery but was afraid to be optimistic.

On the evening of January 30th, the Germans told us to be ready to move out early in the morning. The rumors were true then, the Russians were getting close. The rumor that they had been making a big push must be true and they must be pretty well inside the German border and threatening to overrun us. Everyone was pretty excited now and hopeful that the war would really end very soon. If the Russians were threatening this area and Berlin was only about forty miles from here they couldn't hold out much longer. We wondered where we were going to be taken. At least it would be a change of scenery but we were looking for a tough go of it. No doubt where we would go would be overcrowded and food even scarcer than here. It was our only hope to have the war end very soon. We stayed up very late talking over the situation.

Some were actually afraid of the Russians. They figured if we were over run by the Russians we wouldn't be any better off than we were now, maybe worse. There was talk of being sent to the salt mines. I reminded them that we were supposed to be allies of the Russians. A couple of the fellows seemed to know more about the Russians than I did. They said being their allies wouldn't mean anything to them. I thought surely they wouldn't be that bad. Time would tell I guess.

Before dawn the next morning the Germans were around routing us out. We could hear artillery booming off in the distance plainly now. The Russians were close alright. They we closer than we had hoped for. We were hoping they would reach us before they got us out of the camp.

We tried to stall as much as we could. One company

would be ordered out of the barracks. As soon as they got the next company out, the first one would go back in their barracks. It took them a couple of hours to get us all out and ready to move. Then, when we were all lined up and ready to go, the Germans changed their minds and told us to go back to our barracks. By now we could hear machine gun and rifle fire in the woods not too far to the east of us.

We were wrong though because in a few minutes they began routing us out again. We tried stalling again but weren't all successful. The Krauts weren't fooling around with us this time. They came at us with rifles swinging and Tommy guns threatening.

They finally had us all lined up along the barracks. There were plenty of guards. It seemed as though there were almost a guard for everyman. The whole camp was being abandoned and all of the Germans were going with us. As we stood there lined up with the Germans pointing their guns at us it suddenly dawned on us that as long as they couldn't get us out, they were going to shoot us down. We talked it up among ourselves that if they started shooting, rush them and try to overpower them. It would be a slim chance but it would be our only chance. The Germans dragged one fellow out of line, held a pistol at his head and asked us if we were going to march. We said that we would.

There was plenty of snow on the ground and as we started to move, and it started snowing heavily. We turned right from the camp and headed in the direction of Berlin. The Germans had told us that it would be a couple of days march so we figured we were going to somewhere in the vicinity of Berlin. For the march they had given us each a couple of slices of bread and a small piece of baloney.

The machine gun and rifle fire sounded close, but it looked like we were going to get away.

We carried all of our worldly belongings with us. Mine wasn't much. Just the bread and meat and my blankets. I also had my new G.I. pants rolled up in my blankets. I still had my old crummy ones on. I don't know what I had been saving the new ones for.

We plowed down the road through the snow. We soon discovered that this march wasn't going to be an easy one. We were well run down from not having enough to eat and we hadn't had any real exercise in months.

Most of the Germans had sleds or had fashioned crude ones and were pulling their stuff along with them. They, of course, had considerable more baggage than us but I surmised that they were taking just a small amount of their stuff and abandoning most of it. One guard had a big bag of stuff and handed it to me to carry. I noticed, among other things, in one bag were a couple of loaves of bread. I figured that if I was still carrying the bag by night I would try to hide out from that particular guard and have a couple of loaves of bread to myself. He probably wouldn't recognize me in this mess of G.I.s. He probably wouldn't let me have the bag after dark either.

Our compound had moved out of the camp first. Company One had moved out first and the companies in order following. Our company was number ten so there were about nine hundred men ahead of us. The other compound had followed right behind us. There were about two thousand Americans in the column and our company was just about in the middle.

After about a two mile march we passed through a small village. The villagers just watched us without expression. I saw a good looking blond girl in slacks leaning against the doorway of one of the houses watching us go by. She was the first woman I had seen in four months. I wondered what the people were thinking. They didn't seem excited. It was hard to believe they didn't know the Russians were mighty close.

A short distance out of the village things started happening. The head of our column was probably a half mile ahead. Suddenly we heard a shell smash in up ahead. We looked at one another and then the guards, wondering what had happened. We kept on moving ahead though. Another shell crashed in and then another. Up ahead we could see men scattering out into the snowy fields on both sides of the road. More shells whammed in and a few spent pieces of shrapnel dropped close by.

The word was passed back for us to turn around and head back for the camp. We had run head on into the Russians. Some of the Krauts had gotten between us and the way to Berlin. We didn't need any urging. We turned around and started back at a fast clip. The guards were in a hurry too. Many of them were abandoning their sled and packs. I looked around for the guard who belonged to the big bag I was carrying. I didn't see him so I pitched the damn thing away. We didn't run but moved at a pretty good pace.

We soon reached the village again. I was expecting the Russians to plaster it with an artillery barrage any second. I wanted to get on through it as soon as possible.

I just couldn't understand the attitude of the people in the village. They didn't seem even a bit concerned that the Russians were so close. They just seemed to be going calmly about their business. Either they knew that their route to escape was blocked and they had resigned themselves to their fate or they didn't have any idea the Russians were so close. I was inclined to think the latter theory. I don't know what they thought that artillery was, but I don't think they thought it was the Russians.

We went on back towards the camp. A lone soldier with a panzerfaust (A weapon. Something like our bazooka), pedaled toward the Russians. There was a guy going to his certain death without even a ghost of a chance. A single panzerfaust against no telling how many Russian tanks.

Finally we reached the camp and went back to our barracks. We thought it was all over as far as the Germans were concerned. We figured all we had to do now was wait for the Russians to come and take over the camp.

The Germans weren't through yet though. They got us out of the barracks again by telling us that they were going to shell the camp as soon as the Russian approached. We knew that was possible too because we had heard artillery firing while we were in the camp. The Germans apparently had an artillery range nearby.

We moved out of the camp again, this time turning toward Krustin. A short distance down the road we headed out into the open fields. We went only a few yards. In fact, this second time we never got more than a couple of hundred yards from the camp entrance. Machine gun and rifle bullets began to zip overhead. We looked out and saw Russian Infantry coming across the field in skirmish formation. This really blew the lid off of things.

There was great confusion now. We didn't know what direction to go in. Most of us wanted to go back to the camp. The damned camp seemed like a home, a refuge now. The Germans were screaming for us to move toward Krustin with them. They pulled guns on some of the boys and forced them to go with them. One guard was yelling at me to come along. I turned my back on him and started toward the camp. I held my breath, expecting a bullet any second. Many guards were returning to the camp too.

Machine gun bullets were zipping around thicker now. When I got back inside the camp I first went to the air raid shelter. The shelters were already crammed to capacity. There were only a couple of them and not very well constructed. Some jerk stood in front of one with a shovel. He told me if I took one more step he would bash my head in. I didn't think the air raid shelter was a very good place to hole up anyway. I told the jerk to go to hell and took off for the barracks.

By the entrance to our compound stood the German Officer that had had the Germans classes. As I passed he said, "It's alright lad, it's alright lad". I don't know what he meant. He looked pretty worried. I guess he figured his time was up. I was happy. Our allies, the Russians, were here and we were going to be liberated. I did wonder why they had shelled us back down the road but figured there must be some explanation.

As I walked down the row of barracks toward my room a burst of machine gun bullets ripped into the roof above my head. I was sure the Russians were keeping everything high. Just more or less warning shots. A lot of bullets had zipped overhead. Nothing seemed to be low. I hadn't seen anyone hit anyway.

I was the first to reach our room. Finally, Scotty and Smith came straggling in. We sat there waiting for developments. Most of the fellows, including Graves and Leura, came in.

We heard the Russian tanks grumbling past in front of the camp and could hear them firing guns and machine guns. Then most of them had come down the road toward Krustin, practically ignoring the camp. A couple had stopped in at the camp. We figured it was best to stay in out of the way and let the Russians do what they wanted. I was anxious to get a good look at them and see how they looked and what they dressed like. Well, it was January 31sr, 1945, the day of our liberation.

We got the reports that they had rounded up all the Germans and taken them to the shower house and slaughtered them. A guy that had just come from there told us what he had seen. He wanted me to go back with him and take a look. I didn't go. I wasn't in the mood to see blood and guts right now.

Sometime during the night I got my first glimpse of our liberators. A Russian soldier came to our room. He lighted up a newspaper and looked around. He was looking for any Germans that might be hiding there. I couldn't see him very well but he looked very young, almost a kid. Someone gave him a cigarette and by the tone of his voice he seemed pleased.

We didn't have any Germans hiding in our room but I guess some of the boys in other rooms had hidden them. It seemed odd that a person should feel sorry enough for their enemy to try to hide them from being killed. War is certainly a weird pastime.

Just before dawn the next morning we were startled by a lot of racket. In a second or two we recognized the noise of rockets. At least I recognized what they were, although most had never heard them before. I could remember the sound of the ones that had been fired as we made the Southern France landing. The Russians really laid out a barrage of them. Their artillery was banging away too. We figured they were shelling Krustin. We wondered how the boys that had been forced to go with the Germans to Krustin were making out.

The Germans weren't all through yet either. At the crack of dawn the sky was black with their planes.

Whoever said that the Luftwaffe was dead was crazy. At least it wasn't dead here. I had never seen so many planes, American or German, in the sky at one time as this in the war. They seemed to bring out everything they had including the old Stuka dive bombers. I hadn't even seen a Stuka before. They had quit using them on the Western Front a couple of years ago.

They bombed and strafed all around the camp. We wondered where the Russians Air Force was and where their anti-aircraft guns were. The German planes were flitting around getting no opposition except for a small arms fire. The planes were having it pretty much their own way and seemed to be having a field day.

The G.I.s also got busy. At the crack of dawn we were swarming all over the camp. We raided the warehouses and Officer Headquarters. We found plenty of German cigarettes and some food. One bunch even found a battery set radio and got it going. We chopped down some of the big posts that held the barbed wire and built roaring fires. We actually didn't need hot fires now though. The weather had taken a big change from the day before. We were having one of those winter thaws and the air actually seemed balmy. We wondered what the guards would say now if they could see what we were doing to their camp. They wouldn't get a chance to see now. All of them that had come back to the camp had been killed by the Russians.

Someone had found an American Flag and draped it over one of the barracks. It was a beautiful sight. No one could understand what it represents until they are in a spot like this. Completely away from American authority and from American people. It does mean baseball, hot dogs, freedom, kindness, security and everything good that is available in this lousy world. Some of us, while in the comforts of home or with a bar room orator, can call it corny or flag waving. Get in a position like this and every word is true.

The Russians artillery and rocket barrages and the German anti-aircraft kept up a terrific pace all day. The booming of the artillery and the crashing of shells, rockets and bombs kept the ground constantly trembling.

The Germans were bombing so near the camp we were afraid they would get us. They were bombing and strafing the road in front of the camp and in the fields on all sides. Some of the bombs or bullets could easily go astray. They also might strafe us for the hell of it. We didn't think they would hardly do it having so many more important targets, but you could never tell. Too, it might make someone sore seeing an American Flag flying from one of their prison camps.

We decided that we had better make a move to try to give ourselves a little protection. We tore up part of the barracks floor and dug a trench big enough for all of us to pack into. We ran one of the trenches out to the end of the barracks for an exit. We piled the surplus dirt from the trench on top of the floor for added protection. We figured that our place would now stop at least thirty caliber bullets. Of course, a hit with a bomb and it would all be over.

The battle raged on. There was the constant din from exploding bombs and shells. They sky was full of German planes. It seemed as though the Russians were getting the worst of it right now. They didn't seem to have anything to cope with the German planes. They were losing a lot of men and equipment from the bombing. We still wondered where the Russian Air Force and anti-aircraft were. We hadn't seen a Russian plane yet. All that seemed to be here was a Russian armored spearhead with some artillery and infantry.

I couldn't figure out what had happened and why the Russians were here in the first place. We had heard rumors that the Russians were driving in our direction but we hadn't seen any preparations by the Germans to meet them. Not right around here anyway. It seemed as though as close to Berlin as we were they would have made all sorts of defenses. We figured that the Russian drive had moved a lot faster than they had figured on or they had had their army in this area surrounded and cut to pieces. I guess the Russians were just over whelming them by sheer weight of numbers. Probably the Germans didn't have enough men and equipment to hold them back. It would take a lot of stuff to fight on two fronts like they were and be successful. They didn't seem to be lacking in planes here though. I had never seen anything like it before.

When night fell some big German railroad guns began to throw shells in pretty close. The crash from them made the ground shake. We wished that we could get out of this place. They said the lines were very fluid and unstable. They said in a day or two the bulk of their infantry would be here to consolidate their gains.

During the night those big shells kept whamming in and there was scattered rifle fire. The night did pass rather quietly considering the situation.

Early the next morning the fireworks commenced again. It was a bright sunny day, ideal for an air force. The Germans planes came over again as thick as flies. Again they bombed and strafed all around the camp. Some bullets splattered into the compound.

We had to hand it to the Krauts for not bombing us intentionally. They would have been justified too for there were Russians and a couple of Russian tanks in the camp. They had plenty of targets outside the camp though and it wouldn't have done them any good to kill off a bunch of defenseless men even though we were their enemy. However, they did drop bombs in the camp. I happened to be out watching the planes flitting around. Suddenly I noticed one diving straight in my direction. It gave another little dip and I saw bombs fall from it. I was about twenty feet from the barracks. I raced for the door and by the time I reached it I could hear the bombs whistling. I ran inside yelling that we were being bombed and jumped into the trench with about twenty guys right on my heels. The bombs hit and they shook the ground.

The bombs crashed nearby but not nearly as close as I thought they would. There were two bombs dropped and they landed in the French compound. One bomb made a direct hit on a barracks killing eighteen men by flying shrapnel. They were from the other compound and fellows that knew them buried them there.

It was apparent now that the Russians had been stopped cold. The Germans were making a determined stand here along the Oder River. We wished that the Front would move on. We didn't like being right here in the front lines. Also, we wanted to get out of here and get going. We listened to the BBC (British Broadcasting System) news reports. It told about the gigantic struggle that was going on around Krustin. They were telling us! We were right in the middle of it.

Night came again and with it comparative quiet. Now that the Germans had stopped the Russians and knowing the Germans, I expected a counter attack. If they gained back any ground at all they would be right back with us. I wouldn't care to see them now after the way we had looted and torn up the camp. I imagined they would take a dim view of what we had done. I wanted the Russians to push the Front a little further on. We were all anxious to get out of this place.

We learned what had happened the day the Germans tried to move us. Of course we knew we had run head on into Russian armor. Their story was that seeing a couple of thousand men marching toward them they thought it was the enemy. They said they thought we were Hungarians. Hungarian troops have uniforms about the same color as ours. Their shelling hadn't done our boys any good though. Several had been killed and several were wounded.

The next morning was a repetition of the others. It was another bright sunny day and the German planes were out in force. Still, there was not a sign of Russian air craft. We just couldn't figure it out. I was beginning to wonder if they even had an Air Force.

The Stuka dive bombers would circle around one edge of the camp and release their bombs. We could see the bombs go sailing over the camp and crash into Russian positions on the opposite side of the camp. We kept hoping that those Kraut bombardiers knew what they were doing and wouldn't drop a few short and on us. Sometimes so many bombs went sailing over the camp it looked like it was raining bombs.

The Stuka dive bombers fascinated me. I had never seen any in action before. The M.E. 109's Messerschmitts that they were using here were of course very familiar. The Stuka seemed awfully slow and flimsy. It was easy to see why they hadn't been used against the Americans or British for years. They wouldn't last two minutes over our lines. Here they were having a field day though. They could dive straight down but they were slow. Sometimes several of them would get in a long line and dive down one at a time. When they would get in this formation and start diving it sort of reminded me of a big roller coaster. The Stukas sort of reminded me of a giant wasp. Their landing gear wasn't retractable and it hung there like the legs of a wasp.

I remembered the stories of the dreaded Stuka at the beginning of the war. It showed how much things had improved as far as planes went. These planes were completely obsolete now. Well, almost obsolete. They still seemed to use them against the Russians.

About noon we could see a big flight of American planes over Berlin. They were receiving plenty of flak. After they bombed Berlin they swung wide in our direction. One of the big bombers was dropping behind the formation. When the rest of the formation turned and headed back toward the west this crippled one kept coming in our direction. We didn't know if it was out of control or if it was trying to make it to the Russian lines before the crew had to bail out. In any event it didn't make it. Suddenly smoke began to stream from it and it nosed earthward. We saw four or five parachutes blossom out. All of the guys must not have gotten out because I think a bomber of that size carried a crew of at least eight men. The big plane plunged down whirling faster and faster. Suddenly there was a big roar from its motors and the plane seemed to slow up and start falling to pieces. The plane was almost completely disintegrated when it disappeared behind some distant woods. Dozens of pieces from it floated slowly down. The chutes soon disappeared behind the woods too.

Late in the afternoon the sky began to get overcast. About dark the Russians told us to get ready to move out. We didn't need much urging this time. Within a few minutes we were all lined up and ready to go.

The whole camp was taking off. There were columns

of Italians and French and Russians getting ready to pull out. As we stood there a shot rang out and a bullet zinged by. I thought it might be a German sniper holed up somewhere and doing a little harassing. It may have just been that some Russian had accidently discharged his gun.

We moved out of the camp in the very last rays of daylight. There were supposed to be a couple of Russian guides up ahead someplace to lead us back through the lines.

We moved out of the camp and started down the road we had taken a few days before.when the Germans had tried to get us out. Along the road by the camp lay a lot of stiff, silent bodies. Most of them were former guards. There was also a burned out Russian tank there.

After only a few yards we turned north off the road and started going through open fields. We heard a lone German plane droning overhead. All through the war the Germans had a peculiar habit of sending lone planes over the lines just after dark. Some kind of recon plane I guess. They never dropped any bombs and they never fired on us. The fellows from the Normandy Front called it "Red Check Charlie".

Just ahead we could see a Russian artillery piece firing from a thicket. We could see its shells landing over to our left. I judged that they were falling in the vicinity of that little village we had gone through a couple of days ago. A fire was burning brightly where the shells were landing.

The going was pretty tough. The ground was soft and soggy and we splashed through icy pools of melted snow. The pace of the march increased until we were soon going at almost a run. We kept passing up Russians that had been in the camp with us. They just couldn't keep up the pace. Some would drop from sheer exhaustion and just lay there on the wet ground. They had been in the prison camp too long and just couldn't take it. Most of them had been in prison camps three years and longer. Most of them were in bad shape with T.B. and other diseases.

We kept plunging on through the darkness at a terrific pace. We reached a paved road and turned east on it. We soon reached a woods. There seemed to be some Russian equipment in this area. Occasionally a truck would pass. We even spotted horses and wagons. The trucks that we saw here seemed to be the old model "A" Ford types.

To the north a gigantic artillery duel seemed to be in progress. From the sound of the guns they must have been the huge railroad type guns.

We passed on through the forest. The pace began to slow. It seemed that we were turning back and going around Krustin from the north. Our pace slowed even more, and we stopped often for short intervals.

Once a group of Russian soldiers passed close to us. They reeked to high heaven of perfume. I guess they had gotten some while looting houses and had put it on themselves for the hell of it.

Out of the woods again we could see fires burning brightly all around. It appeared that the Russians had set fire to may farmhouses. I began to wonder about our "liberators". I sensed that these people were a lot different from us. I hadn't actually had much contact with them yet but just sensed something. It seemed we had a lot of things in common with the French, Italians, English and Germans, but these guys were a lot different. Seeing farmhouses burning around the countryside made me think of when the Mongol Hordes swept out of the east and had almost overrun all of Europe. In the darkness it even appeared one of the soldiers was wearing a spotted animal skin of some kind.

It didn't make me think much more of them when the Russian soldiers began to stop us and take watches, rings and other valuables someone might still have been able to hang onto. These were our allies? Hell, the Germans didn't rob you and they were our enemies. I figured that there was a slim possibility that they didn't know who we were. They might have thought that we were German or some ally of the Germans. It was dark and they might not have known but I doubted it.

We turned off the road and started going through a muddy field again. We waded in knee deep mud toward a huge barn. We figured that this was where we would stay for the rest of the night. However, we stood around the barn in knee deep icy mud for some time. No one seemed to know what to do and no order was given to enter the barn. I actually wished I was back in the prison camp right now. Finally, we started moving again. We passed down through a narrow, slippery ravine and then out onto a paved highway again. A few Russian trucks were moving on this road. What seemed strange to me was that the trucks weren't driving black out. They had their lights on. Although there weren't many of them and they didn't seem to be traveling in any sort of convoy, the idea of driving with the lights on so close to the Front seemed odd. In our army it certainly wouldn't have been tolerated.

Everything was in confusion now. There wasn't any kind of organization among us now and no one seemed to know what to do or where to go. Apparently the Russian guides had left. There may not have been any to begin with.

We approached and stopped on the edge of a village.

We stood waiting for someone or something to give us the word what to do. We stood there waiting for about two hours. Everyone was cold and miserable. I was so cold that my legs were absolutely numb from the knees down. In fact, I felt like I was standing on my knees.

At last the word was given to go into the village and bed down for the rest of the night. It was now 3:30 A.M. Everyone was cold, tired and miserable. There was a mad scramble for the village. G.I.s everywhere were scrambling around looking for a half way decent place to bed down. In the turmoil I became separated from everyone I knew.

I wandered into a barn and found some of the fellows I knew including Jack Leura. He said that he had a place for both of us to sleep. He had rounded up some hay and put it on the floor by one wall of the barn. We pooled our blankets and made a pretty good place to lie down. I took off my cold, wet shoes and wrapped my feet in the blankets. As soon as they began to warm up a little I dropped off into a sound sleep.

Jack and I slept late the next morning to about eight o'clock. We woke up talking and laughing. Things seemed much better now that we were free men.

We made our bed right beside two big wooden doors. They were the type of doors that practically all large barns have. They can open wide and are high to let loads of hay and grain in. We heard a couple of voices just outside the doors. We recognized one as German and I said laughingly to Jack that maybe the Germans were making a counter attack. I had no more than gotten the words out of my mouth when a shot rang out and a body plunked on the ground right beside the doors. We looked at one another in surprise. Jack didn't say a word but he reached for his shoes and tip-toed away.

I peeked out a tiny crack in the door and saw the

body lying right beside the door. I couldn't see the face but could see a brown coat. It instantly flashed through my mind that the Russians had shot one of our boys. I hadn't stopped to think that the voices I had heard had been Russian and German. I slowly pushed one of the big doors open a little to take a look. The body wasn't that of a G.I. but a German civilian. He was an old, gray haired man. He had been shot right through the head. I was relieved that it wasn't a G.I. but I began to wonder about our "liberators". I couldn't imagine what an old man like that could have done to them to take him out behind the barn and blow his brains out.

Soon the German planes came swarming all over the countryside bombing and strafing. It was a gray day with low hanging clouds, but it didn't keep the German planes grounded.

We found out that the name of the village we were in was called Zorndorf. It was a very small village. The population was probably around three of four hundred at the most.

We didn't venture out of the barn at all for a while. The German planes were swarming all over the place. There was a constant roar from their motors. Their machine guns chattered madly and there were many explosions from the bombs they were dropping. The Germans were particularly concentrating on the roads running into the village. They didn't bomb right in the village much, probably afraid of killing their own civilians. However, they did strafe and drop small bombs on the main drag running through the town.

From our barn we could see part of the village. There were plenty of Russians around. There were also quite a lot of trucks and horses and wagons around. There were rockets mounted on some of the beds of the trucks.

We got a chance to look the Russians over a little. The uniforms of the enlisted men weren't actually uniforms. For the most part they seemed to be padded and looked like they might be warm. Their footwear was also assorted. Some wore nice leather boots. Others wore shoes with some kind of wrap on leggings. Still others wore what appeared to be rubber boots. On their heads they wore the typical fuzzy Russian hat. They had flaps that could be let down over their ears for protection from the cold.

The officers wore pretty sharp looking uniforms. Their uniforms were brown and seemed to be made from pretty good material. The jacket or tunic was set off by wide green shoulder patches. On these patches were stars, etc. denoting their rank. Practically all of them wore nice leather boots. Their headgear was very similar to that of the enlisted man.

There were also some Russian soldiers in the village. It seemed like their jobs were to direct traffic, sort of like M.P.s. I had heard that there were some women right in the front lines here. I hadn't seen any until now. This was actually almost the front lines. We were only a few miles from the actual front so these women were really on the front lines. These Russian women soldiers were pretty well dressed. They wore green dresses, brown coats and boots of leather. Their hats were similar to the men's only a little fancier. Their hats weren't quite so fuzzy and sometimes the crown had colored braid on them. Most of the girls were on the hefty side but a lot of them were quite cute.

We hung around our barn all day wondering what to do. No one seemed to have any idea what to do or where to go. There was one rumor that at least sounded good. The rumor had it that in the next sizeable town we would come under American control and be taken care of. It was nothing definite but something to cling to. It would be too dangerous to start out right now anyway the way the German planes were working the road over.

Another thing that made us stick close to the barn and try to figure out things was the attitude of the Russians. We didn't know if they even knew that we were Americans and supposed to be their allies. They seemed like a pretty indifferent bunch and not very friendly. Everyone was suspicious of them. There were a lot of G.I.s in this village and you seldom saw one stirring about. It wasn't just the planes, it was mostly the Russians. Everyone seemed to be staying out of their way as much as possible and see if they could figure out what the score was.

These guys shot at anything that moved and some things that didn't. All that I had come in contact with were drunk. It was like being around a bunch of trigger happy drunks. One drunk officer came reeling out of the house that was twenty yards from our barn. He was wearing a top hat and swallow tailed coat that he had picked up in the house. He had his pistol out and was taking pot shots at everything. He began to throw wild shots in the direction of our barn. He was supposedly aiming at the pigeons on the roof. When he reloaded he would almost fall down. We were glad when a couple of Russian gals came out and they all loaded onto a buggy and took off.

Another Russian looped to the gills came into our barn. He fingered his Tommy gun as he looked us over. I wondered what he was thinking. He went out of the barn talking to himself. We heard him go out and around the barn talking to himself. We heard him grind to a halt and stop muttering when he found the body of the old German that had been murdered by the barn doors. After a short pause he pushed in through the doors. He fingered his gun while he told us, mostly through sign language, that the strafing had killed the old man. We nodded and made signs as if to say," Of course the strafing had gotten him". I thought to myself that this guy had done it. I was getting more and more suspicious of our "allies".

I guess this guy didn't turn out to be such a bad fellow after all. After a nasty laugh he left and started feeding some of the Russian horses. Jack and I helped him a little gathering some of the hay for the nags. This apparently pleased him. He went in the house and came rolling out with a bucket. He milked a cow and agave us the milk. The way he leered at us we wondered if he had poisoned the stuff. I guess he was just trying to be friendly in his way.

We figured that from now on food wasn't going to be much easier to get than it had been. It was obvious that we weren't going to get any from the Russian Army. It looked as if we were going to have to live off the land and that might not be too easy. It looked like we were going to have a tough old winter.

Toward evening we ventured out of the barn in search of food. We soon found a few spuds. "Buckshot" Lawrence ran across some of his friends in one of the houses in the village. They had several large jars of homemade meatballs and were kind enough to give Lawrence a couple of jars.

Luera, Rich, Sanders, Cunningham, Lawrence and I were all sticking together so far. One of the bunch had rounded up a frying pan from one of the houses. That evening the six of us had a pretty decent meal of potatoes and meatballs. That night we burrowed in hay in the loft of the barn and had a good night's rest.

The next morning we got up and had a breakfast of potatoes and meatballs. It was a misty, foggy day with the clouds hanging right on the ground. One thing about a miserable day like this, it made the German planes stay on the ground. It was just too cloudy and misty for them no matter how urgent it was to do some bombing. We didn't see or hear a German plane all day. We had yet to see a Russian plane of any kind.

Several of us got together and decided we had to do something. We weren't getting any place hanging around this little town. Some of the fellows had already taken off in small groups. We heard the rumor that the Russians had said that if we got to Landsberg, Germany, which was about forty kilometers from Zorndorf, we would be picked up in trucks and taken where we would get in American control. It sounded good anyway. We figured that it might be possible that the Americans had set up a camp somewhere just for liberated prisoners.

About eight of us decided to take off together. We were centered around Stanley Boruch. He was of Polish decent and we figured we had better be with a guy that could understand some Russian.

We struck out about one o'clock in the afternoon. Someone had gotten the dope from somewhere that we had better try to make it to a little town named Vietz and spend the night there. Vietz was about 15 kilometers (10 miles) away.

We started down the road at a good clip. We wanted to make Vietz before nightfall. It was still misty so no German planes were flying. The road we were traveling on was partly paved. There were plenty of bad, muddy places in it though due to the thaw and melting snow.

Lots of Russian equipment kept coming along the road. There were lots of horses, wagons and buggies. There seemed like miles of horse drawn wagons. What a field day planes could have with a convoy like this. We figured they were taking advantage of the bad weather to move up.

As we sloshed on down the road through the mud and water we passed lots of dead Germans. Most were civilians, lying by the road. In front of nearly every farmhouse lay a corpse or two. Some of the farmhouses had white sheets hanging from a window. This was a sign of surrender I guess. It didn't look like the Russians had paid much attention to the signs of surrender by the number of bodies around. I saw one body in front of a farmhouse with his arms still up as if he had come out with his hands up as a surrender gesture but had been shot down anyway. There were even dogs lying around that had been shot. I imagined a bunch of Russian tanks had come down this road shooting at anything that moved. It was a pretty grim sight.

We reached a tiny village that was about halfway to Vietz. We stopped here long enough to get a drink of water and rest a little. The village was practically deserted except for a few Russians. We stopped to talk to a Russian Officer that was leaning out of a window of one of the houses. There were two girls draped around him kissing him so much that he could hardly talk to us. All three were pretty well loaded. The officer was a good looking fellow and his uniform was nice and neat. He had a Red Star Medal on his chest so I guess he was some kind of a war hero. The gals hanging onto him were civilians so I figured they were German. After seeing the corpses along the road for the last five miles I couldn't see exactly how anyone could be quite this chummy to the invaders. Women are women though and I guess they knew which side their bread was buttered on. We didn't get any information from the guy as to how much further it was to Vietz.

We went on our way again. We passed more farmhouses and through a small ravine. The country around here was very flat as a rule though. Just as we were reaching a main road that ran parallel to the Warthe River we came upon a knocked out Russian gun. It looked like about a 105mm and had been the victim of the German planes. It sat right in the middle of the road. Russians, probably the crew, had taken up quarters in a nearby house. We started talking to the Russians that belonged to the gun. When they found out that we were Americans they were very friendly. This was the first show of friendship I had seen by the Russians. They started handing out bottles of liquor to us. Even though we were all dressed alike and obviously Americans they would ask each one if we were an Americanski. When we said that we were they would hand us a bottle of liquor. They kept repeating, "Roosevelt, Churchill, Stalin, Studebaker, good". They would entwine their fingers to show how close all four of these were. I wondered why they thought the Studebaker was such a buddy. So far the trucks I had seen had been G.M.

The liquor they gave us turned out to be orange flavored gin. We drank the stuff as we hiked down the road. The main road we were on now was a good one. It was well paved and wide. There were plenty of signs of bombing along this road. The German planes must have given the Russian convoys a bad time along here. There were plenty of bomb craters in the highway.

About dusk we reached the little village of Vietz. Boruch asked some Russians where there was a good place to sleep. They pointed to a large house that was deserted. Just as we were entering the house the Russians set fire to a nearby house. Boruch said that they told him they set fire to the house to direct their convoys at night. I think they set fire to it for the hell of it.

The house we moved into was a nice two story place. It was nice and modern with an up to date electric stove, refrigerator and other appliances. There was lots of nice china and silverware in the cupboards along with expensive looking linen table cloths and napkins. The whole house was nicely furnished and everything was intact. Whoever had lived here had taken off in a hurry.

There was plenty of food in the cellar of the place too. There were potatoes, squash, carrots and many kinds of home canned fruits and vegetables. There were also many bottles of wine and other canned juices. We found plenty of eggs out in the hen house.

We all pitched in and began to prepare a meal. Rocco Rich was the head cook and the rest of us just helped. Of course the power was off but the place also had another stove and there was plenty of wood and coal to use in it. We found plenty of candles to light. We set the table with the best china, linen and silverware. We had a meal of potatoes, eggs, meat, stringed beans, bread, several kinds of fruit and wine. It was the best food and best meal I had had since coming over seas. We all got filled up and were in a jovial mood.

A German civilian came into the house, possibly the owner. He asked us not to eat too much or waste any of the food. At first we ignored the guy. Then we got to thinking he had a lot of guts asking us not to eat too much after we had been starving for months. We shooed they guy out of the place in a hurry.

Later we went upstairs to go to bed. In each of the three bedrooms was a corner furnace. We brought coal and wood from the woodshed and stoked up the furnaces. We soon had the bedrooms nice and warm. Smith and I had a bedroom to ourselves. I brought up a couple of quarts of strawberry juice with me for a little bedtime snack. It was delicious stuff. It wasn't a hard drink but like soda pop only better. It tasted like fresh strawberries.

In one of the rooms upstairs Smith and I found some illustrated books on the German armed forces. They were interesting, and we spent some time looking them over. Finally, around midnight we turned in.

The beds were soft, warm and comfortable. This was the first real bed I had slept in since coming overseas. The thing proved too soft for Smitty and me to go to sleep on. We turned and tossed. We had done a good job with the furnace too for it was stifling hot in the room. We just weren't used to being warm and sleeping in a soft bed. Finally, we gave up trying to sleep in the bed. We took a couple of blankets and put them on the floor and lay down on them. We were asleep in minutes.

The next morning, we woke up pretty early. We soon had our breakfast and were ready to go. We were anxious to get to Landsberg and get under American control.

By daylight I got to take a good look around the house we were in. It was a nice place alright. It was comparable to a home in the States of the upper middle income group. It was nicer than anything I had ever lived in or ever expected to live in. What little I had been able to see of Germany so far I was convinced that it had the best standard of living in Europe and maybe even better than the States. Here we were in a strictly farming area in eastern Germany and there were houses like this. No doubt this was above average but more or less standard. Going through Germany on the train I hadn't seen any shanty towns along the way like we have in the States. Towns like Limberg were neat and clean. No rickety buildings in their large cities. I guess it's the nature of the Germans to work hard and have things neat and nice. But why in the hell do they have to spoil it all by liking war. It seems that most of the German people I knew at home had immigrated to the States to get away from the military. While looking around I found three sets of silver in a nice case. I thought it would be a nice to take home for a souvenir.

We left Vietz and headed down the road toward Landsberg at a hot pace. It was another grim gloomy day for which we were thankful. It would keep the German planes away.

There were lots of G.I.s on the highway now. Everyone had the same thought. On to Landsberg! Landsberg was twenty six kilometers from Vietz, in other words about sixteen miles. We kept up a terrific pace all the way. We stopped every hour for a short rest.

The pace began to tell on the boys. Two at a time began to fall out. We figured we would all meet again in Landsberg, so no one thought anything about a buddy dropping out.

Finally, Graves and Smitty dropped out. If I had known that I wouldn't see them again in Europe I would have dropped out with them. Our parting words were, "See you in Landsberg". Ha, ha, ha. That was really going to be a joke. Leura had found a bicycle somewhere and he and a couple of other had ridden on ahead. That was the last time I saw him in Europe too.

I was beginning to feel sick myself. I had eaten too much and drank too much strawberry juice. I was getting to feel downright lousy and it was becoming an effort to keep up.

All along the road were signs of fighting. Wrecked equipment, bodies and dead horses. There were bodies of Germans smashed as flat as pancakes in the road. Apparently if they were killed lying in the road the Russians never even bothered to drag them off the road.

They just ran over them with their tanks and trucks like a rabbit or something. I couldn't help thinking to myself, looking at all this destruction, of an old Nazi Party saying. "Today we rule Germany, tomorrow the world". They sure had fouled up along the line somewhere.

The road we were traveling on was clogged with Russian equipment. There were lots of American trucks as well as their own in the convoy. There were lots of American Sherman tanks too, as well as their Stalin tanks and lighter Russian tanks. There were good sized trucks in the column carrying large barges on them. I figured these were to be used in crossing the Oder and the Warthe Rivers.

Most of the M.P.s (Military Police) who directed traffic along here were women. Boy! They were tough looking characters. They certainly were grim looking individuals with the gun slung across their shoulders. Most looked like they would cut your throat for a dime. I tried to picture our own WACs (Women's Army Corp) in a situation like this. Our girls looked so fragile and delicate compared to these Annie Oakleys.

A Russian Major and his gang stopped us. The major was drunk, in fact stewed. He was surrounded by a weird assortment, most of them seemed to be kids. Most of them didn't look over fourteen. There were both boys and girls. They were a tough looking bunch too. A couple of the girls especially looked rough. They looked like they must have had nails for breakfast instead of Wheaties. The major asked Boruch a few silly questions and finally let us go on our way.

When we finally reached Landsberg we received a shattering disappointment. Instead of trucks to pick us up and American officials to get us straightened out there was nothing. Landsberg was just a battered up town with more Russians. We didn't know what to do or which way to turn. Boruch asked some Russian officers what we should do. They didn't seem to know or care. They said we might as well keep going as there was nothing here for us. They said there might be something at the next town of any size which was a place called Schwerin. It was quite some distance away. In fact, thirty two kilometers.

We were plenty discouraged, and our morale was so low that we would have to reach up to touch bottom. There certainly was nothing for us here. Landsberg was a fair sized town teeming with Russians.

We decided to push on yet today. We finally found the right road to Schwerin. I was really sick now and it was an effort to keep up. We were all tired as we had already walked about eighteen miles today. We weren't in condition for hikes like this.

We hiked on out of Landsberg about ten kilometers and reached a tiny village. We were all pooped and it was getting dark so we decided to spend the night here. We began to look for a place to bed down. There were only a few houses and buildings in this village. A German civilian came out of one of the houses. We were sort of surprised to see him. We had seen only a few Germans since we got out of the camp, alive that is. I guess he had been watching us and knew we were looking around for a place to sleep. He asked us to stay away from his house because his wife was very sick and he didn't want her disturbed. We told him we wouldn't bother them. He was probably telling the truth or he would have been long gone before the Russians got here.

We found a small abandoned house and a mob of us crowded into it. There was a Russian Calvary outfit in the village. They were a rough, tough looking outfit. Their horses seemed a little on the small side and were mangy looking animals. I wondered if these guys were some of the famous Cossacks. These characters looked anything but dashing.

We got some spuds and killed a couple of chickens. I was so sick I couldn't eat a thing. I had chills, felt dizzy and felt like hell in general. I turned in as early as I could. The place we had to sleep in was pretty lousy. We had to sleep on the floor and it was crowded. However, I was able to get a few hours of fitful sleep.

I didn't feel any better in the morning and still couldn't eat. It was another drab day. We figured if this kind of weather kept up, at least a few more days, we might get far enough away from the front lines to be out of too much danger of being strafed.

While browsing around in some nearby buildings I found a bicycle. It didn't have tires on it but I figured that if I could ride it just a short distance it would help. I was feeling so lousy I was willing to take the chance.

We left the village on our journey toward Schwerin. At the edge of the village we had to make our way across a river. The Germans had blown the bridge when they retreated. We wallowed in knee deep mud. The going was tough and I threatened several times to throw my bike away but I kept pushing it along. We finally reached the other side and a little firmer ground. The approaches to the bridge were clogged with the wagons of Polish refugees heading for home. There were lot of them on foot too.

On the firmer ground I tried several times to ride my bike. The tireless wheels would sink down in the soft dirt making riding it real work. I would ride only a few yards and get off and start pushing again.

Soon we reached some smooth pavement. My bike, tires or not, went swell on this road. I was glad I had struggled along with the thing and had not thrown it away. If I hadn't had the bike, I wouldn't have been able to keep up the pace. I still felt sick and very weak.

I would ride up ahead with a few of the other fellows who had bikes. We would then stop and wait for the ones on foot to catch up with us. In this way I was able to get some rest and it seemed as the day wore on I began to feel better. I kept hoping the wheels of the bike would hold together. I knew the wheels without tires couldn't last too long.

I felt almost guilty having the bike. The rest of the fellows were struggling along dog tired. Many dropped out and others dropped back not being able to keep up the pace. Actually we were hurrying faster than need be. We weren't going anywhere anyway. We were on our way to a town named Schwerin and that was about all we knew. I doubt if there was a man in the bunch who believed that we would find any American authority or any help. I knew I didn't.

The G.I.s were getting spread out in the short time we had been out of the camp. We were the first bunch to push up the road. We hadn't seen a G.I. or passed one so we had to be the first ones there. What surprised me was that we hadn't seen a Russian all day. As nice as this road was it had to be a main road of some kind. It was hard to estimate how many G.Is there were in our bunch for they were strung out for a considerable distance. I wondered where Smith and Graves were. I figured they would catch up to me eventually. It was hard to tell though. I imagined fellows were taking off on all sorts of different roads and going in all directions. This particular bunch was heading toward Schwerin because of a rumor of American help. Other groups were probably going in different directions because of similar rumors. It looked like there was going to be a couple of thousand

G.I.s spread all over the landscape before long. It was a case of every man for himself. There was no organization among us. There wasn't anything to organize over. No one, but no one, knew where to go or what to do. It was certain that the Russians weren't going to help us or give us any advice. Everyone felt like me anyway. The further we stayed away from the Russians the better off we would be. No one trusted them. We were more afraid of them detaining us than we were of finding our way home. We all felt like we would very easily wind up in a Siberian salt mine.

In the middle of the afternoon we began to reach the vicinity of Schwerin. We now began to see Russians. The Russians seemed rather friendly and kept asking where our guns were. We wondered what they were talking about.

A little later we found out what they were talking about. As we started passing through a woods on the approach to Schwerin some bullets began to whine round. We turned and headed back the way we had come in great haste. Back with the Russians they said they hadn't been able to take the town yet although they had had it surrounded for a couple of weeks.

I guess that was why they were friendly. They thought maybe we were going to help them take the town. They must have thought we were a tough bunch and were going to take the place with our bare hands.

Now we really didn't know what to do. After a short conference we decided to start back in the direction of Landsberg. It didn't take a great brain to figure that out. It was the only direction to go. After going back down the road a few miles the back wheel on my bike collapsed and I was on foot again.

Finally we reached a "T" road. One road turned back

to Landsberg and the other one straight to where no one knew. We stood at the crossroads for quite a while trying to make up our minds what to do. I figured there wouldn't be much advantage in going back to Landsberg. The whole days travel would be wasted. In fact, we wouldn't be able to get back there before dark. We knew for sure there was nothing for us there. The road straight ahead went into even more unknown. The whole damned mess was frustrating. Actually it didn't make any difference where we went. There wasn't going to be anything we wanted here in this part of the country at all.

Most groups were turning back toward Landsberg. Our little group, for the most part, decided to go straight ahead. Some of the fellows dropped out and started back to Landsberg with the others. I would have given a lot to have a good road map of eastern Germany. I did have a map though. It was the only map in the group and I would bet a dollar the only one in the whole of the "liberated" prisoners. I had a small address book that had a map of Europe in the front pages of it. All of Europe on a map about two inches by three inches. It, of course, was of no use.

The only ones left in our group now were Nick Alfreda, Rex Badder, Junior Haworth, Cecil Robatille, Ray Gagnon, Stanley Boruch, Camelo Virgo and me.

We had gone only three or four kilometers past the crossroad when we came to a tiny village. It was getting dark by now so we decided to stay here all night. The village consisted of a dozen or so houses and was completely deserted. There were no civilians or Russians to be seen.

In front of the house we moved into were the bodies of a couple of dead Russian soldiers. They must have been there several days. They were wearing the white capes that camouflaged them in the snow. The snow had been all melted for about a week now. I wondered if the Russians didn't even pick up their own dead. They must surely do that? This might have been just a small action here and they had been overlooked. We didn't see any Russians around so maybe they hadn't been back down the road since the first time through.

Food was a little tougher to find in this place. However, we were able to find enough potatoes, carrots and eggs to put together to eat. I was feeling much better by now and was able to eat a little.

There was a little bicycle shop in this town. Haworth found a brand new bicycle. In fact, it wasn't quite all assembled yet but all the parts were there. A couple of others found pretty good bikes. I found one that was pretty good except that it didn't have a front tire. I was tickled to get some sort of transportation anyway. It was rough to ride a bike with only one tire. Haworth and Robatille had the only bikes that had two tires. All of us in our group had bikes now and this was pretty encouraging. We could make pretty good time now. We didn't have any idea where we were going but we could make it faster this way.

We talked over the situation and discussed where we should go and what we should do. I suggested that we find a good place right here in Germany and sweat out the war. I argued that it wouldn't last much longer. After all we had been liberated about forty miles from Berlin and the Allies in the west must be driving. A small group like ours could get in a well-stocked house and could take it easy until the end of the war. I argued that this going toward Poland didn't seem too good. We were just getting away from our own troops. I figured that when we got out of Germany food might be much harder to find. The weather was bound to turn cold again and it would get colder the farther east we traveled. I had a lot of good points to argue but was badly out numbered.

The rest of the fellows seemed to think that we would soon reach American aid here somewhere. They even wanted to push on to Warsaw if necessary. They, as well as myself, were suspicious and afraid of the Russians. The Russians hadn't been treating us exactly like we were allies. They made no attempt to help us in the way of food or anything else. They wouldn't even give us any information on what to do or where to go. Maybe they didn't know but it seemed more like they just didn't give a damn. They weren't treating some of the boys any too good either. They held them up on the highways and had taken their coats and valuables. They had even taken some of the bikes from them. If they stopped you and took your stuff it was like robbery. There wasn't a damned thing you could do about it. They were the boys with the guns and they made you understand they wouldn't hesitate to use them.

Everyone wanted to get out of this damned Europe as fast as they could, including me. I couldn't see the advantage of traveling east when home was west. The rest of the fellows wanted to push on. Of course, I was going to go with them. I didn't have any intention of staying here and sweating it out by myself.

We did figure that we would go clear to Warsaw if we had to find some sort of American authority. We reasoned that Warsaw was the capital of Poland and there would surely be some sort of American authority there.

The next morning we took our time getting breakfast and ready to go. It was another foggy day. It had been surprisingly warm the past week. Here it was only the first part of February and we were on the Eastern Front where the winters are supposed to be tough. I guessed we weren't far enough east and north to get in the bitterly cold weather. Still this might just be a February thaw and it could still get awfully cold in a few days. We hoped this warm weather could last a little while longer.

We hit the road and were on our way about nine o'clock. During the night lots of G.Is had taken this road. There were also wagon after wagon loads of Poles heading for Poland. We passed French, Italian, Yugoslavians, Czechs, Belgium and Greek soldiers. All seemed to have the same thought in mind and that was to get out of here and get home as soon as possible. We figured from the amount of refugees on this road it just might go somewhere. We didn't see any Russians or their equipment moving along it.

We hit some good paved road and our little group of eight began to pass everyone up. We were all elated over the fact that we had been lucky enough to get bicycles. We hoped they would hold together for a while. With our bikes we were soon ahead of the hundreds struggling along the road.

Sometime later we reached a small town. The place was completely deserted. There wasn't a living soul here but us. The place was in shambles and depressing. Many of the houses and buildings had been burned down and some were in shambles from shelling. There were the corpses of several German civilians lying around in the streets and sidewalks. I saw one kid that didn't look more than ten lying under a stone bench. There was a big hole in the side of his head. He was wearing one of those Hitler Youth uniforms.

We entered one of the houses in search of food. Here we found a pretty blonde girl in a black riding habit sprawled face up on the floor. She couldn't have been more than nineteen or twenty. We couldn't see any marks on her and we wondered why she had died. The house was completely ransacked.

In a shed in the back of the house I found a good girl's bike. It was a deluxe model with balloon tires, a speedometer and head light. The speedometer and headlight wouldn't work but the tires were in good shape and inflated. I was glad to find the bike because the front wheel on my bike was just about ready to collapse. I wondered if this bike had belonged to the dead girl inside the house.

We made our way around a few more corpses and left the town much to everyone's relief. The death and destruction and the silence of the place gave us the willies. You couldn't escape it though. All along the road since we had left Zorndorf that first day, death and destruction was all we had seen. Dozens of corpses, hundreds of dead horses, burned and shelled out homes. All along the way was wreckage of all kinds. Hundreds of bikes and pieces of bikes, clothes, personal belongings, guns, autos, dead dogs, uniforms and everything imaginable. It looked like a huge tidal wave had swept through the countryside.

I figured the Germans must have been fleeing on all these broken up and abandoned bikes. When one broke down they would throw it in the ditch and go on by foot. Probably the dead horses were for the same reason. When a horse would play out they would kill it to keep it from falling in the Russians hands. It looked to me that the Russian tanks might have caught up with the fleeing Germans and raised havoc. I wondered how much time the Germans had to evacuate. It looked as if they heard the Russians were coming and just rushed out the door. In the houses we had gone into everything seemed to be intact. Of course lots of them had been looted etc. but the ones that hadn't looked as if the owners had just gone down to the corner store. Clothes, personal belongings and everything else was still there. It appeared to me they just didn't have any warning beforehand and just didn't have time to take anything, even their valuables.

Seeing all this carnage made me hope that something like this would never happen in my country. Sometimes I had wondered why we were clear over here fighting a war that seemed only remotely connected to the United States. If there had been even a remote chance that something like this could happen to our country we should jump into the war immediately.

Along the road we would run across groups of dead German soldiers. They would usually be around a culvert, a ditch or some sort of place for protection. This part of the country was as flat as a pancake with very little if any natural obstacles such as hills, swamps or rugged terrain of any kind. So they had to take up positions along culverts and small ditches.

On down the road sometime later, we rode into a town named Driesen. Although it wasn't a large town it was the biggest place we had hit since Landsberg. This place too was practically deserted. There were only a few Russians around and no G.I.s or other refugees yet.

As we entered the town some joker greeted us with open arms. He was a hawk faced looking character and wore shabby civilian clothes. He had a rifle slung over his shoulder. He could speak German and I figured him for some broken down Kraut that was collaborating with the Russians.

He told us that the Polish border was only up the road a few kilometers and we needed a permit from the Russian Commander in this town before we could cross the border. His story made sense and we fell for it. He also told us that the commander wasn't here today but would be back tomorrow and we could get our passes. In the meantime he said we could stay at the local hotel. This guy was too nice and we should have been suspicious.

The hotel he led us to was a pretty nice place. Howarth and I picked out a room that must have been part of the bridal suite. Here too, the Germans had taken off in great haste. The closets were full of clothes as well as the chest of drawers. There was jewelry on the dresser along with combs and brushes. There were cigarettes on the smoking stand. These people had just rushed out the door with what they had on their backs. From the looks of the amount of clothes and other things the people that lived in this hotel had been permanent residents. Food was pretty easy to find around here and we were soon preparing a meal. This place didn't look like a bad place to spend the night.

Soon the joker that had invited us to stay here showed up with a Russian Officer. The Russian was drunk and even had his cap on sideways. They wanted us to go with them. They led us down the street a block or two to a four story building. A fire was burning on the top floor. They gave us a couple of leaky buckets and wanted us to put out the fire. Some way Boruch talked them out of it.

We returned to the hotel cursing. It was apparent now why he had wanted us to put up in this hotel. We would be handy here for work details.

Soon that bastard came up the stairs again. This time he wanted us to help with a blown out bridge. We told him we would be right down. As soon as the characters left we sneaked downstairs, hopped on our bikes and started beating it out of town.

I'll be damned if we didn't pass a building and there was that same son of a bitch. He yelled at us to stop but we ignored him and kept on pedaling. We came to a grinding halt though when he jerked his rifle off his shoulder and pointed it at us. We went over to him resigning ourselves to a grind of putting in a bridge over some icy river.

This character was growling at us when a Russian officer came out of the building. He asked what was going on here. Boruch told him our story. The officer gave the rat faced character hell, telling him we were Americans and on our way home and not to bother us. He told the guy if he wanted men for work details round up some Germans somewhere. This was truly a break for us and we were grateful. We jumped on our bikes and beat it out of town as fast as we could before they changed their minds.

The Russians were like that though. Inconsistent as hell. You would run into one bunch and they seemed friendly and would even try to be helpful. The next bunch you ran into would be just the opposite. They would rob you and cut your throat for a dime. The way I had it figured the real European Russian was a pretty good guy and half way civilized. It was those ignorant bastards from Russia's far reaching, out of the way places that gave us grief. I imagined a lot of those characters had never heard of America, Germany or anything else.

As we left town we passed a spot where there were about twenty five dead German soldiers. It was evident that they had been rounded up and brought to that particular spot. Each had a bullet hole in his head. We sure were having a lovely tour of Germany. Just think we were getting paid for this too.

I reminded the boys how lucky they were to be here. Paid for a lovely, adventurous, exciting tour of Europe. Just like the civilians say, "You G.Is get all the breaks. We civilians have it tough getting all the booze and cigarettes we need. We do more for the war effort than you guys anyway. We work in the defense plants for hundreds of dollars a week of course. Besides that we buy War Bonds that have a nice fat interest. How many do you buy? Yeah you guys get all the breaks." I don't know whether the boys cared for my sense of humor or not.

After a few more kilometers we reached another small village. There were one or two Russians around the place and a couple of wagon loads of Polish refugees. We found out that the Polish border was only a few kilometers away and this was the last town before we reached it. It was getting dark so we decided that we had better stay here for the night. We picked out the best house in town to stay in. There was a civilian body lying in the front yard of the place. This didn't stop us though. We were getting used to that sort of thing by now. We did check the house and beds when we first moved in. We had heard some guys say that the first night out of Zorndorf they had started to crawl in a bed and there were a couple of stiffs in it. I didn't doubt it a bit. In fact, nothing around here would surprise me.

A little later I got a little shock but not a great surprise. I was out in some nearby barns and out buildings looking for fire wood. I opened a door to a barn and went in. I bumped into the feet of someone hanging from a beam. It was pretty dark in there but there were more than two hanging there. The one I had hit swung slowly. I could feel the nape of my neck tighten. I backed out of the door and looked for firewood elsewhere. I think those people had committed suicide. I guess they figured all was lost and they couldn't bring themselves to being under the Russians. I wondered if they were all from the same family. Another example of the million dollar education one can get from tours like this.

When I went back to the house I told the fellows to go out to the place I had made my discovery. I told them there were a bunch of sex starved blonds out there. They wouldn't go of course for they knew it would be something grisly.

We soon had a good fire going and cooked a little food. Later we retired to the bedrooms. This was a nice home with nice modern furniture. I pictured this place belonging to a rather young couple. Whoever had lain here had taken off in a hurry. Here again everything was intact. We helped ourselves to the cigarettes that were in a modern looking container. We had seen millions of dollars' worth of stuff, just in personal belongings that had been left behind in a few short days. We wondered what would happen to the stuff or if the people who had lived here would ever come back. Boy, what a complicated mess. I had thought about picking up some jewelry from some of these places. I figured I would never get home with it, if I got home. The Russians would probably take it from us. Even if we did get as far as any American Authority it still would probably be taken away. I thought, to heck with it, most of it was probably dime store stuff anyway.

The Poles were helping themselves to stuff. All along the way they had their wagons piled high with loot. They wouldn't make a dent in the amount of stuff though. They deserved everything they took and then some. They spent a lot of years here in Germany as slave labor. They deserved anything they could cart off.

That night as I lay in the soft bed between white sheets, I wondered what the people who owned this place were doing. I wondered if the dead guy out in the front belonged here.

The next morning we got ready and fairly early took off down the road. Soon we came to a small creek. We had been told that this was the border. So this was it. On February 9th, 1945 we crossed over into Poland. We kidded Borush about returning to his Fatherland.

Immediately we began to notice a difference in the appearance of the country. Here in Poland the destruction wasn't so great. There wasn't all the stuff strung along the highways. It seemed the minute the Russians knew they were in Germany they began to destroy, loot, plunder, burn and kill as quickly as they possibly could.

We stopped at a couple of farmhouses. At both of the places the Polish families were just coming home. They were very happy to be getting home. They were friendly and invited us in. They didn't have any food to offer but they boiled some ersatz coffee. When Boruch would tell them he was an American Pole they couldn't seem to grasp what he meant. They must have known that plenty of Poles had immigrated to the States in the past.

We continued passing through a couple of villages. In one of the towns we were able to buy a couple loaves of bread. The loaves were really king sized too. They were about two feet long. I had never seen such large loaves in my life. We bought the bread with German Marks. We were rather surprised that the Poles would accept German money. I figured now that the Germans were gone and going to lose the war their money would be worthless. I guess these people had been using it so long they didn't think anything about it. I guess they had to use something for a medium of exchange. In one of the villages we were told that we had better by pass Posan. There were a large number of Germans there and they were still holding out.

We began to see some Russian planes now. A few fighters flew over very high. One of the fellows who seemed to know said they were American Bel Air Cobras.

We hardly saw any bombers or large planes. One kind of plane we did see by the hundreds though were World War I looking models. They were two winged jobs and small. Everywhere we looked we saw them flying or just sitting around in the fields. If they weren't something left over from World War I they looked it and were about that old anyway. I couldn't imagine what they used them for. They certainly couldn't be used in combat and they were too small to carry any freight. I figured they might have been American or British war surplus from World War I. Maybe after the war they had crated them up and shipped them to Russia. Maybe someone had given them plans for a fighter plane twenty years ago and they were still going by it and manufacturing obsolete planes. Maybe it was like their trucks. Although I never examined one real close I'm sure they were Model "A" Fords. They looked and sounded like about 1930 or 1931 Model "A." I saw brand new ones on flat cars going to the front. They had hardly been driven yet. I figured that back in the early thirties Ford must have set up a plant over in Russia to make trucks. They were still making them the same way. At least that was my theory. The only modern trucks they had were American G.M.C.s and Studebakers. I figured when our trucks wore out the Russian Army would be back on horses and on foot again.

One thing they did have that looked good though was their Stalin tank. It was big and formidable. The gun on it looked like a 120mm. Their motors ran smoothly and sounded powerful. To me it seemed like the best tank in the war. It made our Sherman Tanks look like some obsolete things. That little 75mm on our tank seemed pretty small compared with the gun on these things. I'd hate to think of the outcome of a battle between our tanks and these Russian tanks. I could never figure out why the Americans had such lousy tanks. The English had a pretty good tank in their Churchill and of course, the German Tiger was a good tank. I truly believed these Russian tanks had them all beat though and by a big margin. I understood that this Russian tank had actually been built by an Englishman. He had tried to interest his government and other western countries in it. When they had turned it down he had taken it to Russia and they liked what they saw. They bought it and put it into production.

I was now convinced that the Russians had practically no Air Force to speak of. I had only seen a handful of war planes. When we had been in the fighting around Krustin we hadn't seen even one in action. They just didn't seem to have them. I don't know what they did with all these World War I jobs. They seemed to me that they were absolutely useless. I couldn't figure out why they even bothered with them.

As the day wore on we wondered where we would spend our first night in Poland. We couldn't barge into a well-stocked house now. People were living in all of the houses here. I had a feeling we weren't going to have it as good now as far as food and a place to sleep now that we were out of Germany.

A truck that was heading in the opposite direction stopped and a Russian officer got out. He asked us the directions to some place. We were a fine bunch to ask that sort of question. The guy almost fell over with surprise when he found out that we were Americans. He seemed real happy to see us. He got a big loaf of bread and a bottle of vodka out of the truck and gave it to us. That was the Russians though. You couldn't figure out what they would do next. This guy even looked different from most of the rest. I figured he was a "European" Russian.

BYE FOR NOW

We continued on down the road wondering what to do. We passed a railroad station and inquired about trains. We wanted to know if any passed through here and if they did, how often. No one seemed to know much about it. It was doubtful if the trains kept any kind of schedule. A hit and miss proposition.

We got to talking to a man at the station who told us he knew a woman nearby that had spent several years in the States. He said he knew that she would like to have some Americans to talk to. She had a big house and would be able to accommodate several of us for a few days if we liked. It sounded like a good deal so we let him lead the way. He took off on his bike with us right behind him. We rode some distance. Finally he stopped and pointed to a huge house about a half mile off the road. He said that was the place. The guy didn't go to the house with us but took off down the road.

As we approached the place, we could see several Russian wagons around the place. There were a lot of people working in the nearby fields. We were afraid we were walking into a work detail so we beat it back to the road.

We wondered what we were going to do now. It was getting late and we had no place to go. When we reached the next village it was almost dark. We figured the best thing to do was to go to the police. We found the Police Station and told them our sad story. The "police" station seemed to be more of a headquarters of some sort. Men with rifles slung over their shoulders dashed in and out. They weren't dressed as police or soldiers. I guessed they were part of the Polish Underground or something.

We were treated very nicely though. As soon as Boruch told them who, why and what we were the men there sprang into action. Several took off in different directions and were soon back with meat, potatoes and bread. The meat was in huge chunks looking something like steaks three or four inches thick. They took us down to the village school house and told us we could bed down there for the night. We got some hay from a nearby stack and made some beds on the floor. We tried to figure out a way to cook up the food with our limited facilities. The only utensil we had was an old, beat up pot. We tried to make a stew with the meat and potatoes. The stew wasn't very tasty, not having any seasoning to put in it, but it was food.

When we had come to the school house our bunch were the only ones there. Soon more G.I.s began to straggle in. Lots of soldiers of different nationalities began to make their appearance. Beside the Americans there were French, Dutch, Italians, Belgiums, Yugoslavs, and Estonians. The place was bulging at the seams,

The next morning we got off down the road fairly early. We hadn't gone far when the Russians stopped us. They took Gagnon's bike and overcoat from him. The rest of us were lucky enough to escape. Gagnon's buddy, Robatille, decided to stay and move along with him. The rest of us said we would ride on ahead and wait for them in the next town.

The next town was a place called Kruez. It wasn't too big of a place but seemed to have an important cross roads of some sort. Lots of Russians and their equipment were moving on the two main roads through the town. We moved to the outskirts of town and sat down and waited for Gagnon and Robatille.

Sitting here watching the Russians and their equipment go by made me wonder what made the Russian Army tick. It seemed like everyone worked independently. They seemed to have an undisciplined

BYE FOR NOW

army. I saw no saluting or even anyone that seemed to be in charge of anything. There would be a bunch go by all carrying Tommy guns. Maybe right behind them would come a lone artillery piece or a truck with some rockets on it or maybe a couple of supply trucks. It looked to me that everyone was on their own. I wondered how a seemingly unorganized and undisciplined army like this could have rolled back the Germans like they had. I figured it must be sheer weight of numbers. I figured they kept building up at a point until they had several million troops in one spot. Then the word was given to move forward and they just overwhelmed the Krauts with a mass of humanity.

The biggest single thing that made them a mobile army were American trucks and jeeps. In these last few days I had seen thousands of them. They also had thousands of horses, wagons and buggies. I even saw some guys, oriental looking, riding those hairy Asian camels. It was quite a sight to behold this great horde going down the road.

The Russian Army seemed to move on vodka as well as gasoline. A good many of the soldiers seemed about half crocked. I understood, for instance, that the five gallon cans for extra gasoline on the jeeps were mostly filled with vodka. I didn't doubt it for a minute. The drivers of the vehicles drove like maniacs. As we were sitting here a truck loaded with men and women soldiers came roaring by. They were pulling a small portable kitchen behind them. This section of the road was bad and it was muddy and slippery. The guy driving the truck didn't even slow down. They went careening, slipping and sliding past us. Just beyond us he pulled over toward the side a little to let an oncoming vehicle pass but never slowed. The swaying portable kitchen suddenly hooked a tree that was growing close to the edge of the road. There was a big crash and pots, pans, wheels and things went flying in all directions. The impact jerked the kitchen loose from the truck. The truck didn't even stop. The characters on the back just let out a big cheer. It was obvious they were pretty well fortified with vodka and they just didn't give a damn. That was the Russians for you. Whoever said, "the mad Russians" were right. I just couldn't figure out what made them tick.

We waited quite a while for Gagnon and Robatille but they didn't show up. We figured they might have taken a different road out of Kreuz. We decided to push on, thinking they would probably catch up with us sooner or later anyway. We started pedaling down the road at a pretty good clip. The road was good and we were making pretty good time. We didn't know where we were going but we were making good time getting there. Things were going swell until Alfredo hit a bad spot on the road and fell over. I was riding so close behind him I couldn't stop in time and I ran over the back wheel of his bike and smashed it. That was great. Our pace was slowed down now.

Down the road a mile or two we received a surprise. As we neared a town the G.I.s became thicker. Everyone that had been on the road ahead of us had been stopped by the Russians. They wouldn't let us enter the town and had a road block set up to show us they meant business. They gave no reason for not letting us pass. The Russians didn't need a reason I guess. You never knew what they were going to do next.

We were milling around wondering what to do next. Boruch talked to a Russian. He wouldn't say what the holdup was. He probably didn't know. He said that here was a Red Cross place in a small village on the road to our right. We figured it was another bum steer but there wasn't much we could do but go see what was up.

The village was supposed to be about six miles away. It was getting late so we took off as fast as we could. The road was pretty good so we took turns letting Alfredo ride on our bikes and we covered the distance in pretty good time. It was getting to be dusk when we pulled into the village. It was a small village and not too prosperous looking. Things weren't looking too promising.

However, it did have a Red Cross place set up. It was in the largest building in town. The building was pretty small but it was a two story affair. All they had for us in the way of food was a small piece of bread and some ersatz coffee. G.I.s and others were pouring into the place. It was going to be completely overcrowded. As we lined up for our scrap of bread Boruch said, "To hell with this. I'm going to find some place for us to shack up". We held his place in line and he took off.

Soon Boruch came back and motioned for Haworth, Alfredo and me to come with him. He had found a place for us to stay. It was the best looking house in this tiny village and was almost directly across the street from the Red Cross place. Boruch said he had asked the guy there if he and three of his friends could stay for the night. The fellow had said it was O.K. if we weren't lousy. Of course Boruch assured him we weren't. The only one of us that did have lice was Boruch himself. I was glad now that I had thrown in with Boruch. The only reason we had gotten this place to stay was he was a Pole and could talk to these people.

We entered the house and were welcomed by a couple of fellows that were sitting in the living room drinking. They had apparently been drinking quite a while because they seemed pretty high. They were friendly though and seemed real glad to see us and help us out. One of the fellows I guessed to be in his forties and the other, a nice looking blonde fellow, to be about twenty five.

They poured us a big stiff drink of good liquor and they had cigarettes. They kept apologizing to Alfredo, Haworth and me for not being able to talk to us and not being able to speak English. Of course Boruch was the only one of us that could speak Polish. In this language, if you don't know it you can't even catch word now and then. In Italian, French or even German a word now and then is similar to English and even if you don't understand the language very well you are able to get by a little. This language is completely different. We were plenty satisfied to sit there and drink their liquor, smoke their cigarettes and let Boruch make the conversation. Boruch would tell us once in a while what they were talking about.

Soon the young fellow got up and took off. Apparently, he was just a neighbor and didn't live here. We sat there and continued to drink and smoke with the older man. Through Boruch we found out that they didn't like the Russians any better, if as well, as the Germans. He said the people around here were looking forward to help and friendship from the United States.

An hour later a girl burst in the door. I figured her to be about twenty four. She was quite cute. A little on the hefty side but not really bad at all. What you could call "pleasingly plump" I guess. Her name was Anna.

She bustled around the place straightening it up. I wondered if she was this guy's daughter or what. Soon another woman and a couple of small children made their appearance. I figured they were the family of the fellow. I still couldn't figure out where this Anna fit in. This apparently was a dairy and was either owned or operated by these people. There were several large barns out in the back full of cows. Maybe this Anna was a bookkeeper or something for the place. She was much older than the kids to belong to the same family. Maybe a relative.

Alfredo decided to go back across the street to the Red Cross place. He said he had spotted a buddy there from the fighting days and wanted to talk to him. I thought he was crazy to give up a place like this. I wondered if he wanted to see his buddy or was suspicious of something. Anyway he took off.

The women busied themselves getting food together. They were preparing the stuff in a large kitchen adjoining the living room. They brought the food to us in the living room. The meal consisted of a couple of kinds of meat, potatoes and bread. The food was good and it really hit the spot. When we would finish one plate of food it would be filled up again. When we protested that maybe we were eating food that they might need themselves the man said, "You people will pay us back tenfold". I don't know where they got the confidence that the United States would do so much for them. I hoped they would for these were swell people. In fact, all of the Poles I had come in contact in with so far were real nice people.

After we had eaten all we could hold the dishes were cleared and we sat there continuing to drink. The fellow was getting pretty high, but he was still friendly and gracious.

Haworth was sick. He had been sick all day but now he was really feeling grim. He seemed to have a fever like he might have the flu. Anna and the older woman made over him. They got some medicine out that must have been powerful. They got a tablespoon of sugar and put a few drops of this clear looking stuff on it. Haworth was out like a light a few minutes after taking it. They tucked him in on the davenport.

A little later another girl came in. Boruch's eyes just about came out of their sockets when he saw her. I guess mine did too. She was a downright beautiful blonde. She was a friend of Anna's and had come here to spend the night. She was afraid of the Russians and wanted to be around where there were more people. The guy told us that everyone was afraid of the Russians. He said the kids wouldn't even go out to the toilet after dark.

The house we were in was situated close to the street. We could bear Russians crunching up and down outside. There would be an occasional shot. Probably some drunk Russian firing his gun. I didn't blame the people for being leery of them. I was too.

We found out from these people that there was a railroad station about two miles from the village. They didn't know how often the trains came through here but had heard some in the last few days. We planned to go there and wait for one to come through the next day.

Finally, the older couple and their kids retired for the night. They seemed to have sleeping quarters above the kitchen.

Haworth was out cold so that left Boruch and I and Anna and the pretty blonde to ourselves. A cozy situation I suppose or maybe it could be. Boruch hardly took his eyes off the blonde since she had made her appearance. I couldn't understand their conversation but it was obvious old Boruch was trying to make time. I couldn't understand the conversation but could read the message in his Rudolph Valentino "Let's go the bedroom" looks. At first he didn't seem to be having much luck.

Anna and I sat on a divan across the room from Boruch and the blonde. Our conversation was naturally pretty limited. Boruch was so intent on his project he wouldn't even hear us when we asked him to translate something for us. I did learn that Anna was twenty-eight. She said that she could get married now.

Apparently when the Germans were here a woman had to be twenty-eight before she could get married. I guess that this might be a way of keeping the population from growing too fast. Getting a late start would keep the families smaller.

About all Anna and I could do was sit there and smile at one another. This damned language barrier could be bad at times. I wondered what she thought of me. Her smile was friendly if not downright inviting. Still, I didn't want to make a complete ass of myself. Maybe I would get a hard right to the teeth and be ordered out of the house. I didn't like the idea of spending the night outside. Still, the very friendly look meant something. I knew I would be here only one night and would never be back.

It was a weird situation I found myself in. Clear over here in Poland in some tiny village. I estimated I must be at least eight or nine thousand miles from home not knowing where to go or which way to go. It seemed our present plans were to push further east. Going in that direction wouldn't be getting any closer to home either. Of course, a couple of thousand miles more and we would be at the point of no return. It would be just as close to California to keep going as to turn back now. Anyway it looked to me it was the long way home.

Anna grabbed my hand and started tugging for me to get up. I thought to myself, this is it. It wasn't though. There was an ancient phonograph in one corner of the room. The speaker on it was a tin affair and looked something like a morning glory blossom. In fact, everything in this house was old. Most of the stuff looked like it had been handed down for generations. There didn't seem to ne many new modern things.

At least music was something we could both understand. I imagined the records would all be polkas or something but got a surprise because some of the records were in English. I was sure a couple of them were some of the old Bing Crosby records. The ones that had been made before he developed his present style that made him famous. I was sure that a couple of them were Ted Lewis records. I wondered how they happened to have records like that here. I guess some records get all over the world.

While we were listening to the records Anna slowly but deliberately backed into me. About all there was left to do was put my arm around her. She was soft and smelled good. It had been months and months since I had been this close to a woman. War does strange things to an individual as well as nations. People do things during war time that they wouldn't think of doing during normal times. They may even look down on these things as immoral. The war made it a day to day, even and minute by minute proposition for a lot of us. I guess somewhere in the back of your mind you figure you had better live all you can while you still have a chance. Anyway, "C'est la guerre".

The next morning I slept unusually late. In fact, I was the last one up and then Boruch had to wake me up. When he woke me up it took a minute or two to figure out where the hell I was. Oh, yeah, that's right, here in Poland in some village I didn't even know the name of. We had a wonderful breakfast of meat, eggs, biscuits, jam, ersatz coffee and milk. I was amazed to see that these people had chocolate. They must have been hording it for years.

We took our time but finally were ready to go down to the railroad station to see what would develop. We exchanged addresses with the people and hoped to hear from each other after we got back to the States. I left them my bicycle in hopes it would be a tiny payment in return for the wonderful treatment we had received.

We took off for the railroad station. It had snowed during the night and there were a couple of inches on the ground. It was considerably colder than it had been. We plowed across the snowy fields for about two miles until we came to the station. We were about the only G.Is here but the place was teeming with Polish refugees and all of their belongings. They were all lined up along the track as if they were expecting a train. This looked encouraging. Maybe there would be a train by soon.

We hung around the station all day but no trains. In the middle of the afternoon it began to snow quite heavily. Dusk came and still no train. Boruch said we ought to go back to the Polish family for the night. The rest of us didn't want to go. We felt they had done enough for us already and didn't want to take advantage of them. Boruch was pretty persuasive though and the snowy weather helped the rest of us decide he was right.

Reluctantly we returned to the house. They still welcomed us and made us feel at home. It was another evening of good liquor, cigarettes and plenty of food. In some ways it was quite different tough. There were more of us now. Haworth was alive now and Nick Alfredo had come with us this time. Also, the blonde was gone. Maybe she preferred the Russians to Boruch. I spent part of the evening entertaining the kids. One was a girl about nine or ten and the boy a year or two younger. They were teaching me how to count to ten in German. Of course, I knew that much about the German language but I pretended I didn't. They seemed to be getting a kick out of it. When it was time to go to bed all four of us crapped out on the living room floor.

The next morning, after another wonderful breakfast, we were ready to try the railroad again. When we left this time we knew we wouldn't be back. We made our minds up that we would sleep out in a snow drift rather than impose on these people again.

It had stopped snowing but there were several inches of it on the ground. It was overcast and looked like it could snow any minute. At the station we found that the train had already arrived.

The Polish refugees were getting on the flat cars with all their belongings. They were all loaded up and ready to go. The train must have been here for some time. We looked for a place to get on the train. There were two or three passenger cars toward the end of the train. No one seemed to be using them so we decided that we would use one of the cars. I wondered why the Polish hadn't crowded into them. The weather was threatening and it would be a lot warmer than an open flat car. I guess it was easier to get their belongings on the flat cars. The Polish were in gay spirits. I actually wondered why though. Naturally they must be tickled to get out of the "slave labor" camps and be on their way home, but what did they have to go home to? They had probably been gone from their homes for years and things were probably completely different now. The Russians were here now and had probably taken over. Maybe they had hopes of the Russians going home after Germany was defeated and they could live like they had between the wars, independently.

I doubted if the Russians would pull out. I think they thought of Poland as part of their empire anyway. They had taken over half of it in 1939 and now they had it all figured out that they would see no reason to give it up.

We got on one of the passenger cars and took over a couple of compartments. We were the only ones on our car and wondered where this train was heading. Wherever it was going we were going to be riding in pretty good style. I hoped it would go on to Warsaw or even to Moscow. I didn't care. This would be nice traveling along out of the elements.

Soon the train began to move. I couldn't help getting a thrill out of it. I had no idea where we were going but I was glad we were moving. I just liked to be going somewhere. Maybe I have a bit of the wanderlust.

We jolted along at a fair clip. We soon discovered that one of the wheels on our car was frozen up. It was just skidding down the track. We wondered how long it could go on like that before it fell off or something. Maybe the damned thing would come flying up through the bottom of our car. When we would stop ever so often we could see steam coming up from around the wheel. Something was so hot it was melting the snow along the track and turning it into steam.

I was disappointed when the train, after going about twenty five miles, stopped and we found out that this was as far as it was going. I had hoped to go much farther on it. We were now in a town named Rogasen.

We got off the train wondering what to do. It was getting late and we had to try to find a half way decent place to sleep. There were a few G.Is around and they said they were putting up in a building in the town. We went to the building, an office type of a place. We found, to our relief, that there was plenty of room and we would have a place to sleep on the floor. After we got squared away we wandered around the town a little. It was almost dark now so we didn't venture too far from the place where we planned to sleep. There were quite a few Russians in town. In one place a Russian was playing the piano. I don't know if the place was a bar or not but it would have been as far as the Russian was concerned. He was pretty well stewed. He did seem to be able to play the piano well though. He was playing classical music so I didn't know whether he was playing well or not but it sounded O.K. Soon after we returned to our building and turned in early.

The next morning we were up pretty early wondering what to do. We wandered around town for a while. We had eaten the last of our food and were getting pretty hungry. It looked as though food was pretty scarce around here. At one place food was being served to civilians. They had to have ration tickets as well as pay for the food. All they were getting was a piece of bread with some jam and a cup of coffee. I could see whole families lining up for this meager meal. I wondered how much hope these people had for a decent future. Maybe after the war and things were back to normal there would be more food and everything.

We finally decided which road went towards the general direction of Warsaw. We had now determined to get to Warsaw as fast as possible. It was very obvious that there wouldn't be anything for us before we got there. We were beginning to doubt very much if there would be anything there either. If there wasn't, by God we would go all the way to Moscow if necessary.

We plodded on out of town and decided that if we were going to make any time we would have to get a ride some way. Our bikes were gone now and hoofing it to Warsaw would take some time. It still was a good many kilometers away. We decided to try our luck at hitch hiking on Russian trucks. We figured that we were taking the risk of winding up on work details or in the salt mines or something. We had to take the chance though as we could die of old age wandering in this vast area.

As Russian trucks would go by we would stick out our thumbs like hitch hikers did in the States. I doubt if the sign meant anything to these guys. We would also holler at them, "Hey, Ruski, Ruski?" It wasn't long before a truck stopped and we climbed on the back. The truck was empty, probably going after supplies. There were two Russians in the cab. Christ, these guys drove like maniacs. A lot of the road was bad but that didn't slow them down. We slipped, skidded, careened and sloshed down the road. The guys driving were roaring drunk. Once they stopped by the side of the road. They indicated they would be right back and went into a nearby house. I guess they went in to get more vodka. A few more miles up the road they reached their destination and we were on foot again.

Getting a ride and not winding up on a work detail gave us a little more confidence. We figured we might make pretty good time hitch hiking. While we were waiting for another ride we got to talking to a couple of G.Is that came along. They too had been hitch hiking. We told them of our wild ride. They said that was nothing, we should have been with them. They said they were on a truck going like mad right on the heels of a truck in front of them. They said the first truck slowed down and the truck had bumped into it a little before their driver could stop. They said that not much damage had happened but it had made the driver of the lead truck mad. He got out his tommy gun and shot the radiator on their truck full of holes. After that experience they wondered if they weren't better off walking. That was the Russians alright. Mad I tell you.

Their story didn't discourage us though. We soon got another ride. This ride wasn't quite as wild. Maybe these guys weren't so stewed. It could have been because they were driving a Russian made truck while the other one had been an American made one. Maybe their own trucks weren't as capable of the speed as ours and maybe they wouldn't hold together with treatment like that. This was a much milder ride whatever the reason.

We rode a considerable distance on this truck. We arrived at the town of Gnesen. We were dumped off in front of a place where there seemed to be quite a few G.I.s congregated. Near the road was an office type looking building and behind it what looked like a row of stables. We found hay in the stable and could make a fairly comfortable bed. There were quite a few French soldiers here too.

Here at Gnesen was the first time the Russians had offered us anything to eat. That evening we had barley soup. I was hungry, and it really hit the spot.

The next day I saw the first act of kindness by the Russians to help us or even notice us for that matter. In the afternoon an officer told us we were going to be sent to a town a few miles farther on where things would be half way decent for us to stay. He had us go out by the road and he stopped trucks for us to get on. Several trucks were stopped and soon all of the G.I.s and French were on them.

We went down the road perhaps fifteen miles and came to another town named Wreschen. Here we were taken to a place that looked like it could have been a riding academy or a military school or something like that. It consisted of several large buildings scattered over several acres. We were ushered into the place and more or less assigned a room. The number of guys in each room depended on the size of the room.

There was a young Russian that didn't look more than fourteen or fifteen taking down our names and what state we were from. The Russian language seemed funny. It seemed to have a lot more letters in it. There seemed to be letters and numbers all mixed together.

The room I was in was on the second story of the building. One end of it overlooked a street. One side overlooked a plot of ground that had mounds of potatoes and carrots covered with straw and dirt. The windows in the rear of the building overlooked nothing but a barren piece of real estate. On the fourth side, of course, was the hallway.

It looked as if our bunks had just been pushed into the room with no thought given to any arrangement of them. None of us tried to line them up in any order either. We just let them stay in the position in which we found them. However, the bunks were quite nice and well built. They were the traditional one above the other affair. They had no mattresses but still would make a pretty good bed,

The Russians made it pretty clear that this was the end of the line for us, at least for the time being. Some of the boys had tried to move on but were brought back by the point of a gun. We were to stay in this immediate area and not even go downtown. It looked like we were now almost prisoners of the Russians.

At least here the Russians began to feed us. We got soup, usually barley, and a pretty good sized hunk of bread every day. I really liked the soup but the bread was something else again. The bread was a very dark brown, almost black. Most of the time it wasn't thoroughly baked and would be doughy inside. One time I pulled a piece of course fiber rope out of mine. It looked like the kind of cord that is used to sew up grain bags. I guess they just threw bag and all in when they started to grind their wheat up for flour.

We didn't have a thing to do here except just lay around. It made the time drag. We wanted to get going on our way home again. It looked like we were going to have to wait for the Russians to make up their minds what they were going to do with us. We wondered where we would go from here.

We did have a roll call about every two days. We would all assemble in the vacant lot behind our building and that Russian kid would call out our names. He had a hell of a time with the names. He seemed to have an easy time with a name like mine but names like Smith, or Jones really threw him. Finally, with him repeating a name a dozen times and also trying the name of the state the guy was from, we would finally figure out who he was trying to name. This process naturally took quite some time.

I guess the Russians were really doing us a favor making us stay put her at Wreschen. The weather had been pretty bad the last few days. It had snowed frequently and it was quite miserable. It would have been pretty tough to be wandering around over the landscape in this kind of weather. It also was quite apparent that food here in Poland was pretty scarce. That would be another problem if we were on our own. Also, it was foolish to keep pushing east too. We didn't know where we were going and there was an awful lot of territory here to wander around in. I guess if the Russians were going to help us at all they would have to get us all together and make us stay put for a while. The place we were staying wasn't too bad either. At least it was dry and reasonably warm. We also got enough food every day to keep us going. Also, so far they hadn't made us do any work or for that matter even paid much attention to us. So, I guess it wasn't so bad holed up here to wait and see what was going to happen.

Boredom was the worst part of it. There was absolutely nothing to do. Of course, it wasn't any more boring than the prison camp bad been and there was some hope we would be on our way soon. One way of passing the time, of course, was talking among ourselves. The main topic was when we were going to get going. One guy among us kept singing the song "My Blue Heaven". That bastard sang it over and over thousands of times, day and night. I heard it so much I wanted to strangle the guy. He must have liked the number or it reminded him of home or his family or something. It sure got old though. It was funny that no one told him to shut up. I guess we figured if he enjoyed it and it helped him pass the time, let him alone.

From the window on the street side we could see the traffic passing below us. Often Russian troops and equipment would pass. Sometimes there would be convoys of trucks, other tanks, often marching men. We even saw a couple of Polish outfits go by. Sometimes there would be a bunch of soldiers going by carrying big signs with men's pictures on them and other signs with writing. I don't know whether they were honoring some war hero or it was some sort of political deal or what.

One time some Russians came around to the rooms asking for anyone who had any talent. They were going to throw a big party in town and wanted entertainers. They were inviting anyone who could sing, dance or play a musical instrument. No one in our bunch had any talent along these lines. One fellow I knew volunteered though. It was Dorazio. He was supposed to be a singer. He had done a little entertaining in night clubs around Philadelphia before the war.

I never learned what the celebration was about. I don't know whether it was for some great victory achieved or a Russian national holiday or what. Maybe it was just a party for the troops around here.

Early in the evening of the night of the party the Russians brought us all a drink. We each received about a water glass full of vodka. This was my introduction to their national drink. We thought it was quite decent of them to think of us.

One day we got the word that we were going to leave Wreschen shortly. We were going by train to Odessa, Russia. Odessa is way down on the Black Sea. It must be twelve or fifteen hundred miles from here. This was certainly the long way home. Even when we reached Odessa we would be a lot further from home than we were now. We were all anxious to get going anyway.

Late one afternoon we fell out and got ready to move. We hiked to the railroad where there were boxcars waiting for us. The boxcars had quite a bit of straw on the floor. There were quite a few men assigned to each car but at least we would all have room enough to lie down. There were just enough fellows to make it nice and cozy. Each car had a kerosene lantern hanging in a corner. This wasn't going to be too bad. This was almost luxurious compared with some of the ways I had traveled lately. About dark the train pulled out. We bounced along fairly steadily through the night.

Early the next morning we were in the town of Kutne, Poland. We sidetracked here for quite some time. During the day we pushed steadily eastward. In the afternoon we reached Warsaw.

I had heard stories of how badly Warsaw had been damaged and they weren't exaggerating. It looked like everything had been reduced to rubble. You could look out and see mounds that looked like great piles of gravel. I don't know whether our train passed near to the main part of Warsaw or not. But from what I could see it was undoubtedly one of the most destroyed cities of the war. We spent the rest of the afternoon in the railyard of Warsaw. We saw a couple of other trainloads of soldiers on side tracks. One trainload was practically all English. I saw a few of the British get off of one of the boxcars and there was a girl with one of the guys. I imagined these guys had been prisoners for years and had been in a camp somewhere in Poland. I guess he was trying to take her home with him. Boy! They must have had a lot of privacy in a boxcar full of soldiers.

Another side tracked train had a lot of German prisoners on it. I sure would have hated to be in their shoes. I don't imagine the Russians treated them with exactly kid gloves. Those guys, for sure, were going to wind up in the Siberian salt mines.

While we were here we were given a meal of soup and bread. This was the first food we had gotten on the trip and it hit the spot. I noticed that the German prisoners were getting the same food as we were and just as much. During the night we pulled out again.

The next morning, we reached Brest-Litovsk. We were now in Russia proper. Now we would probably head in a southerly direction toward Odessa.

The country we passed through for the next few days was flat. Of course all of the country we had come through since we got out of the prison camp had been flat. I hadn't seen anything to even resemble a good sized hill in Eastern Germany, Poland and now Russia. This country, in the Ukraine, seemed more desolate and not as productive as that in Eastern Germany. It seemed to be more of a wheat growing country. For the most part it could be described as flat but did have sort of long rolling knolls. It kind of reminded me of parts of Nebraska that I had been in. I guess this is one of the biggest wheat producing areas in the world.

The population of the area must not be very great. We went for miles without seeing a town or hardly a farm. On the whole trip from Brest-Livovsk to Odessa we didn't pass through any town of any size. This was a big lonesome looking place.

I noticed isolated farmhouses that had been destroyed. They looked like they had been blown up and burned. I wondered if the Germans had done this back in 1942 when the Germans had invaded. I had heard of the Russians "scorched earth policy" where they had destroyed and burned everything as they retreated so nothing could fall into German hands.

We stopped at every little Russian village. They were small too and few and far between. The villagers would all be down at the tracks when we pulled in. They wanted to buy anything we had. They all seemed to have a pocketful of money and wanted to spend it. They would buy anything too. Any trinket you might have picked up in Germany or clothes or anything you might have. Some of the fellows sold their over coats and blankets. A G.I. overcoat would bring around eight hundred rubles. A good blanket would bring almost as much. Some of the G.I.s had white underwear. The Russian women really went wild over these. They would offer almost any price to get them. They would almost come to blows with one another trying to get them. I guess the big attraction was that they could use them themselves. The G.I, shorts were Government Issue. I guess they had gotten them in the prison camp when we were issued new clothes. Most of the G.I. underwear, at least overseas, was O.D. (Olive drab) in color. Apparently there were a few pairs of white ones still around.

I sold my worst blanket for four hundred rubles. I wasn't quite ready to give up my overcoat and best blanket yet. We weren't too sure what the weather would be ahead. Although we were going south and spring was getting close you could never tell.

I soon found out that you needed a pocket full of money to do any business. In another village down the tracks a woman came out with a cake, pink frosting and all to sell. It was cut out into rather small pieces and each piece cost two hundred rubles. My old ragged blanket hadn't been too high at four hundred rubles at that.

At one village I showed my silver setting to a young couple. The girl just about went wild when she saw it. They offered me several hundred rubles for it. I had no intention of selling it at any price. I wanted to take something home with me of the place. The girl really wanted the set and they kept offering me more and more until they were offering a fantastic price. I didn't intend to sell it. She kept her eyes glued to it all the time and they were really shining.

I don't know what came over me but just as the train pulled out I reached out and handed her the damned thing. I didn't get a cent out of it. I guess it was because I knew how badly she wanted it. It was worth a lot anyway to see how her mouth flew open in surprise and happiness. Oh well, maybe it helped to cement relations between the two countries. I imagined too that the little set of silver was the only real luxurious thing she had in her life. These little villages along here didn't look too prosperous.

We continued on toward Odessa. For hundreds of miles the country had looked the same. It was a monotonous place, dreary and barren looking. Possibly if the weather had been sunny and nice it might have made a difference. We hadn't seen the sun it seemed like in weeks. In route we had a couple of pretty cold nights. One night it got cold enough that frost began to form on the inside of the car.

As we neared Odessa the weather didn't seem to improve much. It might have been slightly warmer but it was still overcast and gloomy. It was getting into March now and the sun ought to come out once in a while it seemed.

Finally we reached the city of Odessa. This was supposed to be a place of six hundred thousand or more during peace time so it was a good sized city. We stopped in railyards on the outskirts of the city. We finally got organized and started walking into the city.

We hiked quite a ways and I figured we must be getting into the heart of the city. We finally drew up in front of a large building that could have formerly been an office or possibly a school building of some kind. We went in and took up rooms in the place. I got a room with a bunch of fellows on the second floor. There were no bunk beds or anything so we would have to sleep on the floor.

Here we were more prisoners than we had even been back at Wreschen. We couldn't leave the building without Russians being with us. As Allies, these Russians were a weird acting bunch. I don't know what they were afraid we would do or what we might see.

Almost every day we were taken for exercise. We would march up and down the streets of Odessa. Of course there were Russians to pick out our route and to accompany us. Once the route was established we took the same one every time we were out. The route of our march was limited to a few blocks around the building where we were staying. I never got to see as much of the city as I would have liked however, there were a few things to see. Near our building was a pretty good sized park or square. It didn't seem to have too many trees or shrubs but it had walkways running through it and lots of park benches. The benches for the most part were occupied by very old people. At each corner of the park there was a loud speaker always blaring. I don't know if the speakers were giving out news, propaganda or what. Also, on our march we would pass fortifications that had been built on a couple of corners. These fortifications were low sort of pill box looking affairs with slots to fire out of. They were built tight up against a building at an intersection and were situated so they could dominate the whole intersection as well as the streets in all directions. They were undoubtedly built by the Germans when they were occupying the city. Along the line of the march we were able to see how some of the average Russian city dwellers lived. Around this section at least, there were big dismal looking apartments that seemed to be homes of the citizens. Then there was the sight that had become familiar to me in the past couple of years. That was the ever present destruction. Here and there we would pass a bombed out or demolished building.

On one of our marches the Russian Officer in charge wondered why we didn't sing while marching like they did and all European Armies do. I guess the guy in charge of us told him that wasn't a custom in the American Army. The Russian wanted us to try anyway. We did and naturally it fizzled. Probably the Russians figured we didn't have any spirit.

I'll say one thing in favor of the Russians. They tried to have a little entertainment for us. There was a large corridor on the ground floor of our building where they put on movies for us. It was crowded in the place and the sound wasn't too good but it was a nice gesture. The movies we saw were both American. One was "Sun Valley Serenade" with Sonja Hiene and the other was "Mission Moscow". We enjoyed them very much. They were the first movies any of us had seen in a long time.

Another time we were going to see an English picture but an accident prevented it. The movie had just gotten underway when there was a terrific crash outside and our whole building shook. One Limey said, "What the bloody hell was that?" We all wondered but no one was curious enough to go outside and see. We just wanted the kid to get the movie going again. I guess most of us had been used to loud and different noises long ago. The movie was about to commence again when one of the American Non-coms, more or less in charge, came dashing in. He said a bomb shattered a wall of the building next door had collapsed and fallen in. He said that there were at least two Americans under the debris. We were all to go back to our rooms so it could be determined how many had been buried under the wall. It also happened that they slept in the same room as I did and as a matter of fact, right next to me. I didn't know them other than to say "Hi". They were very close friends and stuck around together all of the time. Apparently they had been down in the back of the building trying to heat some water to shave with when the wall had collapsed. It was a miracle that more hadn't been killed. The latrine slit trenches were dug there but at that particular time no one happened to be using them.

A thing that made it extra bad about these two fellows being killed was that this very day the Russians had told us that they had sent telegrams home telling families that we were safe in Russia and would be home soon. It sure would be hell on the loved ones back home. All the months of not knowing and uncertainty. Then the joy of knowing they were safe and coming home. Then a few hours later receiving notice they were dead. It was going to be pretty rough on someone.

We still wanted to see the movie and returned to the corridor and told the kid to get the thing going again. The kid just about had the movie going again when a Russian Officer came in and ended the whole thing. He said we ought to show some respect for our fallen comrades. He was right of course and we knew it. We returned to our rooms.

The day after the boys had been dug out they were taken to a cemetery here somewhere in Odessa for burial. They wanted a pretty good turnout to accompany the bodies to the cemetery. No one wanted to go. A few almost had to be forced to go to make any kind of representation at all. Everyone felt so indifferent. Here a couple of poor guys being buried thousands of miles from home and no one even seemed to care. I felt ashamed of myself for not going. It seemed though, that after you see so much death and destruction and all kinds of crap for months, you get numb to a lot of things. You lose sight of things and values. Death is so commonplace that it's just an everyday thing and you think nothing of it. I think you get the idea it's something that's going to happen and will happen and you just accept it and hope it isn't you.

The English have a custom when something like this happens. They have sort of a get together and sing their national anthem, etc. It was decided that on the night of the funeral such a service would be given. The English sang their anthem beautifully and then it was our turn. I was dreading this. Our National Anthem is, as everyone knows, very difficult to sing or even play. A fantastic thing happened though. Dorazio, the professional singer, led us. I was proud of the boys. It was sung the best I have ever heard it sung by any group of amateur singers. I was glad we hadn't hashed it up like I thought we would.

One day we went to a circus. I had no idea what a Russian circus would be like so I was anxious to go. We hiked a short distance from our building to the place. I expected to see a large main tent surrounded by smaller tents like an American circus. Instead there was a large oval shaped building where it was held. They had permanent buildings where they held their circuses. It was a big place and must have had a seating capacity of several thousand. The place was jammed with ex POWs. The Americans sat one side, the English on another, the French and Italians in still different sections. Then there were smaller groups of different nationalities scattered around. The place had one large ring in it.

The show was similar to a circus in the States. They had a band whose theme song was Maine's "Stein Song". The featured clown was dressed like Charlie Chaplin. There were aerialists, tumblers, tight rope walkers and clowns. There were a few animal acts including trained horses and a gal with a trained zebra. I don't know how this particular circus rated among others over here but we enjoyed it. I'm sure of one thing and that was these performers never played before a more appreciative audience. They were applauded long and loud for anything they did. It was a very enjoyable afternoon.

Another day we were taken to have showers and get our clothes deloused. This place wasn't too far from our building either. We entered a huge gym. I had never seen one this large. It seemed to be strictly for working out. I didn't see any seats for spectators although they may have had some portable ones somewhere. At one end of the gym were the large ovens where they put your clothes to bake. We stripped down naked and hung our clothes on a hangar. A Russian gal was taking them from us and putting them on racks in the oven. She was sweating and the water was running off her face. I wondered why she didn't take off her overcoat. Maybe she didn't have anything on underneath it. Or maybe she would be out of uniform if she took it off. She seemed to ignore us standing there naked. We had to walk clear to the other end of the gym for showers. After showers we had to walk clear back across the gym to near the delouser to get a towel. Two gals were handing out the towels to us. They didn't ignore us. When you stepped up in front of them to get a towel they would dangle it just out of your reach while they looked you over really well. They seemed to be enjoying their work. Someone was liable to get the call tonight if they had seen what they liked. In this bunch they had a lot to choose from.

Still, even here in Odessa, there was no American authority. The British had people here to help get their prisoners organized. Those English knew what the score was. They know how to get around and get things done. We wondered why our own government couldn't at least have a team of some kind here to help us get organized. The English hadn't been here long. Turkey had just recently entered the war on the side of the Allies and had opened the Dardanelles and Bosporus. The English were helping us though. We were eating their rations now. Even though we were getting rations form the English the Russians continued to give us soup and black bread. With both rations the easting was pretty good now.

I often talked to some of the English and Canadian ex-POWs. Boy! Those guys had a long old ordeal of it.

One bunch of Canadians hadn't been home since 1937 and here it was 1945. They had been sent to the Middle East for a tour of duty. When their time was about up and they were ready to go home the situation in Europe had worsened and they had gone to England instead of home. The war broke out and they were stuck. They had been captured on the Dieppe raid. They hadn't said too much but I guessed the thing was pretty much of a fiasco. They eventually wound up in a prison camp in Poland. I guess one thing they had to cling to during all this time was that their efforts in the raid hadn't completely been in vain. They had the idea that the raid had drawn the German's attention long enough that some big convoy was supposed to have slipped though in the Mediterranean somewhere. I don't know about that but it had made them feel better anyway.

The English I talked to had been prisoners since June of 1940. They had been with the British troops that had been cut off from their own army and had fallen back to Paris with the French. Most of the rest of the British army had escaped at Dunkirk. Four and a half years of a man's life is a long time to spend in a prison camp.

A rather amusing thing happened between the English and one of our fellows. One night at one of the movies I had just finished talking to these fellows and was sitting by them when the movie started. A young punk American G.I. from the Normandy Front squeezed in by us. He was a little smart aleck punk. When he noticed the British sitting there he began making a lot of smart remarks, not at all complimentary to them. They sat there quietly a while taking it. Finally one got fed up and leaned over to the kid and quietly said, "Listen chum, would you care to step outside?" The kid clammed up then. I nudged him and said, "Go on kid. Why don't you go outside with him?" I imagine if he had gone outside someone wouldn't have come back and it probably would not have been the smart punk. These guys had been through enough crap that they weren't in any mood to take something off some punk like this.

Finally, toward the end of March, we were going to get help at last. This time it looked like we might be taking a step in the right direction. We were going to take a ship and head for Naples. We were all happy to hear this news. We knew for sure that in Naples we would at least get back under American control.

The morning came and we marched toward the harbor. The Russians had a band leading the column. Their bands seem to have more of the deep pitched instruments, like from altos on down. It seemed like their tempo was slightly different and we kept getting out of step. Someone would have to sound cadence every once in a while so we could get back into step. Finally, we reached the docks. While we waited to board the ship the band played a few more numbers. Some Russian was taking moving pictures of us. He wanted us to smile and wave. Probably they were pictures to send to our government to show them how happy we were and how well we had been treated. They would probably enclose a nice bill for our board and room too.

Soon we boarded the ship. It was a fairly large passenger ship. A Scottish ship named the Circassia. Our quarters on the ship were in the galley. There were hammocks strung there for us to sleep in. They were hung right above the tables we were to eat on. No one was allowed in the state rooms much less sleep in them. I guess they didn't want to take any chances of getting the rooms lousy. No one blamed them and no one griped about having to sleep in the galley. Everyone was just happy to be on their way home.

We slowly pulled out of the harbor of Odessa. We were on our way! There didn't seem to be any Russian warships here at Odessa. About the only ship I saw was a ship that seemed to be a pretty good-sized yacht.

They served us plenty of food on this ship. It seemed as though you could get all you wanted. It was a lot different than the English L.S.T, we had come over from the States on. They had been tight with food. Maybe they thought they would help fatten us up. Still that English cooking took some getting used to.

I was amazed at how easy it was to master the art of sleeping in a hammock. I had always visualized it being hard to keep from falling out of one. They made a pretty good bed at that.

That very first day out we had an abandon ship drill. I thought it was rather foolish. There weren't any German subs in the Black Sea and we were way out of range of their planes. Still, I guess it was better to be prepared. I guess it would be possible to run into a mine that had gotten away.

I almost got seasick the first day out. The sea was quite calm though. It just had long swells and made the boat sway only slightly. To me those gentle swells were worse than when the sea was choppy and the boat reacted more violently.

We spent most of our time up on the deck. The weather was quite nice and sunny. Besides Americans, there were English and some British Indian troops on the ship. It was hard to judge how many troops there were altogether. Actually there were not so many on this ship, only a few hundred.

I noticed one fellow throughout the trip that seemed

to be a lone wolf. He seemed to hang around near the British yet didn't seem to mingle right with them. He wore an African Corps cap. Lots of us wore assorted headgear but that was the first time I had seen an African Corps cap. Someone said this guy called himself Oliver Cromwell. That name rang a bell somewhere. Wasn't that the English General who opposed Napoleon at Waterloo? It seemed to me there was something phony about this guy but I wasn't going to worry about it if no one else did. We sailed on all day and night uneventfully.

The next morning we had another abandon ship drill. We went charging up the ladder when the alarm sounded. When we tried to dash out on the deck we were turned back. There was a jagged shaped line drawn on the deck which was supposed to represent a bomb hole right in front of the hatch. A British Officer stood there telling us we couldn't come this way because of the bomb hole. We went back down to the galley and found another way out. I guess they like to make these drills a little more realistic.

On this day the British loaned us each two pounds, in other words about ten dollars. This was so we could buy things from the ship's P.X. (Post Exchange). This was the first time any of us had any money in some time. It seemed nice to be able to buy candy and cigarettes. I didn't understand this English money; shillings, florins, etc. When I would buy something, I just made sure I put down enough money to cover it and depended on them to give me the right change.

Finally we reached Istanbul on the Bosporus in Turkey. We stopped off in Istanbul for quite some time. I was hoping we would get ashore here. Some American Major was brought out and came on board. This was the first time we had seen any American authority. He didn't stay long, just long enough to confer with the Captain of the ship.

Istanbul is located on the Sea of Marmara and the western end of the Bosporus. The Bosporus is a ten or so mile strait connecting the Black Sea and the Sea of Marmara. This is a historical place where Europe and Asia meet. I liked the name of Constantinople better than Istanbul for the name of the city though. Istanbul looked like a good sized city. As well as being old and full of history I understood it was quite a place for the night life. I hoped we would get ashore.

Looking toward the Asian side of the straits I could see something that looked quite familiar. The buildings, spires, domes and palm trees looked just like the scene from the back of a pack of Camel cigarettes.

Finally, we began to move again. This Sea of Marmara was quite small. It wasn't any bigger than a fair sized lake. We never lost sight of either shore. We passed several small islands along the way.

We reached and entered the Dardanelles. This was a considerable longer strait than the Bosporus. This was certainly a famous historical place. Armies for thousands of years had been crossing here. Armies from the east who were invading Europe and vice-versa. Of course the Dardanelles had been a strategic bit of water for centuries.

Out of the Dardanelles we entered the Mediterranean Sea. This particular arm of the sea is called the Aegean Sea but as far as I'm concerned it is still the Mediterranean Sea. The Mediterranean Sea is broken up into several names like the Aegean Sea, Tyrrhenian Sea, Ionian Sea, Liguria Sea, etc. It's actually all the same body of water. I imagined all of these seas were named in ancient times when the sea seemed bigger and the areas of it were called something different for identification.

Anyway we were in the Mediterranean Sea. Just out of the straits we could look back and see the place where the British had landed during World War I and tried to take the Dardanelles for the Turks. It had been an ill-fated attempt. The English also pointed to a spot on the other shore where they say historians think Troy was located.

As we sailed on I was amazed by the amount of islands there were. These of course, were Greek islands, as we were sailing close to the Greek mainland. There seemed to be dozens of islands and all seemed to be occupied. Buildings could be seen on the islands.

The weather seemed to be improving daily and even though it was only the last day or two of March the weather was balmy and warm. I guess this kind of weather is what makes Mediterranean Cruises so popular.

Finally, our cruise of several days was about over. It had been a nice trip, especially with the knowledge that we would soon be in American hands and possibly on our way home.

Our destination for the moment was Naples, Italy. Naples was almost beginning to seem like home. I had spent quite a lot of time in Southern Italy and of course Naples was the Queen City of these parts. Our outfit had spent rest periods near here so I had gone into Naples several times. We had left here to go to the Anzio Beachhead. We had left here on our way for the Southern France Invasion. Now, after making a circle through France, Germany, Poland, Russia and God knows where, I was coming right back from where I had started. I had never expected to ever come back to Naples. Of course I had never expected to make a trip like I did when I left here eight months ago. It didn't seem so much could have possibly happened in eight months. It seemed like I had left Naples eight years ago. I hadn't thought too much of

Naples as a city or anything but I'll be damned if I wasn't glad to be getting back to it. Maybe it was beginning to seem like home.

We were getting pretty close to "home". One evening we passed through the Straits of Messina that separated Italy and Sicily. This was also a very famous and historical bit of water. The water was quite rough passing through the strait.

The next morning, I went up on deck early. There it was! The old indestructible Vesuvius. Naples too.

It was quite early when we docked. We were clamoring down the gangplank. There was a Red Cross worker on hand distributing small cloth sacks which contained toilet articles. These things would be most welcome now. Also in each sack was a card. On the card it said something to the affect that we had not been forgotten and that all of our efforts and sacrifices had been appreciated and thanks for everything. This was the first and only time I had ever heard or seen anything of this nature.

The American ex P.O.W.s were taken to a small American installation. The place seemed to be an old army garrison. It was on top of a hill overlooking the Bay of Naples. It no doubt had been a garrison and fort down through the centuries. It now seemed to be pretty much turned over to returning P.O.W.s. There were a few others here and of course the permanent jobs around here were held down by other G.I.s. There weren't too many P.O.W.s. There were nowhere near the two thousand that had left the camp. I guessed a lot of them were still back in Germany or Poland or somewhere. We heard that one bunch had beat us out of Russia.

At this place we had to go through a certain amount of processing. I was surprised that we got no sort of a physical examination at all. The thing nearest to anything along those lines was that we were squirted with DDT powder to get rid of any varmints that we might have had. I actually didn't feel that any physical examination was necessary as far as I was concerned. I felt good and figured by now I had most of my weight back. One thing I had discovered during this war was how tough the human animal could be. They can take a lot more and recuperate a lot faster than anyone would think. They seem to be actually tougher than other animals in lots of ways. I was still surprised they didn't give us an examination for at least T.B. or V.D. though. Some intelligence officers questioned us about the "Afrika Corps" character that had been on the ship with us from Odessa. I guess I had been right when I thought something seemed fishy about him. The minute we had hit here he had taken off. We were all asked to write what we knew and thought about Keating the collaborator back in Limberg. I'll bet he got reports that could have hung the guy. I didn't care whether they ever caught the Kraut or not but I hoped that Keating bastard got what was coming to him. We were issued new clothes. The new Eisenhower jacket had just come out. At first I didn't think too much of it but when I got used to it I decided it was much better looking than the old long tailed dress tunic. We had the old indoctrination about how much V.D. there was around these part so to be careful, etc.

I was surprised when they cashed fifty dollars of German Marks and converted it into American money. It didn't do me any good though for I didn't even have one mark. I kicked myself because I could have easily picked up that much. I had never bothered because I thought it would be useless because Germany was losing the war. Any pistols or other fire arms that any of the fellows might have happened to bring back with them were taken away. There was some excuse about not being able to take them home. I think these jokers here at this camp wanted to keep them for themselves. I didn't have a gun anyway. They wanted to know if anyone had been wounded and they were giving out Purple Hearts to the ones that had. Parmenter, from our room, tried to show a scratch somewhere that was invisible. Although they wouldn't see the wound and I had my doubts if Parmeter had ever been hit, they weren't asking too many questions and gave him one. I could have gotten one too if I had wanted. I had a couple of scars on my knuckles from shrapnel at Anzio. At least the scars were big enough to see. I figured a Purple Heart should be for someone that was really wounded. You got sent home to your family or when you were killed. The Purple Heart was a pretty thing though and maybe I should have picked one up. Probably the people back home would think of you as some sort of a big hero if you had one.

We didn't have to do anything here at this place in terms of work. About all we did was to eat, sleep and take it easy. We could get a pass into Naples about any time we wanted it.

Another guy and I did go into the town. It hadn't changed much. About the only difference was that they had lights now. In fact, they had just now gotten electric power restored. It was still a pretty gloomy place though. Still the beggars and pimps around. I still couldn't go for the place much. Another thing that sickened me was an incident that happened on my first pass when I came back. It had nothing to do with the town or the Italians either. This fellow and I were wandering around looking for something to do. A G.I. (a rear echelon bastard) came up to us and asked if we could change a twenty dollars invasion note into two tens. We were only too happy to be obliging. We both grabbed for our billfolds. The fellow with me beat me to it and changed the guys twenty. Soon afterward we found the stuff was counterfeit and worthless. He was out twenty dollars and money wasn't any too plentiful with us. Although we didn't know it at the time, most of the men had been in this area for a while knew it. A large counterfeiting ring was printing this invasion money and passing it. I guess the job on the money wasn't too good and it was pretty easily spotted if you suspected it. We hadn't known about it and had been struck. Probably we had been picked on because we looked like guys right over from the States. We had on new clothes, no outfit patches, stripes or anything. I guess we did look like guys right out of Basic Training. Out good old comrades. A thing like that gave you a sour taste. I only left the camp once more while I was there. There really wasn't anything in the city anyway.

There was a little excursion I hated to miss though. They took all that wanted to go down to look through Pompeii. I had my uniform in the tailors getting it fitted, pressed, etc. so wasn't allowed to go. I had wanted to go back to Pompeii when there was plenty of time to look around. I could hardly enjoy it the last time. The guy I was with had no interest in the place and kept wanting to go to some bar.

Time here at the garrison dragged by. It was definite we were going home, and we were anxious to get going. We were supposed to leave any day. The sooner the better as far as I was concerned.

One day we were told we would sail for home the next day. It was almost hard to believe. I wasn't going to get too enthused until I got on that ship. I hoped it wasn't a mistake and that we would really start for home the next day.

As long as this was to be my last night in Europe I thought I'd go into town and celebrate a little. We had received a little pay recently so I had a few dollars. A fellow named Fred Turner wanted to go in too. I didn't know Fred too well. I hadn't known him in the prison camp. I had met him in the box car on the way to Odessa. We had talked quite a bit since we had been here in Naples. Fred was slim, and had a rather dark complexion with black wavy hair. He came from Carbondale, Illinois. He seemed like a nice fellow, always ready with a smile.

That evening Fred and I got ready to go to town. At the gate of our camp were Italians who wanted to change invasion money for real American dollars or English pounds. They would give you two for one. I guess they were afraid the war was about over and when the American and English left the invasion money would be no good. I kept back a few dollars for the trip home on the boat and traded the rest. I wound up with about fifty dollars. Fred had about the same. I guess it didn't matter if we had fifty dollars in invasion money or twenty five dollars in American money. If you started to pay for something in invasion money they would charge you twice as much. We headed into town. All the way we were hounded by pimps and kids advertising their sisters or other places of business. It was, "Hey Joe, want beef steak?" or "Hey Joe, how about a night club?", or "Hey Joe, I know a place to jitterbug?" and so on and so on. They seemed to have picked up the bits about nightclubs and jitter-bugging since I had been here before. The old line about their eager, shapely sister hadn't changed.

We hit good old Via Roma and walked on down. Practically all the side streets along Via Roma were off limits. They did look grim and foreboding. These were the streets where you had to go to have all the pleasures these kids were telling about. Down Via Roma we found a restaurant that had been cleaned up by the Army and made passable. It still was run by the Italians but I imagined under a pretty watchful eye of the Army. The place wasn't bad either. The tables had nice white tablecloths and everything was clean and attractive. You even ate by candle light and a guy walked around among the tables playing a violin. The place wasn't packed but there were quite a few G.I.s in the place. There were no civilians except a few girls with some of the G.I.s. I don't imagine unescorted gals were allowed in here. The ones with the G.I.s looked pretty clean and fairly well dressed.

We ordered an Italian dinner and a couple of bottles of wine. The food was pretty good but not like the Italian food back in San Francisco. The place reminded me of some of the Italian restaurants there though. The guy with the fiddle stopped at our table and played "Lily Marlene". This was all very nice and we enjoyed it but we both craved a little more excitement. I guess this being our last night here and all we decided to look for more excitement.

Of course, we didn't have any trouble finding a kid to guide us. We gave him a buck and told him to lead the way. We headed up one of the narrow "Off Limit" streets. In these sinister looking streets we would be lucky not to get hit in the head and robbed. It was nothing unusual for it to happen. I hoped it wouldn't happen to us. Someone could get killed that way. Besides if we got robbed and hurt and had to go to the hospital we would miss the boat tomorrow. If we were caught in this "off limits" area by the M.P.s we would be in trouble. I sure didn't want to miss the boat now for sure. We shouldn't have taken the chance like this but we did.

We let our guide lead on and of course he soon took

us to a house of ill repute. Neither Fred nor I had any idea of getting next to anything but we wanted to see what the score was. We went into a dingy ill lit place and down a hallway. We came to an open door. There was a small room with a small electric bulb hanging from the ceiling. A single bed with a horrible looking hag sitting on it, naked. She purred at us to come in. Hell, I hated to breathe the air in here much less get any closer. A couple more open doors produced the same scene. A couple of these and we had had enough. I'd bet though any of these whores would tell you they had slept with General Rommel, the Desert Fox. It seemed as though every whore in Southern Italy claimed that. I guess they thought it made them seem more alluring. Poor old Rommel would sure have had to be a busy man if all their claims had been true.

We got the hell out of that hole and followed the kid to a place he claimed was a night club. He left us off at the door and took off. He either thought we would be here some time or figured he had earned his buck. We cautiously went into the building not knowing what to expect but ready to fight or run whichever was the handiest. We could hear racket upstairs so we went up. There we found a large room. It had a few tables and chairs, a makeshift bar and a beat up phonograph. There were about five or six girls there looking like they ranged in age from about twelve to their early twenties. There was also an older woman there. I never did know whether she was the mother of these girls or a chaperone or what. At first we were the only men there so we got a lot of attention. Of course, they wanted to sell us a bottle of champagne. We bought the so called champagne. All that was different from the regular gut wine was that his stuff had some kind of a charge in it. When I pried the cork out a little ways it flew out of the bottle with a big bang and went up and bounced off the ceiling.

We had no more than sampled our "champagne" when a couple of the girls dragged us out onto the floor and wanted to dance. The phonograph had about had it and the record was in the same shape. I couldn't dance but neither could my "partner". We struggled through the record and went back to the table. I reached for the bottle of "champagne". It had been almost full two minutes ago and now there wasn't a drop in it. How those other gals had gotten away so fast with it was a mystery. I suspected they dumped it out somewhere when we weren't looking. They surely wouldn't drink that crap. Anyway, one of them asked sweetly, "Guess you are ready for another bottle, huh Joe?" I guessed we were and had another brought in.

I guess Fred and I acted like the last of the big spenders. We bought several bottles of "champagne" during the evening which was enjoyed by all. One thing I was surprised at was that we weren't propositioned. I guess this bunch used a slightly different approach to making the buck. One example was: I was sitting there trying to enjoy my "champagne" when one of the girls snuggled up to me and said huskily, "how about a tip Joe?" I foolishly asked "What for?" She said, "Well, don't you like me Joe?" I didn't know whether I liked her or not. I didn't even know her name. I gave her a buck anyway. What to hell it was only money. During the course of the evening I ran out of cigarettes. I asked one of the girls if there were any available. She said she could get them on the black market but they would be expensive. I wasn't in any position to be choosy. She told me she could get them but they were a dollar a pack. I gave her a couple of bucks. She left the room and was back in about two minutes with a couple of packs. The "black market" was undoubtedly in the next room or at least somewhere in this building. The girl no doubt had plenty of cigarettes stashed away for just such cases. No wonder we weren't propositioned. They could make money faster this way.

Their "night club" didn't seem to be too popular. There were never more than a half a dozen guys at a time in the place and lot of times there was just Turner and me. Late in the evening three English soldiers came in and took a table. They seemed to be only bent on getting drunk and not looking for other pleasures that could be found. They had about the same attitude that Turner and I had. Do some heavy drinking and to hell with anything else. Still, later on American Merchant Seamen came in.

Actually, I wasn't enjoying myself much. It was either stay here or go back to camp. It was late and anyplace else we went to would be like this or worse. At least this seemed to be "clean" fun. It would have been better if these girls hadn't talked so much. Another thing we had to practically keep one hand on our bottle all of the time or it would be passed around to the whole bunch. We were out to spend our money alright but if they had their way they would have drunk up all our money in a very short time. I thought I'd been in some "clip" joints back home but I'd never seen anything like this.

We sat there and continued to drink most of the night. In the back of our minds was the thought of leaving this place tomorrow. It was still hard to believe. We thought of the poor bastards that were still fighting and dying up there in Germany. The war was almost over. It had to be for sure this time. The Russians were at the gates of Berlin and the Allies were half way across Germany. It would end any day now or even any hour. Still guys were fighting and dying. It would be tough to get killed the last few days of the war. Some would though, even down to the last minute of it. Why in the hell didn't those stupid Krauts give up?

Finally, in the wee hours of the morning Turner and I decided we had had enough. The English and the Merchant Seamen were still there when we left. We left the place and headed back down the narrow and dark streets toward Via Roma. We were feeling pretty good but not real drunk. Maybe we were drunk though for we sang the U.S.C. (University of Southern California) fight song as we walked down the street. At the corner of the street and Via Roma we quieted down and sneaked up to take a look. There were no M.P.s (Military Police) lurking about so we were safe. We managed to get back to camp in good shape.

The next morning we were up early and ready to go. This was the day. I felt real good in spite of the lack of sleep and all the rot gut I had consumed. Turner seemed to be in pretty good shape too.

We finally boarded the huge troop ship that was to take us home. It was a huge ship alright. It had been the second largest passenger liner the United States had. As a luxury liner it had been called the Manhattan but now that it was in the Armed Service it was called the West Point. It was operated by the Coast Guard.

I have no idea how many troops were aboard this ship but it must have been thousands. The staterooms of course were for Officers and WACS (Woman's Army Corps). We soldiers had bunks way down in the bottom of the thing. We were really crammed into this ship too. Bunks had been built everywhere. They were stacked on top of one another several feet high. There was just enough room between one bunk and the bunk above for a man to squeeze into. I had a top bunk on the row against the side of the ship. I had to climb up over several bunks to get into mine. It was quite a chore to get in and out of my bunk. The section I was in was pretty near the bow of the ship. It wasn't too far across it at this point.

We pulled out of the harbor. Leaving good old Naples again. This certainly had been my home port since I had been over here. I wondered if I would ever be in Naples again or for that matter in Europe anywhere. I doubted that I ever would. Right now I felt I never wanted to see any part of the damned thing again. Possibly in a few years when some of the memories wore off a little I might feel differently. I doubted it though. Naturally in peace times things would be vastly different, but still…

This ship we were on was really supposed to fly. I don't know how fast it actually could go but it was a good many knots. I was going to get home a lot faster than I had gotten over here on the L.S.T. It had taken three weeks to get to Oran on that thing. I think this was supposed to get from Naples to home in about a week.

This ship also sailed by itself and not in a convoy. It was fast enough to outrun any sub. I guess the only way it would be hit was if a sub was lying in wait and let it have it as it passed by.

Well, we were on our way. Now to sweat out the next few days. It was plain to see that this wasn't exactly going to be a pleasure trip. There were so many of us on here and things so crowded that there wasn't going to be much moving around or much to do. No one minded though. I know I didn't. In the past couple of years I had learned to be patient and take things like they came without getting panicky. I was going to enjoy this trip regardless.

Most of the trip the fellows just lay in their bunks. There really wasn't much else to do. We would just lie there smoking, reading and thinking of home and what might lie in the future. Little groups in the rear section might carry on a little conversation.

Getting your chow on this ship was quite an undertaking. Long lines of men wound around down somewhere in the bowels of this ship waiting to get their food. It was so much trouble that it seemed hardly worth it and most of us skipped a lot of meals. We were able to get candy bars and cigarettes from the P.X. and for a good part lived on them.

It didn't seem that for the number of troops on board too many went up on deck. There wasn't much use I guess. Most of the time there wasn't much to see but more water and everyone had seen enough of that.

I went up on the top deck several times. I sort of like the ocean breeze blowing in my face. Another fellow, Charley Smekjal, from Stalag 11-C days also spent quite a bit of time on the deck. We talked a lot. We even talked about going into business together after the war. He was interested in starting a novelty business and seemed to know a little about it. We even tried to think up ideas that might go over in the novelty line. I figured it was all talk but it helped to pass the time.

These luxury liners must be something during peacetime. This ship had a big swimming pool up on the deck. Of course it wasn't in use now.

We were two days out of Gibraltar when a shocking message came over the loudspeaker. President Roosevelt had collapsed and died. It was almost unbelievable. He had been our president and leader so long. It was April 12th, 1945.

Everyone was more or less in a state of shock for a while. Roosevelt was considered a great man and a great leader of our country by the vast majority of the G.I.s. Most figured he was the one to get the world more or less back to normal after the shooting was over. He didn't live quite long enough to see that day. A lot of us wondered if the post war world could be shaped as well with him gone. In my own humble opinion I thought he was the greatest president our country had ever had. The problems were so much more complex for America both at home and abroad. At the very least I felt he should be mentioned in the same breath with Washington, Jefferson and Lincoln.

Later we heard Harry Truman taking the Oath of Office of the President of the United States. I actually felt sorry for the poor guy. He was stepping into a hell of a spot. Taking over for a man such as Roosevelt would not be easy. I didn't see why anyone wanted to be the President anyway with all their problems.

If I had been smart or had had any experience along these lines to amount to anything, I could have landed in the states with several hundred dollars in my pocket instead of dead broke.

To pass the time away as well as to try to make a little money, a good many of the guys shot dice. A game would start in almost every little section of the ship. Most of us had only a few dollars. I had only eight left myself. When one or two would win all the money in one little section they would move over and start shooting with the winners from other small groups. This apparently went on throughout the ship. It was sort of like an elimination tournament. Finally, all of the big winners congregated on the top deck where a big game was to be played.

I had refrained from playing in smaller games. I never was much of a gambler and cared nothing about dice. I figured I would make eight dollars go as far as I could.

I happened to be up on deck when the "big" winners began to assemble. I had intended to merely watch the game for a few minutes. They were a little slow getting the game started. I guess they were sizing each other up. About three fellows started playing a low stake game right beside me and the first thing I knew I was in the damned thing. I actually had no business in the game. To start with I had only five dollars to risk. The rest I wanted to save for candy and cigarettes. Another thing I didn't know the finer points of the game, odds on different numbers, etc. Anyway, when it was my time to shoot I put down my five and grabbed the dice. I got lucky and made a couple of sevens and elevens and made a couple of points letting the money ride. I then was only shooting ten when I crapped out. By now the big gamblers were getting into the game. I didn't figure the side betting so well so waited until I got the dice again before I bet. I was lucky again. I didn't count my money but knew I had run it up to at least a couple of hundred dollars. The game was getting big now. A guy would throw out a hundred or so and there were big bets on the side. The third time I got the dice I was still lucky. By now I figured I must have several hundred dollars, maybe a thousand or more. This is where I should have quit but as the old saying goes, I didn't. I was determined however to get out of the game with a pretty good sum. I figured I would shoot pretty big the next time I got the dice and win or lose, I would quit. I figured too that maybe it wasn't the sporting thing to quit when I had won so much so quickly. I would take care of everything next time I got the dice. I did. I was shooting large amounts and made three craps in a row then got a point and crapped out on the next roll. I faced the next guy to get the dice and he made about four passes in a row and I was broke. I figured I hadn't really lost anything because I hadn't started with anything. Easy come, easy go, I guess. I still kicked myself though for not quitting when I was quite a bit ahead. Two or three hundred dollars would come in handy. That was a lot of money to a guy making about sixty bucks a month. Well, it was probably the biggest I would ever gamble in my life so at least it was a pretty good experience for only five bucks.

I watched the crap shooter for a while. The game got bigger and bigger. I imagined before this boat docked a few, probably only three of four, would leave this ship several thousand dollars richer. I was amazed at the number of fellows who gambled. I had never cared about it myself and didn't realize until after I got into the army the amount of people who loved to gamble. The only gambling I had ever done in the army, as well as in civilian life, was a little penny ante poker once in a great while.

Now that we were almost back to the States I began to be filled with anxiety. I wondered how I would find things at home. I hadn't heard a word from anyone since the first of August of last year, almost nine months ago. I wasn't even sure Bernice or anyone had heard from me either or knew I was even alive. I didn't know if any of my letters from the prison camp had reached them. I hadn't heard from anyone so there was no reason to believe anything had gotten through to them. We had been told at Odessa that word had been sent home that we were alive and would soon be on our way home. There I wasn't sure of anything anyway. It was pretty rough not knowing how things might be at home after all these months. Maybe Bernice had another guy by now. You could never tell. It was possible that one or both of my folks were dead. After all they were in their sixties at the age anything could happen quickly. I kept telling myself it had only been nine months since I had heard from anyone. Nine months to me and all the things that had happened seemed like nine years but really it wasn't so long. Still it was the better part of a year. I hoped nothing drastic had happened.

One morning we heard the Captain of our ship had had a sleepless night. Apparently Hitler had ordered all of his remaining subs out for one last all out go at it. It seemed as though a bunch of subs were roaming our part of the Atlantic. No doubt an unescorted troop transport would be a prime target. To sink a ship like this would be spectacular and a great victory with the thousands of troops aboard. It wouldn't have any effect on the outcome of the war of course.

We were almost to Boston where we were going to land. It was announced that messages had been sent to our wives or families that we were arriving in Boston. It advised them not to come there because we would only be there for a matter of hours.

The next morning we docked in Boston Harbor. This was it. We were back in the good old U.S.A. It was almost too good to believe. I think most of us were in sort of a daze and hardly knew what was going on.

We left the ship and began boarding nearby trains. Our bunch, and I suppose many of the rest, were going to nearby Camp Miles Standish.

In the next few minutes I went through the biggest emotional strain that I had experienced during the whole war. The car I got on had all ex P.O.W.s on it. I suppose it had been arranged this way. Everyone just plunked in their seats, stared out the windows and didn't say a word. The car was deathly silent. I know everyone felt like me. I was fighting back the tears and didn't dare look at anyone. While we were sitting there a bunch of WACs came on board with coffee, doughnuts and sandwiches. They sat among us and tried to talk to us. Still no one said a word but just sat there staring out of the windows. I know no one trusted themselves to say anything. It was a weird situation. It did seem odd that the forty or so fellows on this car all felt the same and were going through exactly the same emotional reaction.

A M.P. got in the car and walked down the aisle. When he saw what was going on he said, "It's alright fellows, talk, you're home now, not over there somewhere". Still the silence. The M.P. said no more and left. Soon the WACs left too. I guess they thought we were a bunch of ungrateful bastards ignoring them the way we did.

They, or hardly anyone else, would ever be able to understand what a strain it was. We were back in the States. I know I had given up on ever making it back several times. The people, the civilians, would never know how lucky they were to live in a country like this. It has its faults but it is so far ahead of anything over there that there is no comparison. Even taking into account that the war there made things completely different it was easy to see that even in normal times things were a far cry from things here. Fear, poverty and frustration haunted most of the people over there all the time. Well, it's no use trying to explain the fantastic feeling of being home and in a land such as ours.

To me it did seem like it was worth it to go over and go through all that now. If there was the remotest chance that the war could have been brought to our shores it was worth it. In fact, we should have been in sooner. If all the civilians could have seen what I had seen in Eastern Germany and how a country can be ravaged, raped and destroyed by an invading army, their attitude would be different. There wouldn't have to be a draft. The Armed Forces would have more men and women than they would know what to do with. The defense workers would work for practically nothing and sixteen hours a day. No one would buy bonds, they would give their money to the government. If they could see and know what it was like they would gladly do all this to keep this country, even with its faults, the same. Unless you had been there, experienced and seen it, it was just impossible to even begin to grasp or understand. I had been a civilian the early part of the war too, so I know how civilians looked at things. In short, he just doesn't know what it's all about...

The train pulled slowly out. It seemed odd not to see bombed tracks and buildings lining the tracks. A railroad worker looked up and watched the train as it slowly passed. He looked like he was alive, not one of those moving zombies we had gotten used to seeing in Europe.

The train picked up speed and soon we were out of town. The conversation on the car picked up a little. The first emotional shock of getting home was beginning to wear off a little.

Camp Miles Standish was only a short distance from Boston and we made it there in pretty short order. Here we were assigned barracks and told to stick around because we wouldn't be here long. I wandered down around the telephones with an idea of trying to call someone. The phone situation was impossible. There were only a couple of booths and they were full and long lines were waiting to use them. It looked like it would take days to get up to one of them.

They were right about us tarrying long here. The next day the bunch that was going to the west coast were on shipping orders. Now I only had another three thousand miles to go and I would really be home.

Without much ado we were back on a train and rolling. Soon we were in Rhode Island and then Connecticut and then on into New York City. Although I had lived in western New York for ten years I had never been to the city. In the distance we could see the big sky scrapers. Pretty impressive alright. We didn't waste much time here but kept on rolling.

The train trip west was pretty routine. Our destination was Camp Beale, which was located in Marysville, California.

The fellows on the car I was on weren't all ex P.O.W.s by any means. The P.O.W.s had been pretty well divided up. From Camp Miles Standish they had gone in all different directions. The bunch on this car, of course, were from the west coast.

One fellow on the car came up and said he thought he knew me and introduced himself. He was from Dinuba. His name was Donald Shore. I had heard of him and knew who he was. He was a few years younger than me so I hadn't known him well. My mother had baby sat with him when he was real small. He had also just returned to the States from the European Theater. He had been a radio operator on a bomber. I think he had been overseas four months and was coming home on rotation. The flyers got to come home after fifty missions. He said a lot of their "missions" were just flying supplies somewhere behind the lines. He was a Tech Sgt. for being a radio operator. He didn't have to take anymore words of Morris Code than I had been able to take when I had gotten out of Camp Roberts. The Air Corps men had the life. He showed me a picture that he had taken and was real proud of. In fact, I had seen it before some place and had read the write up about it. It was supposed to be an outstanding picture. Shore had taken it one day while they were flying in formation on the way to some target. It was taken from his bomber looking up towards another bomber. The bomb bay doors of the other plane were just opening. I couldn't see anything so interesting about the thing but I didn't know much about photography.

We continued to roll along westward. We seemed to make pretty good time in the Eastern United States, but it seemed after we crossed the Mississippi River our speed slowed down a lot. We would sidetrack out on some side track miles from civilization and wait for some other train to come along. We did this quite often and some of the waits were quite long.

In Lincoln, Nebraska we side tracked right in the town. A lot of us climbed off and headed for some nearby stores. We found a liquor store and everyone started buying booze. There weren't many brands to choose from and I had to settle for "Four Roses". It looked like the Camel Caravan going back to the train. A bunch of fellows walking along in a line, most of them with a case of beer on their shoulders. Liquor, ordinarily, isn't allowed on troop trains but I guess that this bunch, just back from overseas, made it different. At least nothing was said to anyone. Everyone was drinking and passing their bottles around as soon as the train took off again. Everyone got in a good mood and there was a lot of talking and laughing. Even the two officers in the compartment of the car joined us. They too had just come back from Europe. Everyone was in pretty high spirits that night as our train rattled through Nebraska and on.

It's a funny thing. I can drink all kinds of booze and never get the slightest hangover but there seems to be something about alcohol and trains that don't mix with me. I guess it's that slight swaying motion of the train. This night, here in Nebraska, after I had consumed a large quantity of bourbon and beer, I felt quite sick. I had to go to the restroom and let it go out on the tracks.

In ten minutes I felt healthy again. About the only other time I got sick from over indulgence was also on a train. Bernice and I took the Santa Fe Streamliner to San Francisco one time and the same thing happened. Too much time in the club car. What's this got to do with anything anyway?

On we tolled through Colorado, Utah, Nevada and then good old California. Eventually the train found its way to Camp Beale. Here too we were informed we would be here only a very short time and then be on our way to our respective homes. That sounded good. Here at Beale they had a bunch of German "prisoners"...

EPILOGUE

Sadly, it appears that several of the final pages of the manuscript are missing. Given that my mom guarded this book like a mother hen I am amazed that it was not intact. What I do know is that my father made a surprise return to Dinuba, California where his wife Bernice and his parents were living, on April 21st, 1945. It is interesting to note that Hitler committed suicide on April 30th, 1945 and the war was essentially over in Europe.

The Army gave my father two months leave and my parents, compliments of the Army, spent several weeks of that leave in Santa Barbara at the Mir Mar Hotel. I like to think that I was conceived there as my father's only child. I once lived not far from the Mir Mar. I was born exactly nine months after my father's return. What a circle of life?

After leave, my father had to report to Gatesville, Texas. In Gatesville the war in Europe was declared over and Bernice and Dick went to the town square to drink lemonade in celebration. It was a dry state. Dick was then informed that his Division was going to be sent to the South Pacific. Luckily, he did not have to return to active service and was discharged from the Army at Fort Bliss, Texas in October 1945.

Dick returned to Dinuba where he worked in a lumber yard until he was diagnosed with Parkinson's disease in 1966. He died in 1969 at the age of 49.

Bernice, his wife, remarried and remained in the Dinuba area. She died on June 30, 2013 which would have been she and Dick's 72 wedding anniversary.

Beverly Richard "Dick" Borthwick
October 1945

ACKNOWLEDGEMENTS

My heartfelt thank you to Jodi Miles who proofread and urged me on to preserve this memoir. Without her encouragement I would have probably put the whole thing back in the attic. And, of course, Roger, who helped me in so many ways--proofreader, computer tech, English advisor and consultant extraordinaire. As a veteran himself he knew this story had to be told. And to my Dad and all the other boys---and really, they were all just boys, who fought and died in World War II with courage and determination.

www.ingramcontent.com/pod-product-compliance
Lightning Source LLC
Chambersburg PA
CBHW021421070526
44577CB00001B/4